THE SACRED LITERATURE SERIES

ELIZABETH FRY:
A QUAKER LIFE

The Sacred Literature Series of
the International Sacred Literature Trust

Titles in the series

Further titles in preparation

Elizabeth Fry: A Quaker Life

SELECTED LETTERS AND WRITINGS

Introduced and edited by Gil Skidmore

Published in cooperation with the
International Sacred Literature Trust

ALTAMIRA
PRESS

A Division of
ROWMAN & LITTLEFIELD PUBLISHERS, INC.
Lanham • New York • Toronto • Oxford

For more information about the
International Sacred Literature Trust,
please write to the ISLT at:
1st and 2nd Floors, 341 Lower Addiscombe Road
Croydon CR0 6RG, United Kingdom

Photoset in Sabon by Northern Phototypesetting Co. Ltd, Bolton, UK

ALTAMIRA PRESS
A division of Rowman & Littlefield Publishers, Inc.
A wholly owned subsidiary of The Rowman & Littlefield Publishing Group, Inc.
4501 Forbes Boulevard, Suite 200
Lanham, MD 20706
www.altamirapress.com

PO Box 317
Oxford
OX2 9RU, UK

British Library Cataloguing in Publication Information Available

Library of Congress Control Number: 2005923399

Printed in the United States of America

ISBN 0-7591-0898-6 (cloth : alk. paper)
ISBN 0-7591-0899-4 (pbk. : alk. paper)

♾™ The paper used in this publication meets the minimum requirements of American
National Standard for Information Sciences—Permanence of Paper for Printed Library
Materials, ANSI/NISO Z39.48–1992.

The International Sacred Literature Trust was established to promote understanding and open discussion between and within faiths and to give voice in today's world to the wisdom that speaks across time and traditions.

What resources do the sacred traditions of the world possess to respond to the great global threats of poverty, war, ecological disaster, and spiritual despair?

Our starting-point is the sacred texts with their vision of a higher truth and their deep insights into the nature of humanity and the universe we inhabit. The translation programme is planned so that each faith community articulates its own teachings with the intention of enhancing its self-understanding as well as the understanding of those of other faiths and those of no faith.

The Trust especially encourages faiths to make available texts which are needed in translation for their own communities and also texts which are little known outside the tradition but which have the power to inspire, console, enlighten, and transform. These sources from the past become resources for the present and future when we make inspired use of them to guide us in shaping the contemporary world.

Our religious traditions are diverse but, as with the natural environment, we are discovering the global interdependence of human hearts and minds. The Trust invites all to participate in the modern experience of interfaith encounter and exchange which marks a new phase in the quest to discover our full humanity.

Contents

Slave to no sect, who takes no private road
But looks through nature up to nature's God.
Alexander Pope, *Essay on Man*

Introduction

Elizabeth Fry (1780–1845) – prison reformer, "the angel of Newgate"– is perhaps the one Quaker woman of whom most people today have heard. This iconic status has recently been confirmed by her appearance on the British £5 note. In her lifetime her achievements were great and today Elizabeth Fry Societies throughout the world continue her work.

But there is more to Elizabeth Fry than this deserved reputation. Her actions sprang from her faith and she struggled to make the faith in which she was brought up a real one, the "true religion" on which she longed to rely. Although famous in her day both as a woman and as a Quaker, this very fame in some ways made her path more difficult. Her faith, her family and her work were all the subjects of criticism during her life, from outside the Society of Friends but also from within it.

Elizabeth Fry's background

Elizabeth Fry's parents both came from well-established Quaker families, her mother, Catherine Bell, from the Barclays and her father John from the Gurneys. Both the Barclays and the Gurneys were prosperous banking families and Elizabeth's father was a partner in the famous Gurney bank and an owner of a wool stapling and spinning factory. Quakerism was in many ways a spur to Friends' prosperity. They set up in business because the professions were barred to those who refused to swear an oath in order to gain admittance to a university, but their testimony to truthfulness helped their business reputation. So Elizabeth was born into a wealthy family, established members of the county set in Norfolk, well known in Norwich public life and living from 1786, when she was six, at the pleasant country estate of Earlham on the outskirts of the city.

It was a Quaker family, but in many ways it was indistinguishable from other well-to-do upper-middle-class families in the area. They mixed with other families of their class, which exposed them to a range of opinions and religious allegiances. Elizabeth and her six sisters and four brothers were certainly brought up to be religious but were discouraged from appearing "singular". The traditional "Plain" expression of Quakerism was seen as regrettable "enthusiasm" leading away from a "rational" moderate faith.

As a child, the greatest influence on Elizabeth was her mother. Although not a scholar, one part of Elizabeth's early education that stayed with her was a love of nature and of studying the works of creation. Living near the Norfolk coast, she and her sister Rachel were encouraged to make a collection of seashells and to learn about them. This innocent pursuit Elizabeth kept up until the end of her life, both for her own benefit and in the hope that through this study her children and grandchildren might be enabled to "look through nature up to nature's God".

Her mother also influenced the life of Elizabeth and the rest of her children by dying soon after the birth of her twelfth child when Elizabeth was twelve years old. At the age of sixteen the eldest daughter Catherine took on the care of the numerous brood of children, and the sisters and brothers became even closer. John Gurney never remarried but did his best to bring up his family according to his liberal principles, even when this brought him into conflict with others in his family and the Society of Friends.

Elizabeth's upbringing forged ties with people, particularly her brothers and sisters, and with places, Earlham in particular and Norfolk in general, that were never broken. Her spiritual path, however, diverged in its expression from that of most of those with whom she was brought up.

The Quaker background

In order to understand the conflicts within Quakerism in Elizabeth's time it is necessary to go back and examine the beginning of the movement. Quakerism arose in England in the middle of the seventeenth century out of the tumult of the Civil War and the Commonwealth's attempt to set up a "rule of saints". At this time all the traditional sources of authority were being questioned and it became possible for each individual, not only, as the poet John Milton said, "the wise and learned", to seek her or his own path to God and "true religion".

George Fox was just one among many people dissatisfied with the established church who embarked on a journey, both spiritual and actual, looking for the "Truth". He first found his truth for himself and then went to look for people he could share it with. He encountered a group of "seekers" in Westmoreland in the north of England who were also looking for the "Truth" and were meeting together in silence, waiting to be shown a way forward. It was the combination of Fox's revelations with this group's practice of silent waiting that formed the beginning of the Religious Society of Friends or Quakers.

The main revelation, or "opening" as he called it, which came to Fox and which he shared with these seekers and others, was that "Christ is come to teach his people himself". The second coming, which had been awaited for so long, had already happened inwardly. There was no need for priests or any intermediaries between God and the individual. Everyone had access to Christ the Inward Light or Inward Teacher to guide them, if they would look within and make themselves open.

In Fox's experience the Inward Light acted in two ways. First, the Light worked to reveal the darkness in individuals, not to condemn them for past sin, but to show them the ways in which they must change their behaviour. This challenge was usually different for each person and involved him or her in confronting their "cross", a word used by Quakers specifically for the particular stumbling block on the path to convincement which was most difficult for them to overcome. The Quaker term "convincement" is similar to but not the same as conversion. It is not one moment of redemption but a continuing process of faithfulness and sometimes failure, trying to follow the leadings of the Inward Light step by step.

Silent worship has always been an important part of the power of Quakerism. From the outside it may appear that nothing is going on but in fact at its best this is a vital activity. While sitting in silent waiting, a group of people could feel drawn together like streams running into a river or a fire made up of separate living coals, to use two contemporary metaphors. Out of the living silence any one of them might receive words from God, either for themselves or to share with others. When spoken, these words were called vocal ministry and individuals particularly gifted in this way eventually became known as ministers. The important next step for the newly formed group was to go out and let others know what they had found as widely as possible. Soon pairs of Quakers were travelling as missionaries all over Great Britain, to America, to the Continent and even farther afield: Quakerism grew rapidly.

Quakerism in Elizabeth Fry's time

By the time Elizabeth Fry was born in the late eighteenth century, the Religious Society of Friends had changed considerably from the vital expanding movement of Fox's time. Its spiritual roots remained the same but it was much more tightly regulated. Overseers, in charge of pastoral care and of keeping a watch on Friends' behaviour, and elders, who made sure that meeting for worship was held in the approved fashion, were appointed for life. Ministers too, once their gift for vocal ministry had been officially recognized and recorded, served for life and a high standard of public and private behaviour was expected of them. A network of ministers, usually travelling in pairs, visited meetings throughout Great Britain and often journeyed further afield to Ireland, the Continent and America, spreading their influence wide. This network included visiting American and Irish ministers, and ministers from several countries would often travel together, helping and learning from one another. At home, ministers would make official visits to Quaker families in a district to make an audit of their spiritual condition. Although there was still a hope that converts to Quakerism might be made, the missionary zeal of ministers at this time was mainly directed to those within the Society of Friends rather than to those outside it.

Each generation of Quakers had to face the problem of retaining those brought up in Quaker families as active Quakers. An important component of Quakerism was and is the necessity for each person to come to a conviction of the rightness of the faith for themselves. Education is never enough in itself as Quakerism comes from a personal conviction of the existence of the Inward Teacher, Christ, leading the individual into right action. It is necessary to follow one's guide, but also to be convinced of the Quaker way.

Quakerism in the past, as it remains today, is a combination of the individual's spiritual journey and a corporate worship and witness in the world. As William Penn described early Friends, "they were changed men themselves before they went about to change others". The Quaker faith demanded, and still demands, not only a personal spiritual journey but also a witness, or testimony, to the world through action of different kinds. Each Friend had their own testimony for truth to give, but usually this was expressed through generally accepted corporate testimonies. The basic testimonies were, and remain, a witness for peace, for truthfulness, for simplicity and for equality.

'Plain' and 'Gay' Quakers

Traditional Quakers at the end of the eighteenth and the beginning of the nineteenth centuries believed that it was important that Quakers should show a 'consistent' behaviour in line with the testimonies that would mark them out as Friends. A personal inward conviction was not enough. A 'Plain' Quaker was expected to express the testimonies for truthfulness, simplicity and equality through the conventions of plain dress and plain speech. At this time it was impossible to hold office or have any influence in the organization of the Religious Society of Friends without being 'plain'. But there were others who, like Elizabeth's parents, thought of themselves as Quakers and believed they were bringing up their children as Friends to whom the attitudes of 'Plain' Quakers seemed extreme and unreasonable and who preferred to assimilate with those around them as much as possible. In contemporary terms they were known as 'Gay Quakers' – 'Plain' and 'Gay' describing their outward appearance.

In the beginning plain dress expressed the testimony to simplicity and was a matter of removing superfluous ornament from clothes and deciding on one colour for each person's garments instead of following the changeable and distracting dictates of fashion. During the course of the eighteenth century, however, complicated dress codes were developed and Friends had "plain" clothes made by specialist tailors and dressmakers. Collars on men's jackets were not allowed, grey became universally adopted as the Quaker colour, and much energy was expended in policing proper Quaker plainness.

For Elizabeth Fry much of her early concern with plain dress revolved around caps and handkerchiefs. In later years her dress was certainly simple but her plain grey dress was made of silk and the brown shawl she wore for visits to Newgate was lined with ermine. However, it seems that adopting plain dress in her case did free her from worry about the changes of fashion and left her freer to concentrate on her spiritual state, so that in a way it did achieve its object.

The testimony to plain speech, which had sprung from the testimonies to truth and to equality, also changed in its effect over time. At first a refusal to use any honorific titles when speaking to people or to use the polite plural forms of address, but to say "thou" to everyone of whatever status, brought considerable anger and persecution down upon Friends. Parents, used to being addressed respectfully by their children, sometimes reacted strongly to being called "thou". Judges too reacted with harsh sentences against what they heard as a lack of respect.

By Elizabeth Fry's time, however, the use of plain speech was more likely to result in social embarrassment than in any serious penalties, although this did not make its adoption easy. Elizabeth had some difficulty with calling others "thou", as much within her own family as outside it. Brought up as a lady among the Norfolk county set, she was very aware of polite address and found it difficult to stand out. Another result of her upbringing gave her difficulty not only with plain speech in itself but also with the testimony to equality. Although she was willing to speak to women prisoners as fellow mothers, she was always aware of the different degrees of society and believed that they were divinely instituted. She was always aware of her genteel status and encouraged other "ladies" to visit prisons so that they might give a good example. She did not address the nobility she got to know in plain speech but called them by their "vain titles" – "Lord", "Lady" and "Your Majesty". Again she was talking to them on equal terms, but with respect to their elevated state. It was probably the apparent inconsistency of this attitude to the "great and good" that particularly annoyed stricter Quakers.

Another aspect of plain speech was the rejection of "pagan" names for the days of the week and months of the year. Quakers used only numbers, such as 1st day and 4th month, in order to describe them truthfully. Elizabeth Fry's change to "plainness" can be charted in part from the change in expressing dates in her journal when in April 1799 she writes 4th month and continues in this way for the rest of her life.

The different attitudes among Friends caused difficulties and divided families, as had the convincement of Friends in earlier times. Plain friends had no compunction about rebuking Gay Friends for their behaviour, particularly for the way in which they brought up their children. Elizabeth's father was "spoken to" several times when it was thought that his children were getting too close to non-Quakers and he took notice of these strictures. Elizabeth's uncle, Joseph, was a "Plain Friend", but the brothers worked together in banking without too much conflict and were welcome in each other's houses. As children grew up and tried to find their own spiritual path, the existence of relatives in both camps, in whom they might confide, could be a great help to them.

Plainness marked Quakers out as separate from "the world" and for some the reputation of being a "remnant" or a "peculiar people" was desirable. If Quakerism was to survive, they argued, then it had to keep itself free from worldly contamination, and for a body once persecuted but now allowed freedom of worship, staying quiet and unnoticed was a benefit. Elizabeth Fry's high profile public work went against the grain with many Friends and they did not hold back in their criticism of her.

Disownment

Mild disapproval of one another's life-style was one thing, but there were greater causes of division within the Society of Friends which could lead to deeper rifts with families and to the loss of many to the Society. Because Quakers were so conscious of the way in which they were perceived by those outside the Society and because the upholding of the various corporate testimonies was so important, a system of internal discipline had grown up from the beginning. A Quaker could be disowned and no longer regarded officially as a Friend if they behaved in a way which might bring the public reputation of the Society into disrepute. This covered a multitude of sins, including drinking to excess, adultery, dishonesty, bankruptcy and marrying someone who was not a Quaker, usually called marrying out.

In practice disownment meant that a person lost their membership and was not allowed to attend business meetings or take any part in the decisions of the Society. They were not excluded from meeting for worship or from personal friendship with Quakers. Disownment was not a step taken lightly. The offender would be visited and remonstrated with, sometimes many times over many years, but if the step was taken it was seen as a disgrace. It was possible for someone once disowned to be reinstated, but only if they were willing to apologize publicly for their fault.

In the eighteenth century marrying out was one of the commonest and most divisive reasons for disownment. Quaker marriage had, from the beginning of the movement, been a declaration of two people before God, in the presence of witnesses in a Quaker meeting without the need for a priest or anyone else to officiate. At first there had been difficulties regarding the legality of such a marriage but these were eventually settled by Lord Hardwicke's Act of 1753, which allowed Quakers to solemnize marriage elsewhere then in the parish church. However, this only applied to cases where both parties were Quakers. If one half of the couple was not a Quaker, then the marriage had to take place in a church, before a priest, and this was usually a matter for automatic disownment. Unless in the fullness of time the non-Quaker half of the partnership became a

Friend, it was almost impossible to apologize and be reinstated without seeming to regret that the marriage had taken place. It is not surprising therefore that disownment for marrying out drove many young people, among them several of Elizabeth Fry's children, out of the Society of Friends. The Orthodox solution to the problem was to keep young people out of the company of any but other Quakers, but this was not the way in which Elizabeth had been brought up and was not the way in which she brought up her children. She gave them a Christian education, and although she hoped that they would be Quakers and marry Quakers, she believed that it was God who should do this work, not her. She did not oppose the marriage of any of her children, although as a Quaker minister she could not be seen to approve by going with them to church.

Disownment for marrying out was an ever-present worry for Elizabeth Fry, but it was not this disownment that affected Elizabeth Fry and her family most. In 1828 Elizabeth's husband Joseph Fry was made bankrupt when the banking business he was involved in failed. There was no suggestion that he had been personally at fault and he felt that he had nothing to apologize for, but bankruptcy was seen as failing to fulfil promises to creditors and therefore against the testimony to truth, and disownment was inevitable. Joseph, a Plain Friend all his life, felt the rejection keenly and his children rallied to his side against what they saw as the cruelty and rigidity of the Society of Friends. Elizabeth was torn between her family and her faith for, although not disowned herself and still a minister, she also felt rejected and criticized. She also suffered from the change in her financial circumstances and even the cushioning of the blow by her brothers and sisters, who made sure that she and her family had somewhere to live and money to spare for her charitable work, did not make it easy to bear. Joseph withdrew from any connection with banking and went back to business as a tea merchant, a trade he knew well, in which he never got out of his depth and in which his sons might join him.

Influences on Elizabeth Fry

In spite of the difficulties and disappointments that Elizabeth Fry had to endure as a "Plain" Quaker, she never regretted her decision. Both looking back later on her life and at the time, she acknowledged the influential people who had helped her to discover and be true to her Inward Teacher.

Elizabeth's family were always the greatest influence on her and even when they did not see eye to eye she wanted to please them. It pained her that the inclination she had towards "Plain" Quakerism should give pain to her father and to her brothers and sisters. But none of her family put obstacles in her way once they were sure that she had fully considered the path she was taking. Her father took her to London and to Coalbrookdale, not so much to distract her as to give her a wider experience of life which might help her to judge for herself.

Outside her family the greatest influence on the young Elizabeth was William Savery (1750–1804). He was an American travelling minister who had been away from America for several years travelling on the Continent and in Ireland and Great Britain. On his travels he came to Norwich meeting, and Elizabeth, who had come to hear him out of curiosity, found herself deeply affected by what he had to say. He preached a simple evangelical message, urging his hearers to look within for the truth, to open themselves to Christ as their Inward Teacher and to go further than either deism or a rational belief in science or the natural world. He was fond of quoting Pope in his ministry and recommending people to look "through nature up to nature's god", a concept that already meant much to Elizabeth. He also told his own story, of one who had not known what the Quakerism he had been brought up in meant until he had gone through a spiritual awakening. For Elizabeth, brought up in the way she had been but longing for something more, his words struck home. She wanted to hear more and found opportunities to listen and speak to him. Elizabeth could not get enough of William Savery, indeed her attitude to him was that of an obsessed fan. The trip to London which her father proposed was as attractive because William Savery would be there as for all the amusements she might join in or the people she might meet.

William Savery inspired Elizabeth to begin to "turn plain", but she was confirmed in her difficult change by others nearer home. Taking another journey with her father, she visited Coalbrookdale, home of the Darby ironmasters and centre of a community of Plain Friends. Here Elizabeth stayed for a few days with her cousin Priscilla Hannah Gurney (1757–1828). Priscilla Hannah came from the same kind of background as Elizabeth and from the same Quaker families, the Gurneys and the Barclays. Her mother and sister both remained Gay Quakers, but Priscilla had undergone a long and difficult conversion experience, being baptized into the Church of England before realizing at last what was true for her. In her journal she describes her experience, "my mind was, in the most sudden and powerful manner, arrested in its course, by the irresistible impression of these words, formed within me but not uttered by me 'I must be a Quaker', accompanied by a sense of divine authority which I could not evade". She left her family in Bath in 1792 and went to live in Coalbrookdale with her "parental friends", Richard and Rebecca Reynolds. Described by a friend as "small in person, beautiful in countenance, elegant in manner", Priscilla was the ideal person to help Elizabeth at this stage of her spiritual journey. It is almost certain that Priscilla talked to Elizabeth about her own experience as Elizabeth uses almost exactly the same phrase when describing what she sees as her next step, "I know now what the mountain is I have to climb, *I am to be a Quaker*".

At Coalbrookdale Elizabeth also met the famous minister Deborah Darby (1754–1810), who prophesied what her future service was to be – "a light to the blind, speech to the dumb and feet to the lame" – and that she might become a Quaker minister in her turn. Deborah was an influence for good in the lives of many, including Stephen Grellet, a French aristocrat who had fled the Revolution and whom she had met in her travels in America and brought to Quakerism. It was his disquiet about the conditions of the women in Newgate that was eventually to bring Elizabeth Fry into that field.

Another great influence in Elizabeth Fry's life was her young brother Joseph John (1788–1847). Eight years her junior, Joseph was the one among all her brothers and sisters who took the same path, becoming a Plain Friend at the age of twenty-one and later a travelling minister. He and Elizabeth travelled together in the ministry in the British Isles, in Ireland and on the Continent. They worked together for prison reform and for the Bible Society. He also shared some degree of her fame, particularly within Quaker circles. His evangelical Bible-based preaching was particularly popular in America, which he visited for three years from 1837. Elizabeth and Joseph always supported each other and he was greatly affected by her death. All her brothers and sisters were dear to her, but Joseph had a special place in her affections and influence over her because they had to some extent trodden the same path.

Elizabeth Fry's faith

Elizabeth Fry was from her youth of an extremely nervous disposition, afraid of the dark, of the sea, with a lively imagination regarding possible disasters. Sometimes she was confirmed in her fearfulness when imagined calamities, like the death of her mother, actually happened. This nervous fearfulness often made her ill, frequently manifested in stomach upsets and fainting fits, and her medicine for these illnesses was, as was usual at that time, increasing doses of alcohol and laudanum – the "luxuries" which she did not feel able to do without. Throughout her life, her real remedy for indisposition was always practical action. If she could be doing good, or organizing other people to do good, then her mind was distracted from her own worries and state of health. Practical action on a large scale, particularly when she could see beneficial results and feel that her efforts were appreciated, was what kept her going. If those to whom she did good were not grateful or if she was criticized by her family or by other Quakers, she was both hurt and mystified. As she repeats again and again in her journals and elsewhere, she is only acting as she believes God wants her to, not for her own exaltation.

Although she wanted to "feel" true religion as well as trying to discover it rationally, Elizabeth Fry's faith was not primarily a mystical one. Her faith was evangelical in that she made a very clear identification between the Inward Teacher and Jesus Christ in the same way as William Savery had. Her faith was certainly grounded in the Bible, but the authority she looked to, like that of early Friends, was not Scripture of itself but Christ within. She felt that if she prayed and listened for an answer, she would be led into the right path. Even though she might count herself an Evangelical and certainly allied herself with the position of her brother Joseph, Elizabeth had serious misgivings about the extreme position of some Friends, which was gaining ground towards the end of her life, that stressed the necessity of belief in doctrines such as the Atonement. Such an insistence sounded too much like the imposition of dogma and even superstition to sit comfortably with Elizabeth's Quakerism.

Again and again she states her faith that true religion will "break down the partition walls" which sectarianism builds up. In this belief she is going against the contemporary orthodoxy of Quakerism, which saw the wisdom of raising "a hedge" or wall between the Society of Friends and the world to avoid contamination. Elizabeth moved in circles which to the mind of some Friends showed the danger of contact with the world very clearly. The fact that so few of her brothers and sisters and even fewer of her children remained Friends was proof to some that Elizabeth should have been more careful. Her children should not have been allowed to mix in the circles they had, nor should she and Joseph have allowed them to "marry out". Elizabeth felt the practical impossibility of forcing someone else's life into a particular pattern. She continually prayed that God would seek out her children directly, but she came to believe that this would not necessarily be through Quakerism.

Another important theme in Elizabeth's spiritual life – one with which the modern mind may find it difficult to sympathize – is death. Her close acquaintance with death among her own family and friends is not especially unusual for anyone living at this time. Indeed, the fact that Elizabeth lost only one of her eleven children in infancy marks her out as more fortunate than most. However, it is very important to her, spiritually, that those close to her should make a "good" death – resigned, confident in faith and without regret. Much of this feeling may spring from the early loss of her mother, but it is also related to the growth of her ability as a Quaker minister. She first appeared in the ministry, after years of hesitation, at her father's funeral, and from then on, visiting the sick and dying, she developed her gift for prayer in particular. Several letters and journal entries were written as she sat by the dead body of a loved one. Although Elizabeth was convinced of the absolute wrongness of capital punishment and campaigned against it, she also ministered to prisoners before their execution. She was concerned with their reformation and acceptance of Christianity, so that they might die a "happy death".

The difficult paradox at the heart of this attitude lies in having to reconcile acceptance of God's will in the death of a person and confidence that having made a Christian death they will be going to a happier place, with the real grief of those left behind. This is acceptable if kept within bounds, but there is often a dichotomy between what a person actually feels and what they think they should be feeling. Elizabeth finds this difficult herself, almost impossible when contemplating the death of her daughter Betsy. She is therefore perhaps more generous than many contemporary Friends in recognizing grief in others. Her younger brother Joseph, faced with the sudden death of his second wife, reacts as he ought publicly, but not long after breaks down physically and has to be cared for by his sister.

Although she believed that her public work was an expression of her faith, Elizabeth Fry's position as a Quaker minister was also vital to her spiritual life. This was the reason for many of her travels as much as the opportunity to visit prisons. As ministers, she and other Friends felt that they were mouthpieces for God's words, a belief which added to the aura of calm dignity for which she was known. She had a particular gift for prayer and spoke in simple words rather than relying on the circumlocutions and formulae that often made the ministry of her contemporaries obscure.

Elizabeth Fry's philanthropy

All of Elizabeth Fry's philanthropy sprang from the concern for the plight of the poor and the obligation to do something practical to relieve their practical and spiritual needs that she had learned at her mother's knee. When Elizabeth was young she had taken food and clothes to those in need and had tried to comfort the sick and dying. Under the influence of William Savery, she began a school for local children which during the two years before she left Earlham on her marriage in 1800 had swelled in numbers from two or three to eighty-six. Her teaching largely consisted of reading to her charges from the Bible in her melodious voice. As a young mother she took her children with her to visit the poor. Visiting the Irish Catholic immigrants living near her London home in Plashet, she again tended to their practical needs, read to them and gave them copies of the Bible while never trying directly to change their faith.

So when she began to visit Newgate she was continuing along the same lines she had already begun, bringing food and clothes, reading from the Bible, soothing them with her friendliness and calm manner. Again she started a school for the children in the prison and taught the prisoners too. However, it was soon evident to her that there was such a large task ahead of her that she could not do it alone and so she organized Ladies Committees and joined with other interested women, both Quaker and others. In time, most of the day-to-day visiting was done by others, while Elizabeth Fry campaigned for support from anyone with influence that she could reach. She became an expert who was consulted for advice and wherever she went she visited the local prison and/or lunatic asylum and advised what she thought was needed.

From the 1820s onwards Elizabeth Fry's work in prison reform brought her into the public eye to the extent that she became a "celebrity". Everyone, high and low, wanted to meet the famous Mrs Fry. She was courted, asked for advice, looked to for help, and she embraced the experience in order to further her cause. Her fellow Quakers worried that her extreme popularity might go to her head, but she was all too aware of this danger even as she sometimes succumbed to it. She had novelty value both as a Quaker and as a woman taking a public role, and although she declared her ambivalence, she knew how to exploit her position. When the tide turned later in the 1830s, after her husband's disownment and with a new Whig government inclined to stress punishment rather than reform of prisoners and so less willing to listen to her plans, she missed being at the centre of things, however much she might long for quietness in her journal.

Her concern for the poor remained active. During a holiday in Brighton she was so affected by what she saw that she organized local people to set up a society to visit the poor. These District Visiting Societies soon spread throughout the country and brought together local concerned people of every denomination to do what they could for the poor among them.

Elizabeth was a great believer in the power of the Bible to reach the hearts of people by itself without being preached about and to this end she provided Bibles and tracts for coastguards, sailors and other deprived groups. She also distributed tracts to anyone she met, often books written by her brother Joseph or the book of Bible texts – her "text-book" – which she put together herself. She felt that experience had taught her the best methods to help the poor wherever they might be found and that anyone could follow her example.

Conclusion

Many words have been written about Elizabeth Fry, both during her own lifetime and in the centuries since. Most of these words have been favourable, some might say idolatrous, depicting her as "the angel of Newgate" without fault and wholly concerned for the needs of others.

This book is made up of her own words, which paint a rather different picture of someone aware of her own weaknesses, constantly striving to do what she feels is set before her, but struggling to reconcile the demands of her family and her religion. Her wish to "feel" a "true religion" is always with her, but her loyalty to the "sect" she chose to serve, the Religious Society of Friends, does not overcome a wider outlook, embracing the good of her children, her brothers and sisters and all she met both high and low, "all one in Christ".

Elizabeth Fry was very aware of her own failings. She wanted to be liked and knew that she was fearful of doing the wrong thing or of offending other people. She knew that she was too fond of the company of the great and that the "vain titles of the world" meant more to her than they should have done. She knew that she was prone to excessive anxiety about those close to her and feared that this unfitted her to be really useful to them. She wanted to educate her children without indoctrinating them, but still felt that she had failed when they chose a different religious path from her own. She knew that she was not strong enough to do without the comforts of wealth with which she had been brought up, nor to put aside dependence on alcohol and laudanum which she did not believe her health would allow her to give up.

Above all, she knew that she was not always the calm certain capable "Quaker saint" of her public persona. She did try to follow her Inward Teacher and to be faithful to her understanding of Christianity as a broad church in the best sense. In truth, she was both more and less than the angel of Newgate, and reading some of her words and hearing a little of her voice may allow us in the twenty-first century to understand better and empathize with her spiritual journey.

Gil Skidmore

Note on the text

Elizabeth's spiritual life is mainly evident through her journal, which she wrote almost daily from an early age. She made a summary of the early journals before 1799 and then destroyed them, but all the rest survive in forty-six manuscript volumes. This selection of Elizabeth Fry's writings has been extracted from the two-volume printed version of her Journal put together after her death by her daughters, which includes some of her letters, together with some other letters to be found in Friends House Library and other sources. I have not indicated omissions in the text as the printed volumes are already edited down considerably from the originals. Instead, I have arranged the extracts chronologically with some indication of date and have added comments to explain references when necessary. Although the main emphasis of this selection is not on Elizabeth's Fry's prison reform work, I have included extracts from her 1827 book *Observations on the visiting, Superintendence and Government of Female Prisoners* as they illustrate her attitude to those she was trying to help and to the women she was encouraging to assist her in this work.

The spelling and punctuation of Elizabeth Fry and her past editors have been mostly retained, with only occasional editorial adjustments to avoid ambiguity.

A family chronology

1775 John Gurney married to Catherine Bell
1776 Catherine [Kitty] Gurney born
1778 Rachel Gurney born
1780 Elizabeth Gurney born
1781 John Gurney born
1782 Richenda [Chenda] Gurney born
1783 Hannah Gurney born
1784 Louisa Gurney born
1785 Priscilla Gurney born
1786 Samuel Gurney born
1788 Joseph John Gurney born
1791 Daniel Gurney born
1792 Elizabeth's mother, Catherine Gurney dies
1800 Elizabeth Gurney married to Joseph Fry
1801 Katherine [Kate] Fry born
1803 Rachel Fry born
1804 John Fry born
1806 Louisa Gurney married to Samuel Hoare
    William Storrs Fry born
1807 John Gurney married to Elizabeth Gurney
    Hannah Gurney married to Thomas Fowell Buxton
1808 Samuel Gurney married to Elizabeth Sheppard
    Richenda Fry born
    John Gurney's wife Elizabeth dies
1809 Joseph Fry born
    Elizabeth Fry's father John Gurney dies
1810 Elizabeth [Betsy] Fry born
1812 Hannah Fry born
1814 Louisa Fry born
    Elizabeth Fry's brother, John Gurney, dies
1815 Elizabeth [Betsy] Fry dies
1816 Richenda Gurney married to Rev. Francis Cunningham
1817 Joseph John Gurney married to Jane Birkbeck
1821 Priscilla Gurney dies
    Rachel Fry married to Francis Cresswell
1822 Daniel [Harry] Fry and Francis [Frank] Cresswell born on the
    same day
    Joseph John Gurney's wife Jane dies

1823 Daniel Gurney married to Lady Harriet Hay

1825 John Fry married to Rachel Reynolds

1827 Rachel Gurney dies

Joseph John Gurney married to Mary Fowler

1828 Richenda Fry married to Foster Reynolds

1832 William Storrs Fry married to Julia Pelly

Hannah Fry married to William Streatfield

1835 Louisa Fry married to Raymond Pelly

Joseph John Gurney's second wife Mary dies

1836 Louisa Gurney Hoare dies

1841 Joseph John Gurney marries Eliza Paul Kirkbride

1844 William Storrs Fry dies

1845 Daniel [Harry] Fry married to Lucy Sheppard

Elizabeth Fry dies

1

"I know what the mountain is I have to climb":

The making of a Quaker, 1780–1799

In 1828, faced with the crisis of her husband's bankruptcy and disownment, Elizabeth Fry looked back over her life and wrote with hindsight about her early upbringing

My earliest recollections are, I should think, soon after I was two years old. My father at that time had two houses, one in Norwich, and one at Bramerton, a sweet country place, situated on a common, near a pretty village; here, I believe, many of my early tastes were formed, though we left to reside at Earlham, when I was about five years old. The impressions then received remain lively on my recollection; the delight in the beauty and wild scenery in parts of the common, the trees, the flowers, and the little rills that abounded on it, the farm-houses, the village school, and the different poor people and their cottages; particularly a poor woman with one arm whom we called one-armed Betty; another neighbour, Greengrass, and her strawberry beds round a little pond; our gardener, who lived near a large piece of water, and used to bring fish from it. Here, I think, my great love for the country, the beauties of nature, and attention to the poor, began.

My mother was most dear to me, and the walks she took with me in the old-fashioned garden, are as fresh with me, as if only just passed; and her telling me about Adam and Eve being driven out of Paradise: I always considered it must be just like our garden at Bramerton. I remember that my spirits were not strong; that I frequently cried if looked at, and used to say that my eyes were weak; but I remember much pleasure and little suffering, or particular tendency to naughtiness, up to this period. Fear about this time began to show itself, of people and things: I remember being so much afraid of a gun, that I gave up an expedition of pleasure with my father and mother, because there was a gun in the carriage. I was also exceedingly afraid of the dark, and suffered so acutely from being left alone without a light after I went to bed, that I believe my nervous system was injured in consequence of it; also, I had so great a dread of bathing (to which I was at times obliged to submit) that the first sight of the sea, when we were as a family going to stay by it, would make me cry; indeed, fear was so strong a principle in my mind, as greatly to mar the natural pleasure of childhood. I am now of opinion, that it would have been much more subdued, and great suffering spared, by its having been still more yielded to; by having a light left in my room, not being long left alone, and never forced to bathe; for I do not at all doubt that it partly arose from that nervous susceptible constitution, that has at times, throughout my life, caused me such real and deep suffering. I know not what would have been the consequence, had I had any other than a most careful and wise mother and judicious nurses, or had I been alarmed, as too many children are, by false threats of what might happen.

I had, as well as a fearful, rather a reserved mind, for I never remember telling of my many painful fears, though I must often have shown them by weeping when left in the dark, and on other occasions: this reserve made me little understood, and thought very little of, except by my mother and one or two others. I was considered and called very stupid and obstinate. I certainly did not like learning, nor did I, I believe, attend to my lessons, partly from a delicate state of health, that produced languor of mind as well as body; but, I think, having the name of being stupid really tended to make me so, and discouraged my efforts to learn. I remember having a poor, not to say low opinion of myself, and used to think that I was so very inferior to my sisters, Catherine and Rachel. I believe I had not a name only for being obstinate, for my nature had then a strong tendency that way; and I was disposed to a spirit of contradiction, always ready to see things a little differently from others, and not willing to yield my sentiments to theirs.

My natural affections were very strong from my early childhood, at times almost overwhelmingly so. Such was the love for my mother, that the thought that she might die and leave me used to make me weep after I went to bed, and for the rest of the family, that notwithstanding my fearful nature, my childlike wish was, that two large walls might crush us all together, that we might die at once, and thus avoid the misery of each other's death. I seldom, if I could help it, left my mother's side, I watched her when asleep in the day with exquisite anxiety, and used to go gently to her bed-side to listen, from the awful fear that she did not breathe; in short, I may truly say, it amounted to deep reverence, that I felt for my father and mother. I never remember, as a little child, but once being punished by my mother; and she then mistook tears of sorrow for tears of naughtiness, a thing that deeply impressed me, and I have never forgotten the pain it gave me. Although I do not imply that I had no faults, far from it, as some of the faults of my childhood are very lively in my recollection; yet from my extreme love and fear, many of these faults were known almost only to myself. My imagination was lively, and I once remember, and only once, telling a real untruth with one of my sisters and one of my brothers. We saw a bright light one morning, which we represented far above the reality, and upon the real thing being shown us that we had seen, we made it out not to be it.

My remembrance is of the pleasure of my childhood being almost spoiled through fear, and my religious impressions, such as I had, were accompanied by gloom: on this account, I think the utmost care needed, in representing religious truth to children, that fearful views of it should be most carefully avoided, lest it should give a distaste for that which is most precious. First show them the love and mercy of God in Christ Jesus, and the sweetness and blessedness of his service; and such things in scripture, for instance, as Abraham's sacrifice, should be carefully explained to them. I think I suffered much in my youth from the most tender nervous system; I certainly felt symptoms of ill health before my mother died, that I thought of speaking to her about, but never did, partly because I did not know how to explain them; but they ended afterwards in very severe attacks of illness. I have always thought being forced to bathe was one cause of this, and I mention it, because I believe it a dangerous thing to do to children. What care is needful not to force children to learn too much, as it not only injures them, but gives a distaste for intellectual pursuits. Instruction should be adapted to their condition, and communicated in an easy and agreeable way.

How great is the importance of a wise mother, directing the tastes of her children in very early life, and judiciously influencing their affections! I remember with pleasure my mother's beds for wild flowers, which, with delight, I used, as a child, to attend to with her; it gave me that pleasure in observing their beauties and varieties, that though I never have had time to become a botanist, few can imagine, in my many journeys, how I have been pleased and refreshed, by observing and enjoying the wild flowers on my way. Again, she collected shells, and had a cabinet, and bought one for Rachel and myself, where we placed our curiosities; and I may truly say, in the midst even of deep trouble, and often most weighty engagements of a religious and philanthropic nature, I have derived advantage, refreshment, and pleasure, from my taste for these things, making collections of them, and various natural curiosities, although, as with the flowers, I have not studied them scientifically.

My mother also encouraged my most close friendship with my sister Rachel, and we had our pretty light closet, our books, our pictures, our curiosities, our tea things, all to ourselves; and as far as I can recollect, we unitedly partook of these pleasures, without any of the little jealousies or the quarrels of childhood.

My mother, as far as she knew, really trained us up in the fear and love of the Lord. My deep impression is that she was a holy devoted follower of the Lord Jesus; but that her understanding was not fully enlightened as to the fulness of gospel truth. She taught us as far as she knew, and I now remember the solemn religious feelings I had whilst sitting in silence with her after reading the scriptures, or a Psalm before we went to bed. I have no doubt that her prayers were not in vain in the Lord. She died when I was twelve years old; the remembrance of her illness and death is sad, even to the present day.

The earliest of Elizabeth Fry's existing journals dates from 1797

April 1797 – Without passions of any kind how different I should be! I would not give them up, but I should like to have them under subjection; but it appears to me, as I feel, impossible to govern them, my mind is not strong enough, as I at times think they do no hurt to others. But am I sure they will hurt no one? I believe by not governing myself in little things, I may by degrees become a despicable character, and a curse to society; therefore, my doing wrong is of consequence to others, as well as to myself.

April 25th – I feel by experience, how much entering into the world hurts me; worldly company, I think, materially injures, it excites a false stimulus, such as a love of pomp, pride, vanity, jealousy, and ambition. It leads to think about dress, and such trifles, and when out of it, we fly to novels and scandal, or something of that kind, for entertainment. I have lately been given up a good deal to worldly passions; by what I have felt I can easily imagine how soon I should be quite led away.

May 16th – There is a sort of luxury in giving way to the feelings! I love to feel for the sorrows of others, to pour wine and oil into the wounds of the afflicted; there is a luxury in feeling the heart glow, whether it be with joy or sorrow. I think the different periods of life may well be compared to the seasons. First, we are in the spring, only buds are to be seen, next, our characters are blown, and it is summer; autumn follows, and there are then many remains of summer, and beautiful ones too; there springs also the best fruit from the summer flower. Winter must come, it will follow in its course; there is not much more pleasure then than collecting a few solitary berries, and playing with the snow and ice.

I like to think of everything, to look at mankind; I love to "look through Nature up to Nature's God". I have no more religion than that, and in the little I have I am not the least devotional, but when I admire the beauties of nature, I cannot help thinking of the source from whence such beauties flow. I feel it a support. I believe firmly that all is guided for the best by an invisible power, therefore I do not fear the evils of life so much. I love to feel good – I do what I can to be kind to everybody. I have many faults which I hope in time to overcome.

May 21st – I am seventeen today. Am I a happier or a better creature than I was this time twelvemonths? I know I am happier; I think I am better. I hope I shall be much better this day year than I am now. I hope to be quite an altered person, to have more knowledge, to have my mind in greater order; and my heart, too, that wants to be put in order as much, if not more, than any part of me, it is in such a flyaway state; but I think if ever it were settled on one object it would never, no never, fly away any more; it would rest quietly and happily on the heart that was open to receive it, it will then be most constant; it is not my fault it now flies away, it is owing to circumstances.

May 30th – It is a great comfort to me that life is short, and soon passes away, yet, it is certainly a pleasure or blessing to exist. I think I have now no reason to wish to die, I am so well; but I must own with ill health, such as I used to have, life is a burden. Perhaps I now think worse of it than I did when I had it, for the imagination increases evils at a distance, as it does every thing else; I was supported through it, whilst it lasted: though I was very unhappy, I could not call myself a miserable being. Ill health is certainly a deprivation of the powers of life; we do but half live when ill.

22

My fate is guided by an all-wise and all-virtuous Director, I shall not be ill, unless it is right I should be so.

June – I am at this present time in an odd state. I am like a ship put out to sea without a pilot; I feel my heart and mind so overburdened, I want some one to lean upon.

June 20th – If I have long to live in this world, may I bear misfortunes with fortitude; do what I can to alleviate the sorrows of others, exert what power I have to increase happiness; try to govern my passions by reason, and adhere strictly to what I think right.

July 7th – I have seen several things in myself and others, I have never before remarked; but I have not tried to improve myself, I have given way to my passions, and let them have command over me. I have known my faults, and not corrected them, and now I am determined I will once more try, with redoubled ardour, to overcome my wicked inclinations; I must not flirt; I must not ever be out of temper with the children; I must not contradict without a cause; I must not mump when my sisters are liked and I am not; I must not allow myself to be angry; I must not exaggerate, which I am inclined to do. I must not give way to luxury; I must not be idle in mind, I must try to give way to every good feeling, and overcome every bad. I will see what I can do; if I had but perseverance, I could do all that I wish, I will try. I have lately been too satirical, so as to hurt sometimes; remember! it is a fault to hurt others.

July 10th – Some poor people were here. I do not think I gave them what I did with a good heart. I am inclined to give away; but for a week past, owing to not having much money, I have been mean and extravagant. Shameful! Whilst I live, may I be generous; it is in my nature, and I will not overcome so good a feeling. I am inclined to be extravagant, and that leads to meanness, for those who will throw away a good deal are apt to mind giving a little.

July 30th – Pride and vanity are too much the incentives to most of the actions of men, they produce a love of admiration, and in thinking of the opinions of others, we are too apt to forget the monitor within. We should first look to ourselves and try to make ourselves virtuous, and then pleasing. Those who are truly virtuous not only do themselves good, but they add to the good of all. It is wonderfully ordered, how in acting for our own good, we promote the good of others. My idea of religion is, not for it to unfit us for the duties of life, like a nun who leaves them for prayer and thanksgiving; but I think it should stimulate and capacitate us to perform these duties properly. Seeing my father low this evening, I have done all I can to make him comfortable, I feel it one of my first duties; I hope he will always find in me a most true friend and affectionate daughter.

August 1st – I have done little today, I am so very idle; instead of improving I fear I go back; I think I may improve, being so young, but I also think there is every chance of my disimproving; my inclinations lead me to be an idle, flirting, worldly girl. I see what would be acting right, but I have neither activity nor perseverance in what I think right. I am like one setting out on a journey; if I set out on the wrong road, and do not try to recover the right one before I have gone far, I shall most likely lose my way for *ever*, and every step I take, the more difficult shall I find it to return, therefore the temptation will be greater to go on, till I get to destruction. On the contrary, if now, whilst I am innocent of any great faults, I turn into the right path, I shall feel more and more contented every step I take, and if I do now and then err a little from the proper path I shall not find it so hard to return to it, for I shall by degrees find the road to vice more and more unpleasant. Trifles occupy me far too much, such as dress &c., &c. I find it easier to acknowledge my vices than my follies.

August 12th – I do not know if I shall not soon be rather religious, because I have thought lately, what a support it is through life; it seems so delightful to depend upon a superior power, for all that is good ; it is at least always having the bosom of a friend open to us (in imagination), to rest all our cares and sorrows upon, and what must be our feelings to imagine that friend perfect, and guiding all and everything, as it should be guided. I think anybody who had real faith could never be unhappy; it appears the only certain source of support and comfort in this life, and what is best of all, it draws to virtue, and if the idea be ever so ill founded that leads to that great object, why should we shun it? Religion has been misused and corrupted, that is no reason why religion itself is not good. I fear being religious, in case I should be enthusiastic.

August 30th – "Come what, come may, time and the hour run through the roughest day." A very sad and trying day. Tried by being poorly, by others, and by myself: very far from what I ought to be.

September 3rd – There is much difference between being obstinate and steady; I am obstinate, when I contradict for the sake of contradiction; I am steady, when I keep to what I really think right. I am too apt to contradict, whether I should or not. If I am bid to do a thing, my spirit revolts – if I am asked to do a thing, I am willing.

December – A thought passed my mind, that if I had some religion, I should be superior to what I am, it would be a bias to better actions; I think I am by degrees losing many excellent qualities. I am more cross, more proud, more vain, more extravagant. I lay it to my great love of gaiety and the world. I feel, I know I am falling. I do believe if I had a little true religion, I should have a greater support than I have now; in virtue my mind wants a stimulus; never, no never did mind want one more: but I have the greatest fear of religion, because I never saw a person religious who was not enthusiastic.

January 1798 – I must die ! I shall die! wonderful, death is beyond comprehension. To leave life, and all its interests, and be almost forgotten by those we love. What a comfort must a real faith in religion be, in the hour of death; to have a firm belief of entering into everlasting joy. I have a notion of such a thing, but I am sorry to say, I have no real faith in any sort of religion; it must be a comfort and support in affliction, and I know enough of life to see how great a stimulus is wanted, to support through the evils that are inflicted, and to keep in the path of virtue. If religion be a support, why not get it?

January 18th – I am a bubble, without reason, without beauty of mind or person; I am a fool. I daily fall lower in my own estimation. What an infinite advantage it would be to me, to occupy my time and thoughts well. I am now seventeen, and if some kind, and great circumstance does not happen to me, I shall have my talents devoured by moth and rust. They will lose their brightness, lose their virtue, and one day they will prove a curse instead of a blessing. Dreaded day! I must use extreme exertion to act really right, to avoid idleness and dissipation.

Sunday February 4th – This morning I went to Meeting, though but poorly, because I wished to hear an American Friend, named William Savery. Much passed there of a very interesting nature. I have had a faint light spread over my mind, at least I believe it is something of that kind, owing to having been much with, and heard much excellence from, one who appears to me a true Christian. It has caused me to feel a little religion. My imagination has been worked upon, and I fear all that I have felt will go off. I fear it now; though at first I was frightened, that a plain Quaker should have made so deep an impression on me; but how truly prejudiced in me to think, that because good came from a Quaker, I should be led away by enthusiasm and folly: but I hope I am now free from such fears. I wish the state of enthusiasm I am in may last, for to-day I have felt *that there is a God*; I have been devotional, and my mind has been led away from the follies that it is mostly wrapt up in. We had much serious conversation; in short, what he said and what I felt was like a refreshing shower falling upon earth that had been dried up for ages. It has not made me unhappy: I have felt ever since humble. I have longed for virtue. I hope to be truly virtuous; to let sophistry fly from my mind; not to be enthusiastic and foolish; but only to be so far religious as will lead to virtue. There seems nothing so little understood as religion.

February 6th – My mind has by degrees flown from religion. I rode to Norwich, and had a very serious ride there, but meeting, and being looked at, with apparent admiration, by some officers brought on vanity; and I came home as full of the world, as I went to town full of heaven.

In hearing William Savery preach, he seemed to me to overflow with true religion, and to be humble, and yet a man of great abilities; and having been gay and disbelieving only a few years ago, makes him better acquainted with the heart of one in the same situation. If I were to grow like him, a preacher, I should be able to preach to the gay and unbelieving better than to any others, for I should feel more sympathy for them, and know their hearts better.

Sunday, February 11th – It is very different to this day week (a day never to be forgotten whilst memory lasts). I have been to Meeting this morning. To-day I have felt all my old irreligious feelings – my object shall be to search, try to do right, and if I am mistaken, it is not my fault; but the state I am now in makes it difficult to act. What little religion I have felt has been owing to my giving way quietly and humbly to my feelings; but the more I reason upon it, the more I get into a labyrinth of uncertainty, and my mind is so much inclined to both scepticism and enthusiasm, that if I argue and doubt, I shall be a total sceptic; if, on the contrary, I give way to it, and as it were, wait for religion, I may be led away. But I hope that will not be the case; at all events, religion, true and uncorrupted, is of all comforts the greatest; it is the first stimulus to virtue; it is a support under every affliction. I am sure it is better to be so in an enthusiastic degree, than not to be so at all, for it is a delightful enthusiasm.

February 15th – My mind is in a whirl. In all probability I shall go to London. Many, many are the sensations I feel about it, numbers of things to expect. In the first place, leaving home, how truly I shall miss my best of friends, and all of them [*her brothers and sisters*]. In the next place, I shall see William Savery most likely, and all those plain Quakers. I may be led away, beware! my feelings are far more risen at the thought of seeing him than all the playhouses and gaieties in the world. One will, I do not doubt, balance against the other; I must be careful not to be led away; I must be very careful not to get vain or silly, for I fear I shall. Be independent, and do not follow those I am with, more than I think right. Do not make dress a study, even in London. Read in the Bible, when I can; but if I see William Savery I shall not, I doubt, be over fond of gaieties.

February 24th – At last landed safely here (London); it is very pleasant in some things, very unpleasant in others. On Monday, I do not think it unlikely I shall go to the play. Tuesday, I expect to spend quietly. On Wednesday, I hope to see the Barclays, and to have a dance.

February 26th – Although I told William Savery my principles were not Friendly, yet I fear I should not like his knowing of my going to the play. I think such religion as his must attract an atheist; and if there were many such Quakers as he is, the Society would soon increase.

I went to Drury Lane in the evening. I must own I was extremely disappointed; to be sure, the house is grand and dazzling, but I had no other feeling whilst there than that of wishing it over. I was not at all interested with the play, the music I did not much like; and the truth is, my imagination was so raised that it must have fallen, had the play been perfect.

March 1st – I own I enter into the gay world reluctantly. I do not like plays. I think them so artificial that they are to me not interesting, and all seems so very far from pure virtue and nature. To-night I saw Hamlet and Bluebeard; I suppose that nothing on the stage can exceed it. There is acting, music, scenery to perfection, but I was glad when it was over; my hair was dressed and I felt like a monkey. London is not the place for heartfelt pleasure, so I must not expect to find it.

March 7th – I went to Meeting in the evening. I have not enough eloquence to describe it. William Savery's sermon was in the first part very affecting, it was from the Revelation; he explained his text beautifully and awfully, most awfully I felt it; he next described the sweets of religion, and the spirit of prayer. How he did describe it! He said, the deist, and those who did not feel devotion, looked at nature, admired the thunder, the lightning and earthquakes, as curiosities; but they looked not up through them to nature's God. How well he hit the state I have been in, I trust I may not remain in it; his prayer was beautiful, I think I felt to pray with him.

March 17th – May I never forget the impression William Savery has made on my mind. I thank God for having sent at least a glimmering of light through him into my heart, which I hope with care, and keeping it from the many draughts and winds of this life, may not be blown out, but become a large brilliant flame, that will direct me to that haven, where will be joy without a sorrow, and all will be comfort. I have faith, how much, to gain, not all the treasures in this world can equal that heavenly treasure. May I grow more and more virtuous, follow the path I should go in, and not fear to acknowledge the God whom I worship; I will try, and I do hope to do, what is right. I now long to be in the quiet of Earlham, for there I may see how good I can be, and so I may here, for the greater cross the greater crown; but I there can reflect quietly and soberly on what has passed, there I hope to regulate my mind, which I know sadly wants it. May I never lose the little religion I now have; but if I cannot feel religion and devotion, I must not despair, for if I am truly warm and earnest in the cause, it will come one day. My idea is that true humility and lowliness of heart is the first grand step towards true religion. I fear and tremble for myself, but I must humbly look to the Author of all that is good and great, and I may say humbly pray, that He will take me as a sheep strayed from His flock, and once more let me enter the fold of His glory. I feel there is a God and Immortality; happy, happy thought! May it never leave me, and if it should, may I remember I have felt that there is a God and Immortality.

March 26th – This morning I went to Amelia Opie's and had a pleasant time. I called on Mrs Siddons, who was not at home; then on Doctor Batty; then on Mrs Twiss, who gave me some paint for the evening. I was painted a little, I had my hair dressed, and did look pretty for me. Mr Opie, Amelia, and I went to the Opera concert. I own, I do love grand company. The Prince of Wales was there; and I must say, I felt more pleasure in looking at him than in seeing the rest of the company, or hearing the music. I did nothing but admire his Royal Highness; but I had a very pleasant evening indeed.

Again, looking back thirty years later, Elizabeth comments on this important period of her life

Here ended this important and interesting visit to London, where I learned much and had much to digest. I saw and entered various scenes of gaiety; many of our first public places; attended balls and other places of amusement. I saw many interesting Characters in the world, some of considerable eminence in that day; I was also cast among a great variety of persons of different descriptions. I had the high advantage of attending several most interesting meetings of William Savery, and having at times his company, and that of a few other Friends. It was like the casting die in my life; however, I believe it was in the ordering of Providence for me, and that the lessons then learnt are to this day valuable to me. I consider one of the important results was the conviction of these things being wrong, from seeing them and feeling their effects. I wholly gave up on my own ground, attending all public places of amusement, I saw they tend to promote evil; therefore even if I could attend them without being hurt myself, I felt in entering them I lent my aid to promote that, which I was sure from what I saw, hurt others; led many from the paths of rectitude and chastity, and brought them into much sin; particularly those who had to act in plays, or sing in concerts. I felt the vanity and folly of what are called the pleasures of this life, of which the tendency is not to satisfy, but eventually to enervate and injure the heart and mind; those only are real pleasures which are of an innocent nature, and used as recreations, subjected to the cross of Christ. I was in my judgment much confirmed in the infinite importance of religion, as the only real stay, guide, help, and comfort in this life, and the only means of our having a hope of partaking of a better. My understanding was increasingly open to receive its truths; although the glad tidings of the gospel of Christ were little, very

little, if at all understood by me. I obtained in this expedition a valuable
knowledge of human character, from the variety I met with; this I think
was useful to me, though some were very dangerous associates for so
young a person, and the way in which I was protected among them is in
my remembrance very striking; and leads me to acknowledge that at this
most critical period of my life, the tender mercy of my God was marvellously displayed towards me; and that His all-powerful, though to me
then almost unseen and unknown hand, held me up and protected me.

The contemporary journal continues

Earlham, April 30th, 1798 – To-day the children brought me a letter
from William Savery: I cannot well express what I felt at receiving it. I do
not know the course I am to run, all is hid in mystery, but I try to do right
in every thing. I feel he gives me a stimulant to virtue; but I fear, by what
I expressed in my letter, he suspects that I am turning plain Quaker. I hate
that he should estimate me falsely. I must remember that on the foundation of the doctrine I believe we agree. I must look to One higher than he;
and if I feel my own mind satisfied I need not fear. Look up to true religion as the very first of blessings, cherish it, nourish, and let it flourish and
bloom in my heart; it wants taking care of, it is difficult to obtain. I must
not despair or grow sceptical if I do not always feel religious. I have felt
God, as it were, and I must seek to find Him again.

April 21st – I am so glad I do not feel Earlham at all dull, after the bustle
of London; on the contrary, a better relish for the sweet innocence and
beauties of Nature. I hope I may say, I do look "through Nature up to
Nature's God". I go every day to see poor Bob [*a servant living at a cot-
tage in the Park*], who I think will not live. I once talked to him about his
dying, and asked him if he would like me to read to him in the Testament.
I told him, I felt such faith in the blessings of Immortality, that I pitied not
his state; it was an odd speech to make to a dying man. I hope to be able
to comfort him in his dying hours. I gave some things to some poor people
to-day; but it is not there that I am particularly virtuous, as I only am following my natural disposition. I should be far more so, if I never spoke
against any person, which I do too often. I think I am improved since I was
last at home; my mind is not so fly-away. I hope it never will be so again.
We are all governed by our feelings; now the reason why religion is far
more likely to keep you in the path of virtue than any theoretical plan is

that you feel it, and your heart is wrapt up in it; it acts as a furnace on your character, it refines it, it purifies it; whereas principles of your own making are without kindling to make the fire hot enough to answer its purpose. I think a dream I have had so odd, I will write it down.

Before I mention my dream, I will give an account of my state of mind, from the time I was fourteen years old. I had very sceptical or deistical principles. I seldom or never thought of religion, and altogether I was a negatively good character, having naturally good dispositions, I had not much to combat with; I gave way freely to the weakness of youth. I was flirting, idle, rather proud and vain, till the time I was seventeen, I found I wanted a better, a greater stimulus to virtue, than I had, as I was wrapt up in trifles. I felt my mind capable of better things; but I could not exert it, till several of my friends, without knowing my state, wished I would read books on Christianity; but I said till I felt the want of religion myself, I would not read books of that kind; but if ever I did, would judge clearly for myself, by reading the New Testament, and when I had seen for myself, I would then see what others said.

About this time, I believe, I never missed a week or a few nights without dreaming, I was nearly being washed away by the sea, sometimes in one way, sometimes in another; and I felt all the terror of being drowned, or hope of being saved. At last I dreamt it so often, that I told many of the family what a strange dream I had, and how near I was being lost. After I had gone on in this way for some months, William Savery came to Norwich. I had begun to read the Testament with reflections of my own, and he suddenly, as it were, opened my eyes to see religion; but again they almost closed. I went on dreaming the dream. The day when I felt I had really and truly got true and real faith, that night I dreamed the sea was coming as usual to wash me away, but I was beyond its reach; beyond its powers to wash me away; since that night I do not remember having dreamed that dream.

Odd! It did not strike me at the time so odd; but now it does. All I can say is, I admire it, I am glad I have had it, and I have a sort of faith in it; it ought, I think, to make my faith steady. It may be the work of chance, but I do not think it is, for it is so odd not having dreamed it since. What a blessed thought to think it comes from heaven! May I be made capable of acting as I ought to act; not being drowned in the ocean of the world, but permitted to mount above its waves, and remain a steady and faithful servant to the God whom I worship. I may take this dream in what light I like, but I must be careful of superstition; as many, many are the minds that are led away by it. Believe only in what I can comprehend or feel; don't, don't be led away by enthusiasm; but I don't fear. I feel myself under the protection of One, who alone is able to guide me to the path in which I ought to go.

April 29th – The human mind is so apt to fly from one extreme to another; and why is not mine like others? I certainly seem to be on the road to a degree of enthusiasm, but I own myself at a loss how to act. If I act as they would wish me, I should not humbly give way to the feelings of religion; I should dwell on philosophy and depend more on my own reason than any thing else. On the contrary, if I give way to the religious feelings to which I am inclined (and I own I believe much in inspiration), I feel confident that I should find true humility and humble waiting on the Almighty the only way of feeling that inward sense of the beauties, and of the comforts of religion; it spreads a sweet veil over the evils of life; it is to me the first of feelings; that state of devotion, that absolutely makes you weep, is most fine! I own my dream rather leads me to believe in, and try to follow the path I would go in. But I should think my wisest plan of conduct would be to warmly encourage my feelings of devotion, and to keep as nearly as I can to what I think right, and the doctrines of the Testament; not at present to make sects the subject of my meditations, but to do as I think right, and not alter my opinions from conformity, to any one gay or plain.

May 8th – This morning being alone, I think it a good opportunity to look into myself to see my present state, and to regulate myself. At this time the first object of my mind is religion. It is the most constant subject of my thoughts and of my feelings; I am not yet on what I call a steady foundation. The next feeling that at this present fills my heart is benevolence and affection to many, but great want of charity, want of humility, want of activity; my inclinations lead me, I hope, to virtue; my passions are, I hope, in a pretty good state; I want to set myself in good order, for much time is lost and many evils committed by not having some regular plan of conduct; I make these rules for myself:

First, – Never lose any time; I do not think that lost which is spent in amusement or recreation, some time every day ; but always be in the habit of being employed.

Second, – Never err the least in truth.

Third, – Never say an ill thing of a person, when I can say a good thing of them; not only speak charitably, but feel so.

Fourth, – Never be irritable nor unkind to anybody.

Fifth, – Never indulge myself in luxuries that are not necessary.

Sixth, – Do all things with consideration, and when my path to act right is most difficult, feel confidence in that power that alone is able to assist me, and exert my own powers as far as they go.

May 19th – Altogether I think I have had a satisfactory day. I had a good lesson of French this morning, and read much in Epictetus. Saw poor Bob, and enjoyed the sweet beauties of nature, which now shine forth; each day some new beauty arrives. I love the beauty of the country, it does the mind good. I love it more than I used to do. I love retirement and quiet much more since my journey to London. How little I thought six months ago I should be so much altered; I am since then, I hope, altered much for the better. My heart may rise in thankfulness to that omnipotent power that has allowed my eyes to be opened in some measure to see the light of truth, and to feel the comfort of religion. I hope to be capable of giving up my all, if it be required of me, to serve the Almighty with my whole heart.

May 21st – To-day is my birth-day. I am eighteen years old! How many things have happened to me since I was fourteen; the last year has been the happiest I have experienced for some time.

May 27th – I must be careful of allowing false scruples to enter my mind. I have not yet been long enough a religionist to be a sectarian. I hope by degrees to obtain true faith; but I expect I shall lose what I gain, if I am led to actions I may repent of; remember and never forget my own enthusiastic feeling nature. It requires caution and extreme prudence to go on as I should do. In the afternoon I went to St Peter's, and heard a good sermon. The common people seemed very much occupied, and wrapt up in the service, which I was pleased to see; afterwards I went to the cathedral, then I came home and read to the Normans and little Castleton.

June 1st – I have been great part of this morning with poor Bob, who seems now dying. I read a long chapter in the Testament to him, the one upon death, and I sat with him for some time afterwards. Poor fellow! I never saw death, or any of its symptoms before; sad to see, it truly is; I said a few words to him, and expressed to him how happy we should be in expectation of immortality, and everlasting bliss. Father of mercies, wilt Thou bless him, and take him unto Thee? Though my mind is flat this morning, and not favoured with Thy Spirit in devotion, yet I exert what I have, and hope it will prove acceptable in Thy sight. Almighty God, Thy will be done and not ours. May I always be resigned to what Thou hast ordered for me; I humbly thank Thee, for allowing my eyes to be opened, so as even to feel faith, hope and love towards Thee. First and last of everything infinite, and not to be comprehended except by Thy Spirit which Thou allowest to enlighten our hearts.

June 12th – This evening I have got myself rather into a scrape; I have been helping them to beg my father for us to go to the Guild-dinner, and I don't know whether it was quite what I approve of, or think good for myself; but I shall consider, and do not intend to go, if I disapprove of it. How strange and odd! I really think I shall turn plain Friend; all I say is, search deeply; do nothing rashly, and I then hope to do right; they all, I think, now see it. I do not like to appear a character I am not certain of being. For a few days past, I have at times felt much religion for *me*; humility and comfort belong to it. I often think very seriously about myself. A few months ago, if I had seen any one act, as I now do, I should have thought him a fool; but the strongest proof I can have that I am acting right at the present time is, that I am certainly a better, and I think a happier character. But I often doubt myself, when I consider my enthusiastic and changeable feelings. Religion is no common enthusiasm, because it is pure, it is a constant friend, protector, supporter, and guardian; it is what we cannot do well without in this world; what can prove its excellence so much as its producing virtue and happiness? How much more solid a character I am, since I first got hold of religion! I would not part with what I have for anything; it is a faith that never will leave my mind, I hope most earnestly. I do not believe it will, but I desire always to be a strictly religious character.

June 13th – I have some thoughts of by degrees increasing my plan for Sunday evening; and of having several poor children, at least, to read in the Testament and religious books for an hour. I have begun with Billy; but I hope to continue and increase one by one. I should think it a good plan; but I must not even begin that hastily. It might increase morality among the lower classes, if the Scriptures were oftener and better read to them. I believe I cannot exert myself too much, there is nothing gives me such satisfaction as instructing the lower classes of people.

At this time Elizabeth, with her father and sisters, undertook a journey to the south coast and then to Wales and Coalbrookdale.

Farnham, July 26th – Tonight I am much tired, quite fagged, body and mind, and the text comes strongly before me, "Blessed are they that mourn, for they shall be comforted", for though I feel weak in body, I have truly support in mind. God is a merciful Father, and when His children (though evil like me) mourn, He will comfort them, and preserve them, if they will exert their own powers also, to serve Him in spirit and in truth. How often I fail! He is never-failing, no, never! He makes the sun to rise on the just and on the unjust, and we acknowledge not His blessings, but lament over the few clouds that shade its brightness: and sometimes murmur at the Lord that made us. Weak mortals! and I am weak indeed. But I feel I have to deal with a merciful Father.

Weymouth, July 29th – We dined here, and after dinner went on the sea. I always feel rather afraid when there, for I consider that if the least accident were to happen, I should be drowned; and I do not know if it be right only for pleasure to run the risk of one's life. I always feel doubtful of ever seeing land again; but I believe it to be partly unwise cowardice; if duty led me to it, I do not think I should fear. Some minds, by nature, are more cowards than others, and require more faith to overcome it. This evening, I am sorry to say, I feel a hankering after the world and its gaieties: but what real satisfaction is there in being admired? I am uncertain about going to the Rooms to-morrow. I should not object, I think, if no expense follow it; but if I can keep away I will do so. I have been considering, and believe this subject requires real thought. I hear there is to be a ball, and I don't doubt we may go: if I go, I shall enter the world and fall very likely into some of its snares. Shall I feel satisfied in going, or most satisfied in staying at home? I believe in staying at home. The worst of all will be I shall have to contradict the will of all the others, and most likely to disappoint my father by not going; there is the rub, if I don't go perhaps he will not let the others go. I think I shall leave it on these grounds; if I can stay at home in any way, do – but if I cannot without vexing my father I must go, and try not to be hurt by it.

Dawlish, August 3rd – This morning Kitty came in for us to read the Testament together, which I enjoyed: I read my favourite chapter, the 15th of Corinthians, to them. Oh! how earnestly I hope that we may all know what truth is, and follow its dictates. I still continue my belief that

I shall turn plain Quaker. I used to think, and do now, how very little dress matters; but I find it almost impossible to keep up to the principles of Friends without altering my dress and speech. I felt it the other day at Weymouth. If I had been plain, I should not have been tempted to have gone to the play, which at all events I would not do; plainness appears to be a sort of protection to the principles of Christianity in the present state of the world. I have just received a letter from Anna Savery, and have been answering it, and have written rather a religious letter, which I mean to show them, though it is to me a cross, as I say in it I think I am a Quaker at heart. I hope it will not hurt them; but it is better to be on clear grounds with my best friends, upon that which so nearly interests me. I know it hurts Rachel and John the most. Rachel has the seeds of Quakerism in her heart, that if cultivated, would grow indeed, I have no doubt. I should never be surprised to see us all Quakers.

Plymouth Dock, August 8th – After a good night, as soon as breakfast was over, we went to see the ropes made at the Docks, which was a most curious sight. How thankful I should be, that for all my constant erring from the path of truth, I am yet sometimes allowed to feel I have an Arm to lean upon, superior to human, that will support me in time of trouble. After leaving the Dock-yards, we went on board a ferry-boat, and I felt rather afraid, to my shame. We then went to see a Review, which I feel rather uncertain if it were right for me to go to, as I so highly disapprove of war; but I believe whilst I appear as other people, I must act as they do unless with the greatest difficulty. I do not alter from conformity, but from conviction. Afterwards we went to Lord Mount Edgcumbe's, a very fine place, but I was not in the mind for it. Am I right or not? They have just been to say an officer has come for us to hear a very famous Marine Band; and I do not go, because I have some idea it is wrong, even to give countenance to a thing that inflames men's minds to destroy each other. It is truly giving encouragement, as far as lies in my power, to what I most highly disapprove, therefore I think I am right to stay at home. I will now go on with an account of the day.

We went on board a man-of-war with Judd [*their maid*] and the men-servants; it was a fine but melancholy sight. I may gain some information by it, but it is not what I quite approve of, the same as the band; my heart feels most anxious this night that I may go right, for strait and narrow is the path that leadeth to eternal life, and broad is the way that leadeth to destruction. I must remark, before finishing this journal, that I feel much satisfaction attending my not going to the Review, a thing my heart is so much set upon as military music; as soon as I determined, in my own mind, to give it up, inclination vanished, and now would lead me to stay at home. If I look at it, my path is clearer than I think; for it ought to give me comfort and hope, that in so small a thing I feel so much satisfaction it should help me forward in my journey to that haven, where alone comfort is to be found.

Ivy Bridge, August 9th – The first thing we undertook this morning was to see the Dock-yards, which is a sight too astonishing to describe. But after all the art, expense and trouble that men put themselves to, what do they gain, but the destruction of their fellow-creatures? After that we went by water to Plymouth, and saw many Friends; but one very plain, who was agreeable to us all, even interesting. As I left Plymouth my mind felt deeply hurt on account of the poor sailors and women, of whom I have seen a sad number, and longed to do them good, to try one day to make them sensible of the evil state they appear to be in. Just at that time, I read or thought of that passage in the Testament, where it says, we are to look upon all men as greater than ourselves. Christ truly taught humility, and I reflected that, in all probability, if I had had the same temptations, I should have been equally wicked; for I am sorry, indeed, to say, I fear I mostly give way to temptation, when it falls in my way. Ah! much, much have I to do, much to strive for, before I shall be able to feel my house is built upon a rock. I know how weak is its present foundation; but this night my mind is cheered by the brightening light of religion.

Clifton, August 15th – This morning I have seen much beautiful country about Clifton. I think it very likely we shall go to the Welsh Half-Yearly meeting, where I expect we shall meet most of the Colebrook Dale Friends, whom I quite long to see. We have been a pleasant excursion this afternoon, to a Mr Harford's; I had an interesting drive home, and thought about serious subjects. I often think of home with a longing heart, to set off once more quietly in my career.

Ross, August 16th – We have travelled far to-day; I set out rather thinking I should have Mrs B–'s company, which I had, and enjoyed at times much; experience teacheth knowledge. I think her in all respects not sufficiently practical, but too theoretical. I don't like her theories, she appears to me to think too highly of bringing the things of this world (that do not in my opinion lead to happiness) to perfection. If too much attended to, I think it loss of time and of course I believe, though she has much religion, that this prevents her enjoying it as much as she would otherwise do; for, those who depend too much on this world are apt not to depend sufficiently on the one to come. Some sweet and beautiful scenes we saw from Gloucester to Ross, by moonlight, which I enjoyed.

Abergavenny, August 18th – We went one stage before breakfast from Usk to Pontypool; as soon as we got there, we met two plain Friends, they both preached; my mind had some devotional feelings, which I felt a blessing. I remained and dined with them, and a little of that peculiar love I feel towards plain Friends sprung up in my heart for them. Before the afternoon Meeting, I went with Mrs B– to call on Lady M. I own I felt very uncomfortable. I felt as if I were too much a Friend with Friends, and too worldly with other people. I then went to Meeting and had a very serious reflecting time. I thought I should be acting a better part to say thee instead of you, to other people when I could, for I felt myself to-day, one minute saying thee, the next you; it appeared hypocritical. I had an argument in my own mind, which I will try to remember; I first thought how there could be any difference, in Christian virtue, in saying you or thee to people. I considered there were certainly some advantages attending it; the first, that of weaning the heart from this world by acting in some little things differently from it. But I then thought, is it not better to be remarkable for excellence of conduct, than for such little peculiarities? I find that in a perfect state, such things would not signify, but we are in an imperfect state; and our virtue is hard to maintain, without some fortress to support it; we must combat with imperfection, and at times be obliged to make great things of little things, and use them as arms to defend us from the many wiles and snares of the world.

Landaly, August 21st – A gentleman dined with us, to whom I did not attend, till I discovered he was a Lord. Oh pride, how it does creep in upon me!

Aberystwyth, August 23rd – Is dancing wrong? I have just been dancing; I think there are many dangers attending it, it may lead to vanity and other things. But I think, in a family party, and in an innocent way, it may be of use by the bodily exercise; it animates the spirits, and produces good effects. I think dancing and music the first pleasures in life. The more the pleasures of life are given up, the less we love the world, and our hearts will be set upon better things; not but that we are allowed, I believe, to enjoy the blessings Heaven has sent us. We have power of mind sufficient to distinguish the good from the bad; for under the cloak of pleasure, infinite evils are carried on. The danger of dancing, I find, is throwing me off my centre; at times when dancing, I know that I have not reason left, but that I do things which in calm moments I must repent of. I went and bathed, which required much exertion of courage. After dinner we went to the Devil's Bridge. I was much pleased with the beautiful scenery; but as we were climbing down the rocks, which appeared almost perpendicular over the fall of water, I was taken with the most painful sensation of fear, and dared not go another step, but sat down and thought I should have fainted; if I had, I must have fallen to the bottom. After we arrived safely home to a sort of little inn, where we slept, we had a very happy evening; for we were wet, and were obliged to put on our dressing gowns, and sit over a fine turf fire, in the public-house; singing, and being sung to, by the interesting Welsh inhabitants.

Caernarvon, August 27th – After a good breakfast, we set off on our journey. The first few miles I shall find very difficult to describe, for such a scene I had not an idea of; all surrounded with rocky mountains, lost in the clouds as they passed over them. Sometimes we were on the edge of a precipice, sometimes on the borders of a river, where the road was cut out of the rock and high mountains on each side, now and then the wild goats straying over them. We were obliged to walk part of the way, which was trying to me, as I had the toothache. Since I have been here, I have had a Welsh harper, which I was not quite sure was right, as it was giving, or at least causing money to be given, that might have been spent much better.

August 28th – My mind is in an uncomfortable state this morning; for I am astonished to find I have felt a scruple at music, at least I could not otherwise account for my feelings; but my mind is rather uneasy after I have been spending time in it. These cannot be sensations of my own making, or a contrivance of my own forming, for I have such happiness when I overcome my worldly self; and when I give way to it, am uneasy; not but what I think feelings are sometimes dangerous to give way to; but how odd, yet how true, that much of human reason must be given up. I don't know what to think of it, but I must act somehow, and in some way; yet do nothing rashly or hastily, but try to humiliate myself to true religion; and endeavour to look to God who alone can teach me and lead me right; have faith, hope, and if little things are to follow to protect greater ones, I must, yes, I must do it. I feel certainly happier in being a Quaker, but my reason contradicts it.

Now my fears are these, lately I have had Quakerism placed before me in a very interesting and delightful light; and is it unlikely that inclination may put on the appearance of duty? Now my inclination may, before long, lead me some other way; that is a sad foundation to build the fortress upon which must defend me through life; but I think I am wrong in one thing, though it is right to doubt myself; yet do I not make myself more uneasy, for fear I should be a ridiculous object to the world, and some of my dear friends.

Colebrook Dale, August 31st – Cousin Priscilla's room. This evening I am at Colebrook Dale, the place I have so much wished to be at. I had rather a comfortable drive here from Shrewsbury; read in the Testament, and got by heart one or two verses. I felt it a great pleasure to see cousin Priscilla; but my heart has not been enlarged towards this sweet set. We have taken a long walk this afternoon. It brings me into a sweet state, being with plain Friends like these, a sort of humility. I expect to be here some days, which I delight in. I feel this evening in a calm, and rather religious state of mind. I am blessed a little to feel the existence of my Father who is in heaven; and I have some hope I may one day be confined in the sheepfold, and not stray from the flock.

September 2nd – I cannot easily describe that which I would, for I know not in my own mind what my feelings exactly are. This morning when breakfast was over, I had some talk with Priscilla, and then we sat down to read the account of a young woman of the name of Rathbone, to me striking and interesting; how well she was assured of Immortality, how clearly did she see her path to Heaven! Happy, happy woman; blessed, ah blessed is thy fate! May we also be permitted to accompany thee to glory, immortality and eternal life, with our God and our Saviour; shall I ever be sensible of deserving immortal glory? Too great a blessing I fear for me and my weak self ever to obtain. For hard is the task and narrow is the road that leadeth thereunto.

We then went to Meeting, my mind was clouded, but now and then a small ray enlightened it. Between the two Meetings, I read again with cousin Priscilla, and all my sisters, that account of the young woman. Hard is the task of dedicating the heart unto God; I fear, yet I hope I may with His assistance one day so fortify it, as to become a defender of truth and religion. After the afternoon Meeting, we drank tea at Deborah Darby's; I felt much love towards her, and her friend Appleby particularly; I felt gratified when she said William Savery had mentioned me to her, and that Rebecca Young, who was out, was sorry she could not see me; there is little, ah little indeed in me! When we came home this evening, my father took me aside and gave me some good advice; to beware of passion and enthusiasm, which I hope I do most earnestly pray I may be, for truly they are snares of the enemy.

September 3rd – Got up late. Heard Deborah Darby was here, and went down; during breakfast, I felt my heart beat much; as soon as it was over, Deborah Darby preached in a deep, clear, and striking manner. First she said, God would visit us all, and did visit us, that God was a father to the fatherless, and a Mother to the motherless. My mind felt deeply oppressed by it. She then addressed me in particular; I do not remember her words, but she expressed, first, I was, as I am, sick of the world; and looked higher (and I believe I do) and that I was to be dedicated to my God, and should have peace in this world, and glory everlasting in the world to come. Could more satisfaction be given? Let me be thankful, I really cried, and I think never felt such inward encouragement. Let me be a worthy servant of my Master who is in heaven. May I, Oh! may I do right.

My father has given me leave to stay till Fourth-day morning, kind he truly is. He spoke to me again this morning. I feel myself highly favoured is all I can say, and may my heart bow before its Maker now and evermore! After they all went, I came and wrote my journal, and sat with cousin Priscilla, and we read till dinner. After that we sat again together with the children, and went on with some letters interesting to me, from that young woman to Richard Reynolds. This afternoon I was at the Darbys. I have felt as it were tinctured with the goodness of those I have been with; but little I own. Oh, my inward temptations, shall I ever overcome you! Priscilla Gurney I feel my constant little friend, dearly indeed do I love her.

September 4th – After tea, we went to the Darbys, accompanied by my dear friend Richard Reynolds, and still dearer Priscilla Gurney. We had spent a pleasant evening, when my heart began to feel itself silenced before God, and without looking at others, I found myself under the shadow of His wing and I soon discovered that the rest were in the same state: I was persuaded that it must be that which I felt. After sitting a time in awful silence, Rebecca Young spoke most beautifully, she touched my heart, and I felt melted and bowed before my Creator. Deborah Darby then spoke; what she said was excellent, she addressed part of it to me. I only fear she says too much of what I am to be. A light to the blind; speech to the dumb; and feet to the lame; can it be? She seems as if she thought I was to be a minister of Christ. Can I ever be one? If I am obedient, I believe, I shall. After the meeting my heart felt really light and as I walked home by starlight I looked through nature up to nature's God. Here I am now in Cousin Prissy's little room – never to forget this day while life is in my body. I know now what the mountain is I have to climb. I am to be a Quaker!

Merridon, September 5th – I rose this morning about five o'clock, I did not feel so much as I expected leaving Colebrook Dale. There is a mountain for me to climb over, there is sacrifice for me to make, before I am favoured with faith, virtue, and assurance of immortality. I feel it would appear so like conformity to the opinions of others, to alter just after being with these Friends, but I think that it is a time to do so, for strength and courage have been given me. This day I have said thee instead of you; but still go on soberly and with consideration.

Coventry, September 6th – I rose in good time to write to Priscilla Gurney and felt in a state of darkness and discouragement about my language, but I am happy to say my mind again feels clear. I dare not draw back. I hope to continue in the habit with spirit, and if by yesterday week I have kept up to it, and then feel discouraged, I may give it up. I felt saying thee very difficult to-day to Mrs –, but I perceived it was far more so after I sang to them. I altogether get on pretty well, but doubts came into my mind this morning; yet were I not to persevere I should, I believe, feel unhappy in it.

Earlham, September 9th – My father, Kitty, and myself set out early this morning for Newmarket. When I was there, I saw Henry B–; my sensation was odd when I saw him, for I took to my heels and ran away. I thought I could not get courage to address him in the plain language; but after I collected myself, I did it without much difficulty. How easy it has been made to me! By what nice degrees I have entered it, but I believe the hardest part is to come; I have felt the advantage of it, though at times in a dark and discouraging state. It makes me think before I speak, and avoid saying much, and also avoid the spirit of gaiety and flirting.

Earlham, 10th September – We arrived last night from our long, and in some respects, delightful journey. So far from hurting me, I hope it will act as a fresh stimulus to virtue and religion, at least it should; I have had some bright and clear times that should not be forgotten. In the afternoon, I had a very serious talk with Kitty about my being a Friend. She thinks that my judgment is too young and inexperienced to be able to take up any particular opinions; she may be right. I am willing to give up the company of Friends and their books, if she request it; but I do firmly believe my mind will never be easy or happy unless I am a Quaker.

September 27th – This evening I have been doing exercises, and singing with them; my mind feels very clear to-night and my body much better. I have been thinking about singing, I hope in that, as in every thing else, to do what is right. I cannot say I feel it wrong to sing to my own family, it is sweet and right to give them pleasure. I do not approve of singing in company, as it leads to vanity and dissipation of mind; but that I believe I have no occasion to do, as dear Rachel does not request it, for she does not like it herself. I should be sorry quite to give up singing as the gift of nature, and on her account; as long as it does not lead me from what is right, I need not fear.

October 6th – This morning I awoke not comfortable, the subject of dancing came strongly before my mind. Totally declining it, as a matter of pleasure I do not mind, only as I am situated with the others I find it difficult; the question is, if these may not be scruples of my own forming, that I may one day repent of? The bottom of my heart is inclined to Quakerism, and I know what imagination can do. I believe the formation of my mind is such, that it requires the bonds and ties of Quakerism to fit it for immortality. I feel it a very great blessing being so little in the company of superior fascinating Quakers; because it makes me act freely and look to the only true Judge, for what is right for me to do. The next question I ask myself is, am I sufficiently clear, that dancing is wrong, to give it up? Because I know much precaution is quite necessary. I believe I may, if I like, make one more trial, and judge again how I feel; but I must reflect upon it, determining to give it up, if I think right. I wish to make it a subject of very serious reflection, hoping, as usual, to do right; it will hurt them much, I fear, but time I believe will take that off, if they see me more happy and better for it. Let me redouble all kindness to them.

This day has been very comfortable in most respects, though I have not done much. I have finished my letter to my dear cousin Priscilla; but I cannot feel quite easy to send it, without first speaking to my father, for I do believe it is my duty to make him my friend in all things. Let me be an open, true, kind, and dutiful daughter to him, whilst life is in my body.

October 12th – I have many great faults, but I have some dispositions I should be most thankful for. I believe I feel much for my fellow-creatures; though I think I mostly see into the minds of those I associate with, and am apt to satirise their weaknesses; yet I don't remember ever being any time with one who was not extremely disgusting, but I felt a sort of love for them, and I do hope I would sacrifice my life for the good of mankind. My mind is too much like a looking-glass; – objects of all kinds are easily reflected in it whilst present, but when they go, their reflection is gone also. I have a faint idea of many things, a strong idea of few; therefore my mind is cultivated badly. I have many straggling, but not many connected ideas. I have the materials to form good in my mind, but I am not a sufficiently good artificer to unite them properly together, and make a good consistence; for in some parts, I am too hard, in others, too soft. I hope and believe the great Artificer is now at work, that if I join my power to the only One who is able to conduct me aright, I may one day be better than I am.

October 17th – My journal has not gone on well of late; partly owing to my going out, and having people in this room, now there is a fire. I dislike going out, what my mind wants is peace and quiet. The other night, as I was alone in a carriage, a fine starlight night, I thought, what is it I want? How I overflow with the blessings of this world. I have true friends, as many as I wish for; good health, a happy home, with all that riches can give, and yet all these are nothing without a satisfied conscience. At times I feel satisfied but I have not reason to feel so often; oh that I could! Perhaps this night, with constant exertion all day, I may feel that first of feelings. It is now afternoon. I woke in a bad mind, but I am happy to say I overcame it, by doing as I thought right, which appeared at once to turn the scale from dullness to liveliness; from a bad mind to a good one. This afternoon I have much to correct, I feel proud, vain and disagreeable; not touched with the sweet humility of Christianity; nor is my heart enlightened by its happy doctrines. I have now two things heavily weighing on my mind – dancing and singing, so sweet and so pretty do they seem; but as surely as I do either, so surely does a dark cloud come over my mind. It is not only my giving up those things, but I am making the others miserable and laying a restraint upon their pleasures. In the next place, am I sure I am going upon a good foundation? If I am doing right, God will protect me and them also; if I am doing wrong, what foundation do I stand upon? None: then all to me is nothing. Let me try to take my thoughts from this world, and look to the only true Judge. I believe singing to be so natural, that I may try it a little longer: but I do think dancing may be given up. What particularly led me to this state was our having company, and I thought I must sing; I sang a little, but did not stay with them during the playing. My mind continued in a state of some agitation, and I did not sleep till some time after I was in bed.

October 19th – My mind feels more this morning, if any thing, than it did last night. Can such feelings be my own putting on? They seem to affect my whole frame, mental and bodily; they cannot be myself, for if I were to give worlds, I could not remove them; they truly make me shake. When I look forwards I think I can see, if I have strength to do as they direct, I shall be another person: sorrow, I believe, will remove to be replaced by joy; then let me now act! My best method of conduct will be to tell Rachel how I am situated in mind, and then ask her what she would advise; and be very kind and tell her the true state of the case. Is it worth while to continue in so small a pleasure for so much pain? The pleasure is nothing to me, but it is a grand step to take in life. – I have been and spoken to Rachel, saying, I think I must give up singing. It is astonishing the total change that has taken place, from misery I am now come to joy; I felt ill before, I now feel well – thankful should I be for being directed, and pray to keep up always to that direction. After having spoken to my darling Rachel, where I fear I said too much, I rode to Norwich, after some poor people I went to see many and added my mite to their comfort. Nothing I think could exceed the kindness of my dear Rachel. Though I have no one here to encourage me in Quakerism I must be one before I am content.

7th December – I have had a letter to say my dear friend William Savery is arrived safely in America. Kitty and I have been having a long talk together this evening upon sects; we both seem to think them almost necessary. It is long since I have what I call truly written my journal; writing my journal is to me expressing the feelings of my heart during the day; I have partly given it up from the coldness of the weather, and not having a snug fire to sit by. I wish now, as I have opportunity, to look a little into the present situation of my heart; that is the advantage of writing a true journal, it leads the mind to look inwards. Of late I do not think I have been sufficiently active, but have given rather way to a dilatory spirit. I have been reading Watts's Logic, it tells me how ill regulated are my thoughts, they ramble truly! Regularity of thought and deed is what I much want; I appear to myself to have almost a confusion of ideas, which leads to a confusion of actions; I want order; I believe it difficult to obtain, but yet with perseverance attainable. The first way to obtain it appears to me to try to prevent my thoughts from rambling, and to keep them as steadily as possible to the object in view. True religion is what I seldom feel, nor do I sufficiently try after it by really seeking devotion; I do not warmly seek it, I am sure, nor do I live in the fear of an all-wise Being who watches over us; I seldom look deep enough, but dwell too much on the surface of things, and let my ideas float. Such is my state I can't tell how I feel exactly: – at times all seems to me mystery.

December 8th – Since dinner I have read much Logic and enjoyed it; it is interesting to me, and may, I think, with attention, do me good. Reading Watts impresses deeply on my mind how very careful I should be of judging; how much I should consider before I speak or form an opinion; how careful I should be not to let my mind be tinged throughout, with one reigning subject, to try not to associate ideas; but judge of things according to the evidence they give my mind of their own worth. My mind is like a pair of scales that are not inclined to balance equally; at least when I begin to form a judgment, and try to hold the balance equally, as soon as I perceive one scale is at all heavier than the other, I am apt at once to let it fall on that side; forgetting what remains in the other scale, which though lighter should not be forgotten. For instance, I look at a character, at first I try to judge calmly and truly; but if I see more virtues than vices, I am apt soon to like that character so much that I like its weaknesses also, and forget they are weaknesses. The same if evil may preponderate, I forget the virtues.

December 12th – This day finished with a dance. If I could make a rule never to give way to vanity, excitement or flirting, I do not think I should object to dancing; but it always leads me into some one of these faults; indeed, I never remember dancing without feeling one, if not a little of all the three, and sometimes a great deal. But as my giving it up would hurt many, it should be one of those things I part with most carefully.

December 30th – I went to Meeting in the morning and afternoon, both times rather dark; but I have been a little permitted to see my own state, which is the greatest favour I can ask for at present; to know what I should do, and to be assisted in my duties: for it is hard, very hard to act right, at least I find it so. But there is the comfortable consideration, that God is so merciful and full of compassion, he is tender over His children. I had a satisfactory time with my girls and boys.

January 4th, 1799 – Most of this morning I spent in Norwich seeing after the poor; I do little for them, and I do not like it should appear I do much. I must be most guarded, and tell those who know I do charity that I am only my father's agent. A plan, at least a duty, that I have felt for some time, I will now mention. I have been trying to overcome fear; my method has been to stay in the dark, and at night to go into those rooms not generally inhabited. There is a strange propensity in the human mind to fear in the dark, there is a sort of dread of something supernatural: I tried to overcome that, by considering that as far as I believed in ghosts, so far I must believe in a state after death, and it must confirm my belief in the Spirit of God; therefore if I try to act right, I have no need to fear the directions of Infinite Wisdom. But my most predominant fear is that of thieves; and I find that still more difficult to overcome, but faith would cure that also, for God can equally protect us from man as from spirit.

January 8th – My father, not appearing to like all my present doings, has been rather a cloud over my mind this day; there are few, if any, in the world I love so well, I am not easy to do what he would not like, for I think I could sacrifice almost any thing for him, I owe him so much, I love him so much. I have been reading Watts on Judgment this afternoon; it has led me into thought, and particularly upon the evidence I have to believe in religion. The first thing that strikes me is the perception we all have of being under a power superior to human. I seldom feel this so much as when unwell; to see how pain can visit me, and how it is taken away. Work for ever, we could not create life. There must be a cause to produce an effect The next thing that strikes me is good and evil, virtue and vice, happiness and unhappiness – these are acknowledged to be linked together; Virtue produces good; vice evil; of course the Power that allows this shows approbation of virtue. Thirdly, Christianity seems also to have its clear evidences even to my human reason. My mind has not been convinced by books; but what little faith I have has been confirmed by reading the holy writers themselves.

January 27th – I have had, in many respects, comfortable Meetings; only my thoughts too giddy dwelling too much on what pleased me yesterday; they have, I am sorry to say, been occupied with old subjects such as dress and a little flirting, I fear. I have enjoyed my little party as usual who are now, when complete, fifteen in number. What path I shall go in life is hidden from my view. May I go in that in which I ought to go! Do not forget how much more tempting it is to choose the easiest, and yet do not enter difficulties for difficulty's sake. Try to be led by no person, but by my own conscience.

January 29th – I am in a doubtful state of mind. I think my mind is timid, and my affections strong, which may be partly the cause of my being so much inclined to Quakerism; in the first place, my affections were worked upon, in receiving the first doctrines of religion, and I loved them through a Quaker; therefore it is likely they would put on that garb in my mind. In the next place, my timidity may make me uncomfortable, in erring from principles that I am so much inclined to adopt; so far I should be on my guard, and I hope not to forget what I have just mentioned. But yet, I think the only true standard I can have to direct myself by is that which experience proves to give me the most happiness, by enabling me to be more virtuous: I believe there is something in the mind or in the heart that shows its approbation when we do right. I give myself this advice: do not fear truth, let it be ever so contrary to inclination and feeling. Never give up the search after it; and let me take courage, and try from the bottom of my heart to do that which I believe truth dictates, if it lead me to be a Quaker or not. The last and the best advice I can give myself is, as far as I am able, to look up to the God who is unitedly worshipped by the whole earth, who has created us, and who we feel has power over our thoughts, words and deeds.

February 14th – I hope I have from experience gained a little. I am much of a Friend in my principles at this time, but do not outwardly appear much so; I say "thee" to people, and do not dress very gay, but yet I say " Mr" and " Mrs", wear a turban, &c. I have one remark to make: every step I have taken towards Quakerism has given me satisfaction.

February 25th – This time last year, I was with my dear friend William Savery, at Westminster Meeting. I can only thankfully admire, when I look back to about that time, the gentle leadings my soul has had, from the state of great darkness it was in; how suddenly did the light of Christianity burst upon my mind. I have reason to believe in religion from my own experience, and what foundation so solid to build my hopes upon; may I gain from the little experiences I have been blessed with, may I encourage the voice of truth, and may I be a steady and virtuous combatant in the service of God. Such I think I may truly say is my most ardent prayer. But God, who is omnipresent, knows my thoughts; knows my wishes, and my many many feelings; may I conclude with saying, "cleanse thou me from secret faults".

February 28th – We have had company most part of the day. I have had an odd feeling. Uncle Joseph and many gay ones were here; I had a sort of sympathy with him. I feel to have been so much off my guard, that if tempted I should have done wrong. I now hear them singing. How much my natural heart does love to sing: but if I give way to the ecstasy singing sometimes produces in my mind, it carries me far beyond the centre; it increases all the wild passions, and works on enthusiasm. Many say and think it leads to religion; it may lead to emotions of religion, but true religion appears to me to be in a deeper recess of the heart, where no earthly passion can produce it. However, music may sometimes be of use: and I think our earthly feelings are made use of to lead us to much better things. I think music and dancing the first pleasures in life, not happiness; they elevate too high. They may be right, but I do not feel quite free to enjoy them; I will now leave it, as my judgment is not clear.

March 1st–There is going to be a dance – what am I to do ? As far as I can see, I believe, if I find it very necessary to their pleasure, I may do it, but not for my own gratification. Remember, don't be vain; if it be possible, dance little. I began to dance in a state next to pain of mind; when I had danced four dances, I was trying to pluck up courage to tell Rachel

49

I wished to give it up for the evening; it seemed as if she looked into my mind, for she came up to me at that minute in the most tender manner, and begged me to leave off, saying she would contrive without me; I suppose she saw in my countenance the state of my mind. I am not half kind enough to her, I often make sharp remarks to her, and in reality there are none of my sisters to whom I owe so much.

March 4th – I hope the day has passed without many faults. John is just come in to ask me to dance in such a kind way, – oh dear me! I am now acting clearly differently from them all. Remember this, as I have this night refused to dance with my dearest brother, I must out of kindness to him not be tempted by any one else. Have mercy, oh God! have mercy upon me! and let me act right, I humbly pray Thee; wilt Thou love my dearest most dear brothers and sisters, wilt Thou protect us? Dear John! I feel much for him, such as these are home strokes, but I had far rather have them, if indeed guided by Supreme Wisdom; for then I need not fear. I know that not dancing will not lead me to do wrong, and I fear dancing does; though the task is hard on their account, I hope I do not mind the pain to myself. I feel for them; but if they see in time I am happier for it, I think they will no longer lament over me. I will go to them as soon as they have done, try to be cheerful and to show them I love them; for I do most truly, particularly John. I think I might talk a little with John, and tell him how I stand, for it is much my wisest plan to keep truly intimate with them all; make them my first friends. I do not think I ever love them so well as at such times as these. I should fully express my love for them, and how nearly it touches my heart, acting differently to what they like. These are truly great steps to take in life but I may expect support under them.

March 16th – I know I want correction, for these few days past I have not gone on well, a sort of coldness, darkness, and uncertainty that will sometimes take possession of the mind; it is, I believe, much owing to a want of vigilance and activity on my part, and it does not always please the Almighty to enlighten us equally. I am a very negligent being. If, as Deborah Darby said to me, I will do as far as I know to be right, I may one day be a light to the blind, feet to the lame, &c., &c. Shall such a state ever be mine? If there be any chance of such a thing, I should labour for it. I think the time I spent at Colebrook Dale one of the happiest, if not the happiest time of my life. I think my feelings that night, at Deborah Darby's, were the most exalted I ever remember. I, in a manner, was one of the beginners of the Meeting; suddenly my mind felt clothed with light, as with a garment, and I felt silenced before God; I cried with the heavenly feeling of humility and repentance. Then, when I was in this awful state, there were two sermons preached, one telling me to get the pearl of great price; and the other telling me what I might expect, even happiness in this world, and everlasting happiness in the one to come. But that silence, which first took possession of my mind, exceeded all the rest.

Fourth month, 6th – I have not done a great deal to-day, and yet I hope I have not been idle: I try to do right now and then, but by no means constantly. I could not recover the feeling of being hurt at rejecting, I suppose, the voice of my mind last night when I sang so much; they were not, I believe, feelings of my own making, for it was my wish to enjoy singing without thinking it wrong.

4th month, 15th – I had for my poor wandering thoughts a satisfactory Meeting; partly owing to being nervous, for it leads me to cast my care upon the Lord. I went to Bedlam, and felt glad to see the poor Melton woman going on well. If comfort be once permitted to enter her heart, it will be a cause of true pleasure to me, and I hope of gratitude to the all-wise Director; but He knows better than I what is for her good. Today, at Meeting, I felt such a relief in the thought that God knows all our thoughts, all our temptations, and that He knows also how much power we have to overcome them: for I felt I could not have a just estimate of my own self.

4th month, 24th – I awoke with good resolutions, wishing to obtain that peaceful state of mind, of feeling myself humbly trying to do the will of the Almighty; I took good resolves, but my nature seems not in the mind to act up to them. I feel to have too much volatility of thought to keep that watch so necessary about my thoughts, words and actions. I do not think this has been a bad day; part of it very satisfactory, particularly teaching three little girls. How little the feelings of my heart seem under my own power; I feel them like my body, under another power; yet mankind do not seem willing to allow that God is the Governor and Director of the heart, though they mostly acknowledge, it is He who guides all outward circumstances; we find we have inward and outward evil to combat, but we have a power within ourselves, that will much alleviate the many evils we are subject to.

5th month, 1st – Even acting right will sometimes bring dissensions in a family, as it says in the Testament; we must not be discouraged even when that is our lot, for whatever may be our situation, if we strictly adhere to that which we believe to be our duty, we need not fear, but rest steadily upon Him who can and will support us. I often observe how much weakness of body seems to humble the mind; illness is of great benefit to us, as I have found from experience, if we try to make good use of it; it leads us to see our own weakness and debility, and to look to a stronger for support. So I believe it may be with the mind; dark and gloomy states are allowed to come upon it that we may know our own insufficiency, and place our dependence upon a Higher Power.

7th month, 12th – This day has not been idle, but not religious. I was most part of the morning at Norwich; in the afternoon, I settled accounts; and in the evening, cut out clothes for the poor. I don't think I have looked into the Testament, or written my journal to-day; it leads me to remember what uncle Joseph said to me the other day, after relating or reading to me the history of Mary, who anointed our Saviour with the precious ointment, and His disciples said she might have sold it, and given to the poor, but Christ said, "The poor ye have always with you, but me you have not always." Now, I thought as uncle Joseph remarked, I might this evening have spent too much time about the poor, that should have been spent about better things.

It was before this journey to the North of England that Joseph Fry proposed to Elizabeth for the first time, so that she had much on her mind. Elizabeth was also undertaking her first official duty as a Friend by visiting Ackworth School General Meeting.

7th month, 30th – We had a long day's journey; I hope it has been my object at least to try to act right. The propriety of saying "thou" has lately struck me: if I think it right to say it I hope I shall be able, though any alteration of speech is very difficult to make.

Ackworth, 8th month, 1st – To-day what is called the General Meeting began; we first had a meeting of worship, which was rather agreeable: after which, we dined with a very large party in the boys' dining-room at the School; as I was wandering about in the bustle, I went into the plain

Friends' room (which I often did), where I had not been very long, before
I felt myself fall into silence before God, which the rest of the party
appeared to do also; we had not sat long before William Crotch began to
preach to me. I was much affected; then old Friend Hustler said something to me; may I profit by such refreshing times. At four o'clock, the
Women's Meeting met; I amongst a great number was chosen one of the
Committee to examine the children, school and household: Hannah
Barnard appeared to me to hold rather too high a hand. After Meeting,
we examined the bedrooms, which I thought in good order, and talked a
little to Hannah Barnard.

8th month, 2nd – I arose about six to go to the School to hear the girls
spell, which I was pleased with, but should have liked to have questioned
them more myself. After that, we breakfasted; then met, in the Committee, to fix a little the plans we should go upon. I and Sarah Cookfield were
mentioned to go and attend to the Grammar School; I said that I had only
a slight knowledge of grammar. We then went to the Grammar School;
the writing, ciphering, working, mending, spinning, knitting, and sewing,
all which I liked much, and thought upon the whole they did very well
indeed; we then examined parts of the house; after which we dined, and
at three o'clock met to hear the report of the Committee; I forgot that
before dinner, we met at twelve o'clock to draw up the report of what we
thought of the proceedings of the school. It was some time before any one
would speak; Friends were begging the Committee to say what they
thought, but in vain, till I think Hannah Barnard broke the ice, and
encouraged the young people to say what they thought; for they had been
requested before. As it appeared to me it was delaying the Meeting, I took
courage (as I thought it was more right than wrong) to speak; and said
what I thought of the grammar and ciphering; I felt glad I had done it,
though I trembled at doing it, not a little. Towards the latter part of the
sitting, I was pointedly asked what I thought of their spelling, which I
said; and also that I did not think they attended to the words of one, so
well as to those of many syllables. After the Meetings, I was encouraged
in what I had done, by salutations from the Friends, Hannah Barnard and
Elizabeth Cogshall. After dinner, we met again and heard the report they
had written to bring in to the men. I thought the Meeting paid rather too
much deference to Hannah Barnard, in delaying the Meeting, because she
was not come in. The Meeting concluded, after long waiting to choose a
sub-committee, which after all was not done, and we took the report to

the men; I own my body and mind longed impatiently to have Meeting over. After tea I had a few interesting minutes with Hannah Barnard, to whom I had longed to speak about my beloved friend William Savery; I met her standing against the wall in the long passage, by Dr Binn's door. I went up to her, took hold of her hand and entered into talk with her; I mentioned dear William Savery: we went and sat in the Doctor's room, where was Thomas Scattergood, whom, though I do not think he spoke, yet I liked.

8th month, 3rd – I arose in a bustle and hurried about till the "cold vict-uals" were given to the poor, which plan I did not much like, as it seemed like showing off. William Crotch preached to them very agreeably, after which Thomas Scattergood called us aside, and in a little Meeting expressed the great love he felt for me yesterday, which made it appear to me as if there were a sympathy of soul, and we both were guided by the same spirit; he expressed how much he felt for me at the time I came into Doctor Binn's room, and had then felt it on his mind to say something to me; I also had felt a silent inclination to hear. We then set off on our jour-ney to York.

8th month, 4th – This morning we walked about York, and saw its won-ders. We saw the Friends' Retreat for crazy people, which my father thought extravagantly carried on. The Minster is a beautiful building; how much people spend about a pious building! Would they spend as much time and trouble about their own souls? We got to Darlington to-night.

8th month, 5th – We were at both Meetings, at Darlington, to-day; I was much pleased with the Friends there, and their appearance of unity and hospitality. We reached Durham to-night; I was much pleased with the beautiful scenery entering the town.

8th month, 10th – We spent the day, till about five, at Broom Park; I do not like myself in that sort of company, I am almost sure to lose ground by a sort of foolish wish to please everybody; I do not absolutely deviate from my character but I enter as far as I can into the character of those I am with, and unintentionally give up more than I should. We went from thence to Alnwick Castle belonging to the Duke of Northumberland, a very magnificent place; but seeing such places never leads me to wish for high life, for after all, are the possessors happier, if so happy as others? The only true and lasting source of happiness is an easy conscience.

Shields, 8th month, 19th – I am sorry it is so long since I wrote my journal. We have been to Edinburgh, which is a city well worth seeing, for its beauty and curiosity. There was an American Friend who put me much in mind of dear William Savery. We again went to Broom Park, where we were most hospitably received. On Second-day evening, on our way from Edinburgh, I was rather nervous. I feel, I am sorry to say, little progress in the path of virtue: keeping up that watch and dependence upon God is so difficult; it is hard work to look only to the true Source in our hearts, we are so apt to wish to save ourselves that trouble, and to look to inferior sources. I believe talking much on the subject has not a good effect, for it leads us to an outward rather than deeply inward feeling; it is hard work really to dig deep; I seem to have so many faults or errors encamped round about me, they are out of my power to overcome alone; but can I not do it with looking to God for assistance?

Earlham, 8th month, 29th – On Third-day evening, we arrived safely at home, after altogether a pleasant journey.

9th month, 18th – This morning I went to Meeting, and fully felt my weakness; but I have found myself to-day and yesterday a little under the influence of religion, which is a blessed thing. I had much palpitation at the Meeting of Discipline, because I saw some things so clearly, but being mentioned by others, I thought I might get off giving an opinion. I was proposed to be representative, and said I had no objection, indeed I felt no objection on my own part, because though I know how weak I am, yet even the weak should not fear to exert the little power they have; and I do feel interested for the Society, and for the most part, approve its principles highly.

10th month, 1st – I feel in a state of much mental weakness, real and true discouragement; I have little faith and little hope, and almost fallen so as not to be able to rise. But if there be a God and a Saviour I need not fear; for though I know and find my state of corruption, yet I believe the warmest wish of my heart is, to do the will of God, and to act right: I do most truly hunger and thirst after righteousness. I find one thing very hard to overcome, which is pride and vanity in outward religious matters.

True religion, I believe, will not admit of pride and vanity. Another temptation is, that I have too much formed in my own mind what I think I am to be; which may outwardly encourage me in a path, that nothing but the dictates of conscience should lead me into. I am really weak in faith, and in works; I believe at least I have a hope that if I exert the little power I now have given me, the day will come when I shall feel the power of God within me.

10th month, 24th – I feel this morning as I have felt lately, quite in a hurry about what I have to do; and I do not think that that is the way to do it well; it is better to go soberly and quietly to work about it, and not to flurry and bluster. I think this day has not been quite so idle, and I hope in a little degree I may have done well. I put some things in proper order, read history and grammar, wrote letters and worked. I feel in rather a flat, silent state of mind. May I be thankful that opportunity is offered me to spend my time in doing something.

10th month, 26th – I am rather in a volatile mind this morning, and that state which requires care. I still feel as if I could not act really and minutely well; a sort of lukewarmness that leads to forgetfulness; and a flying off from the centre in my inmost heart. But weak as I am, if I exert my powers, and in times of need pray for more, and try to turn out worldly ideas, till I receive strength by waiting in stillness upon God; to let His will be done in me; I then shall find if the arm of the Lord be sufficient for me. But I feel and know it is much easier to write than practise; for it is hard, a very hard matter, to wait quietly upon God; it is for the time, giving up the world to follow Him. For though I seldom or ever have found more than darkness in my own endeavours to wait (and how seldom I do it?), yet remember, "Ask and it shall be given thee, seek and thou shalt find, knock and it shall be opened unto thee." If I continue steady in seeking, and will try and pray to seek more and more, the day will come when I shall find; let me remember this. I believe at times the door has been in mercy opened, when at the moment I have not been knocking, for I have now and then tested the beauties of holiness; but it appears as if it had mostly been through others, or with others, I have felt it. But how humbly thankful should my soul lie, that my path of conduct has so far been shown me, when I have sought after it, and that I have had my eyes anointed to see the difference of right and wrong in my conduct; that, perhaps, is enough for me for the present; may I be sufficiently thankful for it, for does it not show that the Most High has not forsaken me?

11th month, 17th – In the evening, with my children, I had in some respects a very comfortable time; it was at least my wish to act right with them. In part of one of the chapters, I seemed carried through to explain something to them in a way I hardly ever did before. It was striking the difference in my power this evening, and this day week. This day week I tried and tried to explain, and the more I tried the more I seemed to blunder; and this evening I was determined not to attempt it, unless I felt capable, and that I did, suddenly and unexpectedly to myself; I had a flow of ideas come one after another, in a sweet and refreshing way. The rest of the evening was principally spent with Hannah Scarnell talking about my poor mother, who died this day seven years.

12th month, 12th – I believe the true state of my mind is as follows. I have, almost ever since I have been a little under the influence of religion, thought marriage at this time was not a good thing for me, as it might lead my interests and affections from that Source in which they should be centred, and also, if I have any active duties to perform in the church, if I really follow as far as I am able the voice of Truth in my heart, are they not rather incompatible with the duties of a wife and a mother? And is it not safest to wait and see what is the probable course I shall take in this life, before I enter into any engagement that affects my future career? So I think, and so I have thought. But to look on the other side. If Truth appears to tell me I may marry, I should leave the rest, and hope whatsoever my duties are, I shall be able to perform them; but it is now at this time the prayer of my heart, that if I ever should be a mother, I may rest with my children, and really find my duties lead me to them and my husband; and if my duty ever leads me from my family, that it may be in single life. I must leave all to the wisdom of a superior Power, and in humble confidence pray for assistance both now and for evermore, in performing His will.

1st month 1st, 1800 – This has not been one of the clear and bright days of life: little has been done, and that little as in a nightmare; not feeling able to get forward, and discouraged. None but one Being knows how I spend my time, and how little I really do in the service of God; but I cannot quite judge myself, and I feel I have complained too much to-day of the burdens of life to other people. My uncle Joseph was here, and I felt my own weakness by his side. I had my children, and found them a great burden; at least I thought that I was making more show than reality. So are my down sittings and my uprisings. Have mercy on me, if Thou existest, O God! Forsake not one who does wish to trust in Thee, and be Thy servant in the way Thou mayst see meet for her.

1st month, 7th – This morning, at Meeting, I had rather a trying time in some respects, at least I fully felt the disobedient state of my own heart. I think, as far as I can judge from past experience, my feelings were not those of imagination. I felt, supposing it was my duty to speak in that Meeting, what would it not be to me? And I don't think I felt perfectly clear of that awful duty; not that I now believe it will be at this time required of me, but it appears to me a devotion of heart that I must try to attain; or else my lamp will not be prepared, that I may go when my Master calleth. I have felt, and still feel, "I cannot do it", when required of me. Almost as much as that: though I yet believe, if I were sure it was required by God, it should be done, if I had power; but in our present state of weakness, we are to see so far and no farther, and we can only act as far as we, in our great weakness, think is the best way for us. My faith is as a grain of mustard-seed. But we may all judge from experience; and I think I may truly say, that when I have followed the direction of this Voice in my heart (those feelings that may be enthusiasm or what else), yet I never have failed to feel content in doing so; even to be amply rewarded, and never to have repented following its dictates, but the more I have been wholly and humbly given up to obey, the more I have found my foundation a stable one; and trying as it has been sometimes, yet after I have gone through the trial, reason and inclination and all have applauded. But reason and inclination often leave us in the day of trouble. However, to go on with my tale. I continued most of the Meeting in this state, not clear of this awful duty, and yet by no means seeing it right to act; but as for that, I believe I would hardly let it come into my mind, and in my thoughts; I wished William Crow to preach, as I do sometimes, and when he rose my heart seemed to feel it was right for him to do so. He began to speak of the state of some one present, and did take me surprisingly home to mine; he mentioned how the ministry had come before that mind; but seemed to think it was not an immediate duty, but was to be tried. So I leave it. I am unwilling to think any thing of the kind would be at present required of me. I believe it would be a greater trial than I can describe, my whole appearance being so different from those who are generally ministers among us. But yet I hope if ever duty really requires it of me I may do it, let it be early or late.

2nd month, 9th – In the evening, my father brought two friends with him and Lawrence Candler. As I was reading to my children in the laundry, my father brought them all in; when I had finished reading in the Testament we were all silent, and soon John Kirkham knelt down in prayer and we all rose up; it was a very solemn time; my heart was not much moved, but I believe many of my dear children were much affected by it; he then preached to them, and it was surprising to me to see how much it seems the same spirit that works in all; and how solemn a thing it is to preach and pray only from authority, and how very different an effect it has on the mind to other advice; however, it was an encouraging thing, and I hope it will not be passed over by me or the children.

5th month, 30th – I have written lately many melancholy journals, and I seem rather inclined this morning gratefully to mention the calm and sweet state I feel in. Even if the feelings be but for this time, it is a blessing to have them. My feelings towards Joseph are so calm and pleasant, and I can look forward with so much cheerfulness to a connexion with him.

6th month, 8th – I felt rather nervous and weak this morning. I wrote to Eliza Fry [*Joseph Fry's sister*], and worked and talked. I might talk too much. I received a letter I liked from Joseph, and answered it this afternoon. I felt unwilling to represent my own faults to him, although I told him how faulty I was, yet it is much more unpleasant to acknowledge any real fault committed, than the natural inclination to faults.

6th month, 9th – I have been busy today without doing much. They all went out about twelve. I then put my poor people's things in a little order, and cut out linen till dinner – and from dinner till tea. I am slow in what I do. I have thought seriously upon becoming mistress of a house. I look in that, as in other things, that principle may be my support, for it leads and supports in the smallest occurrences of life. The preparations of clothing, &c., &c., as they lead me into the little things for which I have a taste, if I do not take care may hurt me, and yet they are both pleasant and interesting to me.

6th month, 17th – My state is a truly comfortable one this morning, such peace of mind and body. I seem to have at present no cloud over me – so calm, so easy – partly owing to having lately felt so much bodily pain, ease and rest are peculiarly pleasant; let it be an encouragement to me, next time pain or sorrow surround me, that even when heavily clouded, the sun may not be far off; may enjoying this sort of peace lead me to long for a more durable and lasting one, and may it stimulate me with more vigour to seek after it by more frequent patient waiting upon God, and may I experience an increasing willingness to take up the cross when called to do so.

8th month, 4th – This has been a comfortable day to me. I have been busy, and a little gone on in my old plans; I have great hopes of leaving all things in good order, which is a relief to me. It is a blessing indeed to feel thus healthy in mind and body; for I think we are subject to mental diseases that are not in our power any more than bodily ones, and that require our patience; although it is our duty in both mental and bodily maladies to do our utmost to overcome them.

8th month, 18th – This morning the Fellowes were here; nothing particular happened till evening, when all my poor children came; it was rather a melancholy time to me. After having enjoyed themselves with playing about, I took them to the summerhouse and bade them farewell; there were about eighty-six of them, many of them wept; I felt rather coldly when with them, but when they went away, I shed my tears also; and then my desires took the turn of anxiously longing for the spiritual welfare of all of us, as a family.

2

"I wish to do my duty":
Marriage and motherhood,
1800–1808

Elizabeth Gurney and Joseph Fry were married in Norwich meeting house on 19 August 1800. They lived at first with Joseph's family at Plashet, on the outskirts of London in East Ham, before moving to Mildred's Court in the centre of town. This was another Fry family house next to the premises of their tea, coffee and spice business, so that the whole family treated it as home and expected Elizabeth and Joseph to continue their tradition of hospitality to visiting Quakers. Elizabeth was soon pregnant and her first child, Katherine, was born in 1801, followed by Rachel in 1803, John in 1804, William in 1806 and Richenda in 1808.

8th month, 19th, 1800 – I awoke in a sort of terror at the prospect before me, but soon gained quietness and something of cheerfulness; after dressing we set off for Meeting; I was altogether comfortable. The Meeting was crowded; I felt serious, and looking in measure to the only sure place for support. It was to me a truly solemn time; I felt every word, and not only felt but in my manner of speaking expressed how I felt; Joseph also spoke well. Most solemn it truly was. After we sat silent some little time, Sarah Chandler knelt down in prayer, my heart prayed with her. I believe words are inadequate to describe the feelings on such an occasion; I wept good part of the time, and my beloved father seemed as much overcome as I was. The day passed off well, and I think I was very comfortably supported under it, although cold hands and a beating heart were often my lot

Plashet, 9th month, 8th – From continued change of scene, and the great deal that I am obliged to talk, I seem of late to be continually letting out, and taking nothing in; of course much weakened by it.

9th month, 28th – I had rather a serious evening Meeting. I first wept, I believe, with thinking of them at home; however, I afterwards began to pray as far as my weak spirit could, for I am weak indeed, and even my good wishes are so surrounded with worldly inclinations that it seems to require much strength to get through , and my faith is weak and without faith it is a hard matter to act, but I believe I may find enough for action, if I will seek for it.

10th month, 3rd – I went to town this morning, and walked about some time, ordering plate, &c. My inclination is to have every thing very handsome, but I do not think it right to have things merely for ornament, unless there be some use attached to them.

10th month, 5th – I do not remember ever wishing for worldly good of any kind, as I have for spiritual, but actions show how much the love of the world still remains; indeed, I seem chained down to the world and worldly things, and my habitation seems in the dust. May it ever rise higher.

Mildred's Court, 10th month, 30th – After breakfast, my husband and I set off from Plashet in my father[*-in-law*]'s coach with nurse Barns, for Mildred's Court. I felt rather low at the prospect before me, and more when I saw the state of the house; confusion in every part. I had a bedroom turned into a sitting-room, put in order, and then went and put myself in order for dinner; our brother William dined with us. I spent rather a pleasant afternoon, which is to me quite a rarity. Joseph and I had a comfortable evening, both I believe feeling the true comfort, I may say blessing, of being at last quiet in our own house. All seemed to shine upon us. May we mutually endeavour to hold all in subservience to that Being, to whom all our thoughts, wishes, and actions are known. I sometimes feel the self-interestedness of wishing to be good, for after all what earthly enjoyment is like it? May we not stop short in our career, but try to run the race that is set before us.

11th month, 7th – George Dilwyn [*an American minister*] came to-day; I feel almost overcome with my own weakness, when with such people.

11th month, 11th – After breakfast, I believed it better to propose reading in the Bible, but I felt doing it, particularly as my brother William was here; not liking the appearance of young people, like us, appearing to profess more than they who had lived here before us. However, I put off and put off till both William and Joseph went down; I then felt uneasy under it, and when Joseph came back I told him, as I did before, what I wished; he at last sat down, having told George Dilwyn my desire. I began to read the 46th Psalm but was so overcome that I could hardly read, and gave it to Joseph to finish.

11th month, 12th – I rather felt this morning it would have been right for me to read the Bible again, and stop George Dilwyn and Joseph reading something else. Now stopping G. D. was a difficult thing; for a person like me to remind him! However, I did not fully do as I thought right, for I did not openly tell G. D. we were going to read, but spoke to my husband, so as for him to hear; then he read, I knowing I had not done my best.

11th month, 14th – I again felt some difficulty at reading the Bible, however I got through well. George Dilwyn encouraging me, by saying, he thought I portioned the reading well. After a little bustling we set off for Hampstead. I was there told by Joseph he thought my manners had too much of the courtier in them, which I know to be the case, for my disposition leads me to hurt no one that I can avoid: and I do sometimes but just keep to truth with people, from a natural yielding to them in such things as please them. I think doing so in moderation is pleasant and useful in society. It is amongst the things that produce the harmony of society: for the truth must not be spoken out at all times, at least not the whole truth. I will give an instance of what I mean. Suppose anyone was to show me the colour of a room that I thought pretty, I should say so, although I thought others more so, and omit saying that; perhaps I am wrong, I do not know if I be not, but it will not always do to tell our minds. This I have observed, and I am sorry for it, that I feel it hard when duty dictates to do what I think may hurt others. I believe this feeling of mine originates in self-love, from the dislike of being myself the cause of pain and uneasiness.

11th month, 15th – George Dilwyn said, for our encouragement this morning, that he had seen, since he had been with us, the efficacy of reading in the Bible the first thing, he thought it a good beginning for the day.

11th month, 22nd – I think I have tried to do better to-day, and a bad cold has prevented my saying much, which is so often a stumbling block, for that little member, the tongue, is very hard to command; until the root be mended, I cannot expect the branches to flourish, or to bring forth much fruit. Thoughts, words and actions appear to spring from a corrupt source. I feel my sisters a lesson to me, they seem so much more virtuous.

12th month, 8th – I value being alone with my husband; it is a quiet I have not lately enjoyed and it does seem to me, at this time, one of the great blessings of life: talking of blessings, am I not ungrateful, when thus surrounded with them, to be wishing for more? It is a pity!

12th month, 9th – Anna Savery drank tea here; we had not sat long after tea before we fell into silence. During the time, I first felt a sort of anxiety for the welfare of us young travellers, and it came strongly across my mind, is it not my duty openly to express it? This put me into an agitation not easily to be described; and I continued in this state, which was a truly painful one, nearly feeling it my duty to pray aloud for us; oh, how hard it did seem! I tried to run from it, but I found the most safety in trying to wait upon God; hoping, if it were imagination, to overcome it; if it were duty, that I might be obedient. Towards the latter end, I felt more inclined towards obedience. But what an obstacle is my not holding my will in subserviency to that of my Maker; for perhaps after all it was only a trial of my obedience, that would not have been called for, but to show me how far I was from a resigned state of heart. I felt oppressed the rest of the evening.

12th month, 10th – I awoke in a burdened state of mind; I thought it better to relieve it to my dear husband, and found comfort in doing so; he warned me against imagination. I must try to trust in the Lord, and I hope to find safety. I felt quite in a state of agitation till we went to Meeting; it made me feel almost ill in body, both last night and this morning; however, my mind was sweetly calmed in the Meeting, and I felt vastly relieved from my terrors, and a little love and trusting in the Heavenly Master. I was almost ready to do whatever might be right for me. Oh! may I give up to what is called for at my hand, and may I not be deceived, but follow the true Shepherd, for my feet seem much inclined to wander!

12th month, 14th – I attended both Meetings as usual, and as usual I came from them flat and discouraged. To attend our place of worship and there spend almost all the time in worldly thoughts is, I fear, too great a mark of how my time is mostly spent; indeed, my life appears at this time to be spent to little more purpose than eating, drinking, sleeping, and clothing myself. But if we analyse the employment of most, what do they more than in some way attend to the bodily wants of themselves or others? What is our work, the good we do to the poor, &c., &c., but for the body!

Elizabeth Fry replies to a letter from a friend

Mildred's Court, First Month, 1801.
In referring to thy former letter, I remembered thou there hailed me as a fellow-traveller towards a better country; and I remember feeling encouragement from it: I am doubtful how far thou couldest now do so, but I trust, although I see little and feel hardly any thing of good in my own mind, that I am not yet quite forsaken as one dead to good works. I am at times ready to feel, what shall I do? For if I were sure this state was out of my own power, I need only quietly rest, hoping for better times; but my fear is that, from want of more watchfulness, I am so continually devoted to things of this world, as to blind my spiritual sight from observing things belonging to the other. There are times when my anxiety for good is great indeed, and for a short time it is my endeavour to seek strength where I hope to find it; but alas! my good wishes and good endeavours are of short, very short duration. I often remember that part of Scripture (more particularly at Meeting) where our Saviour says to Simon, "Couldest thou not watch with me one hour?" I feel able to draw some consolation from what I here read, when I see that others so great and good have found it hard to do so; but I experience the force of the question. I have at times great fears that I may be led astray in matters of the first importance, for there is a power that will at times deceive the unwary mind, for we may remember it can even put on the appearance of an angel of light. It was my lot, in very early life, to be much in company with Deists, and to be rather a warm advocate for their doctrines. I now in many shapes feel myself touched with these early imbibed opinions: for it appears to me that, unless I be, by its very superior power, really lifted above these opinions, my poor weak nature is apt to doubt almost every thing. How poor is the enjoyment, how dark is our prospect, when the enlightening rays of true

religion are taken from us! I did not expect thus to have opened my heart to thee, but one thing led on to another. I now and then remember a remark of thine, that thou believed a soul was still living to that which is good, whilst it partook of that unity that the poor travellers Zionward are favoured to feel towards each other; I have sometimes hoped, when thinking of it, that I am not yet quite dead to such things; as I feel my heart nearly drawn towards some of those whom I believe to be truly making progress in this blessed journey, and while I at times so peculiarly love the disciple, I hope I am not an enemy to the Master.

1st month, 15th – I set off early for Newington, to see J. G. Bevan, who I heard was poorly. I think my visit answered. I met with a very kind reception, and he appeared pleased to see me. He proposed to me reading with the family on First-day evening; which is what I have often thought of, but do not wish to practise until my husband and I are unitedly clearer on the subject.

2nd month, 3rd – This morning, after writing notes, &c., I walked out and went to see a poor woman who I half like and half do not, as there is something in her very odd; however, I spent much time about her. I then read the letters from home, which were comfortable and satisfactory. I was just dressed for company; we had a rather pleasant visit, but I think of late I more and more dislike society of every kind, I really wish for a more retired life; my present constant liability to company seems too much for my weak mind.

2nd month, 4th – I went to Meeting as usual: Sarah Lines mentioned to the Meeting the manner in which she had accomplished her late journey, and the feelings of reward she experienced; her account struck me very much; her influence was, on me at least, truly pleasant and satisfactory. She afterwards named her concern to visit some Meetings in the City of London, which was also done with remarkable simplicity, and I may say, almost humility. I longed for her continued good, and almost prayed she might be kept in a state of humility. For striking is it how liable, at all stages, we are to fall. I almost longed for the good of the religious, as of some far distant from me. Before the Monthly Meeting finished, Mary Bevan got up and addressed herself to the young women, saying we were not to be discouraged at not being called like her (Sarah Lines), but that all who endeavoured to perform their duty should and would equally meet with their reward. I felt much, and longed for good. I think myself at this time on rather dangerous ground, for retirement of mind, or that necessary watchfulness which keeps us poor mortals out of danger, is what I am nearly stranger to; and in the state of deadness to religion, that has lately been my experience, I am also tried by great fears about what duty may call me to. If these be fears of my own imagination, how much is truth wanted to overcome them. Seek, seek, until I find, and do not give up till the last!

3rd month, 15th – I felt really better this morning and went to Meeting, but all my small efforts to quiet my thoughts were ineffectual; the same in the afternoon; it is very serious. Really when I awake in the morning I feel a flatness, when I find my great object of the day no longer appears to be even to wish to do the will of my Creator. But I am as one who has in some measure lost his pilot, and is tossed about by the waves of the world. But I trust that there is yet a power that will prevent my drowning; I draw some consolation from my dreams of old, for how often was I near drowning, and yet at last saved

5th month, 15th – We went in the evening to see a Friend (Joseph Lancaster), who kept a school for poor children. I felt a wish that the young man might be preserved in humility; for I know, from experience, it is a hard matter, when we have the apparent approbation of many, and more particularly of those whom we esteem.

5th month, 29th – After dinner, we attended our Women's Meeting, at four o'clock, which lasted till nearly eight o'clock, it was to me very long and very tedious; indeed it may be, and I doubt not is in great part my own weakness, but to hold fast my faith, I found in this Yearly Meeting, no instrument ought to be looked to. I am afresh come to this conclusion, that only the clear dictates of duty should lead us to act, even in matters of religion; that we should be very careful in expressing even a religious sentiment, without great clearness, and more particularly where others are concerned. How exceedingly cautiously should religious advice be given to others! It should not be done, without strong and clear feelings of duty, for I know from experience, such things are apt, even if they be given as encouragement, to discourage or weaken the feeble mind, if out of place; I believe it better to do too little than too much in them. Notwithstanding the many remarks that I have made I trust I shall in the end be better for this time, for I have seen much to love and admire in the instruments and I trust the principle is not weakened within me. May it lead me to seek deeply to serve my Maker in singleness of heart, for that appears the only way to rectitude of conduct; and not to forget the numerous rocks there are to split upon, on every side. Those observations should teach me the necessity of keeping a constant watch and dependence on my Creator.

6th month, 15th – If I can with truth acknowledge it to be my first wish to do my best, although I may not feel the sensible gratification of doing my duty, I may yet be really doing it. If I do all I can, I have no occasion to fear sooner or later meeting with my reward. I was rather disappointed at our having company, indeed we have now little time alone: it is quite a serious thing, our being so constantly liable to interruptions as we are. I do not think, since we married, we have had one fourth of our meals alone. I long for more retirement, but it appears out of our power to procure it; and therefore it is best to be as patient under interruptions as we can, but I think it a serious disadvantage to young people setting out in life.

Plashet, 7th month, 9th – We are so much from home and in such con-tinual bustles, that really when I am here, I feel at a loss for regular employment. I just have time enough to keep things in order; engagement follows engagement so rapidly, day after day, week after week, owing principally to our number of near connexions, that we appear to live for others, rather than ourselves: our plan of sleeping out so often, I by no means like, and yet it appears impossible to prevent it; to spend one's life in visiting and being visited seems sad. Joseph Lancaster came in after breakfast, I had some talk with him about poor people; he enlightened me about his school plans, but not generally about the poor.

7th month, 10th – I had to fix with Jane King about the nursery, and to reprove a servant for something I did not approve, which kept me in a state of agitation for some time, it is so trying to me to reprove any one. It is so very trying to my natural disposition, partly I suppose from a feel-ing of self-love that does not like being the cause of pain; partly I suppose from feeling for others. I mostly feel satisfaction when I take courage to act the mistress, as it is so much out of my nature.

7th month, 11th – It now and then strikes me to how little end are all these employments that occupy us; we seem principally occupied in clothing, feeding and taking care of our bodies, and yet I trust if even that be done in a right spirit, we still are doing our duty, and it is in these actions about our bodies that our minds and principles act also, if it be our object to do all things to the glory of God. But we are apt rather to do things in subserviency to our own will, rather than the will of our Maker; we therefore devote ourselves to these outward and bodily things. Now, when such things are done, which I believe they may be, under a devotional spirit, we are not injured by being occupied with such trifles.

7th month, 15th – I have had an interesting talk with my dear sister Rachel; she appears to me to have perceived that which will direct her steps. But how hard it is deeply, strictly, and for a long time together, to have our first object to serve our Creator – for at first there is a natural glee, as for something new, and then we feel we have to pass through lukewarmness, which is a dangerous state; I believe one, where many are lost. May I be carried through it!

My thoughts are now very often in my nursery, fixing plans for children. I am very full of castles about my good management; but all must be, should be, held in subserviency to a great and divine Power, who alone knows what is best for them and us; and it is to be hoped He will, in His mercy, guide the hands of the parents to lead them in the right path in every way. I am a great friend to close and constant attention to early education, even the very first years of a child's life.

9th month, 12th – I have hardly had time or strength as yet to describe the events I have lately passed through. I did not experience that joy some women describe when my husband first brought me my little babe, little darling! I hardly knew what I felt for it, but my body and spirits were so extreme weak, I could only just bear to look at those I loved. I felt the dear baby at first a quiet source of pleasure, but she early became a subject for my weakness and low spirits to dwell upon, so that I almost wept when she cried; but I hope, as bodily strength recovers, strength of mind will come with it.

9th month, 23rd – Certainly I am ignorant about the management of such young infants, but I do not feel uneasy about the charge of her body, from my self-confidence I fear; but I believe if we endeavour to do our duty, even in such things, we shall find the way. I much wish to avoid my mother-in-law's very "cotting" plan, for a degree of hardiness I think most desirable – I think being too careful and tender really makes them more subject to indisposition.

10th month, 1st – My present feelings for the babe are so acute as to render me at times unhappy, from an over-anxiety about her, such an one, as I never felt before for anyone. Now it appears to me, this over-anxiety arises from extreme love, weak spirits and state of health, and not being under the influence of principle, that would lead me to overcome these natural feelings, as far as they tend to my misery. For if I were under the influence of principle, I might trust that my dear infant was indeed under the care and protection of an infinitely wise and just Providence that permits her little sufferings for some good end, that I know not of. How anxiously do I hope this poor dear baby may be held in resignation by me to the Divine will. Oh! that I might feel dependence on that Almighty arm about her and about other things. Beyond every thing else, I wish to do my duty, idle and relaxed as I am in performing it.

Mildred's Court, 10th month, 10th – I here sit hearing the great noise and bustle of the Illumination for Peace; my dearest babe is sleeping in the room; my husband and the rest of the party are gone out to see it. This evening I am very tired, and the noise of the mob nearly makes my head ache. This is the way in which they show their joy! It does not seem to me the right manner of showing our gratitude, as it appears to lead to drunkenness and vice. I think true gratitude should lead us to endeavour to retain the blessing, or to make good use of it by more virtue in ourselves and encouraging others to the same.

Mildred's Court, 11th month, 25th – My cough has been so poorly that my husband called in Dr Simms. I asked his advice about our little one being inoculated, he strongly recommended the cowpox, and said that he would undertake the care of her if we liked: I think highly of his judgment, and I believe it to be our duty to avoid evil, both bodily and mentally. So trifling a complaint as the cow-pox, being likely to prevent so dreadful a disease as the small-pox, at least it appears justifiable to try it; although the idea is not pleasant it almost looks like taking too much on ourselves to give a child a disease. But I altogether was easy to do it. I felt a good deal about the operation, which was very little and easily performed. What a wonderful discovery it is, if it really prevent the small-pox !

1st month, 26th, 1802 – It is more than a month since I wrote my journal; I am sorry for it, but I have been Martha-like, and so much engrossed in the affairs of this life, that little time has been spent in reviewing my conduct; indeed I appear very much to have taken my flight from spiritual things. It is not my feeling bereft of the comforts of religion that alarms me, it is my not sufficiently seeking after them I fear; for I hardly ever am on the watch for the Master's coming. I may say my heart has now and then been full, almost to prayer, for my husband, child, and myself; particularly for my little infant, that we may not prove stumbling-blocks in its way to salvation; if it please God it should live to an age of understanding. I believe it would be better for me if I were in a more constant habit of daily retirement; for it would afford me time for self-examination, which I am so unaccustomed to, and if I only sit quietly, I believe I may find it useful, although I feel of myself I can do nothing.

1st month, 28th – I do heartily enjoy our being alone, and falling into some plans, not being interrupted, I appear naturally to fall into employment; and it is so sweet to have quiet plans at my own dear home. How much I think my marriage tends to my outward comfort; it is wonderful to me to observe how every act of mine has prospered, that has been done under the anxious wish of serving my Creator in it.

2nd month, 20th – I felt our dearest child in great danger, as did many besides me, indeed I believe all of us. This was indeed a trial, but I was supported with some resignation of soul, feeling the weight of that part of the prayer, "Thy will and not mine be done".

2nd month, 21st – As the morning advanced, my little infant began to change from a very feverish state to an almost deadly languid one, that I believe most present, thought might be the beginning of a more awful change. She sat on my lap, I happened to be also very faint at the time; I think I may say, I felt resigned to the all-wise dispensations of Providence, which was a great blessing; my mind felt depending on that Power that alone can support in the day of trial. I desire to feel that of myself I can do nothing, and that I may remember the blessing of being able to say, "Thy will and not mine be done".

Yearly Meeting, the annual gathering of British Friends, was usually held in London with many Quakers, from all parts of the country and abroad, attending and visiting one another.

5th month, 31st – Yearly Meeting is now, I am happy to say, finished. I attended all the Meetings but one. In some of them I was much more interested than last year, and felt for the interest of the Society. We have seen a good deal of Friends, and I think I admire them more than I did last year. I have had a few more serious feelings than usual, I have been always devoted to the world, except now and then, when my heart has anxiously hoped for something better. I have felt very much how we are all surrounded with continual temptations, and how very hard it is to hold fast that which is good; I see so many faults in myself, that I fear there are many I know nothing of, from not sufficiently seeking for them; for I observe faults in others who are better than myself, that I believe they know nothing of.

Mildred's Court, 8th month, 19th – To-day we have been married two years: time slips through quickly, trials and pleasures before unknown have indeed been felt by me, trials and joys of many kinds. The love of a husband, the unity experienced; the love of a child, the maternal feelings, when under subordination, are real and great sources of enjoyment, they are apt to occupy the mind perhaps too much. My family is to me in more comfortable order than it was, at least I feel more mistress of it. My forgetfulness I find a material hindrance to me in many such concerns. In the afternoon, I was a good deal with my dearest Joseph.

Plashet, 5th month, 21st, 1803 – I have been long prevented writing my journal, by a severe attack of indisposition. It is difficult exactly to express what I have gone through, but it has been now and then a time of close trial; my feelings being such at times as to be doubtful whether life or death would be my portion. One night I was I believe very seriously ill; I never remember feeling so forcibly how hard a trial it was in prospect to part with life. Much as my mind, as well as body, was then tried in this emergency, still I felt forcibly an inward support, and it reminded me of that text of Scripture, "Can a woman forget her sucking child, yea they may forget, yet will I not forget thee". And then I told those around me that I was so ill, I could almost forget my child; but I felt the existence of a Power that I could never forget. I have gone through much since, in various ways from real bodily weakness, and also the trials of a nervous imagination: no one knows but those who have felt them, how hard they are to bear, for they lead the mind to look for trouble, and it requires much exertion not to be led away by them; nothing I believe allays them so much as the quieting influence of religion, and that leads us to endeavour after quietness under them, not looking beyond the present. But they are a regular bodily disorder, that I believe no mental exertion can cure or overcome, but we must endeavour not to give way to them.

10th month, 4th – After reading a little, I went some way off to see a poor woman. After searching a long time in one of the disagreeable parts of London, I could not find her, but I was directed to another poor person who lived near the place, and although I believe the first woman had deceived me, it led me to serve two others that I have reason to think really wanted. I felt quite in my element serving the poor, and although I was much tired with looking about, it gave me much pleasure, it is an occupation my nature is so fond of; I wish not to take merit to myself beyond my desert, but it brings satisfaction with it more than most things.

Upton, 3rd month, 5th, 1804 – Since I last wrote, I have more closely witnessed the scene of death than I ever did before. Last First day morning, about three o'clock, my mother [-*in-law*] died; I was with her at times on Seventh day, and although I have every reason to believe she died happily, I did not experience those awful, sweet feelings I should have looked for, at so serious a time On First day morning, I went into the room, and sat some time with the corpse; it was very affecting to me to see it, and I was a good deal overcome, and felt it much. I have been surprised how little this event has led me into a serious state of mind, I fear it has not had so profitable an effect upon me as it ought.

Plashet, 2nd month, 5th, 1805 – Since I last wrote, I have been much occupied with many things: rather more than usual about the poor. I have been desirous that attending to them as I do may not prove a snare to me, for I think acting charitably leads us often to receive more credit than we deserve, or at least to fancy so; it is one of those things that give my nature pleasure, therefore I believe I am no further praiseworthy than that I give way to a natural inclination. Attending the afflicted is one of those things that so remarkably brings its reward with it, that we may rest in a sort of self-satisfaction which is dangerous; but I often feel the blessing of being so situated as to be able to assist the afflicted, and sometimes a little to relieve their distresses.

73

5th month, 7th – Yesterday, my sister[*-in-law*], Eliza Fry, was here; we were saying something about the children's dress; and she remarked that for the sake of others (she meant the fear of not setting a good example), she would not do so and so. I said it struck me that those who do their duty with integrity are serving others as well as themselves, and do more real good to the cause of true religion than in looking much outwardly, either to what others do or think. I think that conscience will sometimes lead us to feel for others, and not act so as materially to hurt a weak brother; but I believe we should seldom find that we hurt those whose opinion would be worth caring for, if we kept close to witness in our own hearts. If I were going to do a thing, I should endeavour to find whether it appeared to me in any way wrong, and whether I should feel easy to do it; looking secretly for help where it is to be found, and there I believe I should leave it; and if it led me to act rather differently from some, I should probably be doing more good to society than in any conformity, merely on account of others, for if I should be preserved in the way of obedience in other things, it would in time show from whence such actions sprung, and I think this very spirit of conforming in trifles to the opinion of others leads into forms that may one day prove a stumbling-block to the progress of our Society, whereas, if we attend to the principle that brought us together, it will lead us out of forms, and not into them.

Earlham, 6th month, 7th – There is quite a change since I last wrote, I have passed through much illness among the children; the Yearly Meeting, and since that, coming here. After my return from Plashet dear little Rachel was very poorly, and poor John; all these things tried me, but I endeavoured to bear them with patience and cheerfulness. The Yearly Meeting was very interesting to me, I felt a good deal about it; in the first place, I am struck afresh with the beauty of our principles: but so am I also with the great want of simplicity and integrity in us who profess them; for I am willing to believe that if we more closely attended to it, there would be more unity, more clearness, and more promptness in our manner of attending to the business of the Society. I used to fear that a selfish principle frequently rose up amongst us, rather than the simple love and fear of God, which spirit I think alone should rule in the management of the discipline intended to protect our religious principles. The dread I had over me, in Plaistow Meeting, of saying something, impressed me in most of the Meetings. I had such clear ideas in some of the Meetings; but I did not believe it necessary for my salvation to do it, and I believe hardly any motive short of that could induce me. Once in hearing the queries answered, how many were negligent in attending Weekday Meetings? It struck me, it arose from allowing the business of the world to stand too much in competition with the things of God, and of how much more importance one was than the other; for a right attention to religious duties enables us much better to perform our temporal ones. I have enjoyed coming here, and being with them.

Mildred's Court, 2nd month, 15th, 1806 – I have been confined nearly all this week with a bad cough, and still continue poorly. I have particularly felt the vacancy of all outward help, or consolation, or protection; neither reading good books, writing journals, nor anything else, will, or can do: but placing our dependence on the Power that calls us out of darkness into light, and that alone can lead us and point out to us the rocks on which we are likely to split, for though we may certainly profit by the experience of others, yet there is a new way as it were for each to tread in: and they are not the same temptations which assail all travellers Zion-ward, but different natures are differently tried; all must first seek for light to guide them (individually) that will teach them in the right time what to do, and what to leave undone, and prove in the end their strong tower, and preservation from all harm.

Elizabeth Fry was appointed by her local Quaker meeting as a visitor to the Society of Friends' school and workhouse at Islington.

5th month, 15th – Yesterday I went to the workhouse to spend the evening with the children; a prospect I have had in view some time, almost ever since I have been on the appointment. I took them things for tea: I dreaded going on many accounts, fearing I should not feel at liberty to make any remarks I might wish to the children during their reading, which it was my principal object in going to attend. I did not exactly see my way; however, I thought I would (as Friends say) make my way. I found after tea, they did not read till nearly eight, and I could not remain later than a little past seven. I spoke to the governess about it, and she was quite willing to alter the hour, and so was the stewardess. I proposed reading a little pamphlet that has lately come out by Frederick Smith, to children. There was a solemnity during reading it, so that Ann Withers was in tears most of the time, and some of the children were disposed that way; afterwards, when we had finished, I endeavoured to weigh whether I really had anything to say to them or not; I thought that I had, and therefore took up the book as if to explain it; making my own remarks which appeared to affect the children and the governess, so that those who were on the point of tears really wept. Now this event has made me feel rather odd; it is marvellous to me how I got courage to do it before Anti Withers. I have felt so desirous not to stamp such a thing too highly, for I am ready to believe, though the party appeared to feel what I said so much, it was principally owing to their great tenderness, as that which I said seemed rather to flow naturally from my heart and understanding, than anything really deep from the living fountain. I have desired that this little event may not encourage me too much, for hard things seemed made quite easy. Oh! that in anything like a religious duty I may never go beyond the right Guide, nor ever give self the praise. Keep me humble and dependent on Thee, O Lord! even if self suffer in being made so.

Earlham, 12th month, 6th – On Fourth day morning, the 24th, our dear Louisa was married at Tasborough Meeting. A very serious and interesting time to us all. My father, all of us eleven, my husband and Samuel Hoare. The Meeting was very solemn, and did to me sweetly license them in their solemn engagement, it was like a seal set to it. There was testimony upon testimony, and blessing upon blessing, from the ministers present; and what was better than all to me, a sweet inward covering over the Meeting. All appeared unity and love; rather remarkable to see so large a family all so nearly sympathizing, and closely united. My dear brother John was sweet indeed, and deeply feeling; may it last in him, and may he truly find the pearl of great price.

Questions for Myself [1807]

First, – Hast thou this day been honest and true in performing thy duty towards thy Creator in the first place: and, secondly, towards thy fellow-creatures; or hast thou sophisticated and flinched.

Second, – Hast thou been vigilant in frequently pausing in the hurry and career of the day, to see who thou art endeavouring to serve; whether thy Maker or thyself? And every time that trial or temptation assailed thee, didst thou endeavour to look steadily to the Delivering Power; even to Christ who can do all things for thee?

Third, – Hast thou endeavoured to perform thy relative duties faithfully: been a tender, loving, yielding wife, where thy own will and pleasure were concerned; a tender, yet steady mother with thy children, making thyself quickly and strictly obeyed, but careful in what thou requirest of them: a kind, yet honest mistress, telling thy servants of their faults, when thou thinkest it for their or thy good, but never unnecessarily worrying thyself or them about trifles: and to everyone endeavouring to do as thou wouldest be done unto?

5th month, 27th, 1808 – Since I last wrote, I have gone through much trouble. Last Seventh day week, an account was received of the death of our much loved sister [-*in-law*], Elizabeth Gurney. I felt it deeply; during her illness my heart cried unto the Lord for mercy, and He would take her unto Himself, and that her transgressions might be blotted out. Being still so much inclined to trying nervous feelings made me feel it in a more painful way: not finding any rest away from them all, Joseph and I went to Lynn – an afflicting time. On Third day morning, I had a most affecting meeting with dear John, yet felt myself far too weak, poor, and in too painfully nervous a state, to afford him comfort; but rather needed it myself. It was a very melting interview: the remainder of the day being spent in the house with the dear remains was really sweet to me; I had comfort in my sorrow. Fourth day, we left Lynn for Earlham. The next morning was the funeral at Norwich, and poor I, hardened and almost entirely devoted to my own nervous feelings. This was a trial to me, when I had hoped to have been enabled to seek after the best help for the dear afflicted; and also to feel on account of our much loved lost Elizabeth. But I desired that this humiliating dispensation might be for my good.

8th month, 20th – I have been married eight years yesterday. Various trials of faith and patience have been permitted me; my course has been very different to what I had expected, and instead of being, as I had hoped, a useful instrument in the Church Militant, here I am a care-worn wife and mother, outwardly nearly devoted to the things of this life. Though at times this difference in my destination has been trying to me, yet I believe those trials (which have certainly been very pinching) that I have had to go through have been very useful, and brought me to a feeling sense of what I am; and at the same time have taught me where power is, and in what we are to glory; not in ourselves nor in any thing we can be, or do, but we are alone to desire that He may be glorified, either through us or others, in our being something or nothing, as He may see best for us. I have seen, particularly in our spiritual allotments, that it is not in man that walketh to direct his steps; it is in our place, only to be as passive clay in His holy hands, simply and singly desiring, that He would make us what He would have us to be. But the way in which this great work is to be effected, we must leave to Him, who has been the Author, and we may trust will be the Finisher of the work: and we must not be surprised to find it going on differently to what our frail hearts would desire. I may also acknowledge that through all my trials, there does appear to have been a particular blessing attending me, both as to the fatness of the land, and the dew of Heaven; for though I have been at times deeply tried inwardly and outwardly, yet I have always found the delivering Arm has been near at hand, and trials have appeared blessed to me. The little efforts or small acts of duty I have ever performed have often seemed remarkably blessed to me; and where others have been concerned, it has also I think been apparent in them, that the effort on my part has been blessed to both parties. Also, what shall I say when I look at my husband and my five lovely babes? How I have been favoured to recover from illnesses, and to get through them without material injury in any way. I also observe, how any little care towards my servants appears to have been blessed, and what faithful and kind friends to me I have found them. Indeed I cannot enumerate my blessings; but I may truly say, that of all the blessings I have received, and still receive, there is none to compare to believing that I am not yet forsaken, but notwithstanding all my deviations, in mercy cared for. And (if all the rest be taken from me) far above all, I desire, that if I should be led through paths I know not of, which may try my weak faith and nature, I may not lose my faith in Thee; but may increasingly love Thee; delight to follow after Thee, and be singly Thine; giving all things up to Thee, who hast hitherto been my only merciful Protector and Preserver.

11th month, 10th – I have hardly settled at home since my dear father[-*in-law*]'s death. Last First day, I was sent for to see my dear sister Hannah, who was very poorly; it proved to be the scarlet fever, and being the only sister at liberty, I have nursed her. This I consider a great privilege to be able to do; though I have felt it a very serious thing, with a young babe, and the mother of so many little lambs, to enter so catching a disorder. I have desired I might not enter it in my own will, or simply to gratify inclination, which leads me to enjoy nursing those I love so dearly: circumstances appeared to bring me into it, indeed I had hardly an option, as I was in the first instance brought into it, not knowing what the complaint was; and in the second, there was no one else that I thought proper to fill my place, as my sister Louisa was prevented. I have desired that what is really best for me may occur, even if it be to pass through trouble. But if my merciful Creator sees meet to preserve me and my family from any further suffering on this account, may I be enabled to give the praise where it is due, and may it afresh stimulate me to seek with renewed vigilance, to dedicate myself and all that belongs to me, to Him, whom my poor weak unworthy soul loves; I could think beyond every thing, though I know the world has a strong hold, and perhaps my heart is more devoted to it than to its Creator. I feel thankful for my beloved sister being better.

A fragment that occurs at this part of the Journal

Children should be deeply impressed with the belief, that the first and great object of their education is, to follow Christ, and indeed to be true Christians: and those things on which we, the Society of Friends, differ from the world in general, should not I think be impressed on them, by only saying, as is often done, "because Friends do it"; but singly and simply as things that the Christian life appears to us to require, and that therefore they must be done. They should also early be taught that all have not seen exactly the same; but that there are many equally belonging to the church of Christ who may in other respects be as much stricter than ourselves, as we are than they in these matters. But this does not at all lessen the necessity of our employing a simple mode of expressing ourselves, who are permitted to see the consistency and propriety of it.

11th month, 30th – At this time there is no set of people I feel so much about as servants: – I do not think they have generally justice done to them; they are too much considered as another race of beings and we are apt to forget that the holy injunction holds good with them, "Do as thou wouldest be done unto", and I believe in striving to do so, we shall not take them out of their station in life, but endeavour to render them happy and contented in it, and be truly their friends though not their familiars or equals as to the things of this life, for we have reason to believe the difference in our stations is ordered by a wiser than ourselves, who directs us how to fill our different places; but we must endeavour never to forget, that in the best sense we are all one, and though our paths here may be different, we have all souls equally valuable and have all the same work to do; which, if properly considered, should lead us to great sympathy and love, and also to a constant care for their welfare, both here and hereafter.

3

"Be of good courage and He will strengthen your hearts":

A new home and a new ministry, 1809–1812

The death of Elizabeth's father-in-law meant that Joseph inherited the estate at Plashet and the family moved there. More children were born – Joseph in 1809, Elizabeth (Betsy) in 1811, and Hannah in 1812. At this time Elizabeth, after much hesitation, began to appear in the ministry.

Mildred's Court, 2nd month, 14th, 1809 – The thought of forming a new establishment at Plashet, with servants, &c., is to me a very serious one. I find it so difficult fully to do my duty towards them, and even when I do, to give them satisfaction. My mind is often much burdened on this subject; I long to make them my friends, and for us all to live in harmony and love. We greatly (I mean servants and their heads in general) misunderstand each other; I fully believe partly from our different situations in life, and partly from our different educations, and the way in which each party is apt to view the other. Masters and mistresses are greatly deficient, I think in the general way, and so are most servants towards them: it is for both to keep in view strictly to do unto others, as they would be done unto; and also to remember that we are indeed all one with God. Oh! that I may keep watchful and near my Guide; and that if it be consistent with the Divine will, I may be enabled to say, "As for me and my house, we will serve the Lord" – and delight to do His commandments.

2nd month, 18th – I do not think I have ever expressed the pleasure and enjoyment I find in a country life; both for myself and the dear children. It has frequently led me to feel gratefully, for the numerous benefits conferred; and I have also desired that I may not rest in, or too much depend on, any of these outward enjoyments. It is certainly to me a time of sunshine. All I desire is a heart more truly devoted; both inwardly and outwardly, I have lately experienced great sweetness and tranquillity of mind

Earlham, 2nd month, 30th – I hardly know how to express myself: – I have indeed passed through wonders. On the 26th, as we were sitting quietly together (after my dear sister Richenda had left us, and my soul had bowed on my beloved father's account, of whom we had daily very poor reports), an express arrived bringing Chenda back, saying our most dear father was so ill, that they did not expect his life would be spared. Words fall short to describe what I felt, he was so tenderly near and dear to me. We soon believed it best to set off for this place, on some accounts under great discouragement, principally from my own bodily weakness, and also the fever in the house; but it did not appear as if we could omit it, feeling as we did. Therefore, after a tender parting with my beloved flock, my dearest Joseph, Chenda, and I with the baby, set off. We arrived at Mildred's Court the first night, where our dear sister left us in hopes of seeing our parent alive. In very great weakness I set off the next morning, and had at times great discouragements; but many hours were comforting and sweet. Hearing on the road at the different stages that my dearest father was living, we proceeded till we arrived at Earlham, about twelve o'clock that night. We got out of the carriage, and once more, saw him who has been so inexpressibly dear to me through life, since I knew what love was; he was asleep, but death was strongly marked on his sweet, and to me, beautiful face. Whilst in his room all was sweetness, nothing bitter, though how I feel his loss is hard to express: but indeed, I have had abundant cause to rejoice on his account. After very deep probation, his mind was strikingly visited and consoled at last in passing through the valley of the shadow of death. He frequently expressed that he feared no evil, but believed that through the mercy of God in Christ, he should be received in glory; his deep humility, and the tender and loving state he was in, were most valuable to those around him. He encouraged us, his children, to hold on our way; and sweetly expressed his belief, that our love of good (in the degree we had it) had been a stimulus and help to him.

The next morning he died, quite easily; I was not with him, but on entering his room soon after it was over, my soul was bowed within me, in love, not only for the deceased, but also for the living, and in humble thankfulness; so that I could hardly help uttering (which I did) my thanksgiving and praise, and also what I felt for the living, as well as the dead. I cannot understand it; but the power given was wonderful to myself, and the cross none – my heart was so full that I could hardly hinder utterance.

11th month, 3rd – We attended our beloved father's funeral. Before I went, I was so deeply impressed at times, with love to all, and thanksgiving, that I doubted whether it might not possibly be my place to express it there; but I did, the evening before, humbly crave not to be permitted to do so, unless rightly called to it. Fear of man appeared greatly taken away. I sat the Meeting under a solemn quietness, though there was preaching that neither disturbed nor enlivened me much; the same words still powerfully impressed me, that had done ever since I first entered the room where the corpse was. Upon going to the grave this still continued; under this solemn quiet calm the fear of man appeared so much removed, that I believe my sole desire was, that the will of God might be done in me. Though it was unpleasant to me, what man might say, yet I most feared it was a temptation, owing to my state of sorrow; but that, I fully believe was not the case, as something of the kind had been on my mind so long; but it had appeared more ripe the last few weeks, and even months, I had so often had to "rejoice in the Lord, and glory in the God of my salvation"; that it had made me desire, that others might partake, and know, how good He had been to my soul, and be encouraged to walk in those paths, which I had found to be paths of pleasantness and peace. However, after a solemn waiting, my dear uncle Joseph spoke, greatly to my encouragement and comfort, and the removal of some of my fears.

I remained still, till dearest John began to move to go away; when it appeared as if it could not be omitted, and I fell on my knees, and began, not knowing how I should go on, with these words, "Great and marvellous are Thy works, Lord God Almighty, just and true are all Thy ways, Thou King of Saints; be pleased to receive our thanksgiving"; and there I seemed stopped, though I thought that I should have had to express, that I gave thanks on my beloved father's account. But not feeling the power continue, I arose directly: a quiet, calm, and invigorated state, mental and bodily were my portion afterwards, and altogether a sweet day, but a very painful night, discouraged on every side, I could believe by him who tries to deceive. The discouragement appeared to arise principally from what others would think, and nature flinched, and sank, but I was enabled this morning to commit myself in prayer. May I be preserved in future, if my life be spared, from taking Thy holy name in vain; enable me if Thou seest meet, to follow hard after Thee, that I may know Thy voice, Thou Shepherd, and Bishop of souls, and be as one of Thy sheep. It was my prayer this morning, to be able to turn from the subject, as my poor weak mind felt hardly able to look at it, which was in some measure the case.

This day has altogether been a comfortable one, though very low at times, and having to walk in the valley, may I be enabled, if it be right for me, to trust and not to fear. I have greatly felt my beloved father's loss to-day; and yesterday, though calm, yet I suffered much on his account; he was in some things, like my heart's delight, I so enjoyed to please him and was so fond of him, that to hear of the sufferings he passed through, before he came to a state of reconciliation, greatly affected me to-day; but I have had more comfort on his account than anything else. The great love and kindness I have received from them all, and my uncle Joseph, has been encouraging to me; and my husband has been a true helpmate, and sweet counsellor.

Plashet, 11th month, 16th – We arrived here on Third day evening; though plunged into feeling before I arrived, I felt flat on meeting my tenderly beloved little flock. I was enabled coming along to crave help; in the first place, to be made willing either to do, or to suffer, whatever was the Divine will concerning me. I also desired that I might not be so occupied with the present state of my mind, as to its religious duties, as in any degree to omit close attention to all daily duties, my beloved husband, children, servants, poor, &c.; but if I should be permitted to enter the humiliating path that has appeared to be opening before me, to look well at home, and not discredit the cause I desire to advocate.

Last First day morning, I had a deeply trying Meeting, on account of the words, "Be of good courage, and He will strengthen your hearts, all ye that hope in the Lord", which had impressed me towards Norwich Meeting before I went into it; and after I had sat there a little time they came with double force, and continued resting on my mind until my fright was extreme; and it appeared almost as if I must, if I did my duty, utter them. I hope I did not wholly revolt, but I did cry in my heart, for that time to be excused, that like Samuel, I might apply to some Eli to know what the voice was that I heard – my beloved uncle Joseph, I thought was the person – on this sort of excuse or covenant, as I may call it, a calmness was granted the rest of the Meeting, but not the reward of peace.

As soon as Meeting was over, I went to my dear uncle, and begged him to come to Earlham to see me. The conflict I had passed through was so great, as to shake my body as well as mind, and I had reason to fear and to believe, I should have been happier and much more relieved in mind, if I had given up to this little service; I have felt since like one in debt to that Meeting. My dear uncle came, and only confirmed me by his kind advice, to walk by faith and not by sight; he strongly advised a simple following of what arose, and expressed his experience of the benefit of giving up to it and the confusion of not doing so. How have I desired since, not to stand in the fear of man; but I believe it is the soul's enemy seeking whom he may devour, for terrible as it was, as then presented to me, and as it often has been before, yet, when some ability was granted to get through, that same enemy would have had me glory on that account. May I not give way either to one feeling or the other but strive to look to the preserving power of God.

12th month, 9th – Soon after sitting down in Meeting (on Fourth day), I was enabled to feel encouraged by these words, "Though the enemy come in like a flood, the Spirit of the Lord will lift up a standard against him". This appeared my experience, for soon the storm was quieted, and a degree even of ease was my portion. About eleven o'clock, these same words that had done so in Norwich Meeting, came feelingly over me, "Be of good courage, and He will strengthen your hearts, all ye that hope in the Lord". And that which had hitherto appeared impossible to human nature, seemed not only possible, but I believe I was willing; simply desiring, that in this new and awful undertaking I might not lose my faith, and that the Divine will might be done in me. Under this sense and feeling, as if I could not omit, I uttered them. Though clearness still continued, nature in a great measure seemed to sink under the effort afterwards, and low feelings and imaginations to have much dominion, which in mercy were soon relieved, and I have gone on sweetly and easily since, often even rejoicing.

12th month, 22nd – Again on Fourth day, I have dared to open my mouth in public: I am ready to say, What has come to me? Even in supplication – that the work might be carried on in myself and others, and that we might be preserved from evil. My weight of deep feeling on the subject, I believe, exceeded any other time; I was, I may say, brought into a wrestling state, that the work of the ministry in me might, if right, be carried on, if not, stopped short. I feel of myself, no power for such a work; I may say, wholly unable; yet, when the feeling and power continue, so that I dare not omit it, then what can I do?

1st month, 11th, 1810 – It has been strongly impressed on me, how very little it matters, when we look at the short time we remain here, what we appear to others; and how much too much, we look at the things of this life. What does it signify, what we are thought of here, so long as we are not found wanting towards our Heavenly Father? Why should we so much try to keep something back, and not be willing to offer ourselves up to Him, body, soul, and spirit, to do with us what may seem best unto Him, and to make us what He would have us to be? O Lord! enable me to be more and more, singly, simply, and purely obedient to Thy service!

2nd month, 5th – The first part of last week I was much occupied in arranging my new household; at least, two new servants, housekeeper and cook. I much felt the weight of filling my place rightly towards the servants, whom I may say, I love; how did I desire to help them, in the best sense, and that I might feel that, as for me and my house, we will serve the Lord; I may say, there is nothing I desire so much; and the more I know, and the more I wish to follow Him in the way of His requirings, the more sweet do I find the path, and the more desirable does it appear.

3rd month, 31st – My little boy has been very naughty; his will I find very strong. Oh that my hands may be strengthened rightly to subdue it. O Lord! I pray for help in these important duties! I may truly say, I had rather my dear lambs should not live, than live eventually to dishonour Thy great cause; rather may they be taken in innocency, but, if Thou seest meet, O Lord! preserve them from great evils, and be pleased in Thy abundant mercy, to be with them, as thou hast been, I believe with their poor unworthy parents; visit them, and revisit them, until Thou hast made them what Thou wouldest have them to be. Oh, that I could, like Hannah, bring them to Thee, to be made use of as instruments in Thy Holy Temple! I ask nothing for them in comparison of Thy love; and above all blessings, that they may be vessels in Thy House; this blessing I crave for them, that they may be employed in Thy service, for indeed I can bow and say what honour, what joy so great, as in ever so small a measure, to serve Thee, O Lord!

Early in April, Elizabeth travelled into the West of England with her husband and wrote to her children at home

Cowley Bridge.

I suppose my sweet little flock will be glad to hear of the adventures of their dear papa, mamma, Sarah, and baby, and therefore I mean to make as good a story as I can, of what has happened to us in our journey from

Mildred's Court to Cowley Bridge. In the first place, we admired the grand houses, and saw the Queen's Palace, and before we had gone much further we passed near one belonging to the King: but much as I should have liked it, we neither saw King nor Queen.

Of the first day's journey, I do not remember much, except that I often thought of you, who were left at home. There were some beautiful deer feeding in a park, that I think you would have liked very much to see. I almost longed for my little gardeners with our trowels, &c., to get some of the many primroses and violets there were in the hedges. In some places, almost like a carpet of green, blue, and yellow, and the further we have gone, the more we have seen.

On Sixth day night, we slept at Andover, and I felt rather low. I hope, my dear children, you will each try to give me the pleasure when I come home of hearing you have been going on as I should like.

On our second day's journey, we went up and down a great many hills, till we arrived at Dorchester, where we met dear Anna Buxton, and went with her to a Friend's house at Bridport, who had fourteen children, and one nearly the age of each of you; and they quite enjoyed to hear of you.

To-day, we arrived here to dinner, and I hope I find your dear aunt not worse than when we parted from her. The place is very beautiful, hills, vales, and water.

My love to Harriet and Mary Ann, and kind remembrance to all the servants.

> Yours in tender love,
>
> Elizabeth Fry

8th month, 10th – I have thought this morning, I may in a measure adopt the language of the blessed Virgin, "My soul doth magnify the Lord, and my spirit hath rejoiced in God my Saviour". – May my being led out of my own family, by what appear to me duties, never be permitted to hinder my doing my duty fully towards it, or so occupy my attention, as to make me in any degree forget or neglect home duties. I believe it matters not where we are, or what we are about, so long as we keep our eye fixed on doing the great Master's work, and that whatever we do, may be done to His glory. When I feel as I do to-day, what a glorious service it is, though we may have at times to pass through great trial and poverty, and remember how in these little religious services, I have been helped and carried through, and that as I expressed before, my soul hath in a measure been able to magnify the Lord, and my spirit to rejoice in God its Saviour; I fear for myself, lest even this great mercy should prove a temptation, and lead me to come before I am called, or enter service I am not prepared for; but in all these things, I have but one place of safety, to take refuge in. Be pleased, then, 0 Lord! Thou who knowest my heart, and all its temptations; be pleased to preserve me, and enable me if Thou seest meet, to do Thy will, in strength and in weakness, when it leads to the hardest crosses as well as into the way of rejoicing.

Plashet, 1st month, 5th, 1811 – I find it no easy matter to serve the poor, I desire to do right towards them; but it is very difficult either to turn them away, or to give to all, without doing as much hurt as good. I desire a right spirit about them, and ability to know what is best to be done.

1st month, 11th – Felt very low yesterday evening, rather unusually so for me, partly from the children being naughty and trying. I also feel how poorly my duties are performed towards all. If I be clearer in one description of duty than another, I think it is towards servants; but in that I often have to mourn over my defects. I have felt a little encouragement this morning, and am at times brought to leave others, and their interests, and look and depend upon Him, who can help them, and even listens to the cry of His little ones. As for my beloved children, I had rather they should not be, than have them live to go greatly astray; but let me not forget that if they, like myself, should go astray for a time, there is that Power which can bring them back. Oh, that this may be the case; may they eventually become redeemed from the world, and advocates or valiants in the great cause! It is almost my single desire for them; all others are small in comparison – and as for my beloved husband, oh! that we may be preserved, going hand in hand, and bowing before the Holy One in sweet unity; not turning aside to any other gods, or making to ourselves graven images, and worshipping them.

2nd month, 7th – Yesterday was to me an awful and affecting day; there came up a minute from the men, desiring the women to meet them after the next Monthly Meeting, to consider the subject of acknowledging me as a minister. Friends felt so kindly for me, as to call me out of meeting to tell me, lest hearing it should overcome me; this was unnecessary, for though I felt and feel it deeply, that was not likely to be the case. It brings me prostrate before the great "I am" but I have little or nothing to say for myself: certainly, it is cause of humble gratitude, to believe my little offerings in the ministry have not burdened, but been acceptable to the church. O Lord! if it be Thy will to preserve my life yet a little longer, and continue me in this service, preserve me, even if it be through chastisement, from ever hurting Thy great and holy cause, and enable me to walk worthy of the vocation whereunto I am called.

2nd month, 8th – I have thought this morning, whether we, as a Society, do not suffer more than we need, by expecting too much of ourselves; whether our hope and reliance is sufficiently on Him whom we desire to become our all in all; experience has taught me, that Christ in me, or His saying and anointing power in me, is indeed my only hope of glory. I look not to myself, but to that within me, that has to my admiration proved my present help, and enabled me to do what I believe of myself I could not have done. Under a sense of my own unsubjected will, I do not desire too much to give way to the spirit of mourning, or judging myself, but at once endeavour to turn to Him, and wait upon Him, who can alone strengthen for every good word and work, and will I believe undoubtedly arise, in His own time, for the help of His little dependent ones, and make a way for them, where they see no way. Enable me, O Lord! increasingly to put my whole trust and confidence in Thee.

3rd month, 14th – My husband brought me word in the evening, that Friends had agreed to acknowledge me as a minister. This mark of their unity is sweet, and I think strengthening, and I believe will have advantages, as well as trials attending it. I feel and find it is neither by the approbation, any more than by the disapprobation of man, that we stand or fall; but it once more leads me only to desire, that I may simply and singly follow my Master in the way of His requirements, whatsoever they may be. I think this will make a way for me in some things that have been long on my mind.

3rd month, 19th – I feel at times deeply pressed down, on account of my beloved children. Their volatile minds try me, but amidst my trials I have a secret hope concerning them, that all will end well; and a blessing attend them, if they bow to the blessed yoke (for so I feel it), in their youth. May you, if ever you read this, my beloved little ones, hearken to the advice of your tenderly affectionate mother. Submit to the cross of Christ in small matters and in great, there is no way like it; the crown is in a measure partaken of even here. That no enemy of your souls be permitted to overcome you, or turn your feet into another path, is the sincere desire, nay, prayer of her, who feels your souls' welfare very near to her own; may we all so live, that when time to us here shall be no more, we may unite, and sing praises in eternity. Look at it, what folly, for the sake of self-gratification for a few years, to forfeit even the chance of such a prospect! Ah, my children, press forward through all opposition; walking by faith, rather, than by sight, for in that alone you will find strength and safety; looking too much out loses time and creates confusion, whilst humbly looking within, with the eye of faith, and following whatever that may lead into, or out of, tends to confirm, stablish, and strengthen. May the God of peace be with, bless, and preserve you, saith my soul, Amen. O Lord! be pleased to have mercy on them, win them over to Thy love, and teach them that there is no way like Thy way, no joy like Thy joy!

Plashet, 8th month, 23rd – We had three clergymen and their wives, besides another neighbour and his wife here yesterday; I believe good men and I hope good women also; I felt love, and I think that sort of unity with them, that I have with good Friends. From a great fear of hurting others, I feel, though I believe it is not very apparent, a bowing to their opinions, and not openly professing my own, which tries me. There, no doubt, are advantages, as well an disadvantages, in associating with people of different descriptions; especially in being with the Good, we are increasingly led to estimate the good in all, and also to observe, how the mercy of our heavenly Father is extended towards us, and how He sees meet to accept us in our different ways. But at the same time, there is safety in keeping within our narrow enclosure, more particularly for young people not established in principle. It may induce them to make the example of others a plea for more liberty, instead of rightly stimulating them to look at home and examine how far they are doing the work committed to them, which should be the effect of seeing others zealously pursuing their course. It is also important, as children become marriageable, with whom they associate, and parents should in this, as in other things, keep on the watch, and seek the best direction how far to go and where to stop. But my feelings of love would lead me almost to encourage an intimacy with one of these clergymen and his wife: but I desire to be rightly directed, and if we are likely to lose more than we gain by not holding fast the profession of our faith without wavering, then I hope not to encourage it; I leave it, thinking it will make its own way, which I trust will be the right one, but Friends being so much united with others, and brought so forward in works of benevolence, may prove a snare by flattering them and taking them off their guard. It is on account of schools that we have been thus brought together.

9th month, 6th – I have lately been so much-hurried by an almost constant change of company and employments, as to be at times a good deal tried, and I am fearful my temper will be made irritable by it. I think I may truly say, my desire is, to do my duty fully and faithfully to all connected with me, – nearly and remotely, rich and poor; but I find I cannot satisfy all, and often feel to myself doing almost every thing very imperfectly; a little like the old man and his ass, trying to please everybody, and pleasing nobody, and losing his own approbation into the bargain. This I believe is in a measure the case, though not altogether so; perhaps I may one day spend my time to an apparently better account. Be pleased, O Lord, to bless the small feeble endeavours of Thy poor child, to do her duty to others, for without Thy blessing, they are all ineffectual, and with Thy blessing, I need not doubt but they will tend to my own good, and to the good of those I desire to serve, more particularly at home.

With my dear little ones I often feel myself a poor mother, but my hope is not in myself, for I am sensible I do not apparently manage them so well as many others do their children; but, O Lord! Thou knowest my heart, and its desires for them, and that I may not be found wanting towards them. I neither ask health nor riches, nor any thing for them in comparison with this, that as they grow in years, they may grow in favour with Thee, and with those who love Thee, by walking in humility and in Thy fear. My feeling of my own great deficiencies towards them and others, at times leads me to take great comfort from the shortness of life, if I be but ready, and have done faithfully the work committed. I fancy I could willingly leave them and all, trusting that better instruments might be raised up for their help; but poor as I am, if it please the Lord to make me an instrument of good to them and others, and to bless my small efforts to serve Him, I believe I should rejoice in keeping alive for some time longer. I feel every week that is pretty well run and towards the end of the Race, that it is well, and a cause of gratitude.

9th month, 12th – Yesterday was a day indeed: – one that may be called a mark of the times. We first attended a General Meeting of the Bible Society, where it was sweet to observe so many of various sentiments all uniting in the one great object, from the good Bishop of Norwich (Bathurst), for so I believe he may be called, to the dissenting Minister, and young Quaker (my brother Joseph). We afterwards, about thirty-four of us, dined here, I think there were six clergymen of the Establishment; three dissenting Ministers; and Richard Philips, besides numbers of others. A very little before the cloth was removed, such a power came over me of love, I believe I may say, life, that I thought I must ask for silence after Edward Edwards had said grace, and then supplicate the Father of mercies, for His blessing – both of the fatness of the earth, and the dew of Heaven, upon those, who thus desired to promote His cause, by spreading the knowledge of the Holy Scriptures; and that He would bless their endeavours, that the knowledge of God and His glory might cover the earth, as the waters cover the sea; and also for the preservation of all present, that through the assistance of His grace we might so follow Him, and our blessed Lord in time, that we might eventually enter into a glorious eternity, where the wicked cease from troubling, and the weary are at rest. The power and solemnity were very great. Richard Philips asked for silence, I soon knelt down, it was like having our High Priest amongst us; independently of this power, His poor instruments are nothing, and with His power, how much is effected! I understood many were in tears, I believe all were bowed down spiritually. Soon after I took my seat, the Baptist minister said, "This is an act of worship", adding that it reminded him of that which the disciples said, "when He walked with us, did not our hearts burn within us?" A clergyman said, "We want no wine, for there is that amongst us, that does instead." A Lutheran minister remarked, that although he could not always understand the words, being a foreigner, he felt the Spirit of Prayer, and went on to enlarge in a striking manner. Another clergyman spoke to this effect: how the Almighty visited us, and that neither sex, nor any thing else stood in the way of His grace. I do not exactly remember the words of any one, but it was a most striking circumstance, for so many of such different opinions thus all to be united in one spirit; and for a poor woman to be made the means, amongst so many, great, wise, and I believe good men, of showing forth the praise of the great "I Am". After reading last evening, the dear Lutheran minister, Dr Steinkoff, said a few words in prayer. This morning, my desire, indeed I may say prayer, is, that this may not degenerate into a form amongst us, and I should not be surprised, if I had to express as much; however, that I leave.

Be pleased, O Lord, still to preserve me on the right hand, and on the left, and let me in no way do contrary to Thy will; and if called upon to testify that I can only unite in prayer, where I apprehend Thy Spirit leads into it, enable me, I beseech Thee, to do it on, as to strengthen, rather than weaken the love that I feel so sweetly to unite me with those who differ from myself.

2nd month, 1st, 1812 – On reading over my old journals yesterday, it has led me to admire how some of my early prayers and desires have been answered; how gradual has been the arising and opening of Divine Power in my heart. How much has occurred to strengthen my weak faith, and doubting, fearful heart; how much has been done for me, and how little have I done myself; how much have I rebelled, except in the day of power; how often unwatchful, yet in mercy, how has help been administered, even a willing heart, which I consider an unspeakable gift: but I think I should have flourished better, and grown stronger by this time, had I more fully and more faithfully followed the Lamb whithersoever He goeth. My heart's desire and prayer for myself, above everything else, is, that this may be more entirely done by me. O Lord! be pleased still to carry on Thy own work in me, until Thou hast made me what Thou wouldest have me to be; even entirely Thy servant, in thought, word and deed, if Thou only knowest my weakness and fear of suffering; when in Thine infinite wisdom, Thou mayst see meet to afflict, be pleased to mix mercy with judgment, and uphold me by Thine own power; I thank Thee for all Thy benefits towards me, and desire to prove my gratitude by my love and good works. O Lord! enable me so to do ? Amen.

2nd month, 3rd – The prospect I have had for some months of going into Norfolk, to attend the Monthly and Quarterly Meetings, is now brought home to me, as I must apply to my next Monthly Meeting for permission. It is no doubt a sacrifice of natural feeling, to leave the comforts of home, and my beloved husband and children; and to my weak nervous habits, the going about, and alone (for so I feel it in one sense without my husband) is, I have found from experience, a trial greater than I imagined; and my health suffers much, I think, from my habits being necessarily so different. This consideration of its being a cross to my nature, I desire not to weigh in the scale; though no doubt for the sake of others, as well as myself, my health being so shaken is a serious thing. What I desire to consider most deeply is this: – Have I authority for leaving my home and evident duties? What leads me to believe I have! For I need not doubt but that when away, and at times greatly tried, this query is likely to arise. The prospect has come in that quiet yet I think powerful way, that I have never been able to believe I should get rid of it; indeed hitherto I have hardly felt anything but a calm cheerfulness about it, and very little anxiety. It seems to me as if in this journey I must be stripped of outward dependences, and my watchword appears to be "My soul wait then *only* upon God for my expectation is in Him."

2nd month, 6th – My beloved little ones have been ill with a severe cold, and my sweet babe has so very serious an attack, and one that has now lasted some days, that I believe her life is thought to be in danger. I have suffered a good deal, the most in the night; my desire for myself is, to be enabled to submit to the dispensations of Almighty wisdom, and that faith may be granted me to drink the cup, whatever it may be, as coming from the Lord's holy hand; nothing doubting but that it will be ordered in infinite wisdom and mercy. Natural feelings I do not desire to be without, for I had rather have them, if under proper subjection. Jesus wept, may not we? I feel much gratitude that her sufferings appear comparatively small, and rather to decrease; if I could have a prayer on her account outwardly, it would be that she might be spared much suffering; but I desire and pray above all things, that I may leave all to Him, who has dealt with me and my little ones in unspeakable mercy, that He will yet watch over us for good, and not permit us to suffer more than is best for us. How much better to have her life cut short in innocency, than for her to live to that state in which her sins should have separated her from her God. Be pleased, O Lord! to grant Thy poor servant and her little one, strength sufficient for the day, and whether mourning or rejoicing be my portion, may it work together for my good, and make me a better servant to Thee. Amen, and Amen.

Earlham, 3rd month, 14th – Have I not renewed reason for faith, hope, and confidence in the principle which I desire to follow? In the night I had to acknowledge that the work must be Thine, O Lord! and that it is to me wonderful. My fears and causes of discouragement were many, for some little time before I set off, my own poor health, and my little ones; then my lowness and stupidity. In the first place, my health and the dear children's improved so much, and I inwardly so brightened, that I left home very comfortably. As I went on my way, such abundant hope arose, that light, rather than darkness, appeared to surround me. I have now attended the Monthly Meetings, and three other Meetings. I have also had frequent opportunities of a religious nature, in families; the most remarkable were, one in a clergyman's family, in supplication for him and his house, and another, where he had to supplicate for my help. May I ever remember how utterly unfit I am in myself for all these works: unto me alone belongs abasedness. I can take nothing to myself. As Thou hast seen meet, O Lord! Thou who art strength in weakness, thus to make use of Thy poor handmaid, as an instrument in Thy service, be pleased to keep her from the evil, both in reality and appearance, that she never may in any way bring reproach upon Thy cause!

6th month – My press of engagements has been very great, in the first place, the deep affliction of our much-loved friend, Henry Hull [*an American minister*]. He having received letters to say that his wife, son, mother, and brother-in-law were all dead of a contagious fever, and the lives of the rest of the family very uncertain. Much as he suffered, he bore it like a man and a Christian, so as to encourage, rather than try my faith. It of course took up my time and attention to wait upon, and care for him. We have had a very large family party, my brother and sister Fry, three children, and servants; my sister[-*in-law*] Elizabeth, and cousin Sarah, besides many Friends backwards and forwards: also much illness in the house, my sister and her nurse, and also her baby, very dangerously ill. These have all been objects of care, and interest, so that I am sorry to say, I have been at times so weighed down, and panting for rest, that I have been almost irritable, and I fear not enough estimated the value of their company, or the comfort of being able to serve them; but I hope my health may be some excuse for me, for they are very dear to me. I think my temper requires very great watchfulness, for the exercises of my mind, my very numerous interests, and the irritability excited by my bodily infirmities cause me to be in so tender and touchy a state that the "grasshopper becomes a burden". In this, as in all my infirmities, I have but one hope; it is in the power of Him who has in mercy answered my prayers, and helped me in many of my difficulties, and I humbly trust yet will arise for my deliverance.

As to the ministry, I have been raised up and at times cast down, but my heart and attention have been mostly turned to rigidly performing my practical duties in life, which is my object by night and by day. I have felt, as if I could rest in nothing short of serving Him whom my soul loves, but

I desire to watch, and am fully aware that with regard to myself, I have nothing to trust to, but mercy; but leaving myself, I long whilst permitted to remain in mortality, not to be a drone, but to do every thing to the glory of God. I think I desire to do all things well, more for the cause sake, than for the sake of my own soul, as my conviction of the mercy and loving-kindness of Him who loveth us, and who is touched with a feeling of our infirmities, is so great, that whilst my heart is seeking to serve Him (full as I am of defects), I am ready to trust that, that mercy which has hitherto compassed me about, will be with me to the end of time, and continue with me through eternity. The fear of punishment hardly even arises, or has arisen in my mind, it is more the certain knowledge that I have, of the blessedness of serving our Master, and the very strong excitement of love and gratitude, and desire for the promotion of the blessed cause upon earth. Through all my tried states, I have one unspeakable blessing to acknowledge; and that is, an increase of faith.

7th month, 3rd – We have for the last week been alone, which appears greatly to have recruited soul and body; I much wanted this time with my dear husband and children, it has enabled me to turn my attention to my home duties, and I trust I may rest pretty easy in believing things are generally in good order, as to servants, children, &c., &c. The poor may want a little further investigation; I feel thankful in thus being enabled to stop and examine the state of my family and house. How much have I to be thankful for, though all may not be quite what I wish; how many valuable dependants I have: those who I believe love us, and that which is good; some I hope will remain our friends for life. My beloved children who are come almost to an age of understanding, I long to see more under the Cross of Christ, and less disposed to give way to their own wills; I sometimes indulge them too much when young, I mean very little, and perhaps their nurses do so too. I could desire, though it appears asking a great deal, as to things temporal, that if right for us, we may be able through life to live in the open liberal way we do now, endeavouring to make all around us comfortable, and that we may be able to continue generous friends to the poor. I fear to be much limited would be very difficult to me. I desire that my attention being so much turned to things temporal, may not hinder my progress in things spiritual; I do not believe it injurious to have the natural part occupied in natural things, provided all be done under subjection, and with a single eye to the service of our great Master.

Plashet, 9th month, Second day – Yesterday was rather a remarkable one. I rose very low and fearful, though I am almost ashamed of acknowledging how it was, and has been with me after so many deliverances; but my spirit appeared overwhelmed within me, partly I think from some serious outward matters, but principally from such an extreme fear of my approaching confinement, feeling nothing in myself to meet it, and knowing that it must come unless death prevent it. I went to Meeting, but was almost too low to know whether I should go or not; however, being helped in testimony to show the blessedness of those who hope in the Lord, and not in themselves, appeared to do me good, as if I had to minister to myself as well as to others; I had a trust that my help was in the Lord, and that therefore I should experience my heart to be strengthened. A message came requesting my immediate attendance on poor dear Eliza Sheppard, who appeared near her end, of course I went. These visits are very awful; to sit by that which we believe to be a death-bed; to be looked to by the afflicted and others, as a minister from whom something is expected, and the fear at such a time of the activity of the creature arising, and doing that which it has no business to do. After sitting some time quiet, part of which she appeared to sleep, and part to be awake, a solemn silence covered us, and words of supplication arose in due time; when I believed her to be engaged in the same manner, by her putting her hands together, I knelt down and felt greatly helped, but had not so much to pray for her alone, as for all of us there present with her. I had a few words also to say in taking leave; the visit appeared sweet to her by her smiles, and her whispering to her sister expressing this. Thus ended this solemn scene, her husband, her own sister and brother, and dear Elizabeth Gurney were present; dear Eliza Sheppard's mind appeared in a truly calm, resigned state. I returned home in rather more than an hour, when the prospect of the evening felt very serious to me. After poor John's [*a servant's*] funeral, I wished the servants, and those who attended it and were disposed to do so, to be present at our reading. The party were in all about forty, many young people, and others. We first read two chapters in Matthew; after a pause, I knelt down, and had to supplicate, first, for all the party; afterwards, for our own household, more particularly for the servants; in all which I was helped, and a very solemn silence followed. The party broke up; I think I found myself strengthened, rather than weakened, by the day's work, mentally and bodily, though my own great weakness soon returned upon me, and it appeared striking that such an one should have been so engaged, but painful as these feelings of depression are to bear, I know "it is well", as it keeps me humble, at least I hope so, lowly and abased. Oh! saith my soul, after thus ministering to others, may I not become a castaway myself, and neither in trouble, or rejoicing, bring discredit on the cause that I love, or on His name whom I desire to serve.

4

"My mind and time have been much taken up with Newgate":
The beginning of Elizabeth Fry's prison work, 1813–1819

This period marks the beginning of Elizabeth Fry's visits to the female prisoners in Newgate. Her older sons were sent away to school and more children were born – Louisa in 1814 and Samuel in 1816. She also had to bear the deaths of her brother John in 1814 and her daughter Betsy the following year.

Mildred's Court, 1st month, 12th, 1813 – At last I have been enabled to accomplish my desire in having the greater part of our family here, present at the Scripture reading in the morning. It has been to me a very humbling thing, and I may say trying; the difficulty, reluctance, and luke-warmness about it, that appeared to exist, so that I was obliged to beg my beloved husband to ask it for me. It was very exercising on the First day morning when we met; but through all, unusual peace has been my portion, in giving up to it. It has been entered into more by faith than by sight, as it appeared so very discouraging, others not uniting in what seems to me so important a duty; but I have a secret hope and belief, that good will come of it, if the Lord will be pleased to bless and strengthen me in it. Oh! saith my soul, may it tend to our sanctification and redemption. Be pleased, O Lord! so to bless it, that it become not a dead form, but may it enliven our hearts towards Thee; and enable Thy poor hand-maid to be a faithful minister of Thy word amongst them, so as to be made instrumental in drawing some nearer to thee. I am thankful, for being so far helped on my way, and for a little peace within, when dis-couragement was without.

Mildred's Court, 1st month, 15th – My fear for myself the last few days is, that I should be exalted by the evident unity of my dear friends whom I greatly value, by being, as I feel I am, in degree looked up to, by those less experienced than myself in the gift (small as my own is); and also my natural health and spirits being good, and being engaged in some laudable pursuits, more particularly seeing after the prisoners in Newgate. Oh, how deeply, how very deeply, I fear the temptation of ever being exalted or self-conceited. I cannot preserve myself from this temptation, any more than being unduly cast down or crushed by others. Be pleased, O Lord! to preserve me, for the deep inward prayer of my heart is, that I may ever walk humbly before Thee; and also before all mankind. Let me never in any way take that glory to myself which alone belongs unto Thee, if in Thy mercy Thou should ever enable one so unworthy either to do good or to communicate.

Letter from Elizabeth Fry to her sons, then staying at Earlham, 1813

I cannot help longing to see you, my very dear little John and Willy, and give you each a kiss. I am so very fond of my little children, and often feel thankful I have so many; and if they grow better and better as they grow older, they will comfort and please their parents. I have lately been to Newgate prison to see after the poor prisoners, who had little infants almost without clothing. If you saw how small a piece of bread they are allowed every day, you would be very sorry, for they have nothing else to eat, unless their friends give them a trifle. I could not help thinking when in the prison what sorrow and trouble those have who do wrong; and they have not the comfort of feeling amidst their trials that they have endeavoured to do their duty. Good people are, no doubt, often much tried, but they have so much to comfort them when they remember that the Almighty is their Friend, and will care for them. We may also hope if the poor wicked people are really sorry for their faults, God will pardon them, for His mercy is very great. If you were to grow up, I should like you to go to visit the poor sad people, to try to comfort them and do them good. I hope you will endeavour to be very useful, and not spend all your time in pleasing yourselves, but try to serve others and prefer them before yourselves. How very much I love you. Let me have letters written by yourselves. Farewell, my darling children. Remember the way to be happy is to do good.

Your tender mother,

E.F.

4th month, 2nd, Mildred's Court – Richard Phillips called here to day, and I really think I stand too much in awe of his and John Hull's opinions, as regards my religious movements, for I believe they may err; it is far better to look to that Power that cannot err, and whom I know to teach as no man can teach. I think I am far too much a slave to the opinions of the good; I mind it far more than the laugh of the world. May I be preserved from spiritual pride; and yet, I trust, I may live in unity with the good, as long as I live. I feel my own infirmity very much, and see how needful it is for the vessel to be kept clean that contains a gift to hand to others, even if it be through humiliation and crosses. I have been to-day too much engaged trying to serve others; in these duties there is danger of pride creeping in; I have found it in myself, being so consulted and pressed upon. May I watch, and trust in my Redeemer, who is yet able and willing to cleanse and to save.

5th month, 1st – So one month passes away, and another comes. A sweetness and power enlivens my heart this morning. I pray Thee, O Lord! Thou who hast hitherto helped me, be with me this day, preserve me humble and lowly in spirit, enable me to do Thy will; if Thou grantest ability to Thy poor handmaid to speak in Thy name, enable her and all to give wholly unto Thee the glory and honour of Thy own work. We had a very striking time yesterday evening, before our dear friends Edward and Anne Edwards left us, when sitting with them, my sister Priscilla and some others. Dear Edward Edwards [*a clergyman and family friend*] knelt down, and to my feelings expressed himself in a very lively manner; others were led to speak both in testimony and supplication; afterwards, I had to pour forth a little of my soul; there appeared to flow a current of life and love, as if we were owned by the Most High; I felt my own like a song of praise, and have in my misgiving nature feared that those present might think it done in the impetuosity of the creature, which I believe was not the case, being naturally very flat and low. What I experienced I can hardly express, a little like him who thought he could go on till midnight, expressing the goodness of the Lord to him. I certainly was much raised spiritually, and so I believe were all the party, and that we were united together in Christ. I do not think I ever believed so much as I have done since last Third day Meeting, and last evening, that the hand of the Almighty is in the changes that have taken place in our family; one going one way, one another; for it has in so remarkable a degree opened a door of spiritual unity with those who differ in some points from each other. It has a tendency to spread that blessed principle, which we uphold as a Society, of the anointing Power, leading us into all truth – the Spirit of Christ in man, as his only hope of glory. May we each faithfully keep our places, and do the work committed to us, whatsoever it may be. I also trust, we Friends may receive benefit by this intercourse increasingly opening our hearts in love to all, and enlarging us in the gift of charity; and that it may tend not only to our believing, but more openly declaring our faith in Christ, as our Saviour, our Redeemer, and our only Hope of Glory.

1st month, 24th, 1814 – I feel affected by the distresses of the poor, owing to the very sharp weather; and hardly know how to serve them, but I mean to go after them, and desire a blessing may attend my small efforts to relieve them, for it appears very little we can do for them, so as thoroughly to assist them; but I trust a better than ourselves is near to help and support them under their many trials.

Plashet 2nd month, 4th – I am low, under a sense of my own infirmities, and also rather grieved by the poor. I endeavoured to serve them, and have given them such broth and dumplings as we should eat ourselves; I find great fault has been found with them, and one woman seen to throw them to the pigs; however, I truly desire to act in this with a Christian spirit, still persevering to do my utmost for them, and patiently bear their reproach, which may be better for me than their praises.

Plashet, 2nd month, 11th – Tried by my servants appearing dissatisfied by what I believe to be liberal things; I feel these things when I consider how false a view we may take of each other, and how different my feelings towards them are from being ungenerous, which I fear they think. I know no family who allows exactly the same indulgences, and few who give the same high wages, and yet I do not know of any one so often grieved by the discontents of servants as myself. I believe I had rather go without indulgences myself (if I thought it right) than curtail theirs, but the lavish way in which most of their description appear to think things ought to be used is a trial to me, and contrary to my best judgment; but a constant lesson to myself is the ingratitude and discontent which I think I see and feel in many, because I doubt not it is the same with myself. How bountifully am I dealt with, day by day, and yet if there be one little subject of sorrow or apparent discontent, do I not in my heart dwell upon that, and not by any means sufficiently upon the innumerable mercies and blessings that surround me. Feeling that I am so infirm, can I wonder at the infirmities of others? Far from it, and though tried at times by my domestics, yet my belief is, that my small labour of love has not been lost upon all, and that I have amongst them, faithful, valuable, and conscientious servants, who, through all, love us, and are in reality our friends, though they may at times mistake and misconstrue our conduct towards them, and show us their weakness, as well as we may show ours.

Plashet, 2nd month, 30th – None know but those who suffer from them, the deep humiliations such disorders create, as those I have lately had; I mean great bodily weakness, accompanied by nervous lowness of spirits, and much mental fear. In the first place, how deeply do they try us, being in their own nature so painful; in the next, from the difficulty of doing strictly right in them, how far to endeavour to divert by cheerful amusement, or by taking such things as may soonest relieve them: and added to these, I think many are apt falsely to accuse themselves, and to mistake the painful restlessness and fear occasioned by them, for impatience and mistrust; I have sometimes a hope that this is not my case, though at others great fear arises, lest I should in any degree let go my hold, or be impatient after having so abundantly known the goodness, and lovingkindness of the Almighty.

6th month, 21st – My soul cannot help feeling greatly bound in gratitude for the many and great benefits received; thanksgiving is the voice of my heart, though something of anxiety and disquietude has been my portion, more particularly on account of my beloved husband, and children. I also desire to settle my household aright, to walk before them with an upright, humble, and perfect heart, fulfilling the Law and the Gospel. I desire to be scrupulously nice as to my conduct towards servants; if they revile, revile not again, not even in heart; I am not tempted in word to revile them, but I may speak too freely of them, for they at times grieve me by their apparent ingratitude, and want of consideration; but may I bear as I desire to be borne with. In some instances, I am amply rewarded by their gratitude and love; in others much wounded by them. I thought if not saying too much for myself, that I have wept as between the porch and the altar on their account, and on that of my beloved family altogether; I feel it cause for much thanksgiving, so far to be restored to them again, but my natural spirits at times are overcome. Grant wisdom and grace, O

Lord! I pray Thee, to Thy poor child, to order her steps aright before them all, being wise as the serpent and harmless as the dove.

Letter to her brother John Gurney, Plashet,
6th month, 28th, 1814

My dearest John

I have for many days much wished to write to thee, but in my present feeble state I find so many things to take up what strength I have that I have not much to use for writing. I fancy if thee and I had to run a race by what I hear of thee, that thou wouldst soon gain the prize at the end. I just begin to creep out into the garden yesterday and today and rejoice to find that thou hast really walked well lately and a long time together. How sweet and pleasant this must be after thy confinement from thy knee – how very sweet Earlham must look this weather, I do not wonder at your enjoying being at home again. I suppose we are forwarder here than you are, having had peas some time and the last few days strawberries and cherries. With us the country looks beautifully, more so I think than after a wetter season. Rachel and I hope before many weeks are over to pay you a visit at Earlham. Joseph and I felt thy invitation truly kind and acceptable, indeed dear John thou hast been a very kind brother to us. I much enjoy my new baby and desire to feel very thankful for so sweet an addition to our flock. We name it Louisa, it is a very fine child for its age. I think I gradually gain strength but I think it will be some time before I am strong. I look with hope to my Norfolk visit to my strength expecting to be better for it.

Very dearly farewell – thy loving sister

E.Fry

Plashet, 8th month, 15th – Once more arrived at my sweet home, and truly thankful in having finished my visit to my much-beloved brothers and sisters with satisfaction. I feel most tenderly for all, and I humbly trust, all are pressing Zion-ward, though I cannot say that I fully understand or enter into the activity of the creature appearing to show itself so much in things belonging to the soul's salvation; but this I know, inasmuch as it is of God, it will stand, but inasmuch as it is of man, it will fall. It is not for a poor unworthy fellow-mortal like myself to say what is of God, and what is not, though I may apprehend that there is a mixture,

104

not only in them, but in myself, and in us as a body, though our belief and profession is, that nothing short of the Holy Spirit can really help forward the cause of righteousness on the earth, whether it be immediately or instrumentally; and that we can only do good when influenced by this Spirit, and therefore desire to wait for its stirrings. I parted from my beloved sister Rachel who has for months past been to me a tenderly beloved friend, a most watchful and valuable nurse, and a most loving sister; I felt parting from her a good deal.

John Gurney died in September 1814. Elizabeth was with him and describes his death in a letter to her family at home

Earlham, Ninth Month, 8th, 1814,
(by the remains of my beloved brother.)

My much loved Husband and Children,

Believing you will feel with me in what so nearly concerns me and not only me, but you also, I sit down to tell you as nearly as I can what has happened since I came here. I believe you know I arrived about four o'clock yesterday morning. I was then led into the room where my tenderly beloved brother lay in bed; he was awake, but some feared he would not know me, instead of which, upon seeing me, his words were, "My dear sister, come and kiss me", then he expressed his great pleasure at our being together. He looked very sweet, quite easy, may I not say, like one redeemed. After staying some time by him, I went to bed; but I did not rest much, feeling low, burdened, and rather poorly. My dear sister Priscilla came to me a little past nine o'clock, and advised me to come. He was so very bright, his powers of mind appearing much clearer than any dying man I ever witnessed, except our poor servant John. Upon going into his room, he kissed us each again, and again said he wished for all his sisters together, appearing clearly to recollect each, for upon one saying, "Now there is no exception, all the sisters are with thee", he at first misunderstood, and said, "Did you say there is one exception, for there is not", or to that effect; he said it was delightful how we loved one another. It appeared my place to return thanks for such unspeakable blessings. He then said, "What a sweet prayer!" and afterwards, "I never passed so happy a morning; how delightful being together and loving one another as we do". As the day further advanced, he said, "What a beautiful day this has been!" He enjoyed our dear sister Richenda singing

105

hymns to him; he took leave of most of the old servants; to one whom he used not much to like, he spoke the most kindly, said he was glad to see him, and shook him warmly by the hand, and bade him farewell; he appeared deeply impressed with his many blessings and the mercy shown him. About half an hour after it was over, we had once more to approach the sacred footstool (for ability) to bless the Sacred Name, both for His giving and taking away. Thus closed such a day as I never passed; may we not say "Blessed are the dead that die in the Lord?" Oh, my beloved children and husband, may we not only feel, but profit by this striking event.

Plashet, 11th month, 2nd – My beloved husband and girls returned from France, on Second day; my heart was rather overwhelmed in receiving them again. I also had to feel the spirit in which some persons took my having allowed them to go, making what appeared to be unkind remarks. Oh, how do I see rocks on every hand; thus almost all persons who appear to pride themselves upon their consistency, are apt to judge others; whilst some, who no doubt yield to temptations, greatly suffer, and weaken themselves by it. How weak, how frail are we on every hand; my heart was much overwhelmed, seeing the infirmities of others, and feeling my own.

In a letter to one of her sisters in Norfolk, on the subject of hiring a cook, she says

My late letters savour much of the Martha, but whilst here, cooks appear a very important, if not a necessary part of our comfort, as our food must be dressed. I am, and have been for many weeks past, in my best health; what a comfort is this, may I not be unmindful of it; but how prone we are to cleave to the things of the earth, rather than in heart to cleave to a better spirit! I sometimes feel like an earth-worm, though at times raised above it, which is an unmerited mercy; but I find we may be employed in arranging laundries, kitchens, and such things, until our heart is too much in them. Does not all call for watchfulness, that even in the performance of our duties, however small, they become not a temptation, and we go not astray; lest the seed become choked, and no fruit brought to perfection?

Plashet, 9th month, 9th, 1815 – I think I may acknowledge, that although much stripping and deep poverty has at times been my portion, during my visit to the families of Kingston Monthly Meeting, with dear William Forster and Rebecca Christy; yet power, consolation and sweetness have also been felt at times, and I think our way has been remarkably made in the hearts of those we have visited. I came home with the feeling, that he that waters is also watered. The prospect of not having finished and leaving home again, is serious; but oh, for preservation and strength to do the will of God at home and abroad.

9th month, 15th – I returned home last evening, having just finished my engagement with William Forster and Rebecca Christy. Being at home again, and having some heavy clouds, a little, indeed, a good deal dispersed, is a great comfort and relief. We have been much favoured in our goings along; help being granted from season to season, much unity of the Spirit and general sweetness and openness amongst others. But I have felt since my return, this morning, in our frail state, how difficult it is, even when engaged in religious services, to prevent our infirmities creeping in and showing themselves, something like the iniquity of our holy things. Great as is the honour and favour of being employed in the Master's service, and the peace and consolation which attend the remembrance of it; yet I am so much aware of the evil seed not being eradicated from my own heart, that my present feeling is this, "Who can understand his errors; cleanse Thou me from secret faults, keep back Thy servant also from presumptuous sins, let them not have dominion over me"; and how anxiously do I desire that I may not only be as a vessel washed and cleansed from impurities, contracted in being used, but also if these have shown themselves, that the most precious and blessed cause of truth and righteousness may not have been hurt by me, but that our little labours of love may be blessed to ourselves and others; and now that I am come home, oh, may I labour and not faint.

10th month, 14th – I have been of late, principally occupied at home, which has its peculiar exercises, as well as being abroad; having to govern such a large household, where the infirmity and evil propensity of each one, old and young, too often show themselves and deeply try me in many ways. It confirms me in a feeling of my infirmity; it humbles me; yet I trust through till the discipline of the cross may be found amongst us, and through its subjecting influence, the wrong thing in measure is kept under. However, I have my consolations, and great consolations, but I find I am not to rest even in the ruling and order of my household. Many changes in our family circle, among others, my dear sister Richenda is likely to marry Francis Cunningham [*an Anglican clergyman*].

Plashet, 11th month – It has pleased Almighty and Infinite Wisdom, to take from us our most dear and tenderly-beloved child, little Betsy – between four and five years old. In receiving her, as well as giving her back again, we have, I believe, been enabled to bless the Sacred Name. She was a very precious child, of much wisdom for her years and I can hardly help believing, much grace; liable to the frailty of childhood, at times she would differ with the little one, and rather loved her own way; but she was very easy to lead, though not one to be driven. She had most tender affections, a good understanding, for her years, a remarkably staid and solid mind. Her love very strong, and her little attentions great to those she loved, and remarkable in her kindness to servants, poor people, and all animals, she had much feeling for them; but what was more, the bent of her mind was remarkably towards serious things.

11th month, 30th – Once more my supplications were answered – the bitter conflict that I was permitted to feel during the night, and the morning previous to the funeral of my beloved child, was in the needful time mitigated, and strength granted to give up her remains to the grave, I hope without a murmur; but although faith tells us that the spirit is indeed fled from its earthly house, yet the distress felt in parting with the body, I can hardly describe; for the body of little children, their innocent and beautiful faces and forms, we are prone to delight in; and there is a sort of personal attachment towards little children that partakes of the nature of animal life, which I believe is hardly to be described, but only fully known to parents. This perhaps would make us cling more, even to the poor body – which I felt certainly wonderfully vacant after its blessed inhabitant was fled – yet partly perhaps from nervous weakness, my remaining love to the body, its sweet looks, and some thinking we might keep it longer; also feeling that the last relics of my much loved, kind, and to me beautiful lamb were then about to leave us here for ever, was a pinch to the natural part not to be told: I felt really ill. But I may indeed return thanks unto Him who has given us the victory, through our Lord and Saviour Jesus Christ. This I have been permitted to feel, for my child's death at the time had lost its sting, and the grave its victory – for my soul was upheld in the needful time, though so great had been my dread, that I was enabled to pray for help before I left the house, and also to return thanks at the grave for the tender mercy shown to her, and to me, and to all; and afterwards in the room at the Meeting House, to encourage others to serve the Most High, seeing how great was His loving kindness and tender mercy; and that the uncertainty of time called for standing prepared. This morning my poor soul has felt refreshed in once more being enabled, before my household to cast my care upon my Holy Helper, and to pray for fresh ability in performing the duties of life, and indeed that this event might be sanctified to us all.

Plashet, 12th month, 14th – With regard to my tenderly beloved little Betsy, she is in my most near and affectionate remembrance, by night, and by day; when I feel her loss, and view her little (to me) beautiful body in Barking burying-ground, my heart is pained within me: but when, with the eye of faith, I can view her in an everlasting resting place in Christ Jesus, where indeed no evil can come nigh her dwelling, then I can rest even with sweet consolation; and I do truly desire that when her loss is so present with me as it is at times, that I cannot help my natural spirits being much overwhelmed, that I may be preserved from any thing like repining or undue sorrow, or in any degree depreciating the many blessings continued; particularly so many sweet dear children being left us, for through all, I feel receiving them a blessing, having their life preserved a blessing, and in the sweet lamb who is taken, I have felt a blessing in her being taken away; such an evidence of faith has been granted that it is in mercy, and at the time such a feeling of joy on her account. It is now softened down into a very tender sorrow, the remembrance of her is inexpressibly sweet, and I trust that the whole event has done me good, as I peculiarly feel it an encouragement to suffer whatever is appointed me; that being (if it may ever be my blessed allotment) made perfect through suffering, I may be prepared to join the purified spirits of those that are gone before me; and having felt so very deeply, I am almost ready to think has a little prepared my neck for the yoke of suffering.

7th month, 4th, 1816 – I have been at Pakefield with my beloved brother and sister [*Francis and Richenda Cunningham*]; my soul has travailed much in the deeps, on many accounts, more particularly with them, that in keeping to our scruples respecting prayer, &c., &c., the right thing might be hurt in no mind. Words fall very short of expression, of how much my spirit is overwhelmed within me for us all: our situation is very peculiar, surrounded as we are with those of various sentiments, and yet, I humbly trust, each seeking the right way. To have a clergyman for a brother is very different to having one a friend; a much closer tie, and a still stronger call for the sake of preserving sweet unity of spirit, to meet him as far as we can, to offend as little as possible by our scruples, and yet for the sake of others, as well as ourselves, faithfully to maintain our ground, and to keep very close to that which can alone direct aright.

Earlham, 8th month, 17th – I have a fear lest delicate health, and being wearied by the cares of life, and the kind care of others, should induce my indulging the flesh too much, in eating, drinking, and sleeping, which I do not desire, far from it; but sometimes the words addressed to the Church at Ephesus, as it respects the first love and first works, come home to me, when I remember how much, in the day of my first love, I watched over myself in these respects; but my constitution, for many years of my life has had such a stress upon it, that I am fearful in my own will of giving up those indulgences, that appear so evidently to have contributed and yet to contribute to its support; but I desire to be watchful and careful in this respect, which I trust I have in a measure been, but I often feel as if I were too much living to the flesh, and yet I know not exactly how or in what to alter. May I in these and all other things, be helped and guided by the Holy Spirit, for my heart's desire and prayer is, that I may offend neither in thought, word, or deed.

2nd month, 13th, 1817 – I yesterday left my dearest boys, John and Willy, at Josiah Forster's school; it has been a very important step to take but I trust it is a right one, as we could not comfortably see any other opening for them. I was enabled to commend them in supplication to the Lord for His blessing and providential care. It is indeed a very serious thing to me, thus permitting them to enter the world and its temptation, for so I feel it; it caused me great lowness at first, but afterwards, having committed them to the best keeping, my soul was much comforted and refreshed, and much enlarged in love towards them, as well as the kind friends whose house I was at. Oh may it please Almighty Wisdom to bless the boys, and keep them by His own preserving power from any great sin, and may He pardon the follies of their youth.

Elizabeth wrote and gave to each of her sons the following ~~kali~~
Rules for a Boy at a Boarding School ~~br.~~

1st. Be regular, be strict in attending to religious duties; and do not allow
other boys around thee to prevent thy having some portion of time for
reading, at least a text of scripture, meditation and prayer; and if it
appears to be a duty, flinch not from bowing the knee before them, as a
mark of thy allegiance to the King of kings, and Lord of lords. Attend diligently when the Holy Scriptures are read, or to any other religious
instruction, and endeavour in Meeting to seek after a serious waiting state
of mind, and to watch unto prayer. Let First day (the Sabbath) be well
employed in reading proper books, &c., but also enjoy the rest of innocent recreation, afforded in admiring the beauties of nature, taking exercise in the garden, &c., for I believe this is right in the ordering of a kind
Providence, that there should be some rest and recreation in it. Show a
proper, bold, and manly spirit in maintaining amongst thy playfellows a *shame*
religious character, and a strict attention to all the religious duties;
remember these texts to strengthen thee in it. "For whosoever shall be
ashamed of me and of my words, of him shall the Son of Man be
ashamed, when He shall come in His own glory, and in his Father's, and
of the holy angels" – Luke ix. 20. "But I say unto you, whosoever shall
confess me before men, him shall the Son of Man also confess before the
angels of God: but he that denieth me before men, shall be denied before
the angels of God. Now the sooner the dread laugh of the world loses its
power, the better for you. This strengthens principle in ourselves and
others. Remember these words: – "All that will live godly in Christ Jesus
shall suffer persecution"–2 Tim. iii. 12.

   Strongly as I advise thy thus faithfully maintaining thy principles, and
doing thy duty, I would have thee very careful of either judging or reprov-
ing others; for it takes a long time to get the beam out of our own eye,
before we can see clearly to take the mote out of our brother's eye. There
is, for one young in years, much greater safety in preaching to others by
example than in word; or doing what is done in an upright manly spirit
unto the Lord, and not unto man. I conclude this part of my advice by
this short exhortation: "Be sober and watch unto prayer, and do all to the
glory of God."

   2ndly. I shall not speak of moral conduct, which, if religious principles
be kept to, we may believe will be good, but I shall give certain hints that
may point out the temptations to which schools are peculiarly liable. I

111

have observed a want of strict integrity in school-boys, as it respects their schoolmasters and teachers, a disposition to cheat them, to do that behind their backs which they would not do before their faces; and so having two faces. Now this is a subject of the utmost importance – to maintain truth and strict integrity upon all points. Be not double-minded in any degree, but faithfully maintain, not only the upright principle on religious grounds, but also the brightest honour according even to the maxims of the world.

I mourn to say I have seen the want of this bright honour, not only in school-boys, but in some of our highly professing Society; and my belief is, that it cannot be too strictly maintained, or too early begun; I like to see it in small things, and in great, for it marks the upright man. I may say that I abhor any thing like being under-handed or double-dealing; but let us go on the right and noble principle of doing unto others as we would have others do to us; therefore, in all transactions, small or great, maintain strictly the correct, upright, and most honourable practice. I have heard of boys robbing their neighbours' fruit, &c., &c. I may truly say, that I believe there are very few in the present day would do such things; but no circumstances can make this other than a shameful deviation from all honest and right principles: and my belief is, that such habits begun in youth, end mostly in great incorrectness in future life, if not in gross sin, and that no excuse can be pleaded for such actions; for sin is equally sin, whether committed by the school-boy or those of mature years, which is too apt to be forgotten, and that punishment will follow.

Mildred's Court, 2nd month, 24th – I have lately been much occupied in forming a school in Newgate, for the children of the poor prisoners, as well as the young criminals, which has brought much peace and satisfaction with it; but my mind has also been deeply affected in attending a poor woman who was executed this morning. I visited her twice; this event has brought me into much feeling, attended by some distressingly nervous sensations in the night, so that this has been a time of deep humiliation to me, thus witnessing the effect and consequences of sin. This poor creature murdered her baby; and how inexpressibly awful now to have her life taken away! The whole affair has been truly afflicting to me; to see what poor mortals may be driven to, through sin and transgression, and how hard the heart becomes, even to the most tender affections. How should we watch and pray, that we fall not by little and little, become hardened, and commit greater sins. I had to pray for these poor sinners this morning, and also for the preservation of our household from the evil there is in the world.

Mildred's Court, 3rd month, 7th – My mind and time have been much taken up with Newgate and its concerns. I have been encouraged about our school, but I find my weak nature and proneness to be so much affected by the opinions of man, brings me into some peculiar trials and temptations: in the first place, our Newgate visiting could no longer be kept secret, which I endeavoured that it should be, and therefore I am exposed to praise that I do not the least deserve; also to some unpleasant humiliations – for in trying to obtain helpers, I must be subject to their various opinions; and also, being obliged to confer at times with strangers, and men in authority, is to me a very unpleasant necessity. I have suffered much about the hanging of the criminals, having had to visit another poor woman, before her death; this again tried me a good deal, but I was permitted to be much more upheld, and not so distressed as the time before.

Mildred's Court, 3rd month, 11th – My mind too much tossed by a variety of interests and duties – husband, children, household, accounts, Meetings, the Church, near relations, friends, and Newgate – most of these things press a good deal upon me. I hope I am not undertaking too much, but it is a little like being in the whirlwind, and in the storm; may I not be hurt in it, but enabled quietly to perform that which ought to be done; and may it all be done so heartily unto the Lord, and through the assistance of His grace, that if consistent with His Holy Will, His blessing may attend it, and if ever any good be done, that the glory of the whole work may be given where it is alone due.

4th month, 12th – I have found in my late attention to Newgate, a peace and prosperity in the undertaking, that I seldom, if ever, remember to have done before. A way has very remarkably been opened for us, beyond all expectations, to bring into order the poor prisoners; those who are in power are so very willing to help us, in short the time appears come to work amongst them. Already, from being like wild beasts, they appear harmless and kind. I am ready to say, in the fulness of my heart, surely "it is the Lord's doing, and marvellous in our eyes"; so many are the providential openings of various kinds.

7th month, 28th – I am alone at home with my nine children, a great and very precious charge; at times they appear too much for me, at others I

113

greatly enjoy them; I desire that the anxiety for their welfare, and to have them in order, should not prevent my enjoying thankfully, the blessing of being surrounded by so sweet a flock. I sometimes think of these words, "The fruit of the womb is his reward"; and having borne them through much fear and at times much tribulation, I believe I should thankfully enjoy them; not improperly resting in the precious gift. How I delight to see the springings of goodness in them, the blessed seed appearing, as well as mourn when the evil shows itself. Most gracious Lord, be pleased to be with them and bless them; strengthen the good, I beseech Thee, and weaken the evil in their hearts.

8th month, 4th – My having been brought publicly forward in the newspapers, respecting what I have been instrumental in doing at Newgate, has brought some anxiety with it; in the first place, as far as I am concerned, that it may neither raise me too high, nor cast me too low, that having what may appear my good works thus published, may never lead me or others to give either the praise or glory where it is not due.

Plashet, 8th month, 28th – I was yesterday at Newgate with Sheriff Brydges, &c. I have felt of late fears, whether my being made so much of, so much respect paid me by the people in power in the city, and also being so publicly brought forward, may not prove a temptation, and lead to something of self-exaltation or worldly pride. I fear, I make the most of myself, and carry myself rather as if I was somebody amongst them; a degree of this sort of conduct appears almost necessary – yet oh! the watchfulness required not to bow to man, not to seek to gratify self-love; but rather in humility and godly fear, to abide under the humiliation of the cross. Lord, be pleased so to help and strengthen me in this, that for Thine own cause' sake, for my own soul's sake, my beloved family's, and the Society's sake, I may in no way be a cause of reproach; but in my life, conduct, and conversation, glorify Thy great and ever excellent name. In all my perplexities be pleased to help me, and make a way where I see no way.

Mildred's Court, 12th month, 17th – A remarkable blessing still appears to accompany my prison concerns; perhaps the greatest apparent blessing on my deeds that ever attended me. How have the spirits of both of those in power, and the poor afflicted prisoners appeared to be subjected, and how has the work gone on! Most assuredly the power and the glory is alone due to the Author and Finisher of every good work: things in this way thus prosper beyond my most sanguine expectations, but there are also deep humiliations for me. My beloved children do not appear sufficiently under the influence of religion. I am ready to say, Oh! that I could prosper at home in my labours, as I appear to do abroad. Others appear to fear for me, that I am too much divided, but alas! what can I do, but follow the openings. I think that I do also labour at home, but He who searcheth the heart, who knoweth all things, He knows my faith, my goings out, and my comings in; He knows the desires of my heart towards Himself – indeed the deep inward travail of my spirit has been unutterable and indescribable; but my humble trust and strong confidence is, that He who hears and answers prayer, listens to my cry, hearkens to my deep inward supplications for myself, my husband, children, brothers, sisters, and household, my poor prisoners, and all things upon which I crave a blessing.

Plashet, 4th month, 29th, 1818 – I desire thankfully to acknowledge our return to this sweet place, and all the dear children alive and well. May we more evidently live in the best sense, even unto God. Since I last wrote, I have led rather a remarkable life; so surprisingly followed after by the great, and others, in my Newgate concerns; in short, the prison and myself are become quite a show, which is a very serious thing in many points. I believe, that it certainly does much good to the cause, in spreading amongst all ranks of society, a considerable interest in the subject; also a knowledge of Friends and of their principles: but my own standing appears critical in many ways. In the first place, the extreme importance of my walking strictly, and circumspectly, amongst all men, in all things; and not bringing discredit upon the cause of truth and righteousness. In the next place, I desire to live (more particularly in these things) in the fear of God rather than of man, and that neither good report nor evil report, the approbation nor disapprobation of men, should move me the least but that my eye should be kept quite single to the great and good Shepherd and Bishop of souls.

Yesterday, I had a day of ups and downs, as far as the opinions of man are concerned, in a remarkable degree. I found that there was a grievous misunderstanding between Lord Sidmouth and myself, and that some things I had done, had tried him exceedingly; indeed, I see that I have mistaken it, in my conduct in some particulars, respecting the case of poor Skelton, and in the efforts made to save her life, I too incautiously spoke of some in power. When under great humiliation in consequence of this, Lady Harcourt, who most kindly interested herself in the subject, took me with her to the Mansion House, rather against my will, to meet many of the Royal family at the examination of some large schools. Amongst the rest, the Queen was there. Much public respect was paid me, and except the Royal family themselves, I think that no one received the same attention. There was quite a buzz when I went into the Egyptian Hall, where one to two thousand people were collected; and when the Queen came to speak to me, which she did very kindly, there was I am told a general clap. I think I may say, this hardly raised me at all, I was so very low from what had occurred before, and indeed, in so remarkably flat a state, even nervous.

Plashet, 7th month, 1st – Since I last wrote, much as happened to me; some things have occurred of an important nature. My prison engagements have gone on well, and many have flocked after me, may I not say of almost all descriptions, from the greatest to the least; and we have had some remarkably favoured times together in the prison. The Yearly Meeting was a very interesting one to me, and also encouraging. I felt the unity of Friends a comfort and support. I had to go into the Men's Meeting, which was a deep trial of faith, but it appeared called for at my hand, and peace attended giving up to it. The unity the women expressed at my going, and the good reception I found amongst the men, were comforting to me, but it was a close, very close, exercise. Although I have had much support from many of my fellow-mortals, and so much unity expressed with me both in and out of our Society – yet I believe many Friends have great fears for me and mine; and some, not Friends, do not scruple to spread evil reports, as if vanity or political motives led me to neglect a large family. I desire patiently to bear it all, but the very critical view that is taken of my beloved children grieves me much.

In August, Elizabeth Fry left home on a ministerial visit to Scotland and the North of England, accompanied by her brother Joseph John Gurney, his wife and one of her own daughters.

Stonehaven 9th month, 2nd – We left Aberdeen this afternoon, having finished our services there, and at Kilmuck, where several Friends reside. Other Friends besides ourselves, being at Aberdeen, certainly tended to increase my exercise, for fear of the ministry not going on well, or by not keeping in our ranks; but I think that we were enabled to do so, and although much passed, yet we had cause for thankfulness, inasmuch as there appeared to be harmonious labour for the advancement of truth, and the spreading thereof. I had to go into the Men's Meeting, and my brother Joseph came into the women's Meeting. I do not know what Friends thought of us, as our exercises are certainly of rather a peculiar nature, so very often bending the knee in prayer; and the nature of our testimonies so much alike, though Joseph appears to me the most highly gifted young minister I ever remember, as to power, wisdom, tongue, and utterance. What an unspeakable cause of thankfulness to have him thus brought forth as a bright and shining light!

Our General Meeting at Aberdeen was ended under a feeling of quiet peace; but fears crept in for myself, that I had fallen away a little as to life in the truth, and power in the ministry, for I did not experience that over-flowing power which I have sometimes done at such seasons; still gracious help was granted me from season to season. The day after the General Meeting, we went to Kilmuck, about fifteen miles north of Aberdeen. A short time after our arrival there, before I went to Meeting, such a feeling of suffering came over me as I can hardly express, it appeared only nervous, as I was so well in body that I could not attribute it to that. It continued exceedingly upon sitting down in Meeting, and led me into deep strong supplication, that the enemy might by no means deceive us, or cause our ministry to be affected by any thing but the holy anointing. I feared if this awful state had to do with those present, that I should have something very close to express; if only with myself, I considered that it might be a refining trial. However, Joseph knelt down, in the beginning of the Meeting, as well as myself, and afterwards he spoke as if he felt it necessary to warn some to flee from their evil ways, and from the bondage of Satan. This tended to my relief; but it appeared as if I must follow him, and rise with these words, "The sorrows of death compassed me about, the pains of hell got hold upon me"; then enlarging upon the feeling I had of the power of the enemy, and the absolute need there is to watch, to pray, and to flee unto Christ, as our only and sure refuge and deliverer; I had to show that we might be tried and buffeted by Satan, as a further trial of faith and of patience, but that if we did not yield to him, it would only tend to refinement.

After a time I felt greatly relieved, but what seemed remarkable was, that neither Joseph nor I dared leave the Meeting, without once more bowing the knee for these dear Friends; but after all this very deep and remarkable exercise, a solemn silence prevailed, really as if truth had risen into dominion; and after my making some such acknowledgment in testimony, that our low estate had been regarded, that our souls could

117

then magnify the Lord, and our spirits rejoice in God our Saviour, that light had risen in obscurity, and darkness had in measure become as the noon-day, and the encouragement it was for us to run with patience the race that was set before us, &c., the Meeting concluded; and I think upon shaking hands with the Friends, there hardly appeared an eye that had not been weeping amongst those that were grown up. This whole exercise was very remarkable, in a nice little country Meeting, and the external so fair; but afterwards we heard of one or two painful things, one in particular; we visited nearly all the families, were much pleased with some of them; their mode of living truly humble, like our cottagers. The next day we had a Meeting with the few Friends in Aberdeen, where the exercise was not very great, and the flow in the ministry sweet, and I trust powerful.

Plashet, 10th month, 15th – I have had the comfort of finding my beloved husband mending. My first arrival for a few hours was sorrowful; my dearest Kate being seriously ill, but I am thankful to say she soon recovered. My Louisa is now poorly, but I hope not materially so. My prison concerns truly flourishing: surely in that a blessing in a remarkable manner appears to attend me; more apparently, than in some of my home duties. Business pressed very hard upon me; the large family at Mildred's Court, so many to please there, and attend to – the various accounts; the dear children and their education; my husband poorly; the church; the poor; my poor infirm aunt whom I have undertaken to care for; my public business, and my numerous friends and correspondents. I have desired to keep my mind quiet and lifted up to my Redeemer, as my Helper and my Guide; inwardly, I have felt helped, even He whom my soul loves has been near, but I have also had some perplexity and discouragement, thinking that some of those very dear, as well as others, are almost jealous over me, and ready to mistrust my various callings; and are open both to see my children's weaknesses, and almost to doubt the propriety of my many objects. Such are my thoughts! Indeed I too much feel the pain of not being able to please every one; but this cannot be, and if I only may please my Master, I trust that His servants will not greatly disapprove me. I certainly at times feel pressed almost out of measure; but then I do not think that I have brought myself into all this service, therefore I humbly hope that I and my family may be kept in it. I sometimes wish I had more order in my pursuits, but this appears almost impossible.

118

Plashet, 10th month, 28th – Entering my public life again is very serious to me, more particularly my readings at Newgate. They are to my feelings too much like making show of a good thing, yet we have so often been favoured in them to the tendering of many hearts, that I believe I must not be hasty in putting an end to them, or hindering people coming to them; it is the desire and prayer of my heart, that way may rightly open about them, and that when engaged in them, I may do what I do heartily unto the Lord, and not unto man, and look not either to the good or evil opinions of men. The prudent fears that the good have for me, try me more than most things, and I find that it calls for Christian forbearance, not to be a little put out by them. I am confident that we often see a Martha-like spirit about spiritual things. I know by myself what it is to be over-busy.

Plashet, 11th month, 17th – My spirit is brought deeply prostrate within me, my flesh and my heart at seasons feel ready to fail – sorrows have compassed me about. Among other distresses, finding how powerful the enemy is, and how even those I fully believe to be servants of the Most High, give way to what appears to be a gossiping slanderous spirit; so that that which may be imagined by themselves and others to be a spirit of watching over one another for good, degenerates into a spirit of watching over one another for evil, and savours not of that charity which "thinketh no evil", and "rejoiceth not in iniquity"– not going in love to the parties implicated, but expressing their judgment and their fears to others. This I have deeply felt more particularly as it relates to things said of Ministers, for it is a fearful thing to lessen the weight of the instruments of the Lord, lest their services should also be lessened.

Another sorrow just now is, fearing that I have not one child much under the influence of grace, or that appears really bending to the cross, and this is not only serious for themselves, but brings me into many straits. It is difficult to know how in all things to conduct myself towards them, to be neither too strict, nor too much the reverse. Still I have a humble hope that the work of grace is manifest in some of them, and I trust that it will grow and increase. Perhaps, I am hardly tender enough over the temptations of youth, O Lord! make me more so, a better wife and mother, more calculated to bring them all to Christ their Redeemer. As for myself, innumerable fears creep in, I find myself so much more at liberty than many, so little bound by scruples, and so many weak feelings in my heart, that I am ready to fear whether I am not also falling away. Then, what will become of us? Yet sweet hope and strong confidence arise in Him, who has hitherto helped me, and as I do most deeply and most sensibly feel that I have no confidence in the flesh, as far as I know myself, but that my whole confidence, reliance, and hope are on Christ my Redeemer. I cannot, dare not, mistrust. However numerous my temptations, however deep my trials, however great my perplexities, still the everlasting Shepherd of the sheep is able and willing to care for me, to deliver me, and in his love and pity to redeem me. Lord enable me so to hear Thy voice, and to follow Thee, that I may ever be of the number of Thy sheep, and Oh! in Thine own time, visit my dear children by Thy love, Thy grace, and Thy power, that they may serve Thee, that Thou mayst be their God, and that they may be of the number of Thy people; and may an entrance ever be granted us into Thy everlasting kingdom of rest and peace. The 40th and 42nd Psalms spoke comfort to me this morning; I may say they express the language of my spirit at the present time

Mildred's Court, 3rd month, 5th, 1819 – Fears indeed have compassed me about in this illness. I never remember before, the fear of dying taking so much hold of me; though as far as I know, neither reason nor faith have led me to believe death near. I believe these fears to arise from the nature of my complaint, in great measure; and therefore that it is well to turn from them by innocent and amusing reading, and other things that would divert my attention from myself. It is not well to be influenced in conduct by these fears; for I have experienced, as far as I know, that the Spirit of the Lord shows itself by love, by power, and by a sound mind, rather than by nervous apprehensions. Where the nervous system is weak, no one should be discouraged by dark clouds for a season overshadowing the best things. This is our infirmity, that we often see as through the medium of this frail tabernacle. But without any nervous feelings, I know my state to be a serious one, and when favoured by the clouds being a little dispersed, and a more quiet and cheerful mind, I desire to examine my ownself, to prove my ownself, that if any thing stand between me and my God, it may be removed; for surely I am unfit to come and appear before God!

3rd month, 14th – My faith is strong, respecting my dearest children, that in the end they will have in various ways to glorify the God of their fathers, though all may not be led into conspicuous or public services.

Mildred's Court, 5th month, First day – I am at home from Meeting, as I felt easy to be here, it being wet, and my cough bad, though still favoured to feel surprisingly better. But as I return to health and life, so do I return to its cares; yesterday brought several mortifying and discouraging things with it, principally as to my public services, my private cares and sorrows I am also more sensible of, from being less occupied by my own suffering and infirmity. In coming out of this illness (for so I appear to be) I am rather awfully struck with the remembrance of how little I appeared to feel either willing or prepared to die; or as to my illness, fully resigned to suffer according to the will of God, so that the whole has been a deeply humbling dispensation. I cannot say I much depended upon my feelings, for I was in so nervous a state that I do not think I saw things through a right or just medium. I should think much more of it, if there had not been a cloud over me about every thing – however, it is awful and serious to be subject when poorly to such nervousness – yet, surely, through all, the Everlasting Arm was underneath, and the Lord was my stay and surety; He will not leave nor forsake me just in the needful time, even in death He will be my help and my strength. The difference of last winter and this has been striking, though I then had my deep conflicts, I was, as it were, marvellously raised up – the holy anointing oil appeared freshly poured forth. How did the righteous compass me about, from the Sovereign, the Princes, and the Princesses, down to the poorest, lowest, and most destitute; how did poor sinners of almost every description seek after me, and cleave to me – What was not said of me? What was not thought of me? may I not say in public and in private, in innumerable publications, &c. This winter the bed of languishing – deep, very deep prostration of soul and body – the enemy coming in at seasons like a flood, sorrows compassing me about instead of being a helper to others, ready to lean upon all, glad even to be diverted by a child's book. In addition to this, I find the tongue of slander has been ready to attack me. The work that was made so much of before, some try to lessen now. What shall I say to all this – that in my best judgment, in my soundest faith (if I have this faith) it is the Lord's doing, by His permission, and marvellous in my eyes. Deeply as my spirit may feel to have been wounded within me, yet the first desire of my heart is, I believe for myself and for all, that we may run with fresh alacrity the race that is set before us, looking unto Jesus, as the Author and Finisher of our faith, not so much from slavish fear, as from filial love; I long, yea I pant after serving my Master with a perfect heart, the short time of my continuance here.

9th month, 6th – Since I last wrote, I parted from my beloved boys for school, John, William, and Joseph. I felt a good deal in giving them up, but at the same time believing it to be a right thing, I humbly trust that the blessing of the Most High will be with them. My dearest sister Priscilla has been very dangerously ill, raising blood from the lungs, which has brought me into great feeling and conflict. As I mostly find the case in nursing, it has caused me afresh to see my own unworthiness; so little do I feel able to administer spiritual help, so hard is it to my nature, particularly when under discouragement, to wait upon my gift or to give it its free course; but I may thankfully acknowledge, that I appeared to be a great comfort, help, and strength to her, indeed her dependence was so close upon me, that I could not leave the house night or day, for any length of time. Her state appeared to be indeed a bright and a very blessed one; so calm, so gentle, so humble, and so much resigned to live or to die. Since I have left her sick room, sorrow and deep discouragement have been my portion, from the extreme difficulty of doing right towards those most near; it does appear at times impossible for me, but most likely, this arises from want of more watchfulness and more close abiding in the Light and the Life of our Lord. When I exercise a watchful care from seeing the dangers that attend some, it seems to give the greatest pain, and so causes me the deepest discouragement. Still, yesterday, in the great, in the bitter sorrow of my heart, I found in a remarkable manner the power of my Redeemer near, even helping by His own good Spirit and presence. When I felt almost ready to sink – and my footsteps indeed ready to slip, then the Lord held me up. In the first place, after a very little while, from having been deeply wounded, my heart overflowed with love and forgiveness towards the one who had pained me; I felt what would not I do for the individual? and a most anxious desire, if I had missed it, to make it up by every thing in my power. Thus, when I had feared discouragements would have almost overwhelmed my spirit, there was such a calming, blessed, and cheering influence came over my heart, that it was like the sick coming to our Saviour formerly, and being immediately healed; so that I was not oven able to mourn over my calamity. It appeared as if the Holy One who inhabiteth Eternity would not give me over to the will of my enemies.

Letter to John Gurney Fry, at school in Darlington

Mildred's Court, 11th month, 11th, 1819

My dearest John,
I last evening arrived at home after our pleasant visit to Broadstairs and received thy letter. Thy account of you my sweet boy is very pleasant. I

much like the plans for your studies and rejoice in finding that thou are so industrious and studious. With respect to the Deal I think that I said whoever read a chapter first in the Greek testament should have one, but I do not the least remember William's having one, he must write to me all about it. However, my darling boy, as an encouragement to persevere in all that is good thou mayst have the one mentioned provided that it does not cost more than £1. I hope it costs less as we get very nice ones here for less.

With respect to W's having le Dictionary I should have thought that one would have done for both of you and it is a pity to have two of the same book, more particularly as we have one or two already. Let one of you answer whether the one book will do or not between you? for the money flies very fast going to the sea, &c., and we must be careful and not extravagant. Remember what a flock we have to provide for and to educate.

I think I had rather if thou goest on well in natural history give thee one of our handsome books upon that. As thou art our naturalist pray remember to try to procure some shells from the coast near you, not to cost a great deal but about five shillings worth, ready for your father to bring home with him.

Pray my dear boys, in your letters do not omit the possessive pronoun before your relations when you speak of them, as <u>father</u> say <u>my</u> father, &c. – it is so peculiarly vulgar and ill bred. I suppose your father answered dearest William's last letter to me, the 10th in his box he was to take of our customer at Darlington and we would put it to his account here for we thought that might be lost if sent by water.

Believe me, dearest John, thy most <u>tenderly </u>attached mother

EF

5

"My engagements as usual are very numerous":

A growing family, busyness in Brighton and a sister's death, 1820–1827

Elizabeth Fry's campaigns for prison reform and other good works took up so much time that she was seldom able to write her journal. At the same time, her children's marriages began to cause her both joy and worry. Her last child, Daniel (known as Harry), was born in 1822 on the same day as her first grandchild.

Letter to her cousin Priscilla Hannah Gurney

Mildred's Court, 2nd month, 23rd, 1820

My very dear Cousin,

I have for some time past wished to write to thee, but it is very seldom that I can get any quiet opportunity. I wish much to hear particulars of thee; I feel that confidence in our near tie to each other, that I believe communication is not necessary to keep it up, but I cannot help sometimes regretting that I have not more opportunity of opening my heart to one, whom I feel so particularly near and dear to me, and who I am sure so tenderly sympathizes in all my sorrows, and joys also. I have been favoured with health this winter, except being at times a little overdone, and having some cough. My engagements, as usual, are very numerous. I have, from being on a committee of our Quarterly Meeting, visited some of our Monthly Meetings, but I have had no other engagements of that sort. Our prisons continue to prosper, and Newgate goes on well; it does not require much of my time, though the many things it introduces me into occupy me a good deal. And now for my beloved family; I think that they are going on much the same as when thou left us; I long to see more of the advancement of the blessed Truth amongst us, but I still hope that

that day will come. I anxiously desire to be enabled to do my part, and to walk before my household with a perfect heart, but this is a great attainment, almost too much for so weak and unworthy a person to look for; my sweet little ones go on charmingly. We have good accounts of our boys, this is a great comfort for us. I have a little favour to ask of thee. The children and myself are collecting English shells, and as I know my aunt made so fine a collection, we want to know what is the best book for us to procure to direct us in our search, and where, and from what coast, we are most likely to procure the finest; we have written to know whether we cannot buy some in Devonshire. I think this such a good object for the children, and nice amusement for us all in London, where we have not the garden and flowers to enjoy, that I endeavour to cultivate it. My dearest husband is now by me, and desires his love. I hope thy reply to this will be as full of thy concerns as this is of mine. Believe me, thy nearly attached Cousin.

Plashet, 8th month – I may indeed say, dearest Lord, help me in all my difficulties, regard me in my low estate, and let me see the lightings up of the light of Thy countenance on my beloved children. Though I am deeply sensible in bringing to the knowledge of Thyself, Thy ways are not our ways, and that Thou mayst even permit the poor mind to wander in darkness and in unbelief for a season, that it may be more fully prepared to see the beauty of Thy light, to rejoice in the appearance of the day-star from on high, and to feel the excellency of faith; yet if in Thy tender mercy and compassion, Thou wouldest permit Thy unworthy one to see some fruit of the working of Thy Spirit in her children, that she might still rejoice and be glad in Thee; but above all, Lord, strengthen and enable her to cast all her care upon Thee, and to commit herself, and those most near and dear to her, to Thy grace and good keeping.

I think before I conclude this journal, I should express amongst my many blessings, how much I am enabled to take pleasure in the various beauties of nature, flowers, shells, &c., and what an entire liberty I feel to enjoy them; I look upon these things as sweet gifts, and the power to enjoy them as a still sweeter. I am often astonished, when my mind is so exceedingly occupied, and my heart so deeply interested, how I can turn with my little children to these objects, and enjoy them with as great a relish as any of them; it is a wholesome recreation, that I fully believe strengthens the mind. I mention it as a renewed proof that the allowable pleasures of life, so far from losing their zest by having the time and mind much devoted to higher objects, are only thereby rendered more delightful.

8th month, 19th – I have this day been married twenty years; my heart feels much overwhelmed at the remembrance of it – it has been an eventful time. I trust that I have not gone really backwards spiritually, as I think I have in mercy certainly increased in the knowledge of God, and Christ Jesus our Lord; but this has been through much suffering. I doubt my being in so lively a state as ten years ago, when first coming forth in the ministry; but I believe I may say, that I love my Lord above all – as far as I know, far above every natural tie ; although in His infinite wisdom and mercy, he has been pleased at times to look upon me with a frowning Providence. If I have lately grown at all, it has been in the root, not in the branch, as there is but little appearance of good, or fruit, as far as I can see. In the course of these twenty years, my abode has often been in the valley of deep humiliation; still the Lord has been my stay, and I may say through all, dealt bountifully with me, assuredly He has raised me up from season to season, enabled me to speak well of His name, and led me to plead the cause of the poor, and those that are in bonds, naturally and spiritually.

9th month, 4th – I returned yesterday from finishing visiting the Monthly and Quarterly Meetings in Essex. I was carried through the service to my own surprise, I felt so remarkably low, so unworthy, so unfit, and as if I had little or nothing to communicate to them, but I was marvellously helped from Meeting to Meeting; strength so arose with the occasion, that the fear of man was taken from me, and I was enabled to declare Gospel truths boldly. This is to me wonderful, and unbelievers may say what they will, it must be the Lord's doing, and is marvellous in our eyes – how He strengtheneth them that have no might, and helpeth those that have no power. The peace I felt after the services, for some days seemed to flow like a river, for a time covering all my cares and sorrows, so that I might truly say, "There is even here a rest for the people or God". I am sure from my own experience, there is nothing whatever in this life that brings the same satisfying, heart-consoling feeling. It is to me a powerful internal evidence of the truth of revealed religion, that it is indeed a substantial truth, not a cunningly devised fable. My sceptical doubting mind has been convinced of the truth of religion, not by the hearing of the ear, but from what I have really handled, and tasted, and known for myself of the word of life, may I not say the power of God unto salvation?

Swinton, near Hackfall, Yorkshire, 9th month, 29th – We are here staying at a beautiful place, with a brother of Lady Harcourt's. He and his wife, and all the family are exceedingly kind to us; they indeed make too much of us. However much such visits may be to the taste, they always bring me into considerable exercise of mind; in the first place, for fear of not faithfully standing my ground in Christian humility, simplicity, and faithfulness; and in the next, from the fear of not making proper use of such providential openings for promoting the blessed cause of truth and righteousness

Mildred's Court, 11th month, 5th, First day evening – I do not feel exalted by the approbation of men, though being greatly cast down by their disapprobation, leads me to think that I like it. I feel full of love to others, particularly those near me, but I have not towards them that patience and forbearance that I ought to have, and I think I am too easily provoked – not sufficiently long-suffering with their faults. I do not sufficiently remember that the wrath of man worketh not the righteousness of God. I am not willing to speak the truth in love to my neighbours, but too prone to a flattering spirit; being naturally so afraid of man, that it even affects my conduct to my servants, &c. There are many other sins I could state, to which I am very prone, when not under the immediate influence of grace, but I desire, and in some measure endeavour, not to give way to them.

Now for my circumstances – my husband and myself have had a very uniting journey; I deeply feel the separations that attach to this place, and desire to make pleasing him one of my first objects. My children are not likely to be much with me this winter, but they in their various situations claim much of my mind and time. My household cares at times a weighty burden, which peculiarly cast me down, and appear as if they must swallow up much of my powers. It is what I have no natural taste or power for, and therefore it is so difficult to me; however, I believe that I feel it unduly, and I desire to be enabled to do my duty in it. My public field of service in the prison cause affords a wonderful opening for usefulness; if I had time I should have enough to do without attending to almost any thing else; and what is more, the attention paid to this subject brings so much fruit with it. My heart is also very full towards the members of my own Society, and others; that there appears a large field for service, if I could attend to it – but I have (though enjoying so much of the unity of my friends) many deep discouragements and perplexities, particularly in our outward circumstances; and some nearest to me not more decidedly showing their allegiance to their Lord! I truly desire to receive counsel and direction as to what to do, and what to leave undone, and in the simplicity of faith, to cast all my care upon my Lord, and then I may trust that I shall be sustained, and led and kept in the way everlasting.

Plashet, 7th month, 5th, 1821 – I have been favoured to return home in peace, and what is more, with the very consoling hope and belief that I have done right in leaving Rachel at Runcton, to judge for herself in this most important affair [*her possible marriage to a non-Quaker*]. I cannot help thinking that, in tender mercy, a kind Providence has permitted it, and that it will be for good, should it take place. I have indeed had some awful plunges, and deep wadings about it, but have never in any of them believed it right to alter our determination respecting our dear child. I have certainly felt encouraged by the help of a better than myself, which has appeared peculiarly near, enabling me remarkably to commit the cause to Him. And when most cast down, under the inexpressible fear that I was giving her up too soon; or that I should get involved by it, so as to act either inconsistently with my high religious profession, or be thought to do so by others, and so to hurt my services in the church; even at these times, I have felt a power within me, like oil upon the waters, quieting every storm, consoling and helping me. In the low, the very low state I have been brought into, with an acute sense of the reproach of man, so that I almost expected my mouth would have been shut in Meetings, I have been encouraged and naturally surprised to find that I have seldom known the power of the Spirit more near to help, and to be unto me tongue and utterance, wisdom and power. May it be a lesson to all, not too much to judge others for acting a little out of the usual course. I can hardly express the peace, comfort, and sense of blessing I have had this day. Lord, continue to be very near unto thy unworthy servant, and to her children, and if this dear friend be united to her family, let him be unto her as a son and brother in Thee, O Lord! and as a true helper amongst us.

Plashet, 8th month – I have lately been hopeful and tranquil about my beloved child; trusting that all will end well. I have been much devoted to my other children. I feel this rest cause for much thankfulness, but from one cause and another, I have for the last few months gone through so much that I find my general health shaken. I am not so strong, I think, as I used to be; at times the prospect of going down the hill of life is awful, and the natural powers decaying, still it is accompanied by a sweet hope, that my last days may be my best days, and perhaps my brightest days, that, however, I must leave, only may I be ready to live or to die. Better prepared, if I live, to live more entirely to God; and if I die, to die in the Lord. Lord, grant that it may be so with me, and that those most near and dear to me, may be partakers also of the joys, glories, and power of Thy salvation. Amen.

Plashet, 8th month ,29th – My beloved daughter Rachel was married last Fifth day, the 23rd, at Runcton [*to Francis* [*Frank*] *Cresswell*], by my brother-in-law, Francis Cunningham. Great as the trial certainly has been, and is, to my natural feelings of her leaving the Society of Friends, yet I am of opinion that whatever she may eventually settle into, we have done right in not preventing this connexion; for my secret belief is, that it is for good, and a providential opening for her; though I am fully alive to the pains and disadvantages attending her marrying out of the Society of Friends.

Plashet, 9th month, 3rd – I doubt not but that my late tendency to depression of spirits is caused not only by the sorrow which I certainly feel, and great disappointment, from a child not keeping to the principles that I have brought her up in, and also from the deep sense I have of their intrinsic value; but, moreover, that I have to bear my conduct in the affair being misconstrued by others. I have certainly met with much kindness, great love and sympathy, and from quarters where I should have least expected it, also particularly from the Friends of my own Monthly Meeting.

Plashet, 11th month, 17th – Francis Cresswell and Rachel returned home last Sixth day week, 9th. Rachel's external change has of course been much felt by me, and at times I have been overwhelmed, but I consider it a mercy, that even when discouragements have most prevailed, I have been (I think) confirmed in the belief that what I did in the affair was not wrong, and that good will in the end spring out of it to my beloved child, and I trust to her dear husband also; and through all I see many causes for thankfulness in it. I feel it a time of much discouragement when cast in the way of Friends, kind as they are to me, feeling as if a cloud hung over me in their view. I am at times ready to be astonished, after having so loved their principles and made many sacrifices for them, that all these things should be. I desire to examine myself whether it is my fault, my omissions or commissions, or what is the cause; but it at times brings great humiliation, and I am ready to feel as if I never could again labour

Dishonoured
Humiliation ~ Society

out of my own house or in my own Society; but this, I cannot, I dare not give way to; I never sought in my own will to be brought forward publicly as I have been, or could I have prospered in my public labours as I have prospered, had such been the case. It appears to me, that however deep my discouragements, I must follow on to know my Lord in any way that He may require, and put my whole trust in Him, who already has done wonders for me, more than I could either think or ask; and, who through all my trials, I believe will in spirituals and temporals prove Himself to be a wonder-working God, and that I shall yet know the mountains to flow down at His presence. I cannot but believe there will be those of my own house who will magnify His great and ever excellent name. Be it so, saith my soul, it would be more to me than the increase of corn, wine, or oil. I certainly have a strong confidence that spiritually and naturally help will arise, and that it is laid upon One that is mighty.

Plashet, 2nd month, 13th, 1822 – Since I last wrote, I may say that my desires have been renewed to live under the cross, and not to flinch from it; in one instance, a want of prompt obedience led me to withhold a few words of prayer, that rose in my heart, when my beloved sisters, and my dear brother, Samuel Hoare, were here, and I felt afterwards, that we suffered loss, but I desire to take warning, and at three different times afterwards, under rather trying circumstances to myself, I endeavoured to be faithful, and peace accompanied with humiliation followed. I have desired to be watchful over personal indulgences, as my fatiguing life and often delicate health has given me a liberty in these things, that now I am better I desire to curtail, as far as it is right for me; but I find I do not serve a hard Master, nor one that would lead me into any extremes, for sometimes, when in my own will, for appearance sake, economy, &C., I have wished to leave off indulgences, I have not felt easy with it, and as far as I know, the right thing in my heart has warranted my using a sufficient supply of what I require, though of course limited by Christian moderation. But I may thankfully acknowledge my present needs being unusually small.

That which I believe the Spirit of Truth led me into, continues dear and valuable, and confirmed; though I do not certainly now feel small things of so much importance, as when they were peculiarly the seasonable and called for sacrifices, as I fully believe they were; such as dress, food, and perhaps some other things; in speech I think I have in no degree altered, never having seen it my place to conform to all the idiom of some Friends. The only thing that I know of the least alteration in, is in calling places after Saints; I think I now and then do it, and as far as I remember, used not to do so. I am rather doubtful as to the scruple being now called for, as the word saint has so much lost its original meaning, and simply describes the place; but I certainly could not conscientiously call my poor fellow-mortals saints; we know too little of each other, and have, I believe, no right to such titles, either on earth or after we are gone. I am not in the least shaken about our general language, on the contrary, quite confirmed from experience, as it respects the single language, titles to each other, except titles in law which I approve, as marking classes in society appointed by a wise and kind Providence. The names of the days and months, as used by Friends, I much prefer as more consistent with Scripture, and the Christian life; and I believe that the day is come, that even the names of the heathen gods are better not in our mouths as was prophesied would come to pass. Thus far, as it respects the cross in our peculiar views – may we, as a people, never conform to each other, but simply conform to the cross of Christ, as manifested to us individually; and keep to that manifestation, unless the same light and same power clearly lead out of it after it has effected its purpose, or remove it, which may at times be the case with further experience; and if this be the case, that we each follow the Spirit of Truth for ourselves, we shall continue to be in a measure, and become in a very increased measure, a lively and a spiritual body, showing forth the praise of the Most High.

But to return to myself, I trust I endeavour to bear my cross as to temper, for I think my many cares, my sorrows, and also perplexities have made my natural temper much more irritable, and I too often feel condemned for a hurried, and at times provoked spirit, but I desire not to give way to it, and to watch against it, though occasionally I fear, it catches me unawares. I have great dread for myself, of dwelling in any degree in my ministry on good works, or being influenced in life by the good opinion of men, as I feel I naturally like to have it, and my timid and discouraged mind much feels their disapprobation; I do not think I am such a slave to the opinion of others as I was, for I have anxiously desired and endeavoured to serve my Lord, and not my fellow-mortals, and have suffered much from running the risk of their displeasure, in doing what I believed my duty. I trust, though I know it to be a temptation, it does not really influence my conduct more than it ought to do, in ministry, or in works of charity, as I never remember entering either service to please any mortal. My heart says, God forbid that I should do so; though after having obtained their approbation (perhaps when least expected), there may be some danger of desiring and endeavouring too much to maintain it. Dearest Lord, preserve me, even from this, that whatever I do, may be done purely to Thee, and to Thy glory. Amen.

My mind is much engaged by temporal things, managing my house, farm, &c., from a duty this has become quite a pleasure; I desire to be thankful for it, but yet not to have my heart in the earth or the things of it; my mind feels so peculiarly qualified just now to enjoy the beauties of nature, from my children and our various animals, down to vegetation and minerals. May these things lead me upwards, and not draw me downwards. The prayer of my heart is, that in whatever I do I may be enabled to bring my deeds to the light, that it may be made manifest they "are wrought in God", and that my gracious Lord and Redeemer would see, if there he any evil way in me, and lead me in the way everlasting.

Plashet, 5th month, 2nd – I am favoured with general health of body, and cheerfulness of mind; a good deal occupied by temporal things, though I trust not resting in them. My readings in Newgate at this time of year are peculiarly exercising to me, so many attend, and often such a variety; and some of such high rank, I should think so little accustomed to hear the truth spoken. The prospect of them is sometimes really awful to me, and if I know the desire of my heart respecting them it is this – that the cause of truth and righteousness may be exalted, my Lord glorified, and living faith in Him promoted; and for myself and those engaged in the work, that we may dwell low before Him who hath helped us, abide in His fear, and not the fear of man;

Plashet, 5th month, 28th – Since writing the above, I have had fresh cause to raise up my Ebenezer; help having been granted, and to my own feelings way marvellously made for me, in things that I exceedingly dreaded. In the first place, I felt very low, and peculiarly under discouragement, partly from my sense of weakness both of body and mind, and partly from the idea that Friends might not feel unity with me after my child's marriage. In the first place, I had in the meeting of Ministers and Elders to pray for direction and help for myself and others during the Yearly Meeting, which appeared as if owned by the Great Head of the church. The next thing was our Ladies' Prison Meeting, which I dreaded, and had many misgivings about; however, this was got through quite beyond my expectation; the accounts of many instances of reform from different prisons were truly encouraging and comforting, and the whole feeling was as if a blessing were in it; dear Mary Dudley prayed, and several of us had to acknowledge the kindness of the Most High in it, and to Him alone, in all things, did we desire to give the glory. This Meeting gave me a little hope and encouragement.

Plashet 7th month, 4th – I hope it is with much thankfulness that I can acknowledge being safely at home. I expect to-morrow to have all our family with us, our ten children with dear Rachel's husband. There is to my feelings a great blessing in being thus surrounded by our numerous family; and I have real pleasure, and at times joy in it, though I must also say that my longings are beyond expression to have all more devoted to the best of Masters – to see them more under the influence of the Holy Spirit – more under the discipline of the cross of Christ, that it might be more fully, more clearly, and more decidedly manifest, that as for us and our house we serve the Lord. The best of things, the best of causes, not being sufficiently uppermost with us, my soul is brought to cry unto the Lord for help. What can I do? A poor unworthy servant; I am fearful of doing too much, and fearful of doing too little. Oh, that I may be enabled to seek and find counsel of God. I believe there is a good root of principle in all of my children, of an age of understanding, but I long for them to show themselves more decidedly upon the Lord's side, and more openly to profess Christ before men; I trust there is an increase of this work in some of them. Lord work in them in Thine own way, only let none rest till they experience the power of Thy salvation for themselves. Amen.

8th month, 20th – Yesterday was our wedding-day, we have been married twenty-two years; how many dispensations have I passed through since that time, how have I been raised up and cast down! How has a way been made in the depths, and a path in the mighty waters; I have known much of good health, and real sickness; great bodily suffering, particularly in my confinements, and deep depression of spirits. I have known the ease of abundance of riches, and the sorrow and perplexity of comparative deprivation; I have known to the full, I think, the enjoyment of domestic life; even what might be called the fulness of blessing, and also some of its most sorrowful and most painful reverses. I have known the aboundings of the unspeakable, soul-satisfying, and abounding joy of the Lord; and I have been brought into states, when the depths had well nigh swallowed me up. I have known great exaltation amongst my fellow-mortals, – also deep humiliation. I have known the sorrow, of some most tenderly beloved, being taken from me by death; and others given me, hitherto more given than taken. What is the result of all this experience? It is even that the Lord is gracious and very merciful that His compassions fail not, but are renewed every morning; and may I not say, that His goodness and mercy have followed me all the days of my life?

Eleventh month, 27th – Peace and sweetness appear to rest upon me in entering life. Oh! for my sweet infant, if life be granted him, may he be indeed devoted to the Lord. We neither circumcise nor baptize, but may he be baptized by the saving baptism of Christ! and be in spirit circumcised unto the Lord! I have (perhaps in weakness) much set my heart upon this child, rather expecting he may be a comfort to us in our old age, and not only so, but above all, that he may prove a devoted servant of Christ. May this blessed work not be hindered by any false indulgence in us; but may it be truly promoted by example, precept, and the true discipline of love and wisdom.

Plashet, second month, 19th, 1823 – On Second day, I dined at the Mansion House, with my husband; a change of atmosphere spiritually, but if we are enabled to abide in Christ, and stand our ground, we may by our lives and conversation glorify God, even at a dinner visit, as well as in more important callings. Generally speaking, I believe it best to avoid such occasions, for they take up time, and are apt to dissipate the mind; although it may occasionally be the right and proper calling of Christians, thus to enter life; but they must then keep the eye very single to Him, who having placed them in the world can alone keep them from the evil.

2nd month, 29th – Since I last wrote, I have attended Winchmore Hill Meeting to satisfaction, together with my dear sister Elizabeth, William Allen, and my brother Samuel, whose company I enjoyed. My husband has engaged Leslie, the painter, to come and take likenesses of him and me, to which, from peculiar circumstances, I have appeared obliged to yield; but the thing, and its effect on the mind are unsatisfactory to me, it is not altogether what I like or approve; it is making too much of this poor tabernacle, and rather exalting that part in us which should be laid low, and kept low; I believe I could not have yielded the point, had not so many likenesses of me already appeared, and it would be a trial to my family, only to have these disagreeable ones to remain. However, from one cause or another, this has not been a satisfactory week, too much in the earth and the things of it, too little in the spirit; though not without seeking to take up my cross, deny myself, and follow my Lord and Master.

4th month, 12th – Since I last wrote, we have been engaged in various ways, particularly in the sale of work done by the poor prisoners in Newgate; this has been a considerable public exposure, but I trust not without profit. I deeply felt upon entering it, the danger of the pollutions of the world, and the desire that we, who are seeking in this way to promote the cause of truth and righteousness, might maintain the watch on this point. I trust no harm was done; but I feel after being with so many, and associating with so many, much brought down in myself, under a feeling of great infirmity. I think in looking back the two last days, I do not feel condemned, but rather that I have been in my right place, and that some good may result from the whole thing. Still as a poor instrument, I fear greatly for myself; knowing my inclination to stand in awe of men, and greatly to mind their displeasure, although I am not so sensible of being exalted by their approbation. I also fear for myself, lest the enlargement of heart I feel towards all, particularly the members of the Church of Christ, of every denomination, and the sort of liberty I feel, which I apprehend to be "in the gospel", should lead me to outstep my bounds, and give myself a liberty beyond that which I have attained unto; or that in abounding love and good-will to others, I should be induced to cover, bear with, or acknowledge that, which should be decidedly testified against. I long to stand my ground in all things, at all times, and in all situations, faithfully to bear the cross of Christ; at the same time proving what I so abundantly feel, the liberty, joy and glory of that salvation that cometh by Christ. How perfectly true it is, that His followers find His yoke to be easy, and His burden light. I have the comfort to feel, notwithstanding my many fears on the subject, particularly for myself a considerable portion of peace, hope and belief, that the remarkable manner in which we have been brought forward in these services is not of our own ordering, but that we may acknowledge in deep humility of heart that it is the Lord's doing – to Him alone can we look, and upon Him alone depend for help and preservation. Lord, continue to be near unto us in this work, in the various situations into which it may introduce us, may we experience the blessing of preservation, may our labours be blessed in checking the power of evil, and in turning the sinner from the error of his way, unto Thee, our Lord, our Saviour and our Redeemer!

Plashet, 5th month, 3rd – There are times of encouragement and building up, and of discouragement and treading down. I remarkably experienced the latter state yesterday, as it respects the prison cause; I met with ingratitude amongst the prisoners such as I never remember before, for generally their gratitude has been quite remarkable. It called for patience, yet candour and firmness. Some reflections also that I found had been cast upon it, by one who understood the subject, tried me much. Still, on the prison subject, I have this secret feeling which wonderfully upholds me under the difficulties that may arise; in the first place, I believe I have been providentially brought into it, not of my own seeking; and secondly, that if He, who in a remarkable manner, has hitherto appeared to bless the work, should be pleased for a season to permit a cloud to pass over it, that is nothing to me. I have always considered the work not mine, and have desired that self may have no reputation in it; if trials of this kind come they may be for our good who are engaged in it, and for our humiliation, and for an exercise of charity towards those whom we have sought to serve.

Plashet, 8th month, 7th – We have lately had much company, which leads to handsome dinners, and that sort of excitement which I feel painful on account of my family; but I find it very difficult to act rightly under some of these circumstances. Oh! for more ability, in the power, and in the spirit to maintain the standard of truth and righteousness in my own house, in all things; so that others may be induced to do the same.

Plashet, 11th month, 24th, 1823 – Since I last wrote, I have been much engaged in the parish, amongst the poor, which is certainly satisfactory to me, and I have met with much encouragement amongst them. I have also met with unexpected difficulty, discouragement, and opposition, to my real surprise. Yet I trust this way be blessed to myself, in making self of no reputation in the work, and leading me to feel the foundation upon which I act, that all may be simply done as a duty to my neighbour called for from me by the Lord. It is rather difficult even in these laudable works (for so they are in themselves), to be unruffled by the various views of our fellow mortals; and to maintain the spirit of love and charity towards those, who not only view things differently from ourselves, but show towards us an improper feeling. I truly desire to be kept in the spirit of love; and to endeavour by the meekness of wisdom, as far as it is granted to me, to win over my neighbours to what I believe to be a right thing for our parish. Ah for a little help, dearest Lord, in this, as well as many other callings, and let this labour of love tend to establish some in the ways of righteousness, and to lead others to turn from the evil of their way. Preserve thy servants engaged in it in a humble, patient, diligent, and persevering frame of mind.

Brighton, 5th month, first day, 23rd, 1824 – I am once more away from Meeting on this day; but my strength does not appear sufficient, to venture to sit one. It certainly has, until the last few days, been upon the decline; I cannot but feel how unworthy I am of the many comforts that surround me, I am indeed most abundantly and agreeably supplied. It is a favour to be able so greatly to enjoy the beauties of nature as I do; seldom so ill, but I receive pleasure, and I trust profit from them; the sea is now an almost hourly source of pleasure to me, when I am awake, as is my garden when at home. I feel this the most when from being in a weak state, important things and the business of life do not occupy me so much, and my mind and body appear called upon to rest. I felt this morning as I sometimes have before, about the time people generally assemble to worship (when I have been sitting in solemn silence poorly, and alone), peculiar unity with, and sweet love for, the members of the Church of Christ, not only that part of it to which I belong, but to others also. I do believe there is a communion of spirits, that neither separation of person, nor difference of sentiment can obstruct, if we abide in a watchful waiting state, and that so many of the members of the living Church, being engaged in waiting upon, and worshipping our God, through Christ Jesus our Lord, spreads a good and refreshing influence which extends even to those who are absent.

Dagenham [the Frys' country house], 7th month, 30th – We left Brighton last Sixth day, the 23rd, and after what I passed through in suffering, and afterwards in doing in various ways, I may acknowledge that I have no adequate expression to convey the gratitude due to my merciful and gracious Lord. I left it after a stay of nearly ten weeks, with a comparatively healthy body, and above all, a remarkably clear and easy mind; with a portion of that overflowing peace, that made all things natural and spiritual appear sweet, and in near love and unity, not only with Friends there, but many, many others. I felt as if, although an unworthy instrument, my labours there had not been in vain in the Lord, whether in suffering or in doing. It has not been without a good deal of anxiety, fatigue, and discouragement, that this state of sweet peace has been attained, as I am apt to suffer so much from many fears and doubts, particularly when in a weak state of health. The District Society, in which I was interested, I left, I trust in a way for establishment and likely to be very useful to the poor and to the rich. Also an arrangement to supply the Blockade men on the coast with Bibles and other books: and I hope they will be put in the way of reading them, instead of losing their time. But in carrying out these plans, and particularly for the District Society, there were many discouragements, no person, at one time, believing them to be practicable from the great difficulty of bringing parties together, who, through their peculiar religious views, and other causes, never would co-operate; indeed, at one time, the thing appeared to come to an end, but it unexpectedly rose again, and as far as I can judge, is in a fair way of establishment. Some of the poor Blockade men seemed much affected by the attention paid them, as also did their officers; and I am ready to hope that a little seed is scattered there. In Meetings I passed through much, at times going when I feared I should faint from weakness; but I found that help was laid on One who is Mighty, and I may indeed say, in my ministerial services, that out of weakness I was made strong. The Meetings were generally largely attended by those not Friends, of course without invitation, but I trust that they were good ones, and that we were edified together. This was through deep humiliation, and many, many fears. It certainly calls for great care and watchfulness in all things that we enter, to find that they be not of ourselves, but of our Master, whose servants we are; for He alone should point out our work.

Plashet, 1st month, 6th, 1825 – I now wish to look back upon the year that has just passed, and to endeavour to examine my present standing. As for outward circumstances, I have lost none very near to me, but we have known more than common sorrow from illness. I might say I was seriously unwell, from the beginning of the Third Month to the autumn. I passed through many very painful hours, and some peaceful ones, a few of deep suffering; I question, whether in my life comfort and hope were more, if so much, extinct in my mind. Still, "a prayer-hearing, answering God", delivered me out of my distresses, I may say, "plucked my feet out of the mire and clay, and set them upon a rock, again established my goings, put a new song into my mouth, even praises to my God". This has been a year of much increase of property, so as to remove many of those fears that I have had upon the subject. As for myself I have not much to say, still deeply sensible of great unworthiness, many shortcomings, the world too uppermost, too great a tendency to bow to man, rather than purely serve the living God; not what I would be as wife and mother. Yet through all, there is a living desire to serve my Lord acceptably; at times in suffering, not repining; and in doing, although I may flinch, yet taking up the cross; continuing to speak well of the Lord amongst the people, engaged in heart in the prison cause, Bible Society, and other things of the kind; being made use of in them is an honour I feel and know I am unworthy of, and if ever, through grace I am enabled to promote the cause of truth and righteousness, may I never take glory to myself, but give it altogether to Him who alone is worthy. And now, on entering another year, grant, dearest Lord, to Thy servant who trusteth in Thee, more patience, more trust, more watchfulness, more humility, more quietness of mind, and above all, more reliance and faith in Thee, her God and Saviour, and in the influences of Thy Spirit.

1st month, 26th – I returned from a short expedition to Brighton last evening. A very interesting and I trust not unimportant one. My object was the District Society that I was enabled to form there, when I was so ill, or rather recovering from that state. Much good appears done, much more likely to be done; a fine arrangement made, if it be but followed up; and I humbly trust that a blessing will attend the work, and has already attended it. I feel that I have not time to relate our interesting history, but I should say that the short time we spent there was a mark of the features of the present day. A poor unworthy woman, nothing extraordinary in point of power, simply seeking to follow a crucified Lord, and to co-operate with His grace in the heart; yet followed after by almost every rank in society with the greatest openness for any communications of a religious nature; numbers at Meeting of different denominations, also at our own house, noblemen, ladies in numbers, clergy, dissenters and Friends of course; we had most satisfactory religious opportunities together, where the power of the endless life appeared to be in great dominion

Plashet, 4th month, 6th – The state of our house keeps my mind very much occupied by trifles and temporal things. It is very important with my very numerous objects to have outward things in order; indeed I go so far, as not to like to sit down in a room, even for my time of reading and retirement, without having it neat, and things in their places. I think some people are not sensible how greatly some of these smaller matters conduce to the healthy state of the mind, and even in degree to the prosperity of the soul. I often greatly suffer from the great press upon me, making it nearly impossible not to be in confusion both as to my things and papers, and even what is more, in my mind. How I long for a quieter and better regulated mind, and to have all more in order; as to outward things I hope a few weeks will accomplish this. The delightful weather and season; the innumerable beauties of nature, now showing themselves, have, I may say, refreshed my soul, and led it to "look through Nature, up to Nature's God". To my mind the outward works of creation are delightful, instructive, and edifying. I am, I hope, thankful for so much capacity to admire and rejoice in them. How important to cultivate this taste in youth! It is an advantage through life, in many ways.

Plashet, 4th month, 21st – My occupations are just now multitudinous. The British Society, and all that is attached to it, Newgate as usual. Forming with much fear, and some misgivings, a Servants' Society, yet with a hope, and something of a trust, that it will be for the good of this class of persons for generations to come. I have felt so much for such, for so many years, that I am willing to sacrifice some strength and time for their sakes. It is, however, with real fear that I do it, because I am sensible of being at times pressed beyond my strength of body and mind. But the day is short, and I know not how to reject the work that comes to hand to do.

Dagenham, 8th month, 10th – On Fifth day, the 4th of this month, my dear eldest son was married. Upon the previous evening, with a few of the family present, I was enabled to commend him to his God, for direction, and for protection; it was a very serious time. The next morning, we all, in our wedding garments, proceeded to London; my beloved husband and myself alone in the chariot, deeply feeling the weight of the occasion. Upon our arrival at the Meeting House, in Westminster, we found the party generally assembled. Soon after our sitting down in the Meeting there was that which quieted our spirits, and said, "Peace, be still". We sat more than half an hour, when dear Rebecca Christy knelt down, and, in a powerful manner, prayed for the young people, that a blessing might be with them, above all a spiritual blessing; my heart went with her, and I poured forth my tears before the Lord on their account; there was a very solemn feeling over us, a little as if the Master owned the wedding company by His presence. I had to offer fervent petitions for their good, naturally and spiritually, and for grace for them to keep their solemn covenant with each other, and to make fresh covenant with their Lord.

140

We had an elegant and hospitable entertainment afterwards; my dear uncle Barclay was there, he is grandfather to the bride, and great uncle to the bridegroom.

Plashet, 12th month, 15th – Several large banking-houses in London, and many in the country, have stopped payment; a great many are in danger, strong as well as weak ones; what will yet occur none can tell.

12th month, 19th – The country is in a very awful state, the press upon bankers is so very great, that throughout the kingdom many are stopping payment.

5th month, 27th, 1826 – We are in the midst of the Yearly Meeting; to me a very important time, as I am greatly interested in the welfare of the Society. I do most fully unite in most of its practices and principles; but still I may say, I have somewhat against it. I see that we may improve as we go on, if that which first led us to be a peculiar people be kept to by us. I think in our Meetings for Discipline, too much stress is laid on minor parts of our testimonies, such as "plainness of speech, behaviour, and apparel", rather than on the greater and weightier matters of the law; these (lesser things) are well, and I believe should be attended to; but they should not occupy an undue place. I do not like the habit of that mysterious, ambiguous mode of expression, in which Friends at times clothe their observations, and their ministry. I like the truth in simplicity, it needs no mysterious garment. I also can hardly bear to hear Friends make us out to be a chosen people, above others. I have very much kept silence amongst them, being generally quite clear of any thing to do; but as a spectator, I have rejoiced in the love, the sweetness, and the power of good amongst us, and the evidence that our great High Priest is owning us for good.

Dagenham, 7th month, 20th – I am once more come to this quiet abode, and cannot but enjoy its refreshing influence, more particularly, as my soul has of late been too much disquieted within me; a good deal, I think, from the perplexed state of the business world. Also, I have been, perhaps, too anxious respecting the well-being of my children, and too prone to fret myself in spirit about them. I have been frequently tried by many fears respecting myself, whether I might not have done, and might not do, more for my children. I do not think I am naturally gifted with the talent of education, as some of my sisters are. I have had some doubts whether our peculiar views, in many little things, much in the cross to young people, do not in measure turn them from religion itself; on the other hand, I see in others how imperceptibly the standard lowers, when these minor scruples are given up.

I am persuaded, in the education of youth, there are two sides to the question. I have no doubt whatever of the utility of these things, when adopted from conviction; my doubts are, how far they should be pressed upon young persons, through education. However, I see no other way for myself, and believe, that I must bring my children up, as, I have seen with such indubitable clearness, to be right for myself, which has been so wonderfully blessed to my own soul. That happy day may arrive, when, on their own ground, I may see some of my beloved children walking in the same way; if this would too much gratify me naturally and spiritually, then I am indeed ready to say, by any means, or in any way, so they but come to the knowledge of Christ their Saviour, and be saved through Him, I should be satisfied. It is certainly very sweet, for those who are united by natural ties, also to choose the same path in spiritual things, but experience has proved, in the case of my beloved brothers and sisters, that much of the unity of the spirit and the bond of peace may be experienced, when we may not see eye to eye.

Earlham, 9th month, 17th, 1827 – About three o'clock this morning, our most tenderly beloved sister [*Rachel*] departed this life. Late in the evening she fell asleep, from which sleep she never appeared to awake. They came to let me know, about twelve o'clock, how she was going on; but, at first, I felt unequal to going to her, and she did not want me; but, gradually, I found my tribulated, tossed spirit, calmed, animated, and strengthened, so that I joined the company round her bed, where I remained until the solemn close. We sat some time in deep silence; then I knelt down, and asked that mourning and lamentation might not be the garment of our spirits, but thanksgiving, inasmuch as the warfare was accomplished, the conflict over, and through the unmerited mercy of God in Christ Jesus, an entrance was granted through the gates of the City, whose walls are salvation and whose gates are praise. Then I prayed for ourselves, that the loss of such a sister, who had in so remarkable a manner ministered to some of our necessities, might be made up to us by an increased portion of spiritual blessings, and that her various labours of love to us and to our children might receive such a blessing, as to produce an increase to our lasting good. After returning to bed, natural weakness much overcame me; the death of the body, and its terrors, got hold of me, and the heavenly Inheritance appeared hidden from my view, for a time. To-day, I feel able to partake of the repose now granted us, in no longer having to travel through "the valley of the shadow of death", with one so beloved; and, in measure, to partake of her rest, as I believe I did, in no common manner, of her sufferings, as if one with her in them.

9th month, 19th – Blue room, with my beloved sister's remains. All quietness, rest in comparison – over my own mind a solemn feeling of peace, and this truth impressed upon me, "There is a rest for the people of God". Several important lessons, I think, I have learnt by attending this most beloved sister. 1st, That persons are apt to dwell more on the means of grace, about which they differ, than its simple pure operation leading out of evil into good. This I have long believed, but, seeing one who united as she did with the good in all and could hardly be said to be of tiny sect or body of Christians, so grounded in the Christian life and practice, proves experimentally, that being united fully to any set of people is not essential, and all minor points of difference of comparatively little value. 2ndly, I learn to trust more, and be less afraid. She like myself was liable to many fears, particularly in her nervous sinking states – how little cause had she for these fears, and how were the things that she most dreaded remarkably averted; also, That the last part of a death-illness gradually appears to diminish rather than increase in conflict, as with natural life and power, sensibility to suffering lessens. In short the lesson taught us is, to seek to serve and follow our Lord, and He will be with us and make a way for us, even unto the end. 3rdly, That in passing through life, patience should have its perfect work, that we should seek for a more willing mind to suffer, as well as to do the will of God, looking for daily help in this respect; that we should endeavour in all things for an upright, circumspect walk before the Lord, speaking the truth in love; above all, that we should seek after full understanding of, and reliance on, the work of salvation through Christ; and obtain (if possible) more knowledge of the Scriptures, and a better acquaintance with religious books.

Of my very many outward blessings, the brothers and sisters that I yet have are amongst the greatest. Catherine with her simple, powerful noble, yet, humble and devoted mind. Richenda with her diligence, excellence, cheerfulness, vivacity, willingness and power to serve many. Hannah with her chastened, refined, tender, humble, and powerful character. Louisa with her uncommon ability, talent, expansive generosity, and true sympathy and kindness. Samuel always my friend and my companion; more or less my guide, my counsellor, and my comforter. His stable mind, his living faith, his Christian practice rejoice me often. Joseph, the fruitful vine whose branches hang over the wall, my prophet, priest, and sympathiser, and often the upholder of my soul. Daniel, his uprightness, integrity, power and sympathy, and son-like as well as brotherlike attentions to me, invaluable; he has sweetened many of my bitter cups.

The various places, taken in our beloved sister's sick-room by the different sisters, were very beautiful to see, how conscientiously they filled their different allotments. I have been struck in this, as in other instances, how much real principle is needed, to enable us to nurse and do full justice to the sick, particularly, in very long illnesses, and how much patience and watchfulness are required even with the most favoured patients.

I should like to give a little account here of this most beloved sister. We began life very much together, she was a year and a half the elder. We were partners, as children, of almost all that we possessed, we were educated a good deal together, and mostly slept in the same room. She was also very strongly united in early life to Catherine. She was when young, beautiful, lively and warm hearted; she was very attractive, so as even to excite in some of us who were much less so, feelings of jealousy. She formed a strong attachment when quite young, under very painful circumstances, being contrary to our father's wishes. It eventually was broken off, although our father withdrew his opposition, when she reached twenty-one years of age. This produced a wonderful change in her, destroyed her naturally fine spirits; brought her into deep distress, but I believe also led her to seek better consolation, and that love which could satisfy and would remain. She was a most constant, faithful, devoted friend to her own family, most particularly to myself, a companion and helper in illness and distress, such as is rarely met with or heard of, both before and after my marriage. Of her it might in no common degree be said, "self was of no reputation", she was able to give up her own will, her own way, and her own pleasure to others, in an extraordinary manner.

My becoming a Friend was in the outset a trial to her, she would weep over it, and endeavour to show me the folly of it, as at that period her own mind was only opening to receive religious truth; but on perceiving that my peace was concerned in it, and that my desire was simply to obey that which I believed to be the manifestation of duty, she soon became one of the foremost to make my way easy, in any sacrifice or cross that

144

this led me into; and so far from remaining a hindrance, she became a faithful, constant, steady, helper to me. Even to the last, she would in the spirit of love and truth, warn me or any of us of such rocks as she thought our peculiar views would endanger our stumbling against; and I may truly say, I have for one, often found them Watchwords in season-words, that I trust have taken deep root in my heart, and been blessed to me. In religion, her ground was expansive. As it respected worship, I think she united much with Friends, in some other matters with the Established Church. She had peculiarly the power not only to see, but to unite with the good of all persuasions; and according to the ability granted her, to help all on their way. She was cheerful, hopeful, but very sensitive; yet so remarkably grounded on the everlasting Rock, as not to be greatly moved by, though deeply sensible of, the various trials and fluctuations of this life. She owed much also to her well-regulated and self-possessed mind. Her heart was in no common degree affectionate, even so as at times to prove a trial to her, but deep and strong as was her affection for her own family and friends, her dependence was on higher ground; and He who gave himself a ransom for her, and was her Lord and Master, had her first love.

Her sound mind, good understanding, and clear judgment were very conspicuous; her patience and long-suffering, united with natural cheerfulness, very marked, particularly in her last illness; amongst her minor virtues, her order, regularity, and punctuality wore great. She had peculiar power over children, and possessed, in no common degree, the gift of training and educating them; she was strict, though most kind to them; she particularly cultivated habits of industry, and having whatever was done, well done; she also early proved a teacher to bring them to Christ, and was able, not only to instruct them in the Scriptures, but general religious truth, and many bear testimony to her invaluable labours with them on these most important subjects. She not only sympathised particularly with the afflicted in her own family, but was a frequent and faithful nurse to many others in sickness, and a comforter to them when sorrowful. In short, she was greatly gifted by nature and grace, and what is far above all, she "gave diligence to make her calling and election sure".

6

Extracts from "Observations on the visiting, Superintendence and Government of Female Prisoners", 1827

Well knowing my incompetency for the task of writing for the public, I have felt considerable reluctance in sending to the press the following brief observations respecting the principles and plans adopted by the *British Ladies' Society for visiting prisons*; but, my long experience of the nature and effects of the system pursued by that Society, and the numerous applications made to me for farther explanation and information on this interesting subject, induce me to make an attempt, on which I should otherwise not have ventured.

Before, however, I endeavour to develop the system of the British Society, I wish to make a few general remarks which have long impressed me respecting my own sex, and the place which I believe it to be their duty and privilege to fill in the scale of society. I rejoice to see the day in which so many women of every rank, instead of spending their time in trifling and unprofitable pursuits, are engaged in works of usefulness and charity. Earnestly is it to be desired that the number of these valuable labourers in the cause of virtue and humanity may be increased, and that all of us may be made sensible of the infinite importance of redeeming the time, of turning our talents to account, and of becoming the faithful, humble, devoted followers of a crucified Lord, who went about *doing good*.

Far be it from me to attempt to persuade them to forsake their right province. My only desire is that they should *fill that province well*; and although their calling in many respects, materially differs from that of the other sex and may not perhaps be so exalted a one – yet a minute observation will prove that, if adequately fulfilled, it has nearly, if not quite, an equal influence on society at large.

No person will deny the importance attached to the character and conduct of a woman in all her domestic and social relations, when she is filling the station of a daughter, a sister, a wife, a mother or a mistress of a family. But it is a dangerous error to suppose that the duties of females end here. Their gentleness, their natural sympathy with the afflicted, their quickness of discernment, their openness to religious impressions, are points of character (not unusually to be found in our sex) which evidently qualify them, within their own peculiar province, for a far more extensive field of usefulness.

In endeavouring to direct the attention of the female part of society to such objects of Christian charity as they are most calculated to benefit, I may now observe that no persons appear to me to possess so strong a claim on their compassion, and on their pious exertions as the helpless, the ignorant, the afflicted or the depraved of *their own sex*. It is almost needless to remark that a multitude of such persons may be found in many of our public institutions.

During the last ten years much attention has been successfully bestowed by women on the female inmates of our prisons; and many a poor prisoner, under their fostering care, has become completely changed, rescued from a condition of depravity and wretchedness, and restored to happiness, as a useful and respectable member of the community. Most desirable is it that such efforts should be pursued with patient perseverance wherever they have been already made, and that they should be gradually extended to all the prisons in the kingdom.

But a similar care is evidently needed for our hospitals, our lunatic asylums and our workhouses. It is quite obvious, that there are departments in all such institutions which ought to be under the especial superintendence of females. Were ladies to make a practice of regularly visiting them, a most important check would be obtained on a variety of abuses, which are far too apt to creep into the management of these establishments. Such a practice would be the means, not only of essentially contributing to the welfare of the afflicted sufferers, but of materially aiding those gentlemen, on whom devolves the government or care of the institutions. The Roman Catholic ladies, in many parts of the continent of Europe, have set us, in this respect, a bright and useful example; and the result of their care and attention, especially in the hospitals, has been found, in a high degree, salutary and beneficial. Nor have similar effects failed to be produced in the comparatively solitary instances in which women, in our own country, have been in the habit of regularly visiting the public abodes of poverty and disease.

While I would direct the attention of my own sex (in whose usefulness I take a very lively interest) to the importance of their visiting and superintending the females in our public institutions, I am far indeed from desiring to discourage them in other and more private walks of Christian charity. Among the most interesting exertions of female benevolence, will ever be numbered the visiting of the poor in their own habitations, the necessary attention to the supply of their temporal and spiritual wants, and, above all, the diligent promotion of the education of their children; but the economical arrangement of time, and more especially a suitable division of labour, will enable the benevolent females of any place or district to accomplish without material difficulty all their charitable objects. Regard ought always to be had to the age and circumstances of individuals. For example, a young lady may be well employed in attending to a school or in visiting a sick neighbour, who would be far less suitable than the more elderly and experienced for the care of the hospital, the workhouse, the asylum, or the prison; and yet, the one service will in time form an admirable preparation for the other.

Much may be accomplished by the *union of forces*. If, in every parish or district, such ladies, as desire to make the best use of their time, would occasionally meet together, in order to consider the condition of their neighbourhood, and would divide themselves and allot the labours of Christian love to the several parties respectively, according to their suitability for different objects, the employment of but a small portion of their time would enable them to effect more extensive good than could previously have been thought possible; and, instead of being incapacitated for their domestic duties, they would often return to those duties, refreshed in spirit, and stimulated to perform them with increased cheerfulness, propriety and diligence.

To revert, for a short time, to the subject of our public institutions, although I feel it a delicate matter so earnestly to insist on the point, I must now express my conviction, that few persons are aware of the *degree* in which the female departments of them stand in need of the superintending care of judicious ladies. So great are the abuses which exist in some of those establishments, that *modest* women dare not run the risk to which they would be exposed, did they attempt to derive from them the relief which they require. I would have this subject occupy the most serious consideration of the benevolent part of the community. All reflecting persons will surely unite in the sentiment that the female, placed in the prison for her crimes, in the hospital for her sickness, in the asylum for her insanity, or in the workhouse for her poverty, possesses no light or common claim on the pity and attention of those of her own sex who through the bounty of a kind Providence are able "to do good and to communicate".

May the attention of women be more and more directed to these labours of love; and may the time quickly arrive, when there shall not exist in this realm, a single public institution of the kind, in which the degraded or afflicted females who may happen to be its inmates shall not enjoy the *efficacious superintendence* of the pious and benevolent of *their own sex*!

Highly desirable as it is that even *individual* women, who can obtain no coadjutors in the work, should devote part of their time to the important object of visiting prisons, there are many obvious reasons why the formation of *regular committees* for the purpose, wherever found possible, is greatly preferable.

In the first place, since our life and health are uncertain, and even our abode frequently liable to change, the association of two or more persons in the prosecution of such objects is indispensable to their being steadily and constantly pursued: thus, when one labourer fails, the work will not cease, and others will be ready to supply her place.

There are, secondly, a variety of engagements for those who undertake the care of female prisoners; and these engagements will be found suited to a variety of persons.

In the third place, where there are several visitors, no individual among them is required to give up more than a very limited portion of time. If, for example, there are seven ladies on the committee, the prison may be properly attended to, if each visitor will devote to the purpose a part of one morning only in the week.

Fourthly, a committee will often arrive at sounder and wiser conclusions on any practical question than an individual would be likely to form. The ladies who compose such a committee may mutually assist each other's judgment, and support one another in their respective exertions.

Fifthly, the business in hand, under the care of a regular and judicious committee will be generally conducted with greater order, method and regularity, than will probably attach to the efforts of any solitary individual.

And lastly, when representations are to be made, or requests to be preferred, to magistrates or other persons in authority, the deliberation and sanction of a committee will give them their due weight.

On these grounds I would strongly advise any lady, who is disposed to enter upon the important work of visiting a prison, to look round, in the first instance, for persons who may unite with her in its prosecution; and my experience leads me to believe that there are few, if any, prisons in the kingdom, in the neighbourhood of which some benevolent ladies may not be found, who will be both able and willing to engage in this interesting task. When ladies have thus united for the purpose, it will of course be necessary, before they proceed to put their plan in execution, to obtain the sanction of the magistrates under whose authority the prison is placed. And here I remark that, since persons of rank and influence in society are often able, from their peculiar situation, to remove difficulties which might otherwise be insuperable, some lady in the neighbourhood, of this description, ought to be invited to act as patronness or president of the committee. Much advantage will also arise from a regular yearly correspondence with the committee of the British Society in London.

When a Ladies' Association for visiting any particular prison has been formed, and when the sanction of the Magistrates has been obtained for their undertaking, the Committee (consisting probably of but a few, and those judicious, individuals) will of course take an early opportunity of meeting in the females' department of the prison. They will then call the prisoners together, and explain to them their motives and views in undertaking to assist and superintend them. They will express their sympathy with them under their afflicting circumstances, soothe them with words of gentleness and kindness, and endeavour to hold up, in strong colours, the danger and misery of vice, the beauty of holiness, and the innumerable advantages which attach to a life of sobriety, industry, honesty and virtue. When the attention of the prisoners has been thus engaged, and their better feelings excited, it will be necessary to propose a series of rules for their future conduct. To these rules they may be expected, in the first place, to give their deliberate and voluntary assent; and secondly, to consider themselves firmly bound to adhere to them, during their continuance in prison. Experience has amply proved, that when prisoners are tenderly treated, there is a general willingness to submit to such regulations as the ladies who visit them may propose for their conduct and improvement.

The great object which the visitors ought always to keep in view is, the reformation of the prisoners: and to this principal end all their plans must be subservient. In endeavouring to effect this good purpose, it will of course devolve upon them to instruct the unlettered in useful elementary knowledge, to bring all to a personal acquaintance with Holy Writ, and to train these unfortunate females to habits of cleanliness, order, and regular industry. These several objects must be pursued according to the circumstances which may attach to any particular prison or association; and judicious visitors will seldom be at a loss respecting the proper application of their efforts in order to obtain the results which may be desired. I wish, however, to take the opportunity afforded me, by the present section, of throwing out a few hints respecting the general deportment desirable in the visitors themselves, both towards the prisoners and towards those persons in authority, under whose superintending care the prison is placed.

Much depends on the spirit in which the visitor enters upon her work. It must be the spirit, not of judgment, but of mercy. She must not say in her heart "I am more holy than thou" but must rather keep in perpetual remembrance that "*all* have sinned, and come short of the glory of God" – that therefore great pity is due from us even to the greatest transgressors among our fellow-creatures – and that, in meekness and love, we ought to labour for their restoration. The *good principle* in the hearts of many abandoned persons may be compared to the few remaining sparks of a nearly extinguished fire. By means of the utmost care and attention united with the most gentle treatment, these may yet be fanned into a flame, but under the operation of a rough and violent hand, they will presently disappear and be lost for ever.

In our conduct towards these unfortunate females, kindness, gentleness, and true humility ought ever to be united with serenity and *firmness*. Nor will it be safe ever to descend in our intercourse with them, to familiarity; for there is a dignity in the Christian character, which demands, and will obtain, respect, and which is powerful in its influence, even over dissolute minds.

None need be discouraged from expressing amongst them, a detestation and abhorrence of sin, and a strong view of its dreadful consequences. Nevertheless, it is seldom salutary to make a pointed application of such remarks to the cases of individual criminals; for experience proves, that if those persons who visit them are harsh in judging and condemning them, the effect is hurtful rather than beneficial. Neither is it by any means wise, to converse with them on the subject of the crimes of which they are accused or convicted; for such conversation is injurious both to the criminals themselves and to others who hear them; and moreover, it frequently leads them to add sin to sin, by uttering the grossest of falsehoods.

The visiting ladies must show as much confidence in the prisoners as circumstances will possibly admit; and, in order to this end, it will be at once salutary and safe to intrust them with the care of various articles belonging to the committee. Marks of approbation and small rewards ought also at times to be bestowed on them, as an encouragement to good conduct. To miss these rewards is generally found to be a sufficient mortification for the correction of the disorderly. Solitary confinement, which is useful in extreme cases, is, in my opinion, a punishment far too severe to be resorted to on any light and trivial occasion.

Finally, those who engage in the interesting task of visiting criminals must not be impatient if they find the work of reformation a very slow one. Such it will most necessarily be in the generality of cases. Sensible of the natural corruption of our own hearts, let us learn patiently to bear with the hardened and the profligate, and let us be faithful and diligent in directing their attention to "the Lamb of God which taketh away the sins of the world"; for it is only by faith in Him, that these poor wanderers can obtain the forgiveness for their past sins, or be enabled, for the future, to lead a life of true piety and virtue.

Among the various objects to which the visiting Committee of ladies will find it, in any prison, their place to attend, the instruction of the prisoners may be considered the most interesting and important. It is a melancholy reflexion, that so large a proportion of the inhabitants of this country – a country possessed of so many advantages, and so greatly advanced in civilization – are still left in a condition of almost extreme ignorance.

This observation applies with peculiar force to those who are in the habit of breaking its laws. Of the female criminals who come under the care of the Newgate Committee, about one third are unable to read at all – and another third can only read a very little. With regard to the truths of religion, the ignorance which prevails amongst them is extreme; and this is the natural consequence of the disadvantages under which they have been brought up: for many of them have scarcely ever attended a place of public worship, or heard, or read, any part of the Holy Scriptures. Much, therefore, must depend on the instruction which such persons receive *in prison.*

In the first place, they will there have the advantage of a regular attendance of their appointed place of worship – for our prisons are now almost universally provided with a chapel and a chaplain; and this opportunity will, in most cases, be afforded them more than once in the week. When assembled in the chapel, it is indispensable that the women should be completely separated from the male prisoners, and quite out of their sight. Nothing must be allowed to divert their attention, or to interrupt the solemnity of the occasion.

The chaplain of the prison will, of course, find it his duty not only to perform the services of public worship, but to communicate with the prisoners individually, and to endeavour, by private persuasion and instruction, to lead them into the paths of virtue, religion and peace. Greatly is it to be desired, that those who occupy this important and interesting station, should be themselves persons of true piety. I venture to suggest that they ought to be married men of *established* character, with some knowledge of life, as well as religious experience.

Much as the good order of every prison depends on the conduct and character of the chaplain, and desirable as it is that he should fully and faithfully perform his duties, and that the visiting Committee should not interfere with him, I well know that there is a part of the moral and relig- ious instruction of female prisoners, which cannot be communicated to them so well, so safely, or so efficaciously, as by *the ladies who visit the prison*. The instruction to which I allude is all of a private nature; but, besides this, the assembling of the prisoners together, at least once a day, in order to read to them a portion of the Holy Scripture, is a charge which will most suitably devolve on the members of the visiting Committee.

This duty is one of very serious importance. It ought never to be lightly performed as a mere matter of course; but, when we are engaged in it, our hearts ought ever to be lifted up to Him who can alone bless our endeav- ours. The visiters will do well, generally, to select for the purpose the more clear and simple parts of Scripture, especially from the New Testament and the Psalms. Nor must they fail to direct the especial attention of their hearers to those passages which proclaim the salvation offered to lost mankind through a crucified Redeemer, and which are calculated to revive the buried hopes of even the very worst of sinners. The 25th and 51st Psalms, the 15th chapter of Luke's Gospel, and the 12th of Hebrews, among other portions of Scripture, will be found peculiarly applicable to the case of these sinful and afflicted persons. To pursue a regular course of reading in the Scriptures – for example, to read through the whole New Testament, chapter by chapter – is indeed desirable where the prisoners continue under the care of the committee for long stated periods, as may often be the case in houses of correction. But in Newgate the changes which are perpetually taking place prevent the execution of any such plan.

Much good may be effected by instructing the female criminals *indi- vidually* in the truths of the Christian religion. For this purpose, every member of the committee may have a certain number of them under her care. Judiciously selected tracts and other religious books may be lent to them for their perusal in hours of leisure; and they may be encouraged to commit to memory some of our best hymns – such as those in the Olney Collection – and various impressive passages of the Bible itself. The influence of this private religious instruction is powerful, and I have long observed that the greatest change for the better generally takes place in those prisoners, over whom has been exercised the most of this pious Christian care.

According to the provisions of the late Act of Parliament, prayers are to be read daily in all our prisons. It is the duty of the visiters to endeavour to impress upon the minds of the prisoners a sense of the seriousness of this sacred duty – to point out to them what a high privilege it is to hold communion with God – and fully to explain to them, that unless this service be performed with the heart and spirit, it can never be a sacrifice acceptable, well-pleasing, to God. Some of these poor wanderers are so ignorant as to imagine that, if they do but hurry over a daily service of prayer with their lips, they are thereby justified in the sight of God; and that this superficial offering will atone for their daily transgressions. It cannot be too strongly impressed upon them, that true religion and saving faith are in their nature *practical*, and that the reality of repentance can be proved only by good works and by an amendment in life and conversation. It is, however, a great consolation to know, that the simple declaration of the Gospel has a powerful *tendency* to produce these effects – and actually produces them, at times, even in the most hardened offenders. And although, in some cases, such persons, when again beset with temptation – and great are the trials to which they are exposed – fall under the power of it, yet there are many others, in whom the effects of Christian instruction, given to them when in prison, are not only powerful but *durable*. Long observation and experience enable me to say that there are few engagements from which the pious and benevolent may derive more encouragement than the care and religious instruction of poor criminals. And surely such efforts as these are highly becoming for the followers of Him, who came into the world "to save sinners" – "to seek and to save that which was *lost*".

Some part of the time of the visiters may be very usefully employed in the elementary instruction of the more ignorant prisoners. They ought to be taught to read, write and cipher, as well as to make a ready and profitable use of the needle. The prisoners ought also to be supplied with a small assortment of unexceptionable books, not only of a religious but of a generally instructive nature, as it is most desirable to turn the channel of their thoughts, to improve not only their habits but their *tastes*, and by every possible means to raise their *intellectual* and *moral* as well as their religious standard.

I strongly recommend the plan of mutual instruction, as practised in the schools of Bell and Lancaster. Let the women of the first class be employed (under the superintendence of the matron or the visiters) in teaching the lower classes; and let them receive some remuneration, to encourage them in their work.

One observation only remains for me to make, under the head of Instruction – viz. That, in all our religious communications with the prisoners, every thing sectarian must ever be rigidly avoided, and the attention of afflicted hearers exclusively directed to the *essential and saving principles of our common Christianity.*

7

"I felt a little roughly handled":
Bankruptcy, disownment and change of residence, 1828–1834

The bankruptcy and disownment of Elizabeth's husband brought not only financial problems and an enforced change of residence, but deeper divisions between her family and the Society of Friends. Elizabeth had great difficulty reconciling herself to her misfortune and to the change in attitude towards herself.

Plashet, 1st month, 31st, 1828 – During this month, my beloved family, husband and children have occupied most of my time and attention, and in many respects I have had much comfort; but at their present age, when there is so much to excite the susceptible mind of youth, my anxieties are many on their account, and I feel that I have to watch with at times fearful care over them and their associates, and perhaps when they do not know it, sympathise with them in their passing troubles arising from such circumstances. I sometimes pour forth my prayer for them, that if they are to be united to others in life, their affections may settle on the right objects. How deeply, how tenderly, to be felt for, and watchfully to be cared for, are young people at this period of life and how difficult for us, who apprehend ourselves, as Friends, to be bound by unusual restrictions in marriage connexions, exactly to know the right line to pursue.

I have been, as usual, much occupied by public objects, and have met with both encouragement and disappointment. Encouragement, because the government has greatly aided us in the female convict ships; and disappointment, from not succeeding in more generally obtaining permission for ladies to visit prisons. In our own Society, I have had one important call to Birmingham, to attend a funeral; a very serious and weighty occasion it proved; numbers of the children and grand-children of the deceased, of various descriptions were present. There was a crowded meeting, and few ministers, so that the weight of the service appeared to devolve on me, there, and at the house. The help granted me was marvellous in my eyes;

and I was enabled, at these different times to preach the glad tidings, the liberty and the peace of the gospel of Christ. So it is, out of weakness, we are, when dependent on our Lord alone, made strong, and fear is removed in the most remarkable manner. My dearest brother Samuel accompanied me – who has such brothers as I have, to help in the needful time? I think, as it respects the ministry, I am never so much helped as when without other ministers to look to, my dependence being then singly on my Lord and on His anointing.

I yesterday went to see one of my sons at school and attended Epping Meeting, which I thought a satisfactory time. I tried to make my visit pleasant to all the boys, by taking them a walk, and giving them oranges; I like that the instruments, who communicate religious instruction to the young, should be pleasant to them. I have once or twice been to see my sister Hoare, and have felt the value of the near union between us; my dearest sister Rachel is often present with me, the way in which I have been enabled to support this inexpressible loss, is surprising to myself; surely it is only the tender mercy of my God, that has thus healed my wounds and upheld me under it.

2nd month, 2nd – Yesterday was a full day, and one humbling in its effect. In the first place, I earnestly desired preservation, that I might keep my eye single to God, and not bow to man in spirit. I then went to town, and to Newgate, under a feeling of rather deep concern, where I unexpectedly found numbers of persons, a magistrate, foreigners, a Jew, a clergyman, many ladies, some Friends, and my brother Samuel. Before I began to read, I in secret asked for preservation, at least it was my earnest desire to have my eye kept single to my God. But either the fear of man got too much hold of me, or the "unction" was not with me, for I did not feel the power of Truth over us, as it very often has been at such times. I am ready to believe, that if I had not looked at man, but dwelt yet deeper in spirit, I should have openly called upon the Lord, and should have found help and power in so doing. I went away humbled. My sister Elizabeth said something; but of late there has been so much felt and said about our doing too much in those things with the prisoners, and going out of our province, that it makes me fearful, and consider that as far as the Spirit is rightly subject to the prophets, so far, at this critical time, we ought to curtail in these things. I then went with my beloved brother Samuel to the Bishop of London, to talk to him about religious services with prisoners, to inform him of our situation respecting it in Newgate, and the extreme care necessary in the appointment of chaplains for gaols; also to speak to him of the state of our parish. I spoke, I trust, to the point, and that good and not harm will result from the visit; but I always fear, after such times, lest I should have said too much. We then made a call, where I pretty boldly spoke my opinions of theatres and public places; and in reply to the question, "How I went on, in reforming the world?" I replied, that my zeal was strong in my declining years to do what little I could towards reforming things. Afterwards, I feared that I might have said too much.

3rd month, 5th – How have gospel truths opened gradually on my view, the height, the depth, length and breadth of the love of God in Christ Jesus, to my unspeakable help and consolation; principally, I believe, through the dispensations of Almighty wisdom, partly from the soundness of faith of some near to me, my brother Joseph, my sisters Priscilla, Catherine, and Rachel, as well as many others of different religious persuasions. I think that my general religious association has delightfully extended my spiritual borders. I can, from my heart, say, all one in Christ; all dearly beloved, as brethren and sisters, who love His name, and seek to follow Him. Although I remain a decided Friend in principle, and believe for myself and for many others, that it is our calling, for I consider ours to be a highly spiritual dispensation, and that not only we ourselves, but others would suffer much loss by our not keeping to it.

5th month, 21st – The day before yesterday the wedding [*of her daughter Richenda to Foster Reynolds*] was accomplished. The Meeting was solemn and satisfactory. Our bride and bridegroom spoke well, and with feeling. My dearest brother Joseph prayed for them and ministered to them, as did others; I prayed at the close of the Meeting most earnestly for them, for the other young people, and ourselves further advanced in life. After a short solemn silence the certificate was read and signed. In the morning we had a satisfactory reading with our children. Thanks be to our Heavenly Father, there was, I think, throughout the day a great mixture of real solemnity with true cheerfulness. It was certainly no common day. William Foster Reynolds and his wife, my husband and myself, with nineteen of our own children in the two families, besides children-in-law and some grandchildren, and nine of my brothers and sisters. Through everything, order, quietness and cheerfulness were remarkably maintained. After dinner I returned thanks for our many blessings, and could with a few present feel how many outward deliverances we had experienced; that we had had our heads kept above the waters, spiritually and temporally, and were able to have such a day of rejoicing. Our dear bride and bridegroom left us in the afternoon. The evening was fine, and our lawn looked really beautiful, covered with the large and interesting party. In the evening we assembled together, and had a solemn religious time; giving, I trust, the praise that was due alone to Him from whom all good and blessings flow.

11th month, 15th – The storm has now entered my own borders – once more we are brought into perplexity and trial – but I have this consolation, "He will regard the prayer of the destitute, and not despise their prayer". To whom can I go in this time of emergency, but to Him who hitherto has helped me and provided for me and mine in a marvellous manner – made darkness light before me and crooked things straight. Lord! Thou who remainest to be the God of my love, above all things, in this our sorrow and perplexity cast us not out of Thy presence, and take not Thy Holy Spirit from us; keep us from evil and from the appearance of it, that through the help of Thy Spirit our conduct may be kept upright, circumspect, and clean in Thy sight, and amongst men! that in all things, at all times, and under all circumstances, we may show forth Thy praise. But, oh, dearest Lord, if it be Thy holy will, make a way of escape for us, from the calamity we so much dread, and continue in Thy unmerited mercy to provide for Thy unworthy servant, her family and all concerned in this trial, that we may not want what is good and needful for us, and that others may be kept from suffering through us. If it be possible, remove this bitter cup from us; yet, if it be Thy will that we drink it, enable us through the grace and spirit of Him who suffered for us, to drink it without repining, – yet trusting in Thy love, Thy mercy, and Thy judgment.

In the same vein she wrote to her daughter Rachel

Plashet, 11th month, 27th, 1828.

My dearest Rachel,

I have at last taken up my pen to write to thee; but, to one so near, and so much one with myself, it is difficult. I do not like to pour out my sorrows too heavily upon thee, nor do I like to keep thee in the dark as to our real state. This is, I consider, one of the deepest trials to which we are liable; its perplexities are so great and numerous, its mortifications and humiliations so abounding, and its sorrows so deep. None can tell but those who have passed through it, the anguish of heart at times felt; but thanks be to our God, this extreme state of distress has not been very frequent, nor its continuance very long. I frequently find my mind in degree sheathed to the deep sorrows, and am enabled not to look so much at them – but there are also times, when secondary things arise – parting with servants, the poor around us, schools, and our dear Place. These things overwhelm me; indeed I think naturally I have a very acute sense of the sorrow. Then the bright side of the picture rises, I have found such help and strength in prayer to God, and highly mysterious as in some points of view this dispensation may be, yet I think I have frequently, if not generally, come to be able to say, "Not as I will, but as Thou wilt", and bow under it. All our children and children-in-law, my brothers and sisters, our many friends and servants, have been a strong consolation to me; and, above all, a little refreshment to my tribulated spirit has been granted me at times, from what I trust are the well-springs from on High.

Plashet, 12th month, 16th – I have had some quiet peaceful hours, but I continue in the low valley, and naturally feel too much, leaving this sweet home, but not being well makes my spirits more weak than usual. I desire not only to be resigned, but cheerfully willing to give up whatever is required of me, and in all things patiently to submit to the will of God, and to estimate my many remaining blessings. I am sorry to find how much I cleave to some earthly things – health, ease, places, possessions. Lord, Thou alone canst enable me to estimate them justly, and to keep them in their right places. In thine own way, dearest Lord, accomplish Thine own work in me, to Thine own praise! grant that out of weakness I may yet be made strong, and through Thy power wax valiant in fight; and may I yet, if consistent with Thy holy will, see the travail of my soul and be satisfied, as it respects myself and my most tenderly beloved family. Amen!

Mildred's Court, 1st month, 19th, 1829 – My first journal in this year! What an eventful one was the last! Prosperity and adversity were peculiarly our portion. It has been in no common degree a picture of life comprised in a small compass. However, through all, in prosperity and in adversity, however bright or cloudy my present position or my prospects may be, my desire for myself, and all whom I love is this, so strongly expressed by the Psalmist, "I will hope continually, and yet praise Thee more and more!" So be it, saith my soul, and if it be the Lord's will, may light rise in our present obscurity, and our darkness become as the noonday, both as to temporal and spiritual prospects!

Mildred's Court, 3rd month – It appears late to begin the journal of a year; but the constant press of engagements, and the numerous interruptions to which I am liable in this place, prevent my having time for much writing. We are remaining here with our son and daughter, and their children, until there is some opening for having a settled home. However, my desire is that we may in faith and in humility entirely bow. I have of late not visited the prisons, and been much occupied at home; but I trust that I may be permitted to enter this interesting work again, clothed, as with fresh armour, both to defend me, and qualify me for fresh service, that my hands may be taught to war and my fingers to fight; and that if consistent with the will of my God, I may, through the help of the Captain of my salvation, yet do valiantly.

Upton [a smaller house next to Samuel Gurney's home, Ham House, in Essex], 6th month, 10th – We are now nearly settled in this, our new abode; and I may say, although the house and garden are small, it is pleasant and convenient, and I am fully satisfied, and I hope thankful, for such a home. I have at times been favoured to feel great peace, and I may say joy, in the Lord – a sort of seal to the important step taken; though, at others, the extreme disorder into which our things have been brought by all these changes – the pain of leaving Plashet – the difficulty of making new arrangements, has harassed and tried me. But I trust it will please a kind Providence to bless my endeavour, to have and keep my house in order. Place is a matter of small importance, if that peace which the world cannot give be our portion, even at times, as a brook by the way, to the refreshment of our weary and heavy laden souls. Although a large garden is not now my allotment, I feel pleasure in having even a small one; and my acute relish for the beautiful in nature and art is on a clear day almost constantly gratified by a delightful view of Greenwich Hospital and Park, and other parts of Kent, the shipping on the river, as well as the cattle feeding in the meadows. So that in small things and great, spiritual and temporal I have yet reason to praise, and magnify the name of my Lord.

161

6th month, 23rd – I little expected to attend the Yearly Meeting, having of late appeared to be so much taken out of such things and such services, but, contrary to my expectation, way opened for me to attend every sitting, and to take rather an active part in it, to my real consolation, refreshment and help. The unity of Friends was remarkable. I certainly felt very low at its commencement. After having for so many years received dear friends at my house, and that with such heartfelt pleasure, it tried, not to say puzzled me, why such a change was permitted me. But I rest in the weighty import of the words "That which I do, thou knowest not now, but thou shalt know hereafter."

8th month, 29th – Our wedding–day! Twenty-nine years since we married! As far as we can judge from external appearances, mine has not been a common life. He who seeth in secret, only knows the unutterable depths and sorrows I have had to pass through, as well as at other times, I may almost say, joys inexpressible and full of glory. I have now had so many disappointments in life, that my hopes, which have so long lived strong, that I should see much brighter days in it, begin a little to subside, and my desire is, more entirely to look beyond the world for that which can alone fully satisfy me; and not to have my heart so much set upon the things of this life; or even those persons nearest to me, but more set upon the life to come; and upon Him who is faithful, and will be all in all to His dependent ones. At the same time I desire faithfully to perform all my relative duties; and may my heart be kept in tender love to all near to me.

Upton, 10th month, 21st – Something has occurred which has brought me into conflict of mind; how far to restrain young persons in their pleasures, and how far to leave them at liberty. The longer I live, the more difficult do I see education to be, more particularly, as it respects the religious restraints that we put upon our children; to do enough, and not too much, is a most delicate and important point. I begin seriously to doubt, judge whether as it respects the peculiar scruples of Friends, it is not better, quite to leave sober-minded young persons to judge for themselves. Then the question arises – When does this age arrive? I have such a fear that in so much mixing religion with those things which are not delectable, we may turn them from the thing itself. I see, feel, and know that where these scruples are adopted from principle, they bring a blessing with them; but where they are only adopted out of conformity to the views of others, I have very serious doubts whether they are not a stumbling-block.

162

On First-day, we were rather suddenly summoned to Plashet House, to attend Anna Golder who had charge of the house. She was one of the lowly, retired humble walkers before the Lord; she was suddenly taken very ill, and died in half-an-hour after her niece got there. It was apparently a departure without sting, to mind or body; as far therefore as it respected her, all was peace. But to myself it was different. I arrived there after dark, drove once more into the dear old place – no one to meet me but the poor man who lived in the house, no dog to bark, nor any life nor sound, as used to be. Death seemed over the place, such was the silence until I found myself up stairs in the large, and once cheerful and full house; when I entered the bed-room, there lay the corpse, in her gown, she having died in her chair, only our washerwoman and the woman who lived in the house in the room besides. Circumstances combined to touch some very tender feelings, and the inclination of my heart was to bow down upon my knees before the Lord; thankful, surely, for the release of the valued departed – but deeply and affectingly impressed with such a change! That once lively, sweet, cheerful home left desolate the abode of death – and two or three watchers. It brought, as my visits to Plashet often have done, the hymn to my mind,

"Lord, why is this?" I trembling, cried.

Then again I find I can do nothing, but bow, trust, and depend upon that Power, that has, I believe, thus seen meet to visit us in judgment as well as in mercy!

Earlham, 3rd month, 23rd, 1830.

My most beloved Children,

The information received to-day, that you should any of you have admitted a serious thought of attending our kind friend's party on the 31st, surprises and pains me; not but that I am also fully sensible of your willingness fully to be guided by my judgment in it. With respect to those over whom I have authority, I feel it impossible to leave them in any degree at liberty about it – it is a thing that must not be. I look upon it not only as perfectly inconsistent with our views as Friends but perfectly so for all religions professors, because if I did approve of consecrating a church for the worship of the Almighty, I could not possibly conceive it an occasion for amusement or gaiety, but one of real seriousness. I see the thing to be altogether inconsistent with religious truth, both as to the thing itself and this commemoration of it, and I trust that none of you will be present. I am sure it was, in the first instance, your own view of the case, therefore do not, my dearest children, be shaken in your judgments about it; I believe it will be a cross that you will never repent taking up, but on the contrary, be glad you have done so, for, now and then, sacrifices must be made to duty. Can you approve sacred things and the world's pleasures being thus mixed together? Can you think the consecration of churches, as it is too frequently conducted, consistent with the purity and simplicity of the gospel of our blessed Lord?

Upton, 4th month, 26th – My Suffolk and Norfolk journey proved an interesting, instructive, and I think very satisfactory one. My way appeared to be remarkably made in Suffolk, where I almost feared to go. At Ipswich, when the Quarterly Meeting was over, I think for a time I partook of perfect peace; my rejoicing was, I may say, in the Lord. It was well worth suffering, only to taste of such a brook by the way. At Pakefield, we had a highly valuable and edifying visit to my much loved brother and sister Cunningham; although their religious path is certainly in many respects, very different to my dear sister Elizabeth Fry's and mine, yet it appeared, as if it pleased the great Head of the Church, in no common degree to bless our intercourse, Christian love breaking down all partition-walls; – we were sweetly refreshed together. We indeed, have but one Lord, one faith, one baptism, and one God over all, above all and in us all. I have for many years felt much liberality towards those who differ from myself; but I may say, with increased years and experience I know hardly any distinction, all one in Christ. Those in my own family, who have gone to the Church, are so very near to me spiritually.

After our visit to Pakefield, we went to Earlham and met with a cordial reception; but I think that we were all in a low place. My arrival at home was clouded by a party, to which my children were invited and rather wished to go. We had some pains about it – my path is a very peculiar one, and as to bringing my family up consistent Friends, a most difficult one. My husband not going hand in hand with me in some of these things, my children, in no common degree, disliking the cross of the minor testimonies of Friends, and from deeply sorrowful circumstances, often having had their faith in them tried, also their being exposed unavoidably, to much association with those, who do not see these things needful, renders it out of my power to press my own opinions beyond a certain point. I believe it best and most expedient for them in small things and great, to be Friends; it has to me been a blessed path, and my belief is that it would be so to them, if conscientiously walked in, but it is not I, who can give them grace to do it, and if their not walking more consistently brings reproach upon me, even amongst those nearest to me – I must bear it.

I cannot deny that much as I love the principle – earnestly as I desire to uphold it – bitter experience has proved to me, that Friends do rest too much on externals; and that valuable, indeed jewels of the first water, as are many amongst them yet there are also serious evils in our Society and amongst its members. Evils which often make my heart mourn, and have led me earnestly to desire, that we might dwell less on externals, and more on the spiritual work; then I believe that we should be as a people less in bonds, and partake more of the glorious liberty of the children of God. My desire is only to do what is for the real good of my children, and for the good of the cause I love, and leave myself altogether out of the question, whether it bring me into evil report or good report. I have often been brought by these things, especially of late, into deep conflict of spirit, and out of the very depths can only cry, Lord, help and guide me! and give us not over to the will of our spiritual enemies.

6th month, 7th – I had a difficult path to tread during the Yearly Meeting. I did not of course receive Friends, but went as I was kindly asked, to various houses. I could not but at times naturally feel it, after having for so many years delighted to entertain my friends, and those whom I believe to be disciples of Christ, and now in considerable degree to be deprived of it. But after relating my sorrows, I must say, that through the tender mercy of my God, I have many blessings, and what is more, at times such a sweet feeling of peace, that I am enabled to hope and trust, that through the unbounded and unmerited mercy of God in Christ Jesus, my husband, my children, and myself, will eventually be made partakers of that salvation that comes by Christ.

The state of our Society, as it appeared in the Yearly Meeting, was very satisfactory, and really very comforting to me; so much less stress laid upon little things, more upon matters of greater importance, so much unity, good-will, and what I felt, Christian liberty amongst us. Love appeared truly to abound, to my real refreshment. I am certainly a thorough Friend, and have inexpressible unity with the principle, but I also see room for real improvement amongst us; may it take place. I want less love of money, less judging others, less tattling, less dependence upon external appearance. I want to see more fruit of the Spirit in all things, more devotion of heart, more spirit of prayer, more real cultivation of mind, more enlargement of heart towards all; more tenderness towards delinquents, and above all, more of the rest, peace and liberty of the children of God!

8th month – In bringing up our children, it is my solid judgment that a real attachment is not a thing to be lightly esteemed, and when young persons of a sober mind are come to an age of discretion, it requires very great care, how any undue restraint is laid upon them, in these most important matrimonial engagements; we are all so short-sighted about them, that the parties themselves should after all be principally their own judges in it. Therefore, unless I see insurmountable objections, I believe duty dictates leaving our children much at liberty in these matters. May a gracious and kind Providence direct them aright.

On Fifth-day, several of the higher classes were invited to Meeting and to my own feelings, a remarkable time we surely had; it appeared as if we were over-shadowed by the love and mercy of God our Saviour. The ministry flowed in beautiful harmony, I deeply felt the want of local prayer being offered, but I did not see it my place upon our Meeting assembling together, when, to my inexpressible relief, John Rickman powerfully and beautifully offered up thanksgiving and prayer, which appeared to arise as incense and as an acceptable sacrifice. After a time of silence, I rose with this text: "There are diversities of gifts, but the same spirit; differences of administration, but the same Lord; diversities of operations, but it is the same God who worketh all in all." In a way that it never did before, the subject opened to my view whilst speaking; how did I see and endeavour to express the lively bond of union existing in the Christian Church, and that the humbling tendering influence of the love and power of Christ must lead us not to condemn our neighbours but to love and cover all with charity. My sister E. Fry was rather closely and differently led, and I had to end the Meeting by praying for the King, Queen, and all their subjects every where; for the advancement of that day, when the knowledge of God and His glory would cover the earth as the waters cover the sea; for those countries in Europe that are in a disturbed state, and that these shakings might eventually be for good. After a most solemn feeling of union the Meeting broke up. We dined at our dear friends the Elliots where were Charles Simeon, Henry Elliot (valuable clergymen), and others. A pleasant, sweet, refreshing time we had; I think I never feel so able to rejoice in the Lord, as when united with real Christians of different denominations. We went that night to Chichester, and slept at Maria Hack's, and were much interested by her and her family,

166

some of whom have joined the Church of England, but they appeared to us truly valuable and serious, and we were much pleased with our visit.

12th month, 7th – May I be enabled so to give an account of the various dealings of the Almighty with me and mine, that it may be useful to some, at least to my most beloved children and children's children. I have to begin with rather a melancholy tale: – My beloved children, Foster and Richenda Reynolds, lost their sweet baby upon the 4th of last month, after a few days severe illness. Death is awful and affecting, come as it may, and this I truly felt, when seeing the sweet babe in its coffin, still retaining its beautiful colour. I could not but feel the uncertainty of all our possessions, yet the comfort, that death had only entered our family and taken one for whom we could feel no fear for the future. At her grave, the desire was very strong within me, that we might all become like little children, fit to enter the kingdom of God, being washed and made white in the blood of the Lamb. Since then, my dear nephew Harry Buxton has been called hence. His end appeared in no common degree peace, if not joy in the Lord. He was about seventeen years of age – a remarkable instance of the care and religious instruction of parents being blessed; he was greatly protected through life, from any evil influences, and more carefully and diligently instructed by his dear mother, particularly in all religious truth. He was a child, who in no common degree appeared to be kept from evil, and live in the fear and love of the Lord; he was cheerful, industrious, clever, very agreeable, and of a sweet person – a very deep trial it is to his dear parents to lose him. Still I feel as if I could give up all my sons to be in such a state, but I may be mistaken in this, and perhaps my Lord may yet be pleased, to raise them up to His service here below, which would be even a greater blessing than having them taken in the morning of the day. I think the way in which the children of my sisters turn out proves the efficacy of much religious instruction, and not too much religious restraint. It certainly is a very serious thing, to put upon young persons any crosses in their religious course, that Christ does not call them to bear!

1st month, 11th, 1831 – When dressing, last First day fortnight, A– came in to tell me, that my dear and valued uncle Joseph Gurney had suddenly dropped down dead at his house at the Grove, near Norwich, my aunt only with him at the time. It exceedingly affected me, for he was very dear to me, and more like a father than any one living; he was one in whom the religious life was beautifully manifested, more particularly in his humility, in his cheerfulness and in his obedience. He was a lively minister of the gospel, a valuable and a delightful man, and his loss is indeed very great to those nearest to him as well as to many others. I had a painful struggle to know whether I ought to go to his funeral or not. However, I decided to go, in which I felt peace, and then could leave it all comfortably.

I have seldom of late felt more discouraged from a deep sense of the evil of my own heart, than when I first arrived at Earlham. There are times, when with my brothers and sisters particularly, the contrast of my circumstances with theirs pains me; the mode of my feeling these things oppressed me. I walked alone through some beautiful parts of Earlham, and how did it remind me of days that are past! The sun shone brightly, and hardly a tree, a walk, or a view, but brought interesting remembrances before me; how many gone! how many changes! and then how far was I ready for my great change? It was New Year's Day; little did I expect to keep it there. I returned home, wrote to my husband and children, and poured out a little of my heart to them. I went to the Grove – felt my much-loved uncle being really gone – all changed there. I went to Norwich to call on a few sick, &c.; the place the same, but again how changed to me! However, as my dearest family assembled, I became more comfortable.

Upton, 2nd month, 12th – I returned last evening from Earlham with my dear brother Joseph, having been suddenly called into Norfolk, in consequence of my dearest Rachel's alarming illness. I heard of it late on Second-day week, and set off to her on the Third-day morning: the snow so great, I was stopped on the road, and slept at Ely. Upon my arrival at Lynn the next day, I found my child going on favourably. The pleasure is great of having with my children the double tie, not only of mother and children, but a friendship formed upon its own grounds. I certainly think that in no common degree my children feel me their familiar friend.

5th month, 14th – About three weeks ago, I paid a very satisfactory visit to the Duchess of Kent, and her very pleasing daughter, the Princess Victoria. William Allen went with me. We took some books, on the subject of slavery, with the hope of influencing the young princess in that important cause. We were received with much kindness and cordiality, and I felt my way open to express, not only my desire that the best blessing might rest upon them, but that the young princess might follow the example of our blessed Lord, that as she "grew in stature she might grow in favour with God and man". I also ventured to remind her of King

Josiah, who began to reign at eight years old and did that which was right in the sight of the Lord turning neither to the right hand nor to the left, which seemed to be well received. Since that, I thought it right to send the Duke of Gloucester my brother Joseph's work on the Sabbath, and rather a serious letter, and had a very valuable answer from him full of feeling. I have an invitation to visit the Duchess of Gloucester next Fourth-day; may good result to them, and no harm to myself, but I feel these openings rather a weighty responsibility, and desire to be faithful, not forward. I had long felt an inclination to see the young princess, and endeavour to throw a little weight in the right scale seeing the very important place that she is likely to fill. I was much pleased with her, and think her a sweet, lovely and hopeful child.

The Yearly Meeting begins next week; I am rather low in the prospect, having no house to receive my dear friends in London, continues to be a pain to me. I desire to attend it in all humility, looking to my Lord, and not unto man; I desire to be kept in the unity of those with whom I am in religious communion, for I am one with them in principle; but we must forbear with each other in love, and endeavour through every trial of it, "to keep the unity of the Spirit and the bond of peace".

6th month, 3rd – The Yearly Meeting concluded this day week. I was highly comforted by the good spirit manifested in it by numbers. I think I never was so much satisfied by the ground taken by Friends, leading us to maintain what we consider our testimonies upon a scriptural and Christian ground, rather than because our forefathers maintained them. My opinion is, that nothing is so likely to cause our Society to remain a living and spiritual body, as its being willing to stand open to improvement because it is to be supposed that as the Church generally emerges out of the dark state it was brought into, its light will shine brighter and brighter, and we, as a part of it, shall partake of this dispensation. My belief is, that neither individuals nor collective bodies should stand still in grace, but their light should shine brighter and brighter unto the perfect day. My dearest brother Joseph had a valuable Meeting for the youth, further to instruct them in Friends' principles, which delighted me; he was so clear, so sound, so perfectly scriptural and Christian, and so truly in the spirit of charity and sound liberality, not laxity.

6th month, 25th – I must give an account of the British Society Meeting. It was, I trust, well got through, and I feel the way in which its objects prosper cause for humble thankfulness. Surely the result of our labour has hitherto been beyond my most sanguine expectation, as the improved state of our prisons, female convict ships, and the convicts in New South Wales. I desire to feel this blessing and unmerited mercy towards us, and those poor creatures, as I ought, in humility and true thankfulness of heart.

The day before yesterday, I had a very satisfactory interview with the Queen and several of the Royal Family, in rather a remarkable manner. There was a sale on account of the Hospital Ship in the River, in which I was interested; and hearing that the Queen was to be there, whom I wished to see, I went; but was so much discouraged when I arrived, by the gaiety of the occasion, that I should have turned back, had not my sister Catherine made me persevere. We saw the Queen and her party, and quickly passed through the gay scene. When we got out, we found ourselves with a valuable friend of mine, Captain Young, in a quiet airy place, at the head of the staircase; we were told by him, that the Queen would go down that way, and we should have an excellent view of her. We therefore waited until some of the royal family came down; their carriages not being ready, they withdrew into a private room, where Captain Young admitted us; the Duchess of Gloucester met me with her usual kindness, and presented me to the Duchess of Cumberland. The Princess sister to the Queen, Prince George of Cumberland and Prince George of Cambridge were there with them. The Duchess of Gloucester soon withdrew, and the Queen's sister and I had rather a full conversation together with the Duchess of Cumberland and Prince George. Then came the Duke of Sussex and the Princess of Hesse Homburg; the Duke appeared pleased to see me, and we had a good deal of conversation, the Duke said he would present me to the Queen, who soon came into the room, with the Princess Augusta, whom I knew, he did so in the handsomest manner, and the Queen paid me very kind and marked attention. I had some conversation with the Queen, almost entirely on benevolent objects. I expressed my pleasure in seeing the Royal Family so much interested in these things; my belief that it did much good, and that being engaged in them brought peace and blessing. I was enabled to keep to my simple mode of speech as I believe right, and yet to show them every respect and polite attention. I did not enter religious subjects with any of them, though I trust the bearing of my conversation was that way. We spoke with the Princess Elizabeth, of Friends, of the love her father George III had for them, his visit to our great-grandfather Barclay, my meeting Queen Charlotte in the city and many other things.

My dearest sister Catherine's simple boldness certainly got me into the room and made me go through the thing; her company was delightful, helpful and strengthening. It was a very singular opening, thus to meet those, some of whom I so much wanted to see. It is curious, but for days I had it on my mind to endeavour to see the Queen, and by night and day seriously had weighed it, lest my motives should not be right, but when I remembered, that from not having been presented to her, I could never on any point communicate with her in person, I felt that if there should be an opportunity to put myself in her way, I had better do it. It was striking, how the whole thing was opened for me. I may say providentially; for already I believe some good has been done by seeing one of the party, and I look upon it as a very important event in my public objects for the good of others.

Afterwards, I felt as I mostly do, after any thing of this kind, rather anxious, and extremely fearful for myself, how far it was safe for me thus to be cast among the great of this world, how far it was even right to put myself in the way of it, and how far others would judge me for it; however, the next day, my mind was much quieted, my fears much allayed, and my present sober view is, that it was a remarkable opening, and my desire is, that it may please the Most High to bless it that good may result from it. I lately have had a deeply interesting visit to a female convict-ship, surrounded as I am at such times by poor sailors, and convicts, it is impossible not to feel the contrast of the circumstances in which I am placed. The last time I was in the ship *Mary*, there was such a scene round me – parting from them, probably forever. So many tears were shed, so much feeling displayed – and almost all present the low and the poor. Then, within a few days to be in such a scene of gaiety, though the object in view was good, surrounded by royalty and the great of this earth. The contrast was striking and instructive. I ought surely to profit from the uncommon variety that I see, and the wonderful changes that I have experienced in being raised up, and cast down. Oh may it not prove in vain for myself and others.

12th month, 20th – I am once more favoured, after being far from well, with a renewal of health and power, to enter my usual engagements, public and private. Yesterday, I went to town, – first attended the Newgate Committee, then, the British Society, which was very encouraging to me; there were many present, of different denominations of Christians, and a sweet feeling of love and unity pervaded the whole. Elizabeth

171

Dudley spoke in a lively manner, and I had to pray. There is still much ground for encouragement in the prison cause, I believe a seed is sown in it, that will grow and flourish, I trust, when some of us are laid low. It is a work that brings with it a peculiar feeling of blessing and peace; may the Most High continue to prosper it!

Afterwards I went to Clapham to visit a poor dying converted Jew, who had sent a letter to beg me to go and see him; my visit was highly interesting. I often wish for the pen of a ready writer, and the pencil of an artist, to picture some of the scenes that I am brought into. A man of a pleasing countenance, greatly emaciated, lying on a little white bed, all clean and in order, his Bible by his side, and animated almost beyond description at seeing me; he kissed my hand, the tears came into his eyes, his poor face flushed, and he was ready almost to raise himself out of his bed. I sat down, and tried to quiet him, and by degrees succeeded. We had a very interesting conversation; he had been in the practice of frequently attending my readings at Newgate, apparently with great attention; latterly, I had not seen him, and was ready to suppose, that like many others, his zeal was of short duration, but I lately heard that he had been ill. He is one of those Jews who have felt perfectly liberated from keeping any part of the Law of Moses, which some other converted Jews yet consider themselves bound to observe. I found that when he used to come so often to Newgate, he was a man of good moral character, seeking the truth.

But to go on with my story – in our conversation, he said, that he felt great peace, no fear of death, and a full reliance upon his Saviour for salvation; he said that his visits to Newgate had been to him beyond going to any church – indeed, I little knew how much was going on in his heart. He requested me to read a Psalm that I had read one day in Newgate, the 107th. This I did, and he appeared deeply to feel it, particularly as my dear friends and I made our little remarks in Christian freedom as we went along, truly, I believe (as Friends say) in the life. The poor Jew prayed very strikingly; I followed him, and returned thanks; what a solemn, uniting time it was! The poor Jew said, "God is a spirit, and they that worship Him, must worship Him in spirit and in truth", as if he felt the spirituality of the Christian administration. His countenance lightened with apparent joy, when he expressed his undoubted belief that he should soon enter the kingdom, and that I should, before long, follow him; then he gave me his blessing, and took leave in much tenderness, showing every mark he could of gratitude and love. He did not accept any gift of money, saying, that he wanted no good thing, as he was most kindly provided for by serious persons in the neighbourhood.

1st month, 2nd, 1832 – I think I have seldom entered a year with more feeling of weight than this. As the clock was striking twelve, the last year closing and this beginning, I found myself on my knees by my bed-side, looking up to him who had carried me and mine through the last year, and could only really be our Helper in this. We have had the subject of marriage much before us this last year, it has brought us to some test of our feelings and principles respecting it. That it is highly desirable and important to have young persons settle in marriage, particularly young men, I cannot doubt, and that it is one of the most likely means of their preservation, religiously, morally and temporally. Moreover, it is highly desirable, to settle with one of the same religious views, habits and education, as themselves, more particularly for those, who have been brought up as Friends, because their mode of education is peculiar; but, if any young persons upon arriving at an age of discretion, do not feel themselves really attached to our peculiar views and habits, then, I think their parents have no right to use undue influence with them, as to the connexions they may incline to form, provided they be with persons of religious lives and conversation. I am of opinion, that parents are apt to exercise too much authority upon the subject of marriage, and that there would be more really happy unions, if young persons were more left to their own feelings and discretion. Marriage is too much treated like a business concern, and love, that essential ingredient, too little respected in it. I disapprove the rule of our Society, that disowns persons for allowing a child to marry one not a Friend – it is a most undue and unchristian restraint, as far as I can judge of it.

Upton, 2nd month, 21st – We have lately been brought to feel very seriously the approach of the cholera to our own borders, as it is said to have been as near as Limehouse. I have not generally felt any agitating fear, but rather the weight of the thing, and desirous that it should prove a stimulus to seek more diligently after eternal things, and to be ready spiritually for whatever may await us; and outwardly to use all proper precautions. I have desired earnestly, that we should do our very utmost to protect our poor neighbours, by administering to their many wants. This led me to make some efforts with some of our women Friends, also with some other kind and influential people, and although perhaps thought by some a busybody in it, yet more has been already accomplished than I could have looked for. The poor are likely to be really helped and cared for. In such works of charity, I always desire to be preserved from a forward spirit, or an over active one, yet on the other hand, when I feel any thing laid upon me, as I did in this instance, I feel much bound to work in it, even through some discouragement and opposition; I mostly find in such cases, that way has been made for me, as if He, who called me to the work, was indeed with me in it.

I was too poorly to go to our Monthly Meeting to-day, which I do not much regret, as our dearest son Joseph was to send in his resignation of membership; I so much feel it, that I think perhaps, I am better away. I believe he has done what he now thinks best; there I leave it, and though I certainly have much felt his leaving a Society I so dearly love, the principles of which I so much value, yet no outward names are in reality of much importance in my view, nor do I think very much of membership with any outward sect or body of Christians. My feeling is, that if we are but living members of the Church of Christ, this is the only membership essential to salvation. Belonging to any particular body of Christians has, I see, its disadvantages, as well as advantages, it often brings into the bondage of man, rather than being purely and simply bound to the law of Christ; though I am fully sensible of its many comforts, advantages and privileges. Earnestly do I desire for this dear child that his Lord may make his way clear before him, that he may be truly here a member of the militant Church of Christ, and hereafter of His Church triumphant.

Upton Lane, 6th month, 3rd – We have just concluded the Yearly Meeting. It has been in some respects a marked one, and I hope an instructive one. We had much advice, particularly from one Friend, upon the subject of Christian faith holding up much more decidedly to our view, the doctrine of the Atonement, showing that our actuating motive in all things must be faith in Him who suffered for us and love for Him who first loved us. In this I quite agree, but I felt with her, as well as with some others, that they strain the point of all our minor testimonies being kept to, as a necessary proof of this love. I fully believe, that many of us are called thus to prove our love; but I also believe there are some, if not many amongst us, to whom this does not apply, and that we cannot, therefore, lay down the rule for others.

I had to speak decidedly twice in the Meetings; once in the first Meeting, acknowledging the loving-kindness and tender mercy of our God as

174

manifested to us during the year that was passed, and what an inducement it should be to love and faithfulness. This appeared greatly to relieve
and comfort many minds, for they freely spoke to me about it afterwards.
I had particularly to make allusion to the cholera not having made farther devastations amongst us. I had in another Meeting in a similar way
to return thanks, and pray for us, as a Society, and for the Universal
Church. I also had from a deep feeling of duty, to express my thankfulness, that the Christian standard had been upheld amongst us, so much
encouragement given to read the scriptures, and attend to their holy pre-
cepts; but I felt a fear, whether the influence of the Holy Spirit, as our
guide, had been quite enough dwelt upon, which, as a fundamental part
of our principles, I trusted we should ever maintain. I also expressed my
desire, that the fruits of the Spirit should be more manifest amongst us,
not only in our peculiar testimonies, but in the subjection of our tempers
and wills, which I thought to be much wanted, fearing that some maintained our testimonies, more from expediency than principle, which produced great inconsistency of conduct. I then added my earnest hope, that
individually and collectively, we should stand open to improvement,
making this our prayer: "That which I see not, teach Thou me"; that we
should be willing to be taught of God immediately and instrumentally,
that our light might shine brighter and brighter to the perfect day.

6th month, 9th – I yesterday was favoured to get through the British
Society Meeting. It was to me a very serious occasion; our different reports
were highly satisfactory and encouraging; but I felt it laid upon me to
speak so decidedly on some points, that I could not fully enjoy it. After the
British Society report was read, I first endeavoured to show the extreme
importance of the work in which we were engaged, and the best means
of producing the desired effect, of reforming the criminal; but what most
deeply impressed me was, considering the awful extent of existing crime,
and the suffering and sorrow produced by it – how far the conduct of
the higher classes may influence that of the lower, and tend in many ways
to the increase of evil, by ladies not setting a religious example to their
servants, nor instructing them in the right way; by not keeping the Sabbath
strictly, by very late hours, and attending public places, – by vanity in
dress, and by hurrying mantua-makers and milliners, and so causing
them to oppress and overwork their young women, by not paying their
bills themselves, or through some confidential person, but trusting them
to young or untried servants, thus leading to dishonesty on their parts,

or that of the tradespeople, – by allowing their maid-servants or char-women to begin to wash at unseasonable hours, and consequently to require ardent spirits to support them. Then I represented how much they might do to promote good and discourage evil, by educating the poor religiously in infant and other schools, by watching over girls after they leave schools, until placed in service, and by providing for them suitable religious, instructive and entertaining books; also, by forming libraries in hospitals, and workhouses, and by preventing the introduction of irreligious and light books. I also urged the establishment of district societies. These things I had forcibly and freely to express, showing the blessing of promoting good and the woe of encouraging evil.

To the gentleman who accompanied her son Gurney and his young companions on a tour of the continent, Elizabeth gave some written instructions, including the following

Never allow the boys to be out alone in the evening; nor to attend any public place of amusement with any person, however pressing they may be. I advise, thy seeing that they never talk when going to bed, but retire quietly after reading a portion of the holy scriptures. In the morning, that they be as quiet as possible, and learn their scripture texts, whilst dressing. I recommend the party accepting all suitable invitations from German families, as an important means of improving their general knowledge, as well as their German. It must be remembered that no study is equal to that of mankind, and nothing so likely to enlarge the mind as society with the good and the cultivated of every nation. I advise their taste for our best poets being encouraged, by occasionally learning some by heart, and reading it aloud. Also, their being led particularly to observe and admire all the productions of nature, and to study geology, &c., &c., as far as their time will admit of it.

Above all things, and far beyond every other consideration, mayst thou be enabled to teach them, that the first and great object of life is, to seek the kingdom of God and to do His will.

Returning from a journey in the ministry in Ireland she writes:

9th month, 18th – I felt, amongst Friends in Ireland, as if my service was to lead them from all external dependence, either on their membership in the Society, their high profession or their peculiar testimonies, and to show, that these things are only good as they spring from simple Christian faith and practice, and avail nothing, unless the heart be really changed and cleansed from sin, though I believed that these things would follow as the result to those who fill the important place in the church, that in my opinion, Friends are called to occupy. Above everything else, I endeavoured to lead all to the grand foundation of Christian faith and practice. My dear sister was much led in the same line of ministry.

On some occasions, I felt a far greater openness than others. I believe, in places, there was rather a jealousy over me, I apprehend that my believing it right, as much as possible, to avoid mysticism in my mode of expression, is not fully understood by all Friends; I desire to be sound, simple, and clear, and not to clothe anything in a mysterious garb, even if with individuals it might give it more weight. The unfeigned kindness shown me by several persons can never be forgotten by me.

It is proposed, that my dear son William's marriage should take place in little more than a week. I cannot help feeling deeply giving him up. To have this dear child married, and not be able to be with him, is very affecting to me. With three children likely to marry out of the Society, and the life of one of them very uncertain, I have much, very much to feel; but respecting her and all of my children, if they do but get to the kingdom, I may be thankful! And shall I hold them back? My desires are unutterable, my prayers frequent and fervent, to be directed amidst all my difficulties, to do that which is right, – first in the sight of God, then in the view of my family, and lastly in that of the Society to which I belong.

Dagenham, 10th month, 3rd – Here am I sitting in solitude, keeping silence before the Lord; on the wedding day of my beloved son William. As I could not conscientiously attend the marriage, I believed it right to withdraw for the day. Words appear very inadequate to express the earnestness – the depth of my supplications for him and for his – that the blessing of the Most High may rest upon them. I was yesterday enabled, when with him and his sisters alone, to pour forth my soul in prayer for him, and read such portions of scripture as I thought would be for his good and comfort; he was low, and so we were all, but as the day advanced, we brightened, and as dear William himself said, there appeared a spirit of good over us. I stayed with him almost all day, and went in the evening with him to Ham House, where their kindness was almost unbounded. We then went to our dear friends the Pellys, where I had a warm reception; they very sweetly bear with my scruples, for it must appear odd, very odd to them, my not feeling it right to attend the wedding of such a son – but my heart is full of love to them.

Though I do not see as they see, I most deeply feel that all who truly love Him are one in Christ, yet the more simple and spiritual the administration of religion, the more I believe we are enabled to abide in Him, therefore I feel zealous, perhaps too much so, to have my children thorough Friends; but of this I now see little or no hope, though I expect many of them to be serious in another line, and fully believe, that my striving and labours have been blessed, in leading them to a love of holiness and true righteousness, and beyond all of their Saviour. We concluded the evening in quietness, and strange to say, I slept well and peacefully. This morning, we almost all assembled before breakfast, with one or two valuable dependants and William Champion Streatfeild with us; I was enabled to exhort earnestly, and to pray fervently, not only for the beloved couple, but all the children, and those who were to be, or were already united to them, and for their children; for ourselves, household, &c. It was a very solemn time, and I humbly trust that the presence of the Lord was with us. I desired also to return thanks for this dear son in giving him up from my care, that he had been so much preserved from the evil which is in the world, that he had ever displayed such near love to me and to all of us, and had been so good a son to us. There is much to be thankful for respecting him, and though it has been a great disappointment his not marrying a Friend, yet there is also much to value in this connexion. I have a secret hope it may prove in the ordering of a kind Providence for his good.

Upton Lane, 11th month, 5th – Last Fourth-day, the 1st of the Tenth Month, my dearest Hannah was married to William Champion Streatfield. The morning was bright, the different families collected, – of course I was not present at the ceremony. The bride and bridegroom went to Ham House to take leave of their dear party; they then came home, and we soon sat down to breakfast, about thirty in number. There appeared a serious and yet cheerful feeling over us. I felt prayer for them, but saw no opportunity vocally to express it. As we arose to leave the table, William Streatfield, the vicar of East Ham, returned thanks for the blessings received; when, quite unexpectedly to myself, there was such a solemn silence, as if all were arrested, that I was enabled vocally to ask a blessing upon them. After a short further pause, we withdrew, walked in the garden, or rested, until they left us. The tears often flowed from my eyes in parting from this beloved child.

7th month, 10th, 1833 – We have been favoured the last two days, to have all our fifteen children around us, and the day before yesterday, we had all to dine at our table, and our nine grandchildren afterwards at dessert, our dearest sister Catherine Gurney, the only other person present at table. It was a deeply interesting, and to me touching as well as pleasing sight. It is remarkable, their none fully seeing religious truth with me, yet I cannot repine, if I may but see real marks of the Christian life. Outwardly, through all our difficulties, I could not but feel how all have been provided for, and a liberal table spread before us. The married children all provided for, some abundantly – the grandchildren generally bringing up so well, is a great cause of thankfulness – I could not rejoice or give thanks as I desired, at our many unmerited mercies, but I felt bowed in spirit under a sense of them. We had a cheerful dinner, Rachel, the only one really out of health at this time; but she enjoyed herself. After dinner, we walked a little about, then had tea. After tea, we read the 103rd Psalm, and I spoke to my children, earnestly impressing upon them the importance, now most of them were no longer under our restraint, that they might be conformed to the will of God, and be faithful stewards of His manifold gifts, so that if we went by different ways, we might in the end meet, where there will be no partition walls, no different ways, but all love, joy, peace and union of view and of conduct. I blessed them, and most earnestly prayed for all. We then separated in much near love.

Jersey, 10th month, 12th – Since I last wrote, I have visited the islands of Guernsey, Sark, and Herm, accompanied by my husband, and part of the time by my sister and Rebecca Sturges; my children with us when in Guernsey, and my kind and valued servant, C. Golder. It has been a full tide of engagements, with here and there, by the way, a little rest and recreation, although but little. I have deeply and weightily felt two very large Public Meetings in Guernsey, one by invitation, one not. In both of them I think we were much helped to express our concern towards the people; but holding such Meetings, goes to the very extent of what I apprehend women are called to in public service. I view it very differently from ministering in their own assemblies, and I have often thought it rather too lightly entered into; although at times, I believe it is called for. I feel peculiarly bound, when I do hold these great and important meetings, simply to preach the gospel and its practice, more particularly the importance of the unity of all members of the Church of Christ, of every denomination. This I have much to press upon in these islands. In the small island of Sark, with about five hundred inhabitants, they are quite divided religiously, about half of them Methodists, and half members of the Church of England. They will hardly speak to each other. I tried to use influence, and trust it may not be in vain. In the island of Herm, there is neither school nor place of worship; but there appears to be there, a most providential opening for forming a school, – a young lady willing to live on this desolate island, and devote herself to educating the poor. May the Lord be with her, and bless her in this undertaking! Our visit appeared to make way for this opening. In Guernsey, I think some grievous evils are likely to be remedied in the prison, in time; I have also recommended some alterations in the hospital, which is a very large and important institution. A District Society will be probably established, I trust to the great benefit of the poor.

A letter to one of her daughters

I feel in the first place, earnestly desirous that thou shouldest think as little as possible of thy nervous feelings. I know how extremely painful they are, but experience has taught me, the less I think of them the better. It is most important to look upon them as much as possible like the toothache – that it must be endured while it lasts, but is not dangerous in its nature. As for the discoloured view the imagination may at the time give to things, nothing is more important than to set it down as a clear and fixed thing in the mind, that whilst this nervousness lasts it is not sound, and must not be believed or taken heed to. I would not have thee discouraged at this return of it. I believe I never had death brought home very closely, without being brought into a low nervous state, it is after all, so awful; though I increasingly see, that this is real weakness, and that those who are believers in the Lord Jesus, however unworthy, need not fear it, as through Him, its plague and sting will be done away. But it is folly in one sense to look ahead, we have enough to do to seek for help and grace for the present time to do our present day's work. When the day comes that we have to give up "this mortal life", we may and ought humbly to trust, that through the unmerited mercy and love of our Lord, His grace will be found sufficient for us. I observe, for my great encouragement, that what we call nervousness often proves no common blessing, if made a right use of, and not given way to. It so wonderfully humbles, prevents the crea-ture glorying, and makes willing to do any thing to come to that peace, which quiets every storm. Thy uncles and aunts have nearly all been strik-

180

ing instances of this, and I believe hard, very hard as it is to bear, it is a baptism to fit for a fulness of joy and glory rarely partaken of, but it in no common degree calls for patience. I always think both David and Paul largely partook of this sort of humbling experience. Therefore, my dear child, if tried this way, possess thy soul in patience, and look upon it as a suitable, though bitter medicine, prescribed by the Physician of value to promote thy health and cure.

I am thy most tenderly attached mother,

Elizabeth Fry

Upton, 4th month, 12th, 1834 – At Portsmouth, we paid an interesting visit to the Haslar Hospital, the Hulks Hospital Ship, and some prisons; we also paid a delightful little visit to the Isle of Wight. I felt more able to enjoy the great beauties of nature, from having been owned by my Lord and Master, in my religious services. What a relish does true religion give for our temporal as well as spiritual blessings! I have still much to feel respecting the offer of marriage made to my dear Louisa. It is a very serious thing, my children thus leaving Friends, and I have my great fears, that in so doing, they are leaving that which would be a blessing and preservation to them. At the same time, I see there is no respect of persons with God; nor in reality is there the difference some would make out in the different administrations of religion, if there be but a true, sincere love of our Lord, and endeavour to serve Him. What is above all to me, I have felt peace in it rather peculiarly. Still, we at present are exceedingly feeling the weight of the affair; it is also a considerable pain to me to go through the discipline of the Society respecting it – but in bearing it patiently and humbly, I may in that way be enabled to preach Christ.

4th month, 21st – Yesterday (First-day) I attended Meeting, rather oppressed in body and mind. Ministered to by dear Elizabeth Dudley, but had such heaviness of body as to hinder spiritual revival. In the afternoon I went, accompanied by Elizabeth Dudley, Rebecca Sturges, and some others, to visit the female convict ship; the sun shone brightly, the day delightful, the poor women rejoiced to see us, but my spirit was in heaviness, from the difficulty of leaving my family, even for a few hours, on that day. It was a fine sight to see about one hundred and fifty poor female convicts, and some sailors, standing, sitting, and leaning round us, whilst we read the scriptures to them. I spoke to them, and Elizabeth Dudley prayed. Surely to witness the solemn effect, the tears rolling down many

181

cheeks, we must acknowledge it to be the Lord's doing; still I felt flat, though the others thought it a very satisfactory time, but in the evening I became more revived and comforted and thankful that it has pleased the Lord to send me to the poor outcasts, although at times feeling as if I went more as a machine moved by springs than in the lively state I desire; but at other times it is different, and there is much sense of light, life, love and power.

To-day I expect to go to the Duchess of Gloucester, and amongst some of the high in this life. May the Lord be with me, that my intercourse with these may not be in vain in Him. I feel it no light responsibility, having the door so open with the Government of our country and those filling high places, I am often surprised to find how much so; and yet the Lord only knows the depth of my humiliations, and how it has been out of the depths, that I have been raised up for these services. At the Admiralty, I have lately had important requests granted; at the Home Office, they are always ready to attend to what I ask; and at the Colonial Office, I expect that they will soon make some alterations in the arrangements for the female convicts in New South Wales.

A few days ago I visited Plashet – it was almost too much for my natural spirits. When I saw our weedy walks, that once were made and kept up so neatly; our summer-houses falling down; – our beautiful wild flowers, that I had cultivated with so much care, and no one to admire them – the place that had cost us so much and been at times so enjoyed by us, the birth-place of so many of my children, the scene of so many deep and near interests – the tears trickled down my face, and I felt ready to enumerate my sorrows, and say, "Why is this?" But I felt the cheek within, and desired and endeavoured to look on the bright side of the picture, and acknowledge the tender and unmerited mercy of my God, in Christ Jesus.

5th month, 5th – Yesterday was the Sabbath. I can hardly say how deeply I feel these days as they come, first, as it respects the ministry of the word. It wholly resting on two or three women in our rather large assembly, is an exercise of my faith, and a real trial to my natural feelings; then to believe, as I do, that some of our congregation are in an unregenerate state, how must their silent meetings be passed? And for the babes in Christ I have great fears, inasmuch as true, solemn, silent worship, is a very high administration of spiritual worship. I frequently fear for such, that more external aid is wanted, though I see not how it is to be given. I also feel the want of each one openly uniting in some external act of worship, for there is much in taking an absolute part in what is doing, to feel a full interest in it, but I see not with our views (in which I unite) how this can be remedied. Then for myself, as a minister of the Gospel, I desire to be very faithful, and give the portion of meat in due season to the household; but even here, deep humiliation is my portion, in its appearing, that though I preach to others, I cannot manage my own – my children, one after another, leaving a Society and principles that I love, value, and try to build up. My Lord only knows the exercise of my spirit on those days. Then for my home hours, not having space as we had at Plashet, in which my boys can recreate in the way I consider advisable, during part of this day; now, I have anxiously to watch where they go, and what they are about, so that I am not often favoured to know the Sabbath a delight, or day of rest; yet through all these things, and my too anxious nature, help is wonderfully granted to me. I find the spring within that helps, keeps, revives, sustains, and heals, but I feel that I am bound to seek, and to pray not to be so exquisitely anxious.

6th month, 10th – Since I last wrote, I have got through the Yearly Meeting, which I attended nearly throughout. There appeared to me much more apparent love and unity than last year, still it is a serious and shaking time, and some of the Leaders of our Tribes think they differ in some points of doctrine; but I believe it is more in word than in reality, and as they love the Lord Jesus, if they have wandered a little, they will be brought back. I was a good deal engaged, having to take a quiet view, neither on one side nor the other, but seeing the good of both, but I have a very great fear of ever being too forward, a thing I very much dislike and disapprove. May my Lord preserve me from it. I was favoured to get well through the British Society Meeting, and could not but return thanks that our Holy Head had so blessed this work.

With respect to my dear Louisa's engagement of marriage, I have apprehended that the hand of the Lord is in it, and oh! saith my soul, may it prove so. The pain of her leaving our Society, and the steps attending it, have begun to the wounding of my spirit; for though I do not set much value on outward membership in any visible church, yet it has its pains, at times great pains to me, and I am ready to say, in my heart, How is it? When I have one after another of my family thus brought before our Meeting, it has its trials and humiliations. It would be to me a pleasanter, and I think a more satisfactory thing, if the discipline of our Society had not so much of the inquisitorial in it, and did not interfere in some things that I believe no religious body has a right to take a part in; it leads, I think, to undesirable results. Though I approve persons being disowned for marrying out of our Society, I had rather the act of marriage in itself forfeited membership.

I feel it cause for deep and humble thankfulness to see the happiness of my son and his wife; I feel it also a fresh proof in the important step of marriage, how well it is for young persons to choose for themselves, provided there is no insurmountable objection. Indeed, I have unusually felt comfort in my beloved children of late – beginning to partake of that enjoyment in them that I have all along hoped would one day be mine. May I be encouraged, with a thankful heart, to persevere in training up my younger ones in the Lord, and to trust for them, when walking in the slippery paths of youth – not to be too anxious about them; but earnestly seeking for help, strength, and direction in doing my duty towards them, there commit it. I have been unusually discouraged the last day or two, by two people taking a very decided part in things appertaining to our school at East Ham, and in our Newgate Committee. I have not felt them tender over me and my views, which were rather different to theirs; I felt a little roughly handled, but as I firmly believe they did not mean it, and as I attribute it much to their warm zeal, I have truly desired to take all in a humble Christian spirit; I mean to seek to be doubly and unusually kind to those who have hurt me, and admit no other than kind constructions upon all they have done.

I find in most things in the religious Society I belong to – in charities in education – I am so much disposed, from inclination and early habit, to take enlarged liberal ground, that perhaps watchfulness is needed, lest Christian liberty degenerate into laxity; but, oh! the love, the enlargement I feel towards all, at times, inexpressible – the deep unutterable sense I have of the largeness of the foundation, the fulness and real freedom of the Gospel, how it brings glad tidings to all who love the Lord and His righteousness, how it breaks down partition walls, how it unlooses heavy chains, and unlocks prison doors, how it enables us even to bear with the prejudices of our follow-mortals, and yield to them, if in so doing we do not hurt our own consciences.

8

"How the tide turns":
Difficulties with the Society and Joseph Gurney leaves for America, 1835–1840

Elizabeth Fry continued to feel out of sympathy with many in the Society of Friends as more of her children married out, although she rejoiced in her children's happiness and in her grandchildren. Her brother Joseph embarked on a long journey in the ministry to America and she greatly missed his support. Although her popularity in Britain was waning, new opportunities opened as a result of her extensive travels on the continent.

2nd month, 8th, 1835 – The way appears opening with our present Ministers, to obtain libraries for all the Coast Guard Stations, a matter I have long had at heart. My desire is, to do all these things with a single eye to the glory of God, and the welfare of my fellow-mortals, and if they succeed, to pray that He, who alone can bless and increase, may prosper the work of my unworthy hands, and that I may ever wholly give the glory to Him to whom it is due, even my Lord and my God.

2nd month, 26th – The affairs of our Society cause me real anxiety and pain, and reconcile me in measure to so many of my children leaving Friends. Though it is painful and humbling in my own Meeting, my children's names being on the books only for disownment, yet I deeply feel my Lord is still with me and mine and my trust is, that He is working in a "mysterious way His wonders to perform" amongst us. I have a very strong sense of His mercy and pity towards us, and the wonderful loving kindness already shown us in heights and in depths, in riches and in poverty, in strength, and in weakness.

Upton, 6th month, 10th – Alone in my little room, my whole family gone to Church to the wedding [*of her daughter Louisa to Raymond Pelly*]. I feel solitary, but I believe my Lord is with me. Oh gracious Lord!

at this moment be with my child; pour out Thy Spirit upon her, that she may not only make solemn covenant with her husband, but with her God. Help her to keep these covenants, be with, help, and bless her and hers. Grant enough of this world's goods, but above all, far above all, grant them durable riches and righteousness; that joy and peace, which the world can neither give nor take away. Not that I am worthy, to ask for these blessings, but I ask them for the sake of Him, who is our rightousness; and through whom, Thou showest Thy tender mercy towards us. Amen, and Amen.

6th month, 13th – I can hardly express what the desire and prayer of my heart was on the wedding-day, that it might be rightly spent, and that a blessing might be with us, and all our mercies, remembered and acknowledged. I think this was a good deal the case; they returned from Church, soon after I wrote in my little room. The party appeared cheerful, peaceful and soberminded; the dear grand-children, many of them with us, looking truly lovely, they had their wedding meal, a sweet group round a table with some other children. We sat down about fifty at our table, we had fifteen of our children, my sister Catherine, and my sister Buxton, the bridegroom's family, and a few of our dear and valued friends. I have seldom seen a more lovely party, or apparently in a sweeter spirit; really quite a delightful and beautiful sight. I felt that I could not let the party separate, without some expression of my deep feeling, my pleasure, and satisfaction in our table being so surrounded; my gratification at the interest shown for the bride and bridegroom, and ourselves – and my desire, that this fresh union with our friends and neighbours might be blessed indeed to us all; then my prayer for our dear young people, that they might walk with a perfect and upright heart before the Lord, that they might be of good comfort, be of one mind, live in peace, and that the God of love might be with them even unto the end. I also expressed, that I had remembered in my prayers those members of the family that were afar off – that grace, mercy and peace might be with them! We then broke up, and wandered a little about until our dear bride and bridegroom left us. After which, our party dispersed, but an uncommon feeling of love, sweetness, peace, and blessing appeared to me to rest upon us, for which as a token for good, I desire, very humbly and reverentially to return thanks.

Upton, 10th month, 13th – I returned home yesterday with my dear husband, from a very affecting and unexpected visit into Norfolk, in consequence of the severe illness and death of my beloved sister Mary Gurney, my brother Joseph's amiable, devoted, and superior wife. She was in the prime of her day, only thirty-two years of age, a spiritually minded and lively minister, a very intellectual person, and highly cultivated, generous, and remarkably cheerful, a wonderful helper to my brother, adapted to his wants. When I heard how ill she was, I could hardly believe she would die, she had such an apparent call here below, but our ways are not the Lord's ways, nor our thoughts His thoughts. He took her thus early to Himself, but we apprehend, as the shock of corn fully ripe. Our dearest Joseph's resignation and patience are great indeed, and his even cheerful acquiescence to the will of his God is instructive. The funeral was deeply affecting. After dinner we had an extraordinary time. Our dear brother Francis Cunningham prayed, his dear Richenda spoke. Joseph in the most striking manner enlarged on the character of the departed, on his loss, and his consolation, the day went on and ended well, in a reading with the poor neighbours; but words fail me to tell of the solemn, holy, loving feeling over us. Oh! what a blessing is family unity in the Lord – my children who were present, and many others were deeply and powerfully impressed. May it be lasting – may the same spirit that has so remarkably rested upon us, rest on them, the same love, the same peace, the same unity of spirit, the same freeness of spiritual communication. Such a day is almost like being raised above the things of this world; all appeared sanctified, all blessed, even the very beauties of the place. How did I feel called upon to entreat, and to warn, how did I seek to bear testimony to the very truth – and how did dearest Joseph in his affliction beseech all to come to Christ, for salvation.

12th month, 11th – I returned last evening from a visit to my dear brother Joseph, who was so very low and unwell, that I was unexpectedly sent for; my visit was interesting and I trust satisfactory.

Upton Lane, 1st month, 1836 – I have had a hope that the last year has, notwithstanding all our shortcomings, drawn some near to God; but may we all remember, that we cannot stand still in our religious course, and if we do not go forward, there is very great danger of going backward. I have felt unusually bound to encourage all my most tenderly beloved family, to a full and entire surrender of themselves, to the service of the best of Masters, to be willing to be taught of Him, by His Holy Spirit, through the Scriptures, and through the dealings of our Heavenly Father towards us. I want all my children to partake of the same delightful spiritual union that we have partaken of, as a family, that they may be each other's joy in the Lord. I desire in our intercourse with each other, that we should increasingly partake, not only of temporal enjoyments, but also of intellectual pleasures, and above all, of spiritual communion, which gives so lively a relish to all the gifts of God. As to outward religious callings, at present, there appears some diversity amongst us; sweet as it would be to me, to have some led in the same path as myself, yet I may in truth say, my first desire is, that my dearest children may seek to be of God, in Christ Jesus (as it is easier to join ourselves to a sect than to be joined to Christ), and may know their Lord's will respecting them, may seek to be conformed to it, may be fully persuaded in their own minds, and then hold fast, very fast, that which is good; that here, they each may fill their ranks in righteousness, as followers of a crucified Lord, and eventually through Him, be saved with an everlasting salvation. Amen.

Upton Lane, 5th month, 13th – I returned home safely yesterday afternoon [*from another visit to Ireland*]. I think I never had so happy and so prosperous an arrival – I wept with joy; the stream appears to be turned for a while, my tears have often flowed for sorrow, and now my beloved husband and children have caused them to flow for joy. I found not only all going on well, and having done so during my absence, but to please, comfort and surprise me, my dearest husband had had my rooms altered and made most comfortable, and my children had sent me nice presents to render them more complete. Their offerings of love quite gladdened my heart, though far too good for me; I felt utterly unworthy of them, I may say peculiarly so. I have seldom returned home more sensible of the hidden evils of my heart. Circumstances have unusually made me feel this. I fully believe in this going out, much help has been granted me in various ways; my understanding has appeared to be enlightened more fully to see and comprehend gospel truth, and power has been given me to utter it boldly beyond what I could have supposed. The fear of man was much taken away in Ireland, when I had to tell them what I believed to be home truths. I may say I am brought down under a very deep feeling of utter unworthiness; and earnestly desire and pray, that whatever of our labours have been acceptable in the sight of our heavenly Father, they may be truly blessed to many, and not be in vain in Him; and that whatever may have been in any way not according to His will, that He would in His own power prevent any harm from it arising to others.

6th month, 12th, First-day morning – We yesterday had our British Society Meeting, and it was striking to me to observe, how much our various labours had been blessed, and to hear how many poor women from various parts have been induced to forsake their evil courses, and are now either leading good lives, or have died happy Christian deaths.

6th month, 18th – I have felt a good deal pressed in spirit, these last few days. The day before yesterday I counted twenty-nine persons who came here, on various accounts, principally to see me; there are times, when the tide of life is almost overpowering. It makes me doubtful, as to our remaining much longer in this place, which, from its situation brings so many here. I have several things which rather weightily press me just now. I desire to lay my case before the Lord, trusting in Him, and casting myself and my whole care upon Him.

Jersey, 8th month, 6th – My husband and I have been here rather more than a week. I left home on Fourth-day, the 27th, accompanied by my dear sister Gurney, leaving my husband and the rest of the party to follow on Sixth-day, because I believed it my duty to attend the Quarterly Meeting at Alton, in my way to Southampton. In tender mercy, I was permitted to part from my beloved family in peace, in love, and in good hope that our Heavenly Father would bless and protect them. On Second-day, before leaving home, we had our dear children and grandchildren, for a sweet cheerful evening, drinking tea and having strawberries, in the garden, a little farewell frolic – it was a lovely sight. From Alton, I proceeded to Southampton, where we all met, and were favoured with a favourable passage till early in the morning, when so awful a fog came on, just as we were in the midst of the rocks, between Alderney and Guernsey, that the Captain and the crew appeared to be much alarmed. We all felt it very seriously, and I experienced something of my own infirmity and fearful nature, still I was quiet, and I think trustful. It was delightful once more to see land, and to have the sun shine upon us. I can hardly express the feeling. We were detained about four hours in this fog. I must describe our arrival, the sun breaking out, showing us the Island of Guernsey, Herm and Sark. Castle Carey, the place of our destination, on the top of the hill, surrounded by trees, looking beautiful, we met with the most cordial reception from our friends and their children – the place delightful, my room commanding the finest view of the sea and islands, our comforts abundant, far above our deserts.

I had apprehended, previously to leaving home, that I should feel it a duty to visit the island of Alderney, but I became discouraged, the danger of the sea having been so much brought home to me, and the passage being very difficult. But I found upon weighing the subject, that I was not satisfied to omit it, and therefore if a favourable opening occurred, resolved to make the effort, and to go on Fourth-day, the 11th. We tried for a conveyance in vain, till the very morning, when we found a vessel going. The sun shone brilliantly, the wind fair; every thing prospered our setting off, and we appeared to have the unity of all our party. My beloved husband, Edmund Richards, Sophia Mourant, and myself. We had a very favourable voyage, though these little sailing vessels are unpleasant to me, and give me an uncomfortable sensation. We arrived at this curious island, which is rocky, wild, not generally cultivated, covered in parts with a carpet of lovely wild flowers, and scantily inhabited by an interesting people. No inn of course, but we had a very nice lodging, where we might truly say, we wanted for no real comfort, so the Lord doth provide. I was low and poorly, the first part of our visit; but like the fog on the voyage, my cloudy state was suddenly dispersed, as from a ray of the Sun of Righteousness. We held some meetings, we also formed a Ladies' Charity to visit the poor, we proposed sending a library, and Edmund Richards formed a temperance society. We were received with great kindness, by numbers of the people, and by Major Baines the Governor, and his wife. We found no opportunity for our departure at the time we had proposed leaving Alderney, and were literally confined there, until the end of the following week, when the way appeared to be as clear to return as it had been to go. A vessel to take us – the wind fair, and the sun bright. We arrived safely at Castle Carey, on the evening of the 24th of the Seventh Month, and found good accounts from home, and from the party who had preceded us to Jersey; thanks be to my Heavenly Father! My too anxious and fearful mind having been disposed to much anxiety. I had not much public service in Guernsey. Meetings as usual on First-day. I went to see many families of Friends and others, and besides some of the poor, visited the Hospital, and urged the great need of a Lunatic Asylum. The evening before our departure, I had a very solemn Public Meeting, with many interesting persons, afterwards several joined us at Castle Carey, where we had a time of much interest, pleasantly partaking of natural friendship; afterwards we were read to by a clergyman, and then I had a very solemn occasion of thanksgiving and prayer, greatly doubting my ever seeing most of their faces again. The next morning,

John and Matilda Carey, their children, the clergyman, and our friends the Richards, all accompanied us to the shore, some went with us in a boat to the ship, which I entered in peace and comfort, under the belief, that I had been in my right allotment in that island, and Alderney. We had a beautiful passage here, calm, and lovely weather, and had the blessing of finding the party well.

Jersey, 11th, 8th month, 1836

My dearest John and Rachel,

The account received from yourselves to-day is comforting to me, only I could be rather mortified that my many letters have never reached you. I hope you will see my last to Gurney and Mary which so much describes our proceedings. I wrote a long one to all my daughters knowing you were at Southend. I sent it to Chenda but I think I particularly requested you might have it. However, this I know, I write so much in the hope of satisfying and pleasing all that I affront my party here who say they seldom have me with them I am so much in my attic writing. Our visit to the Island is on many accounts very pleasant, our country excursions delightful. Nathaniel is taking the tour of the Island and we go a certain distance of the coast twice a week or more to the beautiful and varied Bays. We take our dinner with us and the plan here is often to take it in the small barouche [*four-wheeled carriage*] in different parts of the coast. Philip Barton & his wife generally accompany us.

I hope you will read my account of our lodgings, dogs so very near to us and our expeditions, in my letter sent to the boys, if not yet sent away which I carelessly ordered. The dog choosing to live with us and alarming us by his violent barking in the night, a house very near to us was robbed & about the same time, was at least a curious circumstance, for several evenings previous to the Robbery there some one came about 10 o'clock to try to intice the dog away. The weight I feel from your aunt Hoare's state & my strong drawings towards those at home rather casts a cloud over me or the loveliness of the country is very refreshing to me.

This week my first day was a full one visiting the Prison and hospital between and after meeting and finding the Prison in a shocking state showing the effect of the extremity of *sin*. Our third day we went to St. Ouen's Bay, a very fine sandy bay with five Martello towers round it. Some of us visited a poor man very ill who was so astonished to see us in that desolate place that he appeared to think us something beyond human and upon my giving him five shillings his surprise was really entertaining. He thought I must have something in return and said if you often do this you must fail. There is so little money they often barter with each other in Alderney almost entirely. I was not a little amused at the excessive pleasure at seeing me again of the poorer people. Though I cannot speak the language, we have found quite a friendship in my little calls and in one of my connections I have found a poor Jersey woman who appears quite a changed character since I used to read to her in the prison and from being a regular drunkard she is now a useful nurse in the Hospital.

Just to go on with my story after our visit to this large Bay, we all dined at a sort of public house belonging to one of the late General Le Cloutens's old servants. We found our dinner was two large chickens roast and four boiled, plenty of bacon, vegetables and a true Jersey pudding – a common sort of rich plum pudding about a yard round. How you would have smiled to see our set out. There is much very entertaining in our curious expeditions as we go a little out of the common course. Last 3rd day we joined Sir Matthew and Lady Blackeston at Gradelace where they have a very large party of agreeable people and after their collation in a barouche we all dispersed over the hills by the sea, then went to their beautiful place to tea on top of a hill with a most lovely view of the country & St. Ouen's Bay. We arrived at home about 10. Yesterday we went to dine at an old Jersey gentleman's, Major Papon. His place is below a sheer rocky hill, a beautiful house and garden and a fine view of the Bay below. All our party were Jersey families of the higher shot but still the whole thing was truly droll, the dinner rather curious and the different gentlemen making *formal* speeches after dinner, getting up and all and all keeping silence during the time, rather complimentary to the ladies present, particularly to the Benevolents as they called us. Today is Meeting Day we have now got a nice little room to ourselves so you would be much amused with our congregation.

So much for ourselves, now for what is much more interesting, you having taken the house in East Ham. May it prove the right place for you in every way & may It be the habitation of true peace to you, May the Lord lift up the light of his countenance upon you and help you in sending you enough outward prosperity to live comfortably, but above all sending you spiritual increase that all your blessings may be sustained. I am glad you have taken the place, though I never felt disposed to use any influence about it, feeling you were the best judges for yourselves. I hope that Kate liked her little presents –

My very dear love to you and your children.

Your tenderly attached Mother

EF

10th month, 2nd, First-day – On Second-day morning, when going into the Select Quarterly Meeting, with my brother Samuel, my son William came to tell us, that a serious accident had happened to my husband and daughter in Normandy. They had been thrown down a precipice, the carriage broken to pieces, and although they had experienced a very Providential deliverance, in their lives being spared, and no dangerous wound received, yet Katharine was so much hurt, and my dearest husband so much shaken, that they wished me to go to them immediately. I gave up the Quarterly Meeting of course, and set off with my much-loved son William to Dover, so as to cross by the first packet to France. I remembered my sorrow, and perhaps undue disappointment in not accompanying them to France. It seemed almost as if my Heavenly Father had heard my murmurings, as He heard the children of Israel in the Wilderness, and had taken me to France, when I did go against my inclination, alas! I received it also as a lesson to have but one prayer and desire in all things, "that the Lord's will be done on earth as it is in Heaven". The accident was most serious; such an escape, I think I never heard of, the carriage, in the first instance, fell with one horse (the driver and the other horse being separated from them before) about four yards perpendicularly; then the carriage was dragged down about twenty-six yards more. The poor peasants came to assist, and fetched the village doctor for the body, and the priest for the soul.

Calais, Ninth month, 26th, 1836.

My dearest John,

William and I reached Dover soon after twelve o'clock last evening. We were settled by one o'clock, and off about half-past seven this morning. Our journey was an anxious one, until as the evening advanced, I became more quieted, and trustful that all was ordered for us in mercy and wisdom. We had a very favourable passage of three hours; and to our great satisfaction, found your father looking for us on the quay. We found our dearest Kate exceedingly bruised and very grievously hurt altogether.

Your dear father looks, I think, shaken and aged by all that he has gone through. Mary has been a very attentive nurse. She looks also jaded, but from her excessive fright, when they were going down the hill, she knelt down and put her head on Katherine's lap, by which means her face was perfectly saved. And so I have at last touched French ground. William and I have not been idle; we have already visited the Prison and Hospital. We hope it may please Providence, in tender mercy to permit us all to arrive at home next Seventh-day, probably by a packet that leaves this place that morning for London.

Upton Lane, 10th month, 15th – William and I went one day to St. Omer, and stayed till the next. We had a very interesting expedition; his company was sweet to me. I was a good deal instructed as well as interested, in visiting the Roman Catholic charities. The sacrifice that must be made to give up the whole life as the Sisters of Charity do, to teach and bring up the poor children and attend to the sick in their hospitals, is very exemplary; and the slackness of some Protestants and coldness of too many led me to think, that whilst on the one hand the meritoriousness of good works may be unsoundly upheld by the Roman Catholics, yet, that it stimulates to much that is excellent, and a fear arose in my mind, that the true doctrine that teaches that we have no merit in any thing that we do, is either so injudiciously represented, or so misunderstood, that in too many cases it leads to laxity as to sin, and a want of diligence in works of righteousness and true holiness. I was much interested in attending High Mass, but here I thought I saw something of the work of true religion under what appeared to me, the rubbish of superstition and show. But I also thought, that much of the same thing remained amongst Protestants. I long to see true religion in its purity and simplicity, spread more and more to the glory of God and the peace of men.

We had a very interesting Quarterly Meeting yesterday, though the ministry of one dear friend tried me much in parts, more particularly her applying to us as a people, those blessed hopes and promises, that I apprehend simply belong to the members of the living Church of Christ, gathered out of all administrations and nations. I doubt not the living members of our body, from their first rise, have been in many instances bright and shining lights in their day, and have peculiarly had to uphold the simple pure spirituality of gospel truth; but I see no authority for our supposing ourselves to be more of a chosen people, the select few, than all who are redeemed by the blood of the Lamb, though I think our calling a high and important one, in the Militant Church of Christ. May our Holy Head establish by His own power, all that is true and of Himself, amongst us, and entirely bring to nought all that is contrary to His will. This I earnestly desire, and may I not say, pray for myself individually, as well as others.

Earlham, 1st month, 5th, 1837 – I am much struck, by observing in my spiritual course how different are the lines we are led in, even those, who may be under the same outward administration. We observe in nature both animal and vegetable, there are different classes, orders, genera, and species; so I think, I see it spiritually, as the flowers of one species differ a little in colour or size, so in the Church of Christ, those who may be said to be of one species, differ in some small things, no two quite alike. May these differences in no degree separate us from each other.

Upton Lane, 1st month, 25th – My heart and mind have been much occupied, by my brother Joseph writing to inform me, that he apprehends it will be his duty to go to America this year, upon religious service. The subject is deeply important and weighty, yet I desire to rejoice in his willingness to give up all for the service of his Lord. Though some fears have arisen from a sort of floating apprehension I have had for many years, that I ought or might go with him if ever he visited that land. Upon viewing it, as it respects myself, I believe I may truly say, I do not at present see any such opening. As far as I can see, home has my first call of duty, what the future may produce, I leave; but as far as I know my own heart, I very earnestly desire to feel continually that I am not my own, but bought with a price, therefore I am my Lord's servant, and must do as I am bidden, even if the service called for, appear to me unreasonable. But I must further observe, that in condescending mercy, I have generally found in services really called for, there has been a ripeness, that may be compared to the fruit come to maturity. For this service for the present, I see no way.

7th month, 20th – I returned home yesterday evening from Lowestoft, after having accompanied my brother Joseph to Liverpool, in his way to America. Our time at Earlham was very interesting; I believe I was helpful to my brother in a large Meeting that he held, to take leave of the citizens of Norwich. It was a highly interesting occasion, and I trust edifying to many. I am very sorry to say, my mind has too much the habit of anxiety and fearfulness. I believe this little journey would have been much more useful to me, but from an almost constant cloud over me, from the fear of being wanted by some of my family. I think it would be better for myself and for them, if they did not always cling so closely round my heart, so as to become too much of a weight upon me.

My beloved brother's leave-taking of Earlham, and the family there, was very affecting; still there was peace in it, and joy in the Lord, inasmuch as there is delight in doing what we believe to be His will. Of this, I think we partook with him. We went from Earlham to Runcton [*the home of Daniel Gurney*], there we dined. Shall I ever dine with my three brothers again? The Lord only knows – my heart was tendered in being with them. I rejoice that I proceeded with Joseph, for I did not before that feel that I had come at his mind, he had been so much engaged, but on the journey I did so very satisfactorily. Samuel, Elizabeth, Joseph and myself, thus had a time together, never to be forgotten. We had much interesting conversation respecting things spiritual and things temporal, ourselves and our families. We proceeded to Manchester, where we met our dear Jonathan and Hannah Backhouse, their children, and Eliza P. Kirkbride; also, William Forster. We were a very united company. That evening, William Forster read the 54th chapter of Isaiah, expressing his full belief, that our dearest Joseph would experience the promises contained in the last few verses.

The next day we went to Liverpool, and spent much of the morning in his very comfortable ship; we felt being in it, for it was very touching parting with one so tenderly beloved. We made things comfortable for him, I attended to the books, and that a proper library should go out for the crew, passengers and steerage passengers. However occupied or interested, I desire never to forget any thing that may be of service to others. We had a delightful morning with Joseph, but the tears often rose to my eyes; still, I desire to be thankful more than sorrowful, that I have a brother so fitted for his Lord's service, and willing to give up all for His name's sake.

That evening again we had an interesting religious time in prayer. The next morning there was a solemn calm over us, the day of parting was come. After breakfast we all assembled with some of our friends. We read the 4th of Philippians, our spirits were much bowed and broken, but the chapter encouraged us to stand fast in the Lord, to help one another in Christ, even the women who laboured in the gospel, and, to be careful for nothing, for that the Lord would supply all our need.

Soon afterwards we went to the ship. I saw the library arranged with some others to help me; then went and devoted my self to my beloved brother, put sweet flowers in his cabin, which was made most comfortable for him. It was announced that the ship was going – we assembled in the ladies' cabin, I believe all wept. William Forster said, the language had powerfully impressed him – "I will be with you always, even to the end of the world"; therefore we might trust our beloved ones to Him who had promised. I then knelt down with these words – "Now, Lord, what wait we for, our hope is in Thee", and entirely committed him and his companions in the ship, to the most holy and powerful keeping of Israel's Shepherd, that even the voyage might be blessed to him and to others. In short, our souls were poured forth before and unto the Lord, in deep prayer and supplication. Joseph almost sobbed, still a solemn quiet and peace reigned over us. I believe the Lord was with us, and owned us at this solemn time. We left the ship, and walked by the side of the Pier until they were towed out, then we went away and wept bitterly – but not the tears of deep sorrow, far from it; how different to the grief for sin, or even disease, or the perplexities of life. It appeared the Lord's doing, though long marvellous in my eyes, yet I now trust and believe it is His call, and therefore it is well, and there is more cause to rejoice than to mourn over it.

We remained at Liverpool till Second-day morning; went by the railroad to Birmingham, meeting with an accident by the way which might have been serious, but we were preserved from harm. I became at last very poorly, and one morning nearly fainted. I was much sunk, and brought once more to feel my deep infirmity in illness or suffering. By the time we arrived at Lynn, I was too ill to go on to Earlham, and there remained to be most affectionately cared for by my beloved son and daughter, and their servants. I afterwards went to Earlham and from thence to Lowestoft. I much valued my visits, only my foolish nature was too anxious, to enjoy them as I might have done, fancying I was wanted at home. We truly partook of the unity of the Spirit in the bond of peace. I am favoured on returning home, to find my children unusually well, and receive good accounts from my husband and sons on the Continent; so that, once more it has pleased the Lord to permit me to rest as beside the still waters. He restoreth my soul!

Upton Lane, 8th month, 18th – I have believed it right to have the poor invited, to attend the Evening Meeting at Ratcliff to-morrow. These are weighty engagements; may the Holy Spirit be poured forth, for the comfort, help, and encouragement of the hearers, and to my own peace.

9th month, 2nd – Since this Meeting, the interest that others have taken with me in the poor of Ratcliffe has led us to look into their deplorable state. We have formed a committee to visit them at their houses, see their state, provide a library for their use and probably an infant school. So one thing springs out of another!

Last Seventh-day, my brother and sister Gurney and I went to Crawley to attend the little Meeting at Ifield, to go to William Allen's, and to Linfield. My brother said, that any serious persons who liked to attend the Meeting might do so, and to our surprise, we found a large congregation of the labouring classes; I should think nearly a hundred men in smock-frocks; it was quite a sight. I felt low, empty, unworthy and stripped in spirit, but my Lord helped me. We certainly had a solemn Meeting, the people were very attentive; we also had a very satisfactory reading with the people at the inn. In the evening we attended another Meeting at Linfield, in which William Allen very acceptably united. Other Friends were there. We also called upon some poor, sorrowful, destitute ones. This little excursion appeared blessed to our comfort, refreshment and peace, and I believe had the same effect on those whom we visited. I observe, with those who may think they differ in sentiment, there is nothing like bringing them together; how often it is then found, that the difference is more in expression than reality and that the spirit of love and charity breaks down the partition walls.

I have for many months past, deeply felt the wish for more religious intercourse with my children, and more uniting with them upon important and interesting subjects. I have turned it in my mind again and again, and at last have proposed making the experiment, and meeting this evening – first, to consider different subjects of usefulness in charities, and then to close with serious reading and such religious communication as way may open for.

Upton Lane, Eighth Month, 15th, 1837.

My dearest Children,

Many of you know that for some time I have felt and expressed the want of our social intercourse at times leading to religious union and communion amongst us. It has pleased the Almighty to permit, that by far the larger number of you no longer walk with me in my religious course. Except very occasionally, we do not meet together for the solemn purpose of worship, and upon some other points we do not see eye to eye, and whilst I feel deeply sensible that notwithstanding this diversity amongst us, we are truly united in our Holy Head, there are times when in my declining years, I seriously feel the loss of not having more of the spiritual help and encouragement of those I have brought up and truly sought to nurture in the Lord. This has led me to many serious considerations, how the case may under present circumstances be in any way met.

My conclusion is, that believing as we do in one Lord as our Saviour, one Holy Spirit as our Sanctifier, and one God and Father of us all, our points of union are surely strong, and if we are members of one living Church, and expect to be such for ever, we may profitably unite in some religious engagements here below.

The world and the things of it occupy us much, and they are rapidly passing away – it would be well if we occasionally set apart a time for unitedly attending to the things of Eternity. I therefore propose that we try the following plan, if it answer, continue it, if not, by no means feel bound to it. That our party in the first instance, should consist of no others than our children, and such grandchildren, as may be old enough to attend. That our object in meeting be for the strengthening of our faith, for our advancement in a devoted, religious, and holy life, and for the object of promoting Christian love and fellowship.

That we read the Scriptures unitedly, in an easy familiar manner, each being perfectly at liberty to make any remark or ask any question; that it should be a time of religious instruction by seeking to understand the mind of the Lord, for doctrine and practice in searching the Scriptures, and bringing ourselves and our deeds to the light, that it may be made manifest if they are wrought in God. That either before or after the Scriptures are read, we should consider how far we are really engaged for the good of our fellow-men, and what, as far as we can judge, most conduces to this object. All the members of this little community are advised to communicate any thing they may have found useful or interesting in religious books, and to bring forward any thing that is doing for the good of mankind, in the world generally.

I hope that thus meeting together may stimulate the family to more devotion of heart to the service of their God, at home and abroad to mind their different callings, however varied; and to be active in helping others. It is proposed that this meeting should take place once a month, at each house in rotation.

I now have drawn some little outline of what I desire, and if any of you like to unite with me in making the experiment, it would be very gratifying to me, still, I hope that all will feel at liberty, to do as they think best themselves.

I am indeed,

Your nearly attached mother, EF

At the beginning of 1838 Elizabeth Fry visited France, travelling in the ministry in the company of her husband and two Friends, Josiah Forster and Lydia Irving. From St. Germains she wrote to her children

3rd month, 5th, 1838.

We arrived here last evening, after quitting the most deeply interesting field of service I think I was ever engaged in. My first feeling is peace and true thankfulness for the extraordinary help granted to us; my next feeling, an earnest desire to communicate to you, my most tenderly beloved children, and others nearest to me, the sense that I have of the kindness and goodness and mercy of my Heavenly Father, who has dealt so bountifully with me; that it may lead all to serve Him fully, love Him more, and follow more simply the guidance of His Spirit.

I mean now to tell you a little of my reflections upon this important period, the last month at Paris. I was at first very poorly, very low, and saw little opening for religious usefulness, though some for charitable and benevolent objects. Soon my health revived, and we had full occupation in visiting prisons and other institutions, and saw many influential persons. This opened a door in various ways, for close communication with a deeply interesting variety of both philanthropic and religious people, and has thus introduced us into a more intimate acquaintance with the state of general society. Religiously, we find some, indeed we may say a great many, who appear much broken off from the bonds of Roman Catholic superstition, but with it, I fear, have been ready to give up religion itself, though feeling the need of it for themselves and others. To these I think we have been helpful, by upholding religion in its simplicity, and most strongly expressing our sense of the necessity of it, and that nothing can alter and improve the moral character, or bring real peace, but true Christian principles. To this we have very faithfully borne testimony, and most strongly encouraged all to promote a more free circulation of the Scriptures, particularly the New Testament, and a more diligent reading of the Bible in institutions and families. I have, in private circles, introduced (frequently by describing what poor criminals wanted in prisons) the simple truths of the Gospel, illustrated sometimes by interesting facts, respecting the conversion of some of these poor women prisoners, and have been thus enabled in numerous parties, to show the broad, clear, and simple way of salvation, through our Lord and Saviour, for all. It has been striking to me in our dinner visits, some of them splendid occasions, how curiously a way has opened without the least formality, or even difficulty in conversation, to "speak the truth in love", especially one day, as to how far balls and theatres were Christian and right; the way in which Roman Catholic priests appeared to hinder the spread of the Gospel – the importance of circulating good books (this has been a very common subject) and above all the New Testament. At our own Ambassador's Lord Granville's, several were in tears during the conversation. I think our dinner visits have been an important part of our service, so much has been done by these communications after, and at them. In many instances, numbers have joined us in the evening, particularly the youth. With these, it has pleased my Heavenly Father to give me some influence. Last First-day evening, I had a very large party of them to a reading, which appears to have given much satisfaction. It has been a most curious opening with persons of many nations. Many have lately flocked to our little Meetings; I wonder how I could feel easy to go away from such a field of service, but I did, and therefore went. On Third-day, when we went to the King and Queen, and therefore could not attend our little week-day Meeting, they said eighty persons came to it who went away. I have found unusual help at these times, to speak the truth with power, my belief is, that there are many unsettled and seeking minds in this country.

We have had much intercourse with the Minister of Instruction, and he gives me leave to send him a large number of books from England, to be translated into French. My full belief is, that many Testaments and valuable books will circulate in consequence of our visit.

The efforts made to form a Ladies' Society, to visit the prisons of France, and particularly Paris (whether they succeed or not), have been important. First, by my taking many ladies to visit the great Female Prison of St. Lazare, and there reading, or having read, small portions of Scripture, and my few words through an interpreter, producing (far beyond what I could have expected) such a wonderful effect upon these poor sinners. The glad tidings of the Gospel appeared to touch their hearts, many wept exceedingly, and it was a fresh and striking proof of the power of the truth, when simply told. In the next place, the large number of ladies that have met at our house upon the subject, has afforded so remarkable an opportunity to express to them my views of salvation by Christ alone, of the unity that should exist amongst Christians, and must do so, if sanctified by the Spirit, and deeply to impress the simplicity and spirituality of true religion. I think something important in the prison cause will eventually come out of it, but it will take time.

We have had very large parties of English and Americans, and some French, at the houses of the Methodist minister, the American minister, and at another serious person's. Also we joined the French Wesleyan Methodists in their chapel, and had a precious meeting with them. Of the highly evangelical Episcopalians and Independents, we have had very large parties at different houses. In all these, we have had solemn religious service. The Episcopalians have been brought into very close union with us. In our own house, we have had two large parties of a philanthropic and religious nature, attended by many. Lady Olivia Sparrow has often been quite a comfort to me; and many others I may say have proved true helpers, French and Americans, and more than these – the Chargé d'Affaires of the Hanse Towns and his wife, also Russians and Swiss. The Greek Ambassador, Coletti, came to me for advice on some points in the state of Greece, in which I believe I shall be enabled to assist him. A Captain B– thinks of having my sister Hoare's "Hints for the Labouring Classes" translated, for the parents of the children who attend the schools upon the mountains in India. We have also seen many of the medical students, English and American, and are anxious to have some efforts made for their moral and religious good, in Paris, where so many come.

Our visit to the King and the Queen was interesting; but alas! what in reality is rank? The King I think in person like the late Lord Torrington, the Queen a very agreeable and even interesting woman. I expressed my religious interest and concern for them, which was well received, and we had much conversation with the Queen and the Princess Adelaide, before the King came into the Room. We strongly expressed to the Queen our desire to have the Sabbath better kept, and the Scriptures more read. She is a sweet-minded merciful woman. There were present Madame Adelaide, the King's sister, one of the young Princesses, and the Marchioness of Dolomieu, principal Lady of Honour to the Queen.

The Queen appeared much pleased with my Text-book; and the Princess Adelaide said, she should keep it in her pocket and read it daily. Indeed no books have given the same pleasure as the Text-books, both in

French and English. I think we have given away many hundreds of them, and next in number my sister Louisa's books on Education; they delight the people; also a great many of Joseph's Letter to Dr. A–, of which we have a beautiful edition in French, and his Sabbath; of these we expect to give many hundreds, and one or two other tracts, upon Christian Duties, and the Offices of the Holy Spirit. Our various books and tracts have had a very open reception, but we have been very careful when, where, and what to give; although in some of the newspapers it was stated that I distributed controversial tracts, which is not true.

I began in my letter to say what a variety we have seen, but I did not say what deeply interesting and delightful persons we have met with; amongst the Protestants particularly, some first rate ladies, who have been as sisters to me, so abundant in kindness and love. One has truly reminded me of my sister Rachel, in her person, her mind, and her excessive care over me; she has felt me, I believe, like her own. We have indeed increased our dear and near friends by this visit, much as it was in Jersey and Guernsey, only in far greater numbers. I think nothing could be more seasonable than our visit; as it respected the prisons, and I believe the influence of our advice has been very decided, with many persons of consideration. The schools we have also attended to and I have encouraged a more scriptural education; some schools of great consequence, kept by serious Protestants in a district of Paris, much want help. There are seven hundred children, and we hear that the Head of the Police in that neighbourhood says the people generally are improved in consequence.

The want of the language, I have now and then much felt, but not very often, so many speak English well, and many understand it who cannot speak it. Also I blunder out a little French.

The entreaties for us to stop longer in Paris have been very great, but my inclination draws homeward; I am a very great friend to not stopping too long in a place. And as I believed I saw a little light upon our departure, we thought it best to leave all for the present, and go, if we even have, before many months more, to return for a short time. We have been a united and often a cheerful little party. At times I have carried a great weight, never hardly having my home party out of mind for long together, however full and occupied. At other times our business has been so great, as almost to overwhelm us – callers almost innumerable, and most of them on important business, and out and in almost constantly ourselves, so that I have sometimes felt as if I could not long bear it, particularly when I could not obtain some rest in the afternoon. Through all I must say, He who I believe put me forth, has from season to season restored my soul and body, and helped me from hour to hour. This day week I sat down upon my chair and wept, but I was soon helped and revived. I long for every child, brother, sister, and all near to me, to be sensible how very near my Holy Helper has been to me, and yet I have exceedingly and deeply felt my utter unworthiness and short coming, and that all is from the fulness and freeness of unmerited mercy and love, in Christ Jesus. I can hardly express the very near love I have felt for you all. My prayers very often have risen for you, and if any labour I have been engaged in has been accepted through the Beloved, may you my most tenderly beloved ones, partake of the blessing attendant upon it. My dearest husband has been a true helper; and Josiah Forster and Lydia Irving, very kind and useful companions. I forgot to say, I think the few Friends in Paris have been greatly comforted and stimulated by our visit.

I end my account by saying, what I trust is true, "The Lord is my Shepherd. I shall not want." We are now quietly at St. Germains. We hear most interesting accounts of the state of Normandy, and have many letters of introduction to the places where we propose to go, if not wanted home, I shall be glad to go there. We propose being at Rouen to-morrow.

I am,

Your most tenderly attached,

EF

5th month, 20th – To-morrow I am fifty-eight, an advanced period of what I apprehend to be not a very common pilgrimage, I now very earnestly desire and pray that my Lord may guide me continually, cause me to know more of the day of His power, that I may have my will subjected to his will. What He would have me to do that may I do, where He would have me to go there may I go – what He may call me to suffer for His name sake may I be willing to suffer. Further, may He keep me from all false fears and imaginations, and ever preserve me from putting my hand to any work, not called for by Him, even if my fellow-creatures press me into it, as I think some are disposed to do about America. Be pleased to grant these my desires and prayers for Thine own Holy and Blessed name's sake.

7th month, 8th – This day I enter with much fear and trembling, as we are looking forward to a very important Meeting to be held at the Westminster Meeting House, at the request of Hannah Backhouse, to which foreigners of rank and our own nobility are invited. The weight is great – very great from various causes, partly from my fears and doubts as to women's holding Public Meetings.

7th month, 14th – The Meeting was attended by many high in rank. Soon after we assembled, William Allen spoke for some time, then I knelt down and felt much unction and power in prayer for the Queen. After Hannah Backhouse had spoken, in a lively, simple, powerful manner, preaching the truths of the gospel, several went out. I then rose, first endeavouring to show that truth must not be despised, because it came through weak instruments. I mentioned, how Anna in the Temple spoke of our Lord to all who looked for redemption in Israel, how the women first told of our Lord's resurrection, and that their fellow-disciples called it "idle tales". After thus showing that the Lord might see right to use weak instruments, I expressed my feelings towards those present. First, from Scripture, I showed that God is no respecter of persons, that from the palace to the very dungeon, I continually saw this. Then I showed the important and responsible situation of those who fill high places in the world. Either they would be blessed themselves and be a blessing to others, as a city set on a hill, their light shining before men; or they would be of the number of those, through whom offences come, and therefore with the "curse of the Lord" resting on them. I showed them some of their peculiar temptations, in being clothed in purple and fine linen, and faring sumptuously every day; and warned them, seeking to lead them to Christ, and to eternal glory through Him. At the close, I had a few words to express in the way of exhortation, as to their example in their houses, amongst children and servants, reading the Holy Scriptures, family worship and other points.

In August and September Elizabeth Fry visited Scotland with her sister-in-law Elizabeth Fry among others, but her thoughts were often with Europe.

12th month, 6th – This morning I felt deeply the seriousness of laying before my Monthly Meeting, my belief that it may be my duty again to visit France and some other parts of the continent of Europe. It is after much weighty consideration that I have come to the conclusion, that it is right to do this. I have long thought that this summer my course might be turned either to my dearest brother Joseph in America, or to the Continent of Europe; after much weighing it, I have believed the latter to be the right opening for me. I laid my prospect before the Friends of our Monthly Meeting, this morning. Several Friends were there, not members of it. We had a very solemn Meeting – for worship first. My sister and I returned our certificates for visiting Scotland, and then I asked for one for Europe, having very earnestly prayed for help, direction, and protection. When under a fresh feeling of its being right to do it, I simply informed Friends that I looked to paying a visit to Paris, then to the Friends in the South of France; and should probably in returning visit some other parts of Europe. Much unity and sympathy were expressed with this prospect of religious duty, by our own members and those who visited us. There certainly appeared to be in no common degree, a seal set to this serious prospect of religious service.

I now desire to leave all to the further openings of Providence, as to when to go, who is to go with me, and where to go. I desire to leave it all to my most holy and gracious Head and High Priest, my All in All, my Lord and my God. Although I am very deeply sensible that it is only through the fulness and freeness of unmerited mercy, love and grace, that I dare call or feel my Lord thus to be my Head and my Helper. I may acknowledge in faith, my belief that through the help of the Holy Spirit, my Lord has been and is unto me "Wonderful, Counsellor, the Mighty God, the Everlasting Father, and the Prince of Peace".

12th month, 28th – Yesterday, excepting our dear Frank and Rachel, all our beloved children dined with us. It really was to me a beautiful sight. Sixteen round our table, happy in each other, a strong tie of love amidst the brothers and sisters; and much united to us their father and mother. I felt the occasion serious as well as sweet, and very earnestly prayed to the Lord that I might be very faithful, if He called me to any religions service amongst them; whether it were to pray for them, or speak to them of His goodness. When the cloth was removed after dinner, I believed it my duty to kneel down, and very fervently to pray and to return thanks to my God, for all these most tenderly beloved ones. Great help and deliverance has been granted to some of our circle; the Lord has been very gracious, He has added to our number and not diminished them. I did from my heart return God thanks, earnestly asking in faith for a continuance of His mercies; more particularly, that our souls should be satisfied more abundantly with the unsearchable riches of Christ; and that we might be still more closely united in our Heavenly Father's love. I asked the Lord that it might please Him to grant us peace and prosperity through his tender mercy in

Christ Jesus; and that wherever we might be, His blessing might be with us; and that when the end came, it might crown all.

After this solemn time, thirteen of the sweet, dear grandchildren came in. We missed dearest Frank and Rachel, and their lovely group; but they were not forgotten by us. We passed an evening of uncommon enjoyment, cheerful yet sober, lively yet sensible of the blessing and peace of our Lord being with us. I seldom if ever remember so bright a family meeting, it reminded me of our Earlham days; but I could not but feel it a blessing, when a mother as well as a father is spared to watch their family grow up and prosper, and to see and enjoy their children's children.

When I remember all that I have passed through on their account, above all the exquisite anxiety about their spiritual welfare, and now so far to see what the Lord has done for me and for them, what can I say ? What can I do? Ought I not to leave them all to His most holy keeping, and no longer "toil and spin" so much for them?

Paris, 3rd month, 17th, 1839 – Here we are once more in this most interesting city, after a favourable journey, and calm passage. Leaving home was very touching to our feelings; I never saw my children feel a separation so much.

Letter to her childen

Nismes, 5th Month, 12th, 1839.

I have been considering which is best, to write one full letter to You, or several notes, and I am come to the conclusion, now we are so far from home, and have so much to do, that it is better to write to you collectively: We thankfully say, we feel peaceful and in our right place, although separated from many so very dear to us.

We paid a very interesting visit to Lyons, and found a good deal new in the Prisons and Refuges. An order of Catholics, called the Brethren and Sisters of St. Joseph, believe it their duty entirely, to take care of prisoners and criminals generally. They do not visit as we do, but take the entire part of turnkeys and prison-officers, and live with the prisoners night and day, constantly caring for them. I thought the effect on the female prisoners surprisingly good, as far as their influence extended. But the mixture of gross superstition is curious, the image of the Virgin dressed up in the finest manner, in their different wards. I feared, that their religion lay so much in form and ceremonies, that it led from heart work, and from that great change which would probably be produced, did these Sisters simply teach them Christianity. Their books appeared to be mostly about the Virgin; not a sign of Scripture to be found in either prison or refuge. I felt it laid on me as a weighty, yet humbling duty, before I left Lyons, to invite Roman Catholics and Protestants, who had influence in the prisons, to come to our Hotel, and there, in Christian love, to tell them the truth to the best of my belief, as to the only real ground of reformation of heart, and the means likely to conduce to this end. It was the more fearful, as I had to be entirely interpreted for. My heart almost sank within me as the time approached. It was about three o'clock in the day, about sixty people came of the very influential Catholics and Protestants, and I was enabled, through a most excellent interpreter, to show them, that nothing but the pure simple truth, as revealed in Scripture, through the power of the Holy Spirit, could really enlighten the understanding or change the heart. My husband and Josiah Forster also, took a very useful and valuable part. Much satisfaction was expressed. We afterwards dined at a gentleman's, who lived in a lovely situation, on the top of a hill near Lyons. Our invitations began to flow in, and we should, I doubt not, had we stayed longer, soon have been in as great a current as at Paris, or greater. We met with some very interesting, devoted Christian characters – a cousin of the Baroness Pelet's almost like herself, her notes and flowers coming in every morning. The last day was most fatiguing; we had to rise soon after three in the morning for Avignon, to go a hundred and fifty miles down the Rhône.

We have passed through the most delightful country I ever saw. Lyons, with the Rhône and Saône, is in its environs beautiful, and the passage from Lyons to Avignon really lovely; mountains in the distance (parts of the Alps), their tops covered with snow; vegetation in perfection, the flowers of spring and summer in bloom at once, grass just ready to be cut, barley in the ear, lilacs, laburnums, syringas, roses, pinks, carnations, acacias in full bloom, yellow jessamine wild in the hedges. It is a sudden burst of the finest summer, combined with the freshness of spring. The olive groves, intermixed with abundant vineyards and mulberry groves, all beautiful from their freshness. The ancient buildings of Avignon, the ruins on the banks of the Rhône, the very fine and wonderful Roman remains of the aqueduct, called the Pont du Gard, really exceed description. This place also abounds in curious buildings. Here, or in the neighbourhood, we expect to remain some time.

6th month, 2nd – We found a great deal of what was highly interesting in Congenies [*where there was a small group of French Quakers including the Majolier family*]. A peculiar and new place to us. The country remarkable, much cultivated in parts, and planted with vineyards, mulberry, olive, and fig-trees, with but little corn. There is a very delightful air; the hills rather barren and singularly grey, with fine ruins upon some of them, and here and there a peep at the Mediterranean. The little dull villages, much strewed about, thickly inhabited, mostly by Protestants, who appear generally in a low neglected state; we visited some of these villages, and had larger or smaller Meetings in them. We found a great inclination in the people to hear the truth, and I believe there is a real thirst after it. I humbly trust that the blessing of the Lord was with us, as I have seldom felt more peace or more sense of this blessing, than when engaged in these labours of Christian love at Congenies, or a more clear belief that I was in my right place.

6th month – Our First-day at Nismes was deeply weighty in prospect, so that I rested little at night, as I had ventured to propose our holding one meeting in the morning, in the Methodist chapel, that whoever liked might attend it; and in the evening, to do the same in a very large school-room, that all classes might attend, as I believed that all would not come to a Methodist Meeting I went prostrated before the Lord, to this Meeting in the morning, hardly knowing how to hold up my head; I could only apply for help to the inexhaustible Source of our sure mercies, feeling that I could not do it, either on account of myself, or because it was the work in which I was engaged; but I could do it for the sake of my Lord, and that His kingdom might spread. Utterly unworthy did I feel myself, but my Lord was gracious. My dear interpreter, Charlotte Majolier, was there to help me in a very large Meeting, and I felt power wonderfully given me to proclaim the truths of the Gospel, and to press upon the point of the Lord Himself being our teacher, immediately by His Spirit, through the Holy Scriptures, find by His Providences and works; and to show, that no teaching so much conduced to growth in grace, as the Lord's teaching. There was much attention; at the close, I felt the spirit of prayer much over us, longed for its vocal expression, and felt a desire some one might pray, when a Methodist minister, in a feeling manner, expressed a wish to offer something in prayer, to which, of course, we assented – it proved solemn and satisfactory.

We dined at our dear friends, the Pasteur Emilien Frossard's; he and his wife have been like a brother and sister to us; we were also joined by a

Roman Catholic gentleman and his daughter. He has, I think, been seriously impressed by our visit, and it has led him to have the Scriptures read to his work men. There were also Louis Majolier, his daughter and a young English friend. I think I have very seldom in my life felt a more lively sense of the love of God than at his table. I may say, our souls were animated under its sweetness. I think we rejoiced together, and magnified the Name of our God.

In the evening, we met in a large school-room that would contain some hundreds, where numbers assembled, principally the French Protestants and some of their pastors. There, again, I was greatly helped. I really believe, by the Holy Spirit, to speak to them upon their very important situations in the Church of Christ, and the extreme consequence of their being sound both in faith and practice. I also felt it my duty to show them, as Protestants, the infinite importance, not only in France, but in the surrounding nations, of their being as a city set upon a hill that cannot be hid. I showed them how the truth is spreading, and how important to promote it, by being preachers of righteousness in life and conversation, as well as in word and doctrine. There was here also much attention; and our dear and valued friend and brother in Christ, Emilien Frossard, prayed beautifully, that the word spoken might profit the people, and particularly, that the blessing of the Lord might rest upon me. It was no common prayer on my behalf. Thanks to my Heavenly Father, the Meeting broke up in much love, life, and peace.

To her children in England

Bagnères de Luchon, 6th month, 23rd.

Here I sit before breakfast, with a most lovely scene before me. On entering this solemn Sabbath morning – my soul and body refreshed, not only in admiring the wonderful works of the outward creation, and being revived by the delightful air, fresh from the snowy mountains before me; but what is more, my soul refreshed. I have been enabled to lift my heart to my Heavenly Father, for every brother, sister and child individually, and for my dear husband; and collectively, for my many beloved ones; committing all to His holy keeping, I feel rest. And now my beloved children, I will tell you a little how we go on.

My attraction homewards grows stronger and stronger, but I desire patiently to wait the right time: – the openings for religious service are greater than I expected, more particularly amongst the Protestants, at Montpellier, Toulouse, and Montauban. At Montauban, without expressing any other wish, than to have an evening party at one of their houses, to meet some of the professors and students of the College (the only one in France for educating pasteurs for the Reformed Church). We found, to our dismay, all arranged to receive us in the College; and on arriving there, imagine how I felt, when the Dean of the College offered me his arm, to take me into the chapel. There, I believe, the whole of the collegians were assembled, in all at least a hundred. It was fearful work. There were also numbers of the people of the town; we thought about three hundred. Josiah Forster spoke first, explaining our views at some length. Then I rose, with an excellent interpreter, one of their pasteurs; I first told them something of my Prison experience, and the power of Christian principle and kindness; then, I related a little of the state of their prisons in France; then, my ideas as to the general state of France; and afterwards, endeavoured to bring home to them the extreme importance of their future calling, as pasteurs in their church. I reminded them of that passage of Scripture, "the leaders of the people caused them to err". I endeavoured to show them how awful such a state of things must be, and the extreme importance of their being sound in doctrine and practice. Simple duty led me to Montauban. Josiah F. was my kind and useful companion. We were united in much Christian love to many there. I forgot to say, that at the close of the occasion, the pasteur who interpreted for me, prayed beautifully and spiritually, that the words spoken might profit the people; he also prayed for us: this has frequently occurred at the close of some of our interesting meetings, a pouring forth of the spirit of prayer has been granted. My not knowing the language has obstructed my offering it, and it has appeared laid upon others instead. I have seldom felt sweeter peace in leaving a place than Montauban. At Toulouse, we were deeply interested by the Courtois brothers: they appear, body, soul, and spirit, devoted to the service of their Lord, quite a bright example to all of us. The world appeared as nothing to them. I have seldom seen men so wholly given up to good and useful objects; they were most kind to us. We had various calls of duty in that town, and I had a most excellent interpreter in François Courtois. We arrived here yesterday evening, after serious consideration, believing it the best to pursue this course. A certain time of quiet appears really needful to make representations to the French government, and to those in authority, of the various evils that want remedy in prisons, &c. We understand there are many seeking, serious minds, to whom we may be of some comfort, which helps to reconcile us to the measure.

First-day, 11th month, 10th – My time at Lynn was spent very satisfactorily with my beloved children and grandchildren, and my attention particularly occupied by the intention they had, of our dear eldest grandson going into the army. My prayers were first offered in secret, that my Lord would open some way of escape from a life, that I felt to be so unchristian and fearful a one. At first I said little, but kept my heart much lifted up on his account; but afterwards, I fully represented my views to him and to his parents, and I found they had great weight with them. I partook of rather unusually sweet spiritual unity and intercourse with those dear children, much as they outwardly differ from me in many things, still we are, I believe, united in some most essential points of religious truth. My dear grandson Frank and I visited together where I highly valued the company of my sisters, Catherine and Richenda, also of the rest of the party. I travelled home with my dear niece, Catherine Buxton.

Upton, 2nd month, 1st, 1840 – Our beloved daughter Louisa was confined on Fourth-day. The babe a lovely girl, breathed for twenty-four hours, and then died. They had the child named and baptised. I happened to be present, and certainly some of the prayers were very solemn, and such as I could truly unite with; but part of the ceremony appeared to me superstitious, and having a strong savour of the dark ages of the Church.

I have for some time believed that duty would call me to have a meeting in London and the neighbourhood, previous to leaving home. I see many difficulties attached to it, and perhaps none so much, as my great fear of women, coming too forward in these things, beyond what the Scripture dictates; but I am sure the Scripture most clearly and forcibly lays down the principle that the Spirit is not to be grieved, or quenched, or vexed, or resisted; and on this principle I act, under the earnest desire that I may not do this, but that whatever the Lord leads me into by His Spirit may be done faithfully to Him, and in His name; and I am of opinion, that nothing Paul said, to discourage women's speaking in the Churches, alluded to their speaking through the help of the Spirit, as he clearly gave directions how they should conduct themselves under such circumstances, when they prayed or prophesied.

Elizabeth Fry was soon travelling in the ministry again, with her brother Samuel among others, this time not only to France but also to Holland and Germany from where she wrote to her family at home

Amsterdam, Third Month, 19th.

My dearest Harry,

We find this a very interesting place. How amused you would all be at some of our curious Meetings. The other evening we went to drink tea at the house of a converted Jew, where we met numbers of the Pietists; he read the 14th chapter of John in French, I spoke, and gave a little advice on Christian love and unity; then the Jew spoke, and another Jew prayed, and afterwards William Allen. The serious, the sweet, the good, and the ludicrous were curiously mixed up together. Yesterday was very full: first company, breakfast and reading, then preparation for two meetings, one for prisons in the afternoon, and one in the evening for philanthropic objects. At three o'clock about twenty gentlemen came to discuss with us the state of the prisons of Holland, an excellent meeting. A gentleman named Surengar was present, who has followed us from Rotterdam, and has kindly invited us to his house in the North of Holland. Your uncle is very clever in his speeches, and real knowledge of the subject. I received blessing and thanks from many, far too much; our visit appears most seasonable here, so much wanting to be done in the prisons, and other things.

Fifth-day morning – We went to our Friends Meeting. When we arrived the numbers round the door were so great that we doubted whether we could get in, however, way was soon made for us, and we found a large and highly respectable congregation needing no interpreter. We had certainly a flowing Meeting in every sense, I think the cup flowed over with Christian love. I believe it has been a most unusual thing the way in which hearts have been opened towards us. I then went off to the prison to launch the Committee of Ladies in visiting it, several gentlemen also with me. I had just time to go home, rest and dress, and set off to a dinner at our friend Van der Hope's where there are the most exquisite paintings by the Dutch masters. I think I never saw any so much to my taste.

I can assure thee my dearest Harry when I see how ripe the fields are unto harvest every where, I long and pray that more labourers may be brought into this most interesting, important, and, may I not say, delightful service, but there must be a preparation for it, by yielding to the cross of Christ, and often deep humiliations and much self-abasement are needful, before the Lord makes much use of us, but above all we must yield ourselves to God, as "those that are alive from the dead". He will then fit for His own work in His own way.

Dearest love to all of you,

I am, thy most tenderly attached mother, E. F.

Hanover, Fourth Month, 2nd.

My Dearest Husband and Children,

Whilst stopping at a small inn, I mean to finish my account of our visit to Pyrmont. After I wrote we went shaking on such bad roads from house to house, to see the Friends, that I almost feared we must break down. We twice dined with them, in their beautiful spot at Friedensthal (or the valley of peace), surrounded with hills, and a river flowing through it. Roebucks wild from the woods abounding. We were very pleasantly received. I must describe the dinner. Many Germans were present, young and old, and our English party; the table was well covered with cakes, and dried and stewed fruits, the produce generally of their grounds. The soup on the table, and one large Westphalia ham. We had veal handed round afterwards in different forms; and plum-puddings, of course for us, in the middle of dinner. I much liked the true German hospitality, and also seeing the mode of living in the country. Our visits were very satisfactory to these very valuable and agreeable people. Tears and kisses abounded at our departure.

I must tell you of an interesting event: – I went to buy something for little John at a shop, where a very agreeable lady spoke to me in English, and I was so much attracted by her, that I requested her to accept a book, and sent a work on the rites and ceremonies of the Jews. I asked her to attend our Meeting on Second-day morning. She proved to be a Jewish lady of some importance; she came to Meeting with several other Jews, and truly I believe her heart was touched. I invited her to come and see us the next evening, when we expected several persons to join our party. The following day we agreed to form a District Society, to attend to the deplorable state of the poor. The Jewish lady capitally helped us, she then appeared in a feeling state; but this morning when the ladies met to finish our arrangements, and I felt it my place to give them a little advice, and my blessing in the name of the Lord, the tears poured down her face. I then felt it my absolute duty to take her into my room to give her such books as I thought right, and to tell her how earnest my desires were that she should come to the knowledge of our Saviour. I think in our whole journey no person has appeared to be so affected or so deeply impressed; may it be lasting, and may she become a Christian indeed.

Your much attached,

E. Fry

Hildesheim, Fourth Month, 6th.

My much beloved Family,

We left Hanover to-day about five o'clock, after rather a singular visit. We arrived there on Fifth-day evening. On Sixth and Seventh-day our way did not open quite so brightly as sometimes. We saw a deplorable prison; poor untried prisoners chained to the ground until they would confess their crimes, whether they had committed them or not, and some other sad evils. Several interesting persons came to see us. Seventh-day evening we spent at a gentleman's house, where we met some very clever and superior persons, and had much important communication upon their prisons, &c., &c. On First-day we had our little Meetings; such a tide on a Sabbath I think I hardly ever had; it was like being driven down a mighty stream; we had allowed persons to come to us, supposing it would be the last day there. I made some calls of Christian love. The principal magistrate came for an hour about the prisons, and very many other persons. In the evening we had also a party of a select nature to our Scripture reading, and after a very solemn time we represented many things wanted in Hanover.

I forgot to tell you, amongst other visitors, the Queen's Chamberlain came to say that the Queen wished to see our whole party on Second-day at one o'clock. We had proposed going that morning early, but put it off on this account. I think I never paid a more interesting visit to royalty – my brother Samuel, William Allen, and myself. In the first place we were received with ceremonious respect, shewn through many rooms to a drawing-room, where were the Queen's Chamberlain and three ladies-in-waiting to receive us. They showed us some pictures of the family, until Prince George and his half-sister came in to us; he appeared much pleased to be with me again. His sister appeared a serious and interesting young lady.

215

After some little time we were sent for by the Queen; the King was too ill to see us. She is a stately woman, tall, large, and rather a fine countenance. We very soon began to speak of her afflictions, and I gave a little encouragement and exhortation. She was much affected, and after a little while requested us to sit down. We had very interesting and important subjects brought forward: the difficulties and temptations to which rank is subject – the importance of their influence – the Objects incumbent upon them to attend to and help in, Bible Societies, Prisons, &c. We then read our address to the Queen, wishing her to patronize ladies visiting the prisons; it contained serious advice, and our desires for her, the King, and the Prince; then I gave the Queen several books, which she accepted in the kindest manner.

I am indeed,

Your most tenderly attached,

E. F.

Leipzig, Fourth Month, 30th.

My dearest Louisa,

The deeply weighty exercises at Berlin had so much expended all my powers, that I concluded to remain here alone, with my maid and our young friend Boyerhaus, whilst the rest of our little company went to Dresden. I have had a quiet time, and am much refreshed. I enjoy this fine weather. How beautiful is the breaking forth of spring! It is almost hot in the middle of the day, and the country very pleasant.

We have been particularly interested in visiting Luther's abode at Wittemberg, being where he was, and sitting where he sat by his table. Though in an old monastery, he appears to have had very comfortable apartments. We saw a beautiful painted ceiling in his sitting room, though now much defaced. I hope you have all read Merle D'Aubigne's History of the Reformation, we have found it so very interesting, we expect to visit many of the places mentioned in it, and to see the castle in which Luther was confined.

When left alone here I really was amused to find how kind friends gathered round me; one brought me beautiful flowers and oranges, another books, another a very fine print of prisoners in their place of worship. In the morning of Second-day I took a little recreation, accompanied by two gentlemen, and drove about to see this pretty town and environs, the longest excursion for pleasure I have had. I spent the evening at the house of one of these gentlemen where were many to meet me. Two or three spoke English, some French, I am absolutely obliged to communicate my ideas in French, when by myself, and visitors come to see me, who cannot speak English, I manage to hold much communication with them, although no doubt in a very blundering manner. It often surprises me how little real obstruction the want of knowledge of languages has proved to me; but it makes me long for my children and grandchildren thoroughly to know the modern languages What should I have done, had not numbers here known English? Indeed, every well-educated person abroad appears instructed in English and French. As to French, our young people ought to know it as well as they do English, for it is a passport everywhere. I hope the greatest pains will be taken with it, with all the grandchildren, both girls and boys. I must now say, in much near and tender love, farewell.

Your most tenderly attached,

E. F.

Upton, 5th month, 19th – There certainly is the most extraordinary opening in the hearts of those in authority on the Continent, to receive me. I felt much drawn to go to Denmark, but the way did not open for it; if I am called still to go, may my Lord make my way plain before me, though I do not see it now. My present position is this – I consider my health has been almost in a precarious state for many months; I have not recovered my usual strength, and there is a feeling of delicacy throughout, I do not think that I am nervous, but my spirits are low. I am, however, so much revived and strengthened by generous living and a little care and quietness, that I rather look to a general revival of health. On the other hand, I query whether a step downwards is not taken, that I shall never fully recover – at all events, I have been poorly enough to have the end of life brought closely before me, and to stimulate me in faith to do quickly what my Lord may require of me; but above all, it leads me to desire to cast myself more entirely on the fulness of His love, mercy, and pity, and to entreat his care over me, not permitting more to be brought upon me than my extremely weak and infirm nature can bear, and that He will undertake for me at the last, and through the freeness of His grace, and the fulness of the merits of His dear Son, grant me a place within the gates of His city. I long, before I go hence, to have a clearer and more certain view of the Heavenly inheritance.

6th month, 28th, First-day – Since I last wrote I have called upon the Duchess of Beaufort, and the Duchess of Sutherland. The Duchess of

Beaufort received me with much true Christian friendship; the Duchess of Sutherland, in a remarkably kind manner: soon after I entered the room, the Duke and his daughters came in. We had much interesting religious conversation. I felt the spirit of Christian love and prayer arise in my heart for them, that the blessing of God might rest upon them, that as He had given them so liberally of the fatness of the earth, He would also cause the dew of Heaven to descend upon them. The next day, I wrote to ask the Duchess whether she wished to attend a Meeting, on account of the Anti-Slavery Society, at Exeter Hall, as I fancied she might like it, I had a cordial answer, saying that she would go. We sat near the Duke of Sussex and the French Ambassador. To find my poor unworthy self thus placed in the face of this immense assembly (I think three thousand persons) was rather fearful, and yet very interesting, from the cause we were engaged in, the numbers interested in it and the honour of appearing on the side of the afflicted slaves.

Upton Lane, 7th month, 7th – We had the French Ambassador, and a large party to dinner here yesterday, these occasions are serious to me. The query comes home, how far the expensive dinner is right to give, and further, whether good results from it, and whether, if death was approaching, we should thus spend our time; on the other hand, after the extraordinary kindness shown us in France, and even by the French Government, some mark of attention was due from us. Also, to show hospitality to strangers is right and Christian, and in some measure to receive them as they are accustomed to live, does not appear wrong. My fear is, that the time was not turned to account, by the most important subjects being enough brought forward, I tried to do a little in this way, but I fear not enough. May my Lord keep us from in any way lowering the cause we love, may He help us by His grace more continually to exalt it, and may neither our omissions or commissions injure it. Grant gracious Lord that this may be the case.

8th month, 6th – There has been some fear of a war with France, which has been really sorrowful to me; I could have wept at the thoughts, so dear are the people of that country to my heart, and so awful is it to think of the horrors of war, whichever way we look at the subject, religiously, morally or physically. The longer I live, and the greater my experience of life, the more decided are my objections to war, as wholly inconsistent with the Christian calling. O may the Almighty grant, that through His

Omnipotence and unutterable love and mercy in Christ our Saviour, the day may not be very far distant, when the people shall learn war no more, – when peace and righteousness shall reign in the earth.

8th month, 16th, First-day, morning – After being unwell for some days, I set off with my dearest husband and Harry for Sea View, a lovely little spot on the Isle of Wight, where Foster, Chenda, and their children are staying. We met with the kindest, and warmest reception, and were, I may truly say, cherished and comforted by them, How the tide turns; my dearest children, for whom I have felt so deeply, are in their turns becoming my helpers and comforters – thanks be to my Heavenly Father. The place beautiful – the sea air very refreshing, and I almost like another person. On First-day morning we had a very solemn Meeting together; and in the evening, a large number came to our reading, the gentry, sailors, &c. One day I visited Parkhurst, an interesting new prison for boys, which gave me much satisfaction. It was curious to see some of the very things that in early life I in part begun, carried out in practice. I have lived to see much more than I expected of real improvement in prisons.

We are expecting our dearest brother Joseph home this week from America, and I mean to accompany him into Norfolk, if it be my Lord's will. May a blessing rest upon his return! I am increasingly of opinion, that these long separations are liable to serious objections; I think, where it is clear that the great Head of the Church calls any of us far off for a long time, it is most important to have those nearest to us, join us for part of the time, and I believe it would be according to the will of our God.

Earlham, 8th month, 21st – My dearest brother Joseph is safely returned home, after his absence of three years, on his religious visit to America and the West India Islands. I think I never saw any person in so perfectly peaceful a state; he says, unalloyed peace, like a sky without a cloud, and above all, enabled thankfully to enjoy his many blessings. He arrived at Liverpool on the 16th, and I first met him at my son Gurney's, as he called there for me. We all went together to Upton, after our visit to Gurney and Sophia, and a delightful time we had together. The next morning our dearest brother Joseph returned God thanks for his unspeakable mercies; his many deliverances, his great preservations spiritually and temporally, his labours of Christian love being blessed and prospered and many fruits of it seen. He then returned thanks for my brother Samuel and his family, and earnestly prayed for them, that the windows of heaven might be opened, and blessings be poured forth upon them; he also returned thanks for our brother Fowell, and for his having been prospered in his work of Christian charity for the poor slaves; then for me, and for the blessing attending on me and mine; and lastly, for his own children, wholly giving them up to the Lord and to His service. After dinner the same day, he made a beautiful and striking acknowledgment of the mercies shown him; and what delighted me, he appeared to stand fast in true gospel liberty, and to feel true unity of spirit with all that love the Lord Jesus in sincerity. I also returned thanks for these innumerable mercies. We left home the next morning, and I had a very interesting journey here with dearest Joseph, Fowell and Hannah; but I was fatigued.

12th month, 31st – I deeply feel coming to the close of this year, rather unusually so, it finds me in a low estate, and from circumstances, my spirit is rather overwhelmed, although I am sensible that blessings abound through unmerited mercy. I think the prison cause at home and abroad much prospering, many happy results from our foreign expedition, and much doing at home. Among other things, the establishment of a Patronage Society for prisoners, by which many poor wanderers appear to be helped and protected, and a Society for Sisters of Charity to visit and attend the sick. I have had much to do with those in authority, in other countries and our own; and have been treated with great kindness and respect by them.

I have been really interested for our Queen in her marriage with Prince Albert, and lately in her confinement with a little girl.

9

"Breaking down the partition walls":
Last years and death,
1841–1845

Although her health was not good Elizabeth made one more
journey to the Continent in the company of her brother Joseph.
There was still work to be done at Newgate and elsewhere, but
she was often ill and dependent on the care of her family.

Upton, 5th month, 25th, 1841 – Yesterday, I accompanied Hannah Backhouse into the Men's Meeting. When she had spoken, I rose, saying, that
I feared to make any addition, but that I had a few hints to offer. After
expressing my earnest desire that they might all be washed and sanctified,
and justified in the name of the Lord Jesus, and by the Spirit of our God,
I began with my hints. I said my views of the state of the Society were not
so discouraging as those of many others. I remembered, that our first
Friends were gathered out of various religious denominations, and from
the most spiritual of these, therefore they were a spiritual and seeking
people; but in our day, most were Friends from birth and education, and
not conviction, though I believed there were really spiritual ones amongst
us; but I saw much wanting, arising partly from these causes, first, the tendency to be a formal people, resting in a high spiritual profession, like the
foolish virgins with lamps but no oil in them, this did much harm.

Then I feared, being so much a commercial people, that there were too
many who bowed to the idols of gold and of silver, and this hindered their
serving only the living God; but above all, I apprehended that too many
grieved, quenched and resisted the Holy Spirit of God, and this was most
injurious to us. I feared an unwillingness to be taught the first simple
lessons of the Spirit, because humbling to the human heart, and that this
hindered arriving at greater knowledge. I thought our deficiencies in faith
and practice much to arise from this quenching the Holy Spirit. I believed
if there was more faithfulness at all times and in all places – in the Market
place – in the Counting-house – they would be preachers of righteousness,

and there would be judges raised up as at the first, and counsellors as at the beginning, that we should as a people, arise, shine and show that the glory of the Lord had risen upon us, and that we should uphold our important testimonies in the spirit of wisdom and meekness.

I also showed those who were young, how gently our Lord dealt with us, how He fitted us for His own work, how He gave us, not the spirit of fear, but of love and of power and of a sound mind. I also expressed my desire for all those engaged in the discipline, that their spirits might be covered with charity, that they might seek to restore the offender, remembering themselves, lest they should also be tempted, and that they might be enabled to strengthen the things that remain that were ready to die. I concluded by expressing my desire, that all might fill their places in the militant Church on earth, and eventually join the Church triumphant in Heaven in never-ending rest, peace, joy and glory.

6th month, 27th, First-day – After most deeply weighing the subject, and after very earnest prayer for direction, I felt boot satisfied to inform my friends of my belief that it might be right for me to accompany my dearest brother Joseph to the Continent, and to visit some of the more northern countries of Europe. I had very decided encouragement from the Friends, particularly the most spiritual amongst them, which I felt helpful to me; but I was surprised at the degree of relief and peace that I felt afterwards, as from a voice before me, saying, "this is the way, walk in it".

Upton, 7th month, 30th – All difficulties and obstructions, which have been serious and numerous, are removed, as far as I can see; the way is made plain and open before us, to set off to-morrow for our visit to Holland, Germany, Prussia, and Denmark. My brother Joseph, his daughter Anna, my dear niece Elizabeth Gurney, and my own maid go with me, with the prospect of every comfort this life can afford; and, I humbly trust, the Lord Himself calling us into His service, that His blessing will be with those who stay, and those who go. Grant, gracious Lord, through the fulness of Thy love, that this may indeed be the case.

In Holland the party were received by the royal family and then made their way to Copenhagen. Their visit to Denmark is described by Elizabeth Fry in a letter home.

On board the packet after leaving Copenhagen, Eighth Month, 30th

My dearest Husband and Children,

We have been favoured to leave Denmark with peaceful minds, having endeavoured to fulfil our mission as ability has been granted us; a more important one, or a more interesting one, I think I never was called into. On First-day morning, when we arrived in the harbour, we were met by Peter Browne the Secretary to the English Legation, to inform us that the Queen had engaged for us apartments in the Hotel Royal. The appearance of the Hotel was, I should think, like the arrangements of one of our first-rate Hotels about a hundred years ago.

The next morning the Queen came to town, and we had a very pleasant and satisfactory interview with her, she certainly is a most delightful woman, as well as truly Christian and devoted character: she is also lovely in person, and quite the Queen in appearance. She took me in her carriage to her infant school, it really was beautiful to see her surrounded by the little children, and to hear her translating what I wished to say to them. After staying with her about two hours, we returned to our Hotel; and that evening took a drive to see the beautiful Palace of Fredericksburgh in a most lovely situation, the beauties of land and sea combined, with fine forest trees around it. The following morning we regularly began our prison visiting, very sad scenes we witnessed in some of them. We saw hundreds of persons confined for life in melancholy places; but what occupied our most particular attention, was the state of the persecuted Christians. We found Baptist ministers, excellent men, in one of the prisons, and that many others of this sect suffered much in this country, for there is hardly any religious tolerance. It produces the most flattening religious influence, I think more marked than in Roman Catholic countries. We were much devoted to this service of visiting prisons. Third and Fourth days, we received various persons in the evenings, but saw as yet but few Danes. On Fourth day we dined at Sir Henry Watkyns Wynn our ambassador, and here we became acquainted with several persons, they live quite in the country, and we saw the true Danish country-house and gardens.

The King and Queen were kind enough to invite us all to dine at their palace in the country, on Fifth-day. This was a very serious occasion, as we had so much to lay before the King – slavery in the West Indies – the condition of the persecuted Christians here and the sad state of the prisons. I was in spirit so weighed down with the importance of the occasion, that I hardly could enjoy the beautiful scene. We arrived about a quarter

223

past three o'clock; the Queen met us with the utmost kindness and condescension, and took us a walk in their lovely grounds, which are open to the public. We had much interesting conversation, between French and English, and made ourselves understood; when our walk was finished, we were shown into the drawing-room to the King, who met us very courteously, several were there in attendance. Dinner was soon announced: imagine me, the King on one side, and the Queen on the other, and only my poor French to depend upon, but I did my best to turn the time to account. At dinner we found the fruit on the table; first we had soup of the country, secondly, melons, thirdly, yams, anchovies, caviar, bread and butter and radishes, then meat, then puddings, then fish, then chickens, then game, and so on. The fashion was to touch glasses; no drinking healths. The King and Queen touched my glass on both sides; when dinner was over we all rose and went out together. The afternoon was very entertaining, the King and Queen took us to the drawing-room window, where we were to see a large school of orphans, protégés of the Queen. I took advantage of this opportunity and laid the state of the prisons before the King, telling him at the same time, that I had a petition for him which I meant to make before leaving the palace. After an amusing time with the poor children, my brother Joseph withdrew with the King into a private room, where for about an hour he gave him attention, whilst he thoroughly enlarged upon the state of their West India islands. I stayed with the Queen; but after awhile went in to them, and did entreat the King for the poor Baptists in prison, and for religious toleration. I did my best, in few words to express my mind, and very strongly I did it. I gave also Luther's sentiments upon the subject.

We slept at our friends the Brownes, a beautiful place by the sea-side. An agreeable serious gentleman, Julius Schesteed, was our interpreter, and remained with us, helping us to prepare our document for the King, he has become our constant companion, and is now with us in the packet, going to Lubeck, to interpret for us there. On Seventh-day, one of our fullest days, we drove into the country to visit the King's sister the Landgravine of Hesse, the Prince her husband, brother to the Duchess of Cambridge, and the lovely Princesses her daughters. We endeavoured to turn these visits to account, by our conversation. In the evening, we held one of our very large Meetings, I may say a splendid one, as to the company, room, &c. I trust that we were both so helped to speak the truth in love on various and very important subjects, as to assist the causes nearest our hearts, for our poor fellow mortals; it did not appear desirable to allude to the persecuted Christians, as we had laid their case before the King, we might have done harm by it; but I feel the way in which Protestant Europe is persecuting to be a subject that cannot and must not be allowed to rest.

Where we now are, the same old Lutherans whom we found persecuted in Prussia are persecuting others. The way in which ceremonies are depended upon is wonderful, no person is allowed to fill any office civilly or religiously, until confirmed, not even to marry; and when once confirmed, we hear that it leads to a feeling of such security spiritually, that they think themselves at liberty to do as they like, sadly numerous are the instances of moral fall. These very weighty subjects so deeply occupying my attention, and being separated from so many beloved ones, prevent the lively enjoyment I should otherwise feel, in some of the scenes we pass through; but I see this to be well, and in the right ordering of Providence. I have the kindest attendants and everything to make me comfortable.

On First-day morning, we had a very interesting Meeting with the poor Baptists. We then again went into the country, to lay all our statements before the King and Queen. I read the one about the prisons and the persecuted Christians; and my brother read the one about the West Indies: we had had them translated into Danish, for the King to read at the same time. After pressing these things as strongly as we felt right, we expressed our religious concern and desires for the King and Queen. I read a little to them in one of Paul's Epistles; after that I felt that I must commit them and these important causes to Him who can alone touch the heart. We had a very handsome luncheon, when I was again seated between the King and Queen. I may say their kindness was very great to me.

We arrived at Lübeck, after a calm voyage; but I do not like nights in steam-packets. I believe that we were sent to Copenhagen for a purpose. May our unworthy labours be blessed to the liberation of many captives, Spiritually and temporally.

Cassel, Ninth Month, 26th.

My most tenderly beloved Husband and Children,

I am glad, and I trust thankful, to be so far on our way homewards, and I hope and expect that we may this day week have the inexpressible consolation of being once more in England; my longings for it are almost inexpressible, and I have to pray and seek after faith and patience not to be too anxious, or in too great a hurry. I have continued very far from well, with latterly a considerable stiffness in my limbs, so that I am obliged to be assisted to walk up stairs, and helped into the carriage, sometimes by one or two men. I might have had the same attack at home; but one thing is certain, we may fully trust in our Heavenly Father, who is constantly protecting us under the wing of His love, and who knows what is best for us. I have sometimes thought that after being so helped on my way, from the palace to the prison, it was likely that the poor instrument should need a little further refining and purifying, for our works are to be tried as by fire. I have very earnestly desired not to repine, or to be unwilling to drink the cup that may be given me to drink. We travel with six horses to make the greatest speed home. I have a board in the carriage, that when your uncle and Anna are outside, I can quite rest and make a real sofa of it, when I need it, which I do for one or two stages in the day. Mary and François are very attentive and kind; indeed how differently am I cared for to many poor missionaries. I wish you to feel for me, but not to be too anxious about me; commit me entirely to Him who only knows what is best for me. Your aunt Elizabeth's letter was very seasonable and acceptable. I wish her and all my children to know how it is with me, for I need their sympathy and prayers, at the same time that I feel best help to be near, and the Power that says to the waves, "So far shall ye go and no further". Often in my wakeful and at times distressing nights, a sweet peace comes over me to calm my troubled spirit. We hear from newspapers, that the poor Baptists in Copenhagen are to be released from prison, a small sum being paid by way of fine. What a comfort! And the poor Lutherans in Prussia say they are now so well off, that they do not wish us to ask for any more liberty for them of the King.

I am indeed yours most faithfully and lovingly,

E F

Lynn, 10th month, 21st – At Ramsgate, I met with the utmost love and kindness, constant and faithful care, which were very useful to me until the time of my departure.

My visit to Upton Lane, to our dearest William and Julia, has really been cheering to my heart; the day appears come, that my beloved children for whom I have passed through such deep travail of spirit, and for whom I have exercised such tender care, and felt such wonderful love, are to take care of me; indeed, their kindness has been delightful and very comforting, quite enlivening and consoling. I see in this an advantage in coming home so broken in health. I have fallen upon them for care, first at Ramsgate, then at Upton Lane, ministering to my wants in the kindest way, Katharine doing all she can for me; and now Frank and Rachel are abundantly kind. I already feel better for their care over me, and that my suffering is more than made up to me, by the tender love and sweetness it has drawn forth from my most beloved ones.

Earlham, 11th month, 1st – We had a very delightful reception here. This is our son Harry and grandson Frank's birthday, – nineteen. We have cause for deep thankfulness on behalf of these dear sons; they have known many deliverances, and are, I trust, alive unto God as well as alive naturally. I humbly trust they may this year grow in grace, in the knowledge of God and of Christ our Saviour. Grant, gracious Lord! for Thine own name sake, that it may be so.

Upton, 12th month, 5th, First-day morning – I have been favoured to be much better the last few days, – far more easy, – thanks to my Heavenly Father: though I suffer still at times. I look upon this late indisposition as a very privileged one, and have felt, and deeply feel, the mercy extended towards me, in all my wants being so wonderfully provided for. The luxuries of life and generous living that I have had, I accept as gifts from a gracious and merciful Providence, that have been greatly blessed to my help, and, I believe, have greatly promoted my recovery. I exceedingly regret what I consider the intemperate and unchristian views some take of these things, judging all who feel it right to take stimulants in moderation. I believe Christians may use and not abuse these outward blessings, and that we have the highest authority for doing so; as He who set us a perfect example, and exactly knows our wants spiritual and temporal, certainly took wine. May He guide me in this and all other things, and guard me from being injured myself, or injuring others. Grant that this may be the case, gracious and most adorable Lord God and Saviour!

Upton, 1st month, 23rd, 1842, First-day – I find that the newspaper report of the dinner at the Mansion House has excited some anxiety at my being there, from the toasts, the music, &c. It is thought I set a bad example by it, and that it may induce others to go to such dinners, and that my being present appeared like approving the toasts. I quite wish to be open to hear all sides and to be instructed, and if I had erred in going, to do so no more, should such an occasion occur again. At the same time, I felt so much quietness and peace when there and afterwards, and until I heard the sentiments of others, that I fear being now too much cast down or tried by these remarks. I desire to keep near to Him who can alone help me and defend His own cause, that no harm should be brought upon it through me. I desire and pray to be kept in unity with those who love the Lord Jesus, and particularly with the people with whom I am in religious connexion. May I be guided at this time through what I feel a difficult place, by my Lord Himself, through the fulness of His love, mercy, and pity.

1st month, 29th – To-morrow, the King of Prussia has appointed me to meet him to luncheon at the Mansion House. I have rather felt its being the Sabbath; but it still is to be conducted in a quiet, suitable, and most orderly manner, consistent with the day, I am quite easy to go. May my most holy, merciful Lord, be near to me as my Helper, my Keeper, and my Counsellor. My dearest husband and Katharine are to go with me. Oh! may my way be made plain before me as to what to do, what to leave undone; when to speak, and when to be silent.

30th, First-day – I felt low and far from well when I set off this morning for London; but, through the tender mercy of my God, soon after sitting down in Meeting, I partook of much peace. I was humbled before my Lord in the remembrance of days that are past, when I used to attend that meeting (Gracechurch Street), almost heart-broken from sorrow upon sorrow, and I remembered how my Lord sustained me, and made my way in the deep waters. He also raised me up, and then He forsook me not. I was enabled very earnestly to pray to my God for help, direction and preservation. After this solemn and refreshing Meeting, we went to the Mansion House. We waited some time in the drawing-room before the King arrived from St. Paul's Cathedral. I have seldom seen any person more faithfully kind and friendly than he is. The Duke of Cambridge was also there, and many others who accompanied the King. We had much deeply interesting conversation on various important subjects of mutual interest. We spoke of the christening. I dwelt on its pomp as undesirable, &c.; then upon Episcopacy and its dangers; on prisons; on the marriage of the Princess Mary of Prussia; on the Sabbath. I entreated the Lord Mayor to have no toasts, to which he acceded, and the King approved; but it was no light or easy matter. I rejoice to believe my efforts were right. I told the King my objection to any thing of the kind being allowed by the Lord Mayor on that day; indeed, I expressed my disapprobation of them altogether. I may at the end of this weighty day return thanks to my most gracious Lord and Master, who has granted me His help and the sweet feeling of His love.

At the Mansion House, the King of Prussia arranged to meet Elizabeth Fry the following morning at Newgate, and afterwards to lunch at Upton Lane.

2nd month, 1st, Third-day – Yesterday was a day never to be forgotten whilst memory lasts. We set off about eleven o'clock, my sister Gurney and myself, to meet the King of Prussia at Newgate. I proceeded with the Lady Mayoress to Newgate, where we were met by many gentlemen. My dear brother and sister Gurney, and Susannah Corder, being with me, was a great comfort. We waited so long for the King that I feared he would not come; however, at last he arrived, and the lady Mayoress and I, accompanied by the Sheriffs, went to meet the King at the door of the prison. He appeared much pleased to meet our little party, and after taking a little refreshment, he gave me his arm, and we proceeded into the prison and up to one of the long wards, where every thing was prepared; the poor women round the table, about sixty of them, many of our Ladies' Committee, and some others; also numbers of gentlemen following the King, Sheriffs, &c. I felt deeply, but quiet in spirit – fear of man much removed.

After we were seated, the King on my right hand, the Lady Mayoress on the left, I expressed my desire that the attention of none, particularly the poor prisoners, might be diverted from attending to our reading by the company there, however interesting, but that we should remember that the King of Kings and Lord of Lords was present, in whose fear we should abide, and seek to profit by what we heard. I then read the 12th chapter of Romans. I dwelt on the mercies of God being the strong inducement to serve Him, and no longer to be conformed to this world. Then I finished the chapter, afterwards impressing our all being members of one body, poor and rich, high and low, all one in Christ, and members one of another. I then related the case of a poor prisoner, who appeared truly converted, and who became such a holy example; then I enlarged on love, and forgiving one another, showing how Christians must love their enemies.

After a solemn pause, to my deep humiliation, and in the cross, I believed it my duty to kneel down before this most curious, interesting and mixed company, for I felt my God must be served the same everywhere, and amongst all people, whatever reproach it brought me into. I first prayed for the conversion of prisoners and sinners generally, that a blessing might rest on the labours of those in authority, as well as the more humble labourers for their conversion; next I prayed for the King of

229

Prussia, his Queen, his kingdom, that it might be more and more as the city set on the hill that could not be hid, that true religion in its purity, simplicity, and power, might more and more break forth, and that every cloud that obscured it might be removed; then for us all, that we might be of the number of the redeemed, and eventually unite with them in heaven, in a never-ending song of praise. All this prayer was truly offered in the name and for the sake of the dear Saviour, that it might be heard and answered. I only mention the subject, but by no means the words.

The King then again gave me his arm, and we walked down together; there were difficulties raised about his going to Upton, but he chose to persevere. I went with the Lady Mayoress and the Sheriffs, the King with his own people. We arrived first, I had to hasten to take off my cloak, and then went down to meet him at his carriage-door, with my husband, and seven of our sons and sons-in-law. I then walked with him into the drawing-room, where all was in beautiful order – neat, and adorned with flowers: I presented to the King our eight daughters and daughters-in-law (Rachel only away), our seven sons and eldest grandson, my brother and sister Buxton, Sir Henry and Lady Pelly, and my sister, Elizabeth Fry – my brother and sister Gurney he had known before – and afterwards presented twenty-five of our grandchildren. We had a solemn silence before our meal, which was handsome and fit for a King, yet not extravagant – every thing most complete and nice. I sat by the King, who appeared to enjoy his dinner, perfectly at his ease and very happy with us. We went into the drawing-room after another solemn silence, and a few words which I uttered in prayer for the King and Queen. We found a deputation of Friends with an address to read to him – this was done; the King appeared to feel it much. We then had to part. The King expressed his desire that blessings might continue to rest on our house.

Upton, 3rd month, 15th – My son and daughter Cresswell, and several of their children are staying here; their little Gurney just going into the navy. It really oppresses me in spirit, I so perfectly object to war on Christian principles; it is so awful in its devastating effects, naturally, morally, and spiritually.

4th month, 17th – I feel the prospect seriously of our dear grandchild's going to sea; he leaves us to-morrow! It is no light matter. May our God, through His tender mercy, bring good out of this apparent evil. I have exceedingly regretted his going, but I am now more reconciled.

About this Elizabeth wrote a letter to her eldest son, on his becoming a magistrate

My dearest John,

Ever since I heard of the prospect of thy being a magistrate, I have had it on my mind to write to thee; but, alas! such is the press of my engagements, that in my tender state I cannot do what I would. I now, however, take up my pen to tell thee a little of my mind. I think the office of magistrate a very weighty one, and often, I fear, too lightly entered, and its very important and serious duties too carelessly attended to; and this I attribute to a want of a due feeling of the real difficulty of performing any duty; particularly one where much true wisdom is required in doing justice between man and man, unless governed and directed by that wisdom that cometh from above, which is pure, then peaceable, gentle, easy to be entreated, full of mercy and good fruits, without partiality and without hypocrisy. I believe it is thy desire to be governed by this wisdom, and to do justice, and love mercy; but remember this requires a very watchful and subjected spirit, and those who have to sit in judgment on others must often sit in judgment on themselves: this fits the mind for sympathizing with the wanderers, and adopting every right measure for their reformation and improvement. I think it is of the utmost importance to enter the duties attached to a magistrate in a very prayerful spirit, seeking the help and direction of the Spirit of God, and that the understanding may be enlightened to comprehend His will.

I am perfectly sensible that a justice of the peace must keep to the laws of his country in his decisions, and further, that he should be well acquainted with these laws; but I also know much rests with him, as to leaning on the side of mercy, and not of severity; and I know from my experience with so very many magistrates, how much they do in the prisons, &c., &c., to instigate or increase suffering; and also how much they may do for the improvement, and real advantage of criminals. Much is in their power; they may do much harm or much good: too many are influenced by selfishness, party spirit, or partiality, both in individual cases and where public good is concerned; but the simple, upright, faithful, just and merciful magistrates, are too rare, and they are much wanted. Mayst thou, my dearest John, be of this number; but remember it can only be by grace, and being thyself directed and governed by the Holy Spirit of God.

I advise thy reading Judge Hale's life – I know a judge and a justice are different things; but the same wise, truly impartial spirit, should govern

231

both. I wish to remind thee, that in petty offences, much is left to the magistrate's own judgment, and the utmost care is needful that crime is not increased by punishment, and the offenders become hardened, instead of being brought to penitence. I fear for young people. Our prisons in Essex generally only harden; therefore, try any other means with boys or girls: get them to Refuges, or try to have such measures adopted as may lead them to repentance and amendment of their ways. My very dear love to thy wife, and all thy children; and with deep and earnest desires that through the grace of God thou mayst perform all thy duties, domestic and public, to His glory, thy own peace, and the good of mankind.

I am thy very affectionate mother,

E Fry

Cromer, 7th month, 6th – Here I am, in what was my dearest sister Hoare's little room, looking on the sea, but poorly after my journey, feeling the air almost too cold for me; but I am favoured to be quiet and trustful in spirit, and desire to leave all things to Him, who only knows what is best for me. My sister Catharine being with us, and my brother Joseph and his Eliza and dear Anna near to us, is very pleasant, and our dear brother and sister Buxton and Richenda being still at Northrepps.

Letter to one of her grandchildren

Cromer 7/19/1842

My dearest Maria,

As the first letter to thyself I begin upon gilt paper & in this way to prove that I show thee all due respect.

I was much pleased to hear from thee my very dear grandchild and to have an account of you all. I think you must very enjoy your rides on horseback with your dear father. We drive about this lovely country frequently. I think very few sea places exceed it and it is now in its perfection. There are hills, fine cliffs, beautiful woods near, the sands excellent for driving and riding to a considerable distance and much to be found on the shore which I like when I can go down but I have as yet been only once.

We have a most pleasant and comfortable house so that we do not miss the indulgences of Upton. Indeed we may say from the kindness of the Buchans we really have luxuries, and I may thankfully say that I think I am really better than when I arrived here and if it should please Providence that I do not go back again as I so very often have done, I think I shall return in a very different state to what I was when I left home.

I much want to borrow a book of seaweeds that I think we sent you at Wailey as I like to know the names of them. I think you might send it by post. I delight to see the wonderful works offered in small things and in great. As Pope says, "To look through nature to nature's God", I think the earlier the mind is led to do this the better as it gives such a sweet relish to the gifts of Our Heavenly Father; I therefore think the study of natural history and philosophy excellent. Geology is a delightful branch which if I can get time, old as I am, I mean to study.

I am with dear love to you all thy tenderly attached grandmamma – Elizth Fry.

First-day, 8th month, 14th – I have deeply and sorrowfully felt our grandson Frank determining to go into the army. I truly have tried to prevent it, but must now leave it all to my Lord, who can, if He see meet, bring good out of that which I feel to be evil.

I have felt the weight of undertaking to establish a library and room for the fishermen, and something of a friendly society, as in my tender state the grasshopper becomes a burden. I was encouraged however in the night by these words, "Stedfast, immoveable, always abounding in the work of the Lord". In weakness and in strength, we must, as ability is granted, abound in the work of the Lord. May our labour not be in vain in Him! I have had very comforting accounts from Denmark – our representations attended to respecting the prisons, and likely to have much good done in them; also from Prussia. Surely our Lord has greatly blessed some of our poor efforts for the good of our fellow mortals.

Upton Lane, 1st month, 1st, 1843 – Another year is closed and passed never to return. It appears to me that mine is rather a rapid descent into the valley of old age.

2nd month, 6th – I am just now much devoted to my children and all my family, and attend very little to public service of any kind. May my God grant, that I may not hide my talents as in a napkin; and on the other hand that I may not step into services uncalled for at my hands. May my feeble labours at home be blessed. Gracious Lord, heal, help, and strengthen Thy poor servant for Thine own service, public or private.

Sandgate, Seventh Month, 29th – We arrived here yesterday. I have been permitted to pass through rather an unusual time of late. Our house was rather too full for me, and I got too anxious (my easily beset-ting sin), about some nearest to me. I was uncommonly pressed by other people, and then business of various kinds, and from a fine state of health, such as I have not enjoyed for a long time, and the most excel-lent refreshing nights, I have lately frequently been awake nearly all night, and from some cause become in so irritable a state of constitu-tion as to be for hours in the day really distressing. It particularly depresses, and flurries the spirits, and this with an extraordinary press of engagements has almost overwhelmed me. I have very earnestly prayed for help and patience, night and day, and it has been hard to come at a resting place, bodily or mentally. I find myself here in a lovely place by the sea, the air delightful, and the house pleasant. Thus the Lord provides for me in this my tried estate. If it please my Holy Helper, may He soon see meet to heal me.

First-day afternoon – No one of the family at home but myself, how very unusual a circumstance. I have at times passed through a good deal of conflict and humiliation in this indisposition, and it is a real exercise of faith to me, the way in which I am tried by my illness. I suppose it arises from my extremely susceptible nerves, that are so affected when the body is out of order, as to cast quite a veil over the mind. I am apt to query whether I am not deceiving myself, in supposing I am the servant of the Lord, so ill to endure suffering, and to be so anxious to get rid of it; but it has been my earnest prayer that I might truly say, "Not as I will, but as Thou wilt." Lord! help me. I pray that I may be enabled to cast all my burthen [*burden*] and all my care upon Thee, that I may rest in the full assurance of faith in Thy love, pity, mercy and grace.

First-day – Again alone, or nearly so; the rest gone to Meeting. I have passed a humbling week, still poorly by day and night. I think a place so remarkably void of objects does not suit my active mind, but it is well to be brought where I may rest on my oars; for there is a danger of depend-ing on active occupation for comfort, and even for a certain degree of diversion. I feel this when at the sea, at night in my wakeful hours; generally in the day I have something to occupy me; but this place has been unusually dull to me, though I have the sweet company of several of our own dear family. I think I mend a little, but it is very slowly. But truly do I pray night and day for mercy and help. I feel so peculiarly in need of it, seldom more so; however, perhaps when we feel most in danger we may be more safe, than when we apprehend ourselves in a place of safety. Gracious Lord, keep Thy poor servant by Thine own power and Spirit, who cannot keep herself even for a moment!

From this time on, Elizabeth Fry's health gradually declined but she bore this patiently, often repeating the words, "Come what, come may, Time and the hour run, through the roughest day." She was much brought down by bereavement as many of those closest to her died at this time.

Walmer, 8th month, 29th, 1844 – Sorrow upon sorrow! Since I last wrote, we have lost by death, first, my beloved sister[-*in-law*], Elizabeth Fry; second, Gurney Reynolds, our sweet, good grandson; third, Juliana Fry, my dearest William and Julia's second daughter; and fourth, above all, our most beloved son, William Storrs Fry, who appeared to catch the infection of his little girl, and died on Third-day of scarlet fever, the 27th of this month. A loss inexpressible – such a son, husband, friend, and brother! but I trust that he is for ever at rest in Jesus, through the fulness of His love and grace. The trial is almost inexpressible. Oh may the Lord sustain us in this time of deep distress. Oh ! dear Lord keep thy unworthy and poor sick servant in this time of unutterable trial; keep me sound in faith, and clear in mind, and be very near to us all – the poor widow and children in this time of deepest distress, and grant that this awful dispensation may be blessed to our souls. Amen.

Letter to her son John, 1st month, 1845

Dearest John & Rachel,

I find that you have kindly asked Mary to pay you a visit for a night or two, I like very much being with you and your dear girls and desire that you may take dearest Harry by the hand, <u>as he needs a little encouragement</u> and I think he missed William's valuable influence as he so often saw him living in the same neighbourhood.

I feel grateful, very grateful, for every kindness from him, for I think how much he misses me at this critical period of life and how much he is to be felt for in my long illness & his father's lowness. He is a kind dear son and I think just now he requires the kind hand of encouragement.

Farewell, my much loved children. My very dear & tender love is for you and your children. May the blessing of the Most High God rest upon you spiritually and temporally. I am your tenderly attached Mother. E.F.

The last letter she ever addressed to her husband was from North Repps, dated fourth month, 10th, 1845

My dearest Husband,

I am anxious to express to thee a little of my near love, and to tell thee how often I visit thee in spirit, and how very strong are my desires for thy present and thy everlasting welfare. I feel for thee in my long illness, which so much disqualifies me from being all I desire to thee. I desire that thou mayst turn to the Lord for help and consolation under all thy trials, and that, whilst not depending on the passing pleasures and enjoyments of this world, thou mayst at the same time be enabled to enjoy our many remaining blessings. I also desire this for myself in my afflicted state (for I do consider such a state of health a heavy affliction), independent of all other trials. I very earnestly desire for myself, that the tribulation I have had to pass through for so long a time may not lead into temptation, but be sanctified to the further refinement of my soul and preparation for eternal rest, joy, and glory. May we, during our stay in time, be more and more sweetly united in the unity of the Spirit, and in the bond of peace.

In the summer Elizabeth Fry and her husband took a house in Ramsgate where she continued to become weaker.

On 9th month, 13th, she wrote to her son Joseph

I am rather blanked to hear that we cannot see thee and thine this week. I rather particularly long to see a dear son again, as it feels long since John left us and you are sure your beloved wives have also a true welcome. I feel myself much broken, and finding that neither sea air, nor any other thing appears much to raise me up; I do feel that while here (I mean in this life), a great desire to be as much as I can with those most dear to me. My heart overflows with love and most earnest desire for your present and everlasting welfare, particularly that all may be of the number of those who "die in the Lord", "who rest from their labours, and whose works do follow them".

236

I feel certainly very poorly and unless there be some revival more than I now feel, I think that you cannot expect that you will very long have a mother to come to, but I know the Lord can raise me up again, and I should not be surprised if it should be His holy will, but into His hands I commit my body, soul and spirit, humbly trusting that He will be my Keeper, Guide, and Guard, even unto the end; through the fulness of His love, pity, mercy in Christ our Saviour. I know this is a low letter, may it lead to your sympathy, love, and prayers. I think I am low from parting with Julia and the children; my heart is so bound to you all. I am encouraged by remembering the 13th chapter of the First of Corinthians, because I feel that I may humbly trust that that love or charity there spoken of lives in my heart, and is as the apostle John says it is, a mark of having passed from death unto life, "because ye love the brethren".

The following day she wrote to her brother Samuel Gurney as follows

I was very low when I wrote to thee yesterday, therefore do not think too much of it. There is One only who sees in secret, who knows the conflicts I have to pass through. To Him I commit my body, soul and spirit, and He only knows the depth of my love and earnestness of my prayers for you all. I have the humble trust that He will be my Keeper even unto the end, and when the end comes through the fulness of His love and the abundance of His merits, I shall join those who after having passed through great tribulation, are for ever at rest in Jesus, having washed their robes, and made them white in the blood of the Lamb.

I am in nearest love,

Thy grateful and tenderly attached sister,

E. F.

Pray remember the books for the poor old women, we must work whilst it is called "to-day", however low the service we may be called to, I desire to do so to the end, through the help that may be granted me.

Ramsgate, 9th month, 16th – My dearest son Harry was married to dear Lucy Sheppard last Sixth Month, 26th. We had a very solemn Meeting; peace appeared to rest upon us at the Meeting, and at her father's house afterwards. My humble trust is, that the blessing of the Most High God is in this connexion. They spent some very satisfactory time with us before we left home. May grace, mercy and peace rest upon them, and neither the fatness of the earth, nor the dew of heaven, be withheld from them, through the fulness of the love, mercy and pity of our God, in Christ Jesus our Lord.

Our dearest niece Elizabeth was also married the latter end of the Seventh Month to my dear young friend Ernest Bunsen. May the blessing of the Most High God also rest upon them naturally and spiritually. I pray the same for them as for Harry and Lucy.

This is the last entry in her journal. Elizabeth Fry died on 13 October 1845 at the age of 65 and was buried at the Friends Burial Ground in Barking.

so that's how!

Timesavers, Breakthroughs, & Everyday Genius for
2007 Microsoft® Office System

Evan Archilla
Tiffany Songvilay

PUBLISHED BY
Microsoft Press
A Division of Microsoft Corporation
One Microsoft Way
Redmond, Washington 98052-6399

Library of Congress Control Number: 2006935893

Printed and bound in the United States of America.

1 2 3 4 5 6 7 8 9   QWT   2 1 0 9 8 7

Distributed in Canada by H.B. Fenn and Company Ltd.

A CIP catalogue record for this book is available from the British Library.

Microsoft Press books are available through booksellers and distributors worldwide. For further information about international editions, contact your local Microsoft Corporation office or contact Microsoft Press International directly at fax (425) 936-7329. Visit our Web site at www.microsoft.com/mspress. Send comments to mspinput@microsoft.com.

Microsoft, Microsoft Press, ActiveSync, AutoSum, Excel, Hotmail, InfoPath, Internet Explorer, MSN, OneNote, Outlook, PivotChart, PivotTable, PowerPoint, SharePoint, Windows, Windows Live, Windows Media, Windows Mobile, and Windows Server are either registered trademarks or trademarks of Microsoft Corporation in the United States and/or other countries. Other product and company names mentioned herein may be the trademarks of their respective owners.

The example companies, organizations, products, domain names, e-mail addresses, logos, people, places, and events depicted herein are fictitious. No association with any real company, organization, product, domain name, e-mail address, logo, person, place, or event is intended or should be inferred.

This book expresses the author's views and opinions. The information contained in this book is provided without any express, statutory, or implied warranties. Neither the authors, Microsoft Corporation, nor its resellers, or distributors will be held liable for any damages caused or alleged to be caused either directly or indirectly by this book.

Acquisitions Editor: Juliana Aldous Atkinson
Developmental Editor: Sandra Haynes
Project Editor: Valerie Woolley
Editorial and Production Services: Custom Editorial Productions, Inc.

Body Part No. X13-24188

Contents at a Glance

Table of Contents

What do you think of this book? We want to hear from you!

Microsoft is interested in hearing your feedback so we can continually improve our books and learning resources for you. To participate in a brief online survey, please visit:

www.microsoft.com/learning/booksurvey/

Part Two

We've Got to Start Meeting Like This: An End-to-End Solution for More Effective Meetings

Chapter Three

Smile on Your Brother—Better Ways to Organize Meetings with Customers and Colleagues 36

Part Three

All Work and No Play...(You Know the Rest): Create More Professional-Looking Documents in Less Time

Chapter Six

Frustration-Free Formatting—Get the Most from the New Document Structure and Formatting Capabilities of the 2007 Microsoft Office System   86

Chapter Seven

Easy on the Eye Candy—Create Documents, Spreadsheets, and Presentations That Pop   112

Part Four Trust Exercises: Letting Go Through Controlled Collaboration

Chapter Eight Prepare to Share—Share Any Document with Confidence

Chapter Nine Life in the Sandbox—Better Ways to Distribute, Review, and Manage Shared Work

What do you think of this book? We want to hear from you!

Microsoft is interested in hearing your feedback so we can continually improve our books and learning resources for you. To participate in a brief online survey, please visit:

www.microsoft.com/learning/booksurvey/

Acknowledgments

"But who am I, and who are my people,
that we should be able to give as generously as this?
Everything comes from You,
and we have given You only what comes from Your hand."

1 Chronicles 29:14

Sometimes it takes the 20/20 vision afforded only by hindsight to see how God works in the lives of those who trust Him. When I look back over this process and the parallel happenings in my life, I see that He who began a good work in me is still working—just as He promised. Everything I have is from Him and to Him goes all the glory. I give thanks for the talent, opportunity, and people He provided to make this book a success.

People like:

- Tiffany Songvilay—This book was your idea. Thank you for sharing the ride.

- Juliana Aldous and the team at Microsoft Press—Thank you for rolling the dice on a couple of newbies.

- Tawni Christensen, Marcus Ruyle, and Tiffany Wentzel at Microsoft— Thank you for believing in this book as much as we did.

- My Mom and Dad—Thank you for always being my biggest fans.

- My wife, M'Emily—Thank you for your never-ending love and support.

- My daughter, Idalia Corinne—Thank you for being you.

- And Scarecrow—I'll miss you most of all.

Tiffany would like to add:

- Evan—I would have gone stark-raving mad trying to work full time and complete this project on my own. Thank you for returning me to my husband a ~~sane~~ the same woman.

- Tawni C. at Microsoft who introduced me to Stephanie K., who put me in touch with Juliana A., and to Tiffany W., who told me I should get Evan involved. Other Microsoft thanks go to Jared A., Kelly P., Michele F., and my mentors—Monique V., Lesley R., James L., and Brian P.

- Greg G. and Steve G. at Marathon Oil Corporation for giving me the time off I needed to finish this work.

- My official fan club—International Association of Administrative Professionals (www.iaap-hq.org). I came back from your annual conference with the idea to write this book. Thanks to Jenny S. and Karlena R. out of California for representing the warmth and support of thousands of members.

- The writing group—Gwendolyn Z., Brie M., and Yvonne E.

- The teachers who set me on this path—Mr. Gorman, Mrs. Johansson, Dr. McDonald and Bob Darden.

- Thep, my amazing, self-sacrificing husband—who quit playing WoW every night so as not to tempt me away from writing this book. I always wondered what I could do if I didn't play video games all the time and now I know.

- My sister who believes I am fearless—so I am.

- To my father whom I respect and love, and my mother who has always known my purpose in this world.

- And to my grandparents, who walk with the Lord, live in the Word, and serve as a constant reminder that we are here to love one another unconditionally.

Ready for a New Day?

Have you ever seen a Smart Tag? If you use Microsoft Office XP or later, the answer is probably yes. If you're unsure, let us ask the question another way. Have you ever had your work interrupted by a pop-up button and you had no idea what it was for or how to make it go away? *That* was a Smart Tag.

Most Microsoft Office users have a love/hate relationship with Smart Tags; how you feel about Smart Tags depends largely on whether or not you know what to do with them. After all, it's not the Smart Tag itself but what the Smart Tag *does* that really matters. For example:

- When copying between Microsoft Office Word documents, you can use a Smart Tag to match the new text to the existing document formatting in *one* click.

- When Microsoft Office PowerPoint automatically capitalizes something you didn't intend to be capitalized, you can use a Smart Tag to undo the action and change future autocorrect behavior.

- When pasting formulas in Microsoft Office Excel, you can use a Smart Tag to select Paste Special options on the fly—like Values Only and Link Cells—thereby saving you trips to the Edit menu.

Again, it's what the Smart Tag does that makes a difference in your work. And it's that difference that determines whether or not you use, and eventually fall in love with, Smart Tags.

Now, before you close this book and place it back on the shelf, let us assure you—this is *not* a book about Smart Tags (though we will touch on them). Rather, this book grew out of our experience arming end users like you with an understanding of the full capabilities of the Microsoft Office system, along with tips and tricks to help you apply new and existing features to your daily work.

It's not enough to simply say "Office has Smart Tags" or whatever the other flavor-of-the-month feature happens to be, and then leave you to your own devices to figure out why, where, and how a feature should be used. In this book, we explain why a particular feature exists, where it can help you, and how you can take advantage of it. Our hope is that the tips and tricks contained herein become indispensable allies in your daily battle for better results.

The Sum of Its Parts

We believe better results begin with better tools. With the 2003 release, Microsoft introduced the concept of the Microsoft Office System. The idea being that typical workplace productivity has grown beyond the boundaries of the desktop. Advances in Internet speed and connectivity, along with the proliferation of electronic communication methods like e-mail and instant messaging, make it easier for people to work together even though they may be miles apart physically. What began as a glorified typewriter, the PC is now the gateway to a connected world, visiting Web sites, sending and receiving electronic documents, and participating in virtual meetings and conversations.

As we adapt to this new world of work, Microsoft Office must adapt to us. The familiar tools we use for document creation should be equally adept at sharing and facilitating collaboration on document content. We should be free to communicate with the people we need at any time from any location. And we must have the confidence that whatever happens, the integrity of our work will remain intact.

The 2007 Microsoft Office system represents the newest iteration of Microsoft's integrated productivity vision. All of the individual applications, servers, services, and solutions offer productivity benefits to end users. However, Microsoft *designed* the products of the 2007 Microsoft Office system to *work together* for a greater purpose—to solve the real-life business problems you face every day. This book takes Microsoft's vision to heart, offering a comprehensive set of tips and tricks you can use to boost your productivity across the 2007 Microsoft Office system products and technologies.

For All You Do, This Book's for You

We hear what you're saying. "My company doesn't have all of these products." That's okay. If you're simply looking for tips and tricks to help you format an Office Word document or create an Office Excel PivotTable, you won't be disappointed. However, experience has taught us that most users are doing a whole lot more—whether they realize it or not.

Consider that Word document. Did the idea for the document originate in a meeting? Or was it written in response to a flood of like-minded e-mails? Are you the sole contributor to the document? Do you have the authority to approve the final version? How will you share the document with others? Does it contain personal or confidential information? What will happen to the document five years from now?

Place your daily work into a broader context and suddenly something as simple as formatting a document doesn't seem so simple anymore. This book helps you understand the big picture and provides the tools you need to succeed no matter where you happen to be in the frame.

So, who is this book for? You! And everyone else who:

- Is ever overwhelmed by e-mail.
- Wastes too much time in meetings.
- Thinks documents always look better in their heads.
- Wonders why working with others is so difficult.
- Ever feels chained to their desk.
- Is just like us.

That's right. We too have received the "mailbox is full" message from the elusive system administrator. We've twiddled our thumbs in more meetings than we can remember. We've been left for dead among the towering ruins of file menus and dialog boxes. The good news is we found a way out. And now we're here to show you.

A Day in Your Life with the 2007 Microsoft Office System

Peel back the layers of your own daily onion and chances are you'll find each day can be broken down into four basic activities—sending and receiving e-mail, attending meetings, working on documents by yourself, and working on documents with others. Throw in the monkey wrench of mobility, where you complete each of these activities away from your desk, and you've got the makings of a typical day at the office.

And typical days turn into typical nights responding to e-mails. Nights turn into another weekend trying to catch up on paperwork and it looks like you're going to have to miss that training class you had scheduled so you can reconcile five different versions of the same document instead.

Over the next ten chapters, you'll find tips and tricks you can use to put the 2007 Microsoft Office system to work managing your e-mail, making meetings more effective, helping you create more professional looking documents, and facilitating better collaboration between you and your co-workers. We've even included a section to help you accomplish these basic tasks on-the-go.

By focusing on these horizontal scenarios, you'll learn tips and tricks for specific applications within the context of the ultimate problem you are trying to solve—world peace. Okay, so maybe this book doesn't do that exactly, but it can help you be more productive, giving you more time to solve problems that affect your company's bottom line and your next promotion.

Beyond Nip and Tuck—The New Face of Microsoft Office

The first step to moving up is dressing up. Unless you've been living under a rock for the past twelve months, you've probably heard that the core 2007 Microsoft Office applications are sporting a brand new look. The traditional menus and toolbars are gone. In their place is a new user interface (UI) centered around what Microsoft calls the Ribbon (more on this in a minute). In order to take advantage of many of the tips and tricks in this book, you need to have a basic understanding of the Ribbon and how to use it.

Why change the Microsoft Office user interface? It seems that while we were all busy working, Microsoft Office grew up—fast. So fast, in fact, that it outgrew itself. Microsoft Office Word alone grew from 50 menu items and 100 commands in Word 1.0 to 300 menu items and 1,500 commands in Word 2003.

The technology advanced so rapidly, with Microsoft adding so many new features, that the original structure of menus and toolbars became too complex for most users to deal with. The result? A lot of new and important functionality going undiscovered, and therefore unused, by the people it was designed to help. Here is what you need to know about the new Microsoft Office UI.

The Ribbon

Now appearing in Microsoft Office Word, PowerPoint, Excel, Access, and Outlook—the Ribbon! The Ribbon features a set of application-specific tabs, each one containing groups of commands relevant to a major task area. For example, the Word 2007 Ribbon includes tabs for writing, inserting, reviewing documents, and so forth. Likewise, the PowerPoint 2007 Ribbon includes tabs for Slides, Animations, and Slide Show. (See Figure 0-1)

Figure 0-1 The New Microsoft Office User Interface—Office Word 2007.

Some tabs are considered contextual. That is, they appear or disappear depending on the context in which you are working. For example, if there are no tables in your document, there is no need to clutter up the Ribbon with table-related tabs. Insert a table and...voila! The Table Tools tabs appear with design and layout options for your table. Click off the table and the Table Tools tabs are gone.

Galleries

Some command groups offer a more visual set of options to choose from. These groups are called Galleries. Galleries display commands as the result the command will achieve. For example, a style gallery presents the style options as visual samples of what each style actually looks like. A table design gallery displays thumbnails of available table styles. Click the selection in the gallery to apply it directly to your document.

Live Preview

Live Preview takes the concept of Galleries to the next level. By hovering over a command in certain galleries, Live Preview shows you the impact of the command within your document *before* you actually apply it. For example, the font gallery shows you samples of each available font. If you select a block of text in your document, then hover over the gallery choices, you will see a preview of the currently selected font as applied to your document. When you find the font you want, click it and you're done.

Microsoft Office Button

The Microsoft Office Button, represented by the Microsoft Office jewel icon in the upper left of the UI, contains many of the functions formerly found under the File menu. The familiar Save As and Print commands are here, as well as new commands relevant to Finishing and Publishing documents. The Save, Undo, and Redo commands are accessible from a customizable quick access toolbar next to the Microsoft Office Button.

Tip or Treat   To add commands you use frequently to the Quick Access Toolbar, click on the down arrow next to the Quick Access Toolbar. Select from available commands or click More Commands. You can also click on the Microsoft Office Button, click Word Options in the bottom right of the drop down window, then select Customize. Click the command you want in the left column, then click Add to add that command to the right column. Click OK. You can also use this window to customize your keyboard shortcuts.

The Ribbon, Galleries, Live Preview, and the Microsoft Office Button. While there is more to the new Microsoft Office UI than these, an understanding of these core elements is enough to get you started using Microsoft Office 2007.

Volume Value—Office Professional Plus 2007 and Office Enterprise 2007

While home users will appreciate many of the tips and tricks in this book, we wrote this content specifically with the business user in mind. If you use Microsoft Office at work, your organization is most likely covered by some type of Microsoft volume license agreement. If your organization is not a Microsoft volume license customer, chances are someone in IT is evaluating the benefits of becoming one.

Over the years, Microsoft has worked hard to add additional value to their volume-license programs. With the 2007 release, Microsoft is offering two new editions of the Office suite—Office Professional Plus 2007 (a revamped version of Office Professional 2003 Enterprise Edition) and Office Enterprise 2007—exclusively to volume license customers. You can see the product lineup for each of these at *http://office.microsoft.com/en-us/suites/FX101635841033.aspx*. In addition to more products, both Office Professional Plus 2007 and Office Enterprise 2007 include some important application feature-level differences. For example, Outlook 2007 as it appears in Office Standard 2007 does not have all of the features of Outlook 2007 as it appears in Office Professional Plus 2007 or Office Enterprise 2007.

These feature-level differences revolve around three key scenarios—integrated enterprise content management, integrated electronic forms, and information rights and policy. A few of the tips referenced in this book (Document Information Panel, document workflows, slide libraries, and Information Rights Management) are examples of this enhanced technology. You will need Office Professional Plus 2007 or Office Enterprise 2007 (in addition to any necessary server requirements) to take advantage of these particular tips, so you may want to verify with IT which suite of Office 2007 you are licensed for.

A Few Words About Windows Vista

Now, to the question on everyone's mind—what about Windows Vista? While we don't specifically discuss Windows Vista in this book, everything we talk about can be accomplished on a Windows Vista PC (though it's not required). With so much to cover related to the 2007 Microsoft Office system, we felt it would be unfair to you, the reader, if we bit off more than we could chew with Windows Vista. Besides, we had to save something for our next book.

That said, there are some definite advantages to using the 2007 Microsoft Office system in conjunction with Windows Vista. As a platform, Windows Vista and the 2007 Microsoft Office system deliver powerful solutions for improving your insight into business information, helping you protect and manage content, and simplifying how you work with other people.

To learn more about Windows Vista, look for these Windows Vista titles from Microsoft Press at your favorite bookstore:

- Windows Vista Inside Out
- Windows Vista Plain & Simple
- Windows Vista Step by Step
- Breakthrough Vista

About this Book's CD

The companion CD included with this book contains recordings of courses taught by Evan and Tiffany. The CD also includes a searchable electronic book in PDF format.

System Requirements

To view the CD, your computer needs to meet the following minimum hardware requirements:

- 500 megahertz (MHz)
- 256 megabytes (MB) RAM
- 1.5 gigabytes (GB) available space
- CD or DVD drive
- 1024x768 or higher resolution monitor

Support for This Book

Every effort has been made to ensure the accuracy of this book and the contents of the companion CD. As corrections or changes are collected, they will be added to a Microsoft Knowledge Base article.

Microsoft Press provides support for books and companion CDs at the following Web site:

http://www.microsoft.com/learning/support/books/

Questions and Comments

If you have comments, questions, or ideas regarding the book or the companion CD, or questions that are not answered by visiting the sites above, please send them to Microsoft Press via e-mail to

mspinput@microsoft.com

Or via postal mail to

Microsoft Press
Attn: So That's How! Editor
One Microsoft Way
Redmond, WA 98052-6399

Please note that Microsoft software product support is not offered through the above addresses.

Carpe Diem—Seize Your Documents

Congratulations! You've reached the end of the Introduction. You know what this book is about and who this book is for (look in the mirror). You understand the basics of the new 2007 Microsoft Office UI. And you know what to expect and not to expect concerning coverage of Windows Vista.

Now, it's time to get down to brass tacks. Every day is a new day with new opportunities and challenges. Our goal is to show you how to seize today and mine it for everything it's worth. Of course, the 2007 Microsoft Office system is here to help.

But first, you've got to get your head out of your Inbox...

Part One

Drinking From the Fire Hose: Tips and Tricks for Managing Information Overload

In this part

Based on your experience using e-mail at work, would you agree or disagree with the following statement:

"E-mail at work: few feel overwhelmed
and most are pleased with the way e-mail helps them do their jobs."

If you agree, good for you. You are truly the master of your e-mail domain.
If you disagree, then this might be the book for you. If you are still rolling
on the floor, holding your belly, and laughing until it hurts, congratulations; this is *definitely* the book for you.

The statement in question was actually the title of a 2002 report by the Pew
Internet and American Life Project. An initiative of the Pew Research Center, the Pew Internet and American Life Project examines the many ways
the Internet affects our social and business culture. Just like some said rock
'n roll was a fad in the 1950s, there has been a significant shift in the average business user's perception of e-mail in the past five years.

How do we know? We've been there. We've talked with literally thousands
of business users. We've seen the heads nod and the eyes roll. We've heard
the sighs of frustration and the sucking sound of lost time. What used to be
a convenient mode of communication has become an overwhelming chore.
Many times, complete business transactions are conducted entirely
through e-mail without ever picking up the telephone or, in some cases,
even meeting the customer or colleague you are working with.

While few will disagree that when it comes to doing business in a connected world, too much e-mail is better than no e-mail at all, the average
user can tread water for only so long before going under. And the water is
only getting deeper.

- A 2006 Microsoft study ranked e-mail as the most popular computing activity, with 95 percent of Windows-based PC users in the
  United States sending and receiving e-mail.
- According to a 2005 IDC study, there were 465 million business e-
  mailers worldwide in 2002. That number is expected to grow to 795
  million by 2009—an increase of over 70 percent.

- Of course, more business e-mailers means more business e-mail. A lot more. The 12.5 billion (that's *billion*, with a "b") business e-mails per day IDC estimated for 2002 will almost double to 24 billion by 2009. How long would it take to deal with 24 billion e-mails? Consider this: if you deleted one e-mail every second, it would take you almost 32 years to delete one billion e-mails. And unless your name is Methuselah, forget about the 768 years required to clean out the world's Inbox in 2009.

The result of this global trend is a growing number of users unable to stay on top of the daily onslaught of electronic information. Documents are lost, deadlines are missed, and the message from the system administrator telling us that our mailbox is over the size limit comes in faster than a speeding bullet.

The good news is it doesn't have to be this way. In this section, you'll learn how to put the power of Microsoft Office Outlook 2007 and other Microsoft Office system products and technologies to work for you to manage your daily deluge of information. With time-saving tips and tricks you can use right now, you'll be able to:

- Comfortably navigate the redesigned Outlook 2007 user interface.
- Find *and* act on important information in your mailbox.
- Cut your mailbox size in half through better management of your attachments.

Most importantly, the tips and tricks in this section are meant to complement—not replace—formal e-mail and time management strategies. So what are you waiting for? The tide is rising and, when it comes to e-mail, your seat cushion cannot be used as a flotation device.

Chapter 1

I Can See Clearly Now— Easy Ways to Read, Sort, and Store Ever-Increasing Quantities of E-Mail

Learn how to:

- ❏ Get the most out of the Outlook 2007 user interface
- ❏ Sort and categorize your information for easy access
- ❏ Protect yourself from junk e-mail

The New Look of Outlook

Outlook. Your work day revolves around it. It's the first thing you look at when you come into the office and the last thing you look at before you leave. Sometimes, Outlook even follows you home at night. So if you know Outlook like the back of your hand, why does Microsoft Office Outlook 2007 resemble *someone else's* hand entirely?

As the way we work with e-mail changes, so must our e-mail application. Simply put, it was time for a makeover. The new Office Outlook 2007 user interface is designed to handle today's more e-mail-centric workplace. Building upon the three-pane default view introduced in Outlook 2003, you'll find Outlook 2007 even easier to read, sort, find, and store ever-increasing quantities of e-mail. And the redesigned messaging interface—complete with the Microsoft Office 2007 Ribbon—puts the tools you need to compose, format, and act on individual e-mail messages at your finger-tips (see Figure 1-1).

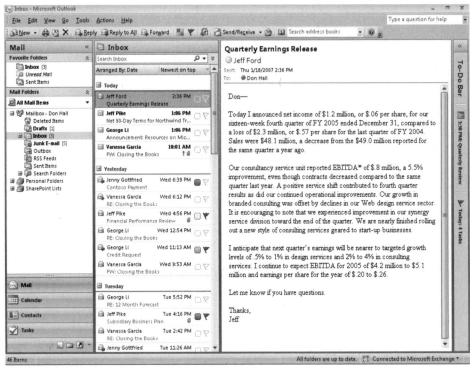

Figure 1-1   The Redesigned Messaging Interface.

So, while you *can* make parts of Outlook 2007 look the way they did when pagers were all the rage, Outlook 2007 is meant to work differently. This chapter will show you how to use the redesigned user interface to your advantage. Unlike your former classmates at your last high school reunion, we think you'll agree Outlook is looking better than ever.

No Pane, No Gain

With more and more e-mail finding its way into your Inbox, knowing what to focus on can be a challenge. Time is at a premium and you need to quickly differentiate between messages that are important, irrelevant, and sometimes downright junk. You also need easy access to your calendar, task list, and other mission-critical information that can make or break a productive day. Following are some ways Outlook 2007 can help.

Enhanced Reading Pane

One of the visual changes made in Outlook 2003 was to move the Reading Pane to the right side of the screen. This gave you *40 percent* more information in the window with easier-to-read, vertical orientation. Less scrolling through the message allowed you to make a split decision to act, skip, or delete it.

In Outlook 2007, Microsoft went a step further. Now, you can preview your file attachments in the Reading Pane. With one click, you can gain insight into the files that are taking up precious space in your mailbox. This allows you to quickly decide whether to save them or delete them (more on dealing with attachments in Chapter 2). To preview an attachment, click the filename in the Reading Pane. If you see a message warning you to "only preview files from a trustworthy source," you may uncheck the box and the warning will stop appearing (see Figure 1-2). Click Preview File. To return to the e-mail message, click Message.

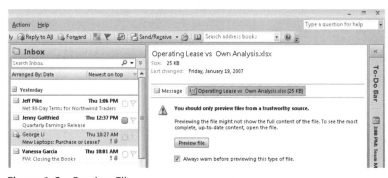

Figure 1-2   Preview File.

Tip or Treat   Do you have access to someone else's Inbox but don't want messages you check to appear read for your coworker? Click the Tools menu, then Options, then select the Other tab. Click Reading Pane and uncheck Mark items as read when viewed in the Reading Pane and uncheck Mark item as read when selection changes. Now an unopened message will only appear read if you right click it and select Mark As Read or use the keyboard shortcut Ctrl+Q.

To-Do Bar

Mail. Calendar. Tasks. Mail. Tasks. Calendar. Why is clicking through Outlook's Navigation Pane like playing a game of Whack-a-Mole? If the vast majority of our time in Outlook is spent reading mail, checking our schedule, and managing tasks, wouldn't it be nice to have everything visible in

Urban Legend Alert

In the past, some companies encouraged their users to turn off the Reading Pane in Outlook to safeguard against virus infections. That memo probably went out in your office about the same time they started casual Fridays. While this may have been a concern in the early days of HTML e-mail content, today's Reading Pane isn't any more of a threat to the organization than khaki pants.

Why the fuss over HTML content? HTML is a Web format. If you've ever visited a Web page with some type of interactive content, chances are you've knowingly or unknowingly downloaded something to your local computer. HTML e-mails can work the same way—and therein lies the rub. Prior to Outlook 2003, previewing an HTML e-mail in the Reading Pane would instruct the message to retrieve any necessary components, like graphics, from a Web server. Any time you download information from an untrusted source, you run the risk of infection or, at the very least, confirming for a junk e-mailer that your e-mail address is valid.

In Outlook 2007, images and other linked content in HTML messages are blocked by default, giving you the choice of whether or not to download them. If you wish to view the content, click the InfoBar at the top of the message and select Download Pictures. If you prefer a deeper level of protection, open the Trust Center from the Tools menu, then check the Read all standard mail in plain text box on the E-mail Security tab. This will display all messages in plain text along with an option in the InfoBar to revert back to the original HTML or Rich Text format.

one view? Allow us to introduce the To-Do Bar (see Figure 1-3). The To-Do Bar provides a consolidated and persistent view of your calendar, upcoming appointments, tasks, and flagged mail, making it easy to act upon your information. The To-Do Bar even shows tasks created through Microsoft Office OneNote 2007, Microsoft Office Project 2007, and Windows SharePoint Services Web sites (more on tasks in Chapter 2). To open the To-Do bar, click To-Do Bar on the View menu. Choose between Normal and Minimized views.

Figure 1-3   The To-Do Bar.

> **Tip or Treat**   Minimized view displays the To-Do Bar as a thin sliver on the right side of the screen, preserving the full width of the Reading Pane. Click the minimized To-Do Bar to temporarily expand it and view your detailed calendar and task information. Right-click the To-Do Bar's title bar and select Options on the short cut command list to adjust the number of months and appointments displayed.

Minimized Navigation Pane

E-mail is stored in folders in Outlook's left-hand Navigation Pane. Many people create folders directly under their Inbox to sort and store messages. Others create ArchiveFolders on the hard drive to move messages out of the Inbox for offline (and less server space-consuming) storage. Public folders are also accessible from this pane.

With all of these folders, you may find yourself doing a lot of scrolling up and down to find and access the particular folder you're looking for. Instead of scrolling, move your mouse over the thin blue line dividing the folder list from the Outlook buttons. Click and drag down to reduce the Outlook buttons to smaller clickable icons at the bottom (see Figure 1-4). To restore the buttons to their original view, simply grab the blue line again and drag it back up.

Figure 1-4   Outlook's version of a quick launch bar.

To move the Navigation Pane out of the way completely, click the minimize icon at the top right of the pane. This will reduce the Navigation Pane to a thin sliver on the left side of the screen. Click the minimized Navigation pane to temporarily display your list of folders.

> **Tip or Treat**   Favorite Folders, introduced in Outlook 2003, are shortcuts to your most commonly used mail folders. Think of them the same way you think of desktop shortcuts to a file in My Documents. They are not copies of your folders and therefore do not take up any additional space.
>
> To create a favorite folder, simply drag any folder (in Mail view) up to the Favorite Folders area and drop it. The next time you need access to the folder, don't waste time expanding your Inbox and scrolling for dollars through your nested subfolders. Just click the favorite folder and...voila! The folder you need, right when you need it.

Really Simple Syndication (RSS)

All we want for Christmas are our two blog feeds. And our industry and news subscriptions. And our Hollywood celebrity baby updates. And we want to manage all of these Really Simple Syndication (RSS) feeds from one place—the same place we manage the rest of our e-mail communication. Fortunately, we don't have to wait until Christmas to take advantage of this functionality. And neither do you.

You can now fully subscribe to and interact with RSS feeds from within Outlook 2007, the most natural place to manage this kind of information. To add an RSS Feed, right-click the RSS Feeds folder in the Navigation Pane and select Add A New RSS Feed. Enter the URL for the RSS Feed you want to manage. For more detailed management options, click Tools, then Account Settings, and select the RSS Feeds tab.

To remove a favorite folder you no longer need, right-click it and choose Remove from Favorite Folders. Do NOT click Delete *"Folder Name"* as this will delete the original folder and you will be very, very sad.

New Mail Desktop Alert

The New Mail Desktop Alert, introduced in Outlook 2003, uses your peripheral vision to teach you that not every e-mail you receive is the most important thing happening to you right now. Today, how many of us even flinch when the home phone rings? We let the answering machine get it because if it's important, they'll call our cell phone, right?

The New Mail Desktop Alert is like Caller ID for your Inbox. It shows you the sender, the subject, and the first few lines of text in a dialog box that takes seven seconds to fade in and fade out. You can continue to type and click in your current application while the alert is on the screen. The days of hearing the incoming mail sound, stopping work, and maximizing Outlook only to discover it was someone saying "Thanks!!!" are over.

In fact, you can prevent e-mails like "Thanks!!!" from ever making it into your Inbox again by clicking the Delete button on the New Mail Desktop Alert. You can also click the alert's flag icon to mark important messages for follow-up as they arrive, instead of hunting for them later in your Inbox.

To turn the New Mail Desktop Alert on or off, click Options on the Tools menu. On the Preferences tab, click E-mail Options, then Advanced E-mail Options. Check or uncheck the box for New Mail Desktop Alert. You can also click Desktop Alert Settings and adjust the length of time the alert is visible (see Figure 1-5).

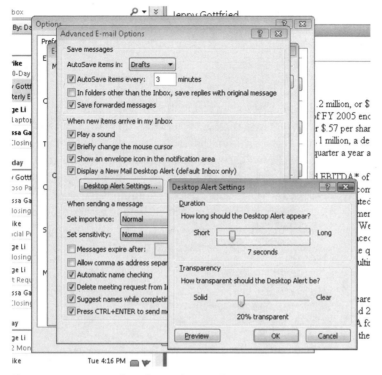

Figure 1-5   New Mail Desktop Alert Settings.

We Like Short Sorts

Think of your Inbox like a child's piggy bank. All of your messages with different priorities and subjects and sizes are all mixed together like so many dimes, nickels, and pennies. When it comes time to pull a butter knife out of the drawer and go fishing for money for the vending machine, you have to get through all the nickels and dimes and pennies to find the quarters. That's like arranging your Inbox by date and scrolling through the entire list to find a message. Wouldn't it be great if we could just have all the quarters fall out of the piggy bank instead? Well, in Outlook, you can arrange your mail folders by group, which makes pulling out the biggest e-mails or the e-mails that are from your boss a lot easier. That's way better than using a butter knife.

The key is organization. An effective process for sorting and storing e-mail today can cut down on the time it takes to find the same e-mail tomorrow. Again, the emphasis is on maintaining an at-a-glance approach. If the e-mail you need is right in front of your face (or accessible in a click or two) there's no need to waste time looking for it. In other words, the days of arranging all of your e-mail by the date they showed up in your Inbox are over.

Show in Groups

Outlook 2007 offers a number of ways to arrange your messages. To take full advantage of this powerful sort functionality, you should first turn on message grouping, a feature introduced in Outlook 2003. To do this, click Arranged By at the top of the column, then select the Show In Groups option (see Figure 1-6). This will arrange your messages in logical group-ings. For example, arranging by date groups messages from "Today," "Yes-terday," "Last Week," and so on. If your message column is too wide or the Reading Pane is not on the right, the Arranged By field is replaced by indi-vidual sort criteria. You can sort your messages by clicking an existing field, or by clicking View, then Arrange By and selecting a sort option.

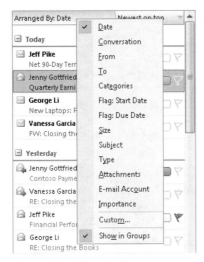

Figure 1-6   Show in Groups.

Click the minus sign next to any of the group headers to collapse an entire section. This is a great way to quickly hide messages that do not pertain to your current activity. To view and entire conversation, click the down arrow next to the subject header. Right-clicking the group header and selecting Delete is an effective way to delete all the messages in a particular group with a couple of keystrokes. In the same way, you can use the Arranged By menu to sort and manage messages according to who they are From, or stack your messages according to Size for quick clean-up.

Tip or Treat   Sorting your e-mail by size is a great way to find large items within a particular folder. To see how much total space your Mailbox is taking up, click Folder Size in the Folders list view. You can also right-click the word Mailbox in Mail view and click Properties. Click the Folder Sizes option in that screen and you will be able to see the total size of your Mailbox and which folders are your biggest offenders.

Arranged by Conversation

As e-mail usage continues to proliferate around the world, more and more people find themselves conducting entire conversations within the confines of their Inbox. The days of picking up the telephone to ask a question or communicate a response are going the way of the floppy disk. However, more e-mail conversations mean more individual e-mails—often spread out over days or weeks—to contend with.

When you use the Arranged By menu to arrange your Inbox and subfolders by Conversation, you are able to see the entire e-mail thread. How is this different than arranging by Subject? Arranging by Subject sorts messages *alphabetically* by subject line first and the individual e-mails within the grouping by date. Arranging by Conversation groups messages by subject and then arranges the entire *groupings* by date. The messages within each grouping are then broken down based on who replied to whom. This way you can see all of the messages in a thread as they arrived and simply jump to the latest e-mail to read or respond.

If a new e-mail arrives that is part of an existing conversation, the entire thread grouping will move to the top of your Inbox. So, when you walk away from your desk and return, all your new e-mails will still be at the top of your Inbox but they will be listed under the related e-mails you read before you left. You know that an e-mail has been responded to if it has a message indented underneath it. If two messages line up directly underneath one another, that is an indication they are a response to the same e-mail.

Arranging by Conversation is another great way to delete redundant e-mail in a snap. Simply right-click the conversation thread header, select Delete, and say goodbye to all of the messages in the thread at once. No more hunting and pecking through weeks of e-mail to clean out unwanted "thread droppings." Before you delete any e-mail, however, take care to save any necessary attachments to another location (see Chapter 2).

Tip or Treat   You followed the instructions above and freed yourself
from an e-mail conversation thread that had long since run its course. To
make doubly sure the thread would never visit you in your sleep again, you
emptied your Deleted Items folder. And now you realize the only place you
had your customer's mobile phone number was in one of those now-
deleted messages. Not to worry.

If your Outlook client is connected to Microsoft Exchange Server 2003 or
2007, you can restore deleted e-mail items for a default period of two
weeks *after* you empty your Deleted Items folder. (IT can shorten or extend
this period, or disable this functionality altogether.) Click the Tools menu,
then select Recover Deleted Items.

Color Categories

Outlook 2003 introduced the concept of color-coding messages and
appointments. Outlook 2007 turns a set of nice-to-have features into an
essential tool for organizing and identifying important information. With
Outlook Color Categories, you can easily categorize and personalize related
e-mail messages, meetings and appointments, and tasks. These Color Categories are a visual way to identify related information on specific projects,
people, or activities.

To assign a Color Category to an e-mail message or task, right-click the
square category icon to the right of the message or task. To assign a Color
Category to a calendar item, right-click the item and choose Categorize.
Then, choose the color you want and click it. To customize the category,
right-click the category icon to the right of a message or a task or go to the
Categorize menu by right-clicking an appointment and selecting All Categories. From here, you can Rename a category or create a New category using
one of 25 different color options (see Figure 1-7). You can also assign and
customize Color Categories using the Categorize button on the Standard
toolbar. Use a Color Category as search criteria to locate related items across
your e-mail, calendar, contacts, and tasks.

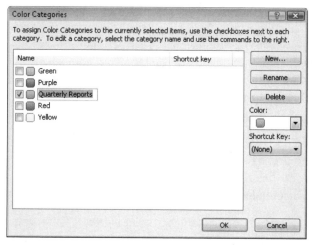

Figure 1-7   The Color Categories dialog box.

Junkyard Dog 2.0

These days spam, or unsolicited junk e-mail, flows like the Nile in flood season. Spam is always intrusive, often offensive, and takes time away from other work. And despite governmental attempts to regulate spam, it's not going away any time soon. The same Pew report referenced at the beginning of Part I (you know, the one that said few people were overwhelmed by e-mail) estimated that, in 2002, spammers worldwide clicked "send" on over 7 billion pieces of spam e-mail a day. If 7 billion pieces of spam was not particularly overwhelming to business users in 2002, consider this: the number is expected to grow to almost 45 billion spam messages a day by 2009—an increase of more than 500 percent!

Despite the increase in spam, most people respond to junk e-mail by hitting the Delete key and sending the offending message to their Deleted Items folder. While this may provide instant gratification, it does nothing to stem the flow of offers for unwanted home equity lines, insider stock tips, and cures for various...er, dysfunctions. Fortunately, Outlook 2007's improved Junk E-mail capabilities give you the tools you need to fight back. Here's how you dam the River Spam.

Junk E-Mail Folder

Introduced in Outlook 2003, the Junk E-mail Folder helps you divert spam away from your legitimate e-mail. To mark a message as junk, right click it, select Junk E-mail, then Add Sender to Blocked Senders List. This moves the message into your Junk E-mail Folder and prevents another message from the same sender from making its way into your Inbox. By comparison, if you merely delete the message, that sender is free to keep sending you more junk. The system won't allow you to add anyone from your company's domain name to this list, but you can add the external contact that keeps sending you all those bad jokes. Sorry, Mom, not at work.

To block entire domain names, right click any message and select Junk E-mail, then Junk E-mail options. Click the Blocked Senders tab and scroll through the listings to find any junk e-mail messages whose domain name is listed more than once. To add a domain name to your Blocked Senders List, click Add and type **@example.com**.

If you find an item in your Junk E-mail folder that shouldn't be there, you can mark it as Not Junk by clicking the Not Junk button on the toolbar. The message will automatically move back into your Inbox. You'll also be given the opportunity to add the sender or the domain to your Safe Senders list, thus preventing these messages from ending up in the Junk E-mail folder in the future. The Safe Senders list can also be managed through the Junk E-mail Options dialog box. Keep in mind, once you mark a message or sender as safe, any HTML message content will be downloaded automatically.

Perhaps most importantly, don't forget to check and empty the Junk E-mail folder on a regular basis as these messages are taking up space and count against the size of your mailbox. To do this, right-click the Junk E-mail folder and select Empty Junk E-mail Folder.

Word to the Wise   Be careful when adding domains to your Safe and Blocked Senders lists. If you block spam from a domain that is widely used (for example, hotmail.com, msn.com, or aol.com), you may be inadvertently blocking e-mail from your friends and family. Likewise, adding these common domains to your safe list may open you up to all kinds of unsolicited communications.

E-Mail Postmarks

Remember when a first-class stamp cost a quarter? At 39 cents and rising, doing business by postal mail is not as cost-effective as it used to be. The same applies to funny business, aka spam. Which is why the amount of junk you receive in your Inbox is ten times the amount you receive in your post office box—infrastructure aside, e-mail is for all intents and purposes a free method of communication. What if there was a way to place a cost—not a financial cost, but a computational cost—on e-mail? Something that would be easy for users to bear, but a nightmare for spammers.

An Outlook E-mail Postmark is a set of unique message characteristics that ensure the e-mail you send will be trusted by the recipient. Outlook 2007 applies the Postmark to the outgoing message, causing the e-mail to sit in the Outbox a little longer than normal, thus adding a computational cost to the message. When the recipient receives the Postmarked message, the receiving Outlook 2007 client is more likely to route the message past the Junk E-mail Filter and into the recipient's Inbox.

Spammers are unlikely to use E-mail Postmarks for their own evil purposes because of the computational cost involved in sending Postmarked messages. When you're sending thousands of e-mails an hour, you can't afford the delay caused by applying Postmarks to each message. Spamming at the pre-Postmark rate would require an increase in infrastructure, something spammers usually want to avoid.

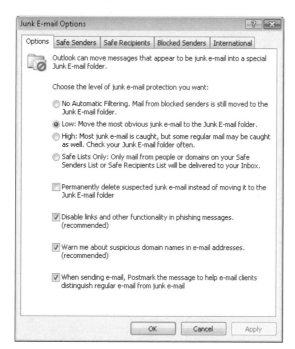

Figure 1-8   Junk E-mail Options.

Outlook E-mail Postmarks are enabled by default in Outlook 2007. To turn Postmarks off, click Options on the Tools menu, select Junk E-mail on the Preferences tab, then clear the box next to When sending e-mail, Postmark the message to help e-mail Clients distinguish regular e-mail from junk e-mail (see Figure 1-8).

No Phishing

You've seen the e-mail: "My husband, Dr. Neil Sturgeon, is a political prisoner in a war-torn nation. The government (such as it is) has agreed to release Dr. Sturgeon for a large handful of cashola. Unfortunately, all of Dr. Sturgeon's funds are tied up in Martian hedge funds and can only be accessed by Dr. Sturgeon himself. Please help me secure the release of my husband by replying to this e-mail with your bank account number, a major credit card, and the combination to your high school locker. Please provide your home address so we can steal...er, mail your money back to you along with a hefty reward immediately upon Dr. Sturgeon's release."

In case you haven't figured it out, you were just invited on a phishing expedition. Phishing is a sneaky spamming practice in which an e-mail poses as something legitimate—a cause, a company you patronize, even your bank—and tricks you into providing the sender with some type of personal information like an account or credit card number. Your information is then used against you as the spammer helps him or herself to your identity, your money, and ultimately your peace of mind.

Outlook 2007 helps protect you from phishing e-mails by tracking suspect messages and warning you of the potential threats contained therein. It also disables any links to prevent you from inadvertently clicking through and starting something you may not be able to stop. To turn the anti-phishing feature on, right-click any message, then click Junk E-mail, then Junk E-mail Options. Check the box next to Disable links and other functionality in phishing messages. If you feel a disabled link is legitimate, or the e-mail as a whole was incorrectly identified, you can click the InfoBar to restore the original functionality.

Tip Jar

Here's a review of the top 10 tips covered in Chapter 1:

- **Preview Attachments** Click the attachment, then select Preview File. To return to the e-mail message, click Message.

- **To-Do Bar** Click View, then To-Do bar. Select Normal. Right click the To-Do Bar and select Options from the command list to adjust the number of months and appointments displayed.

- **Resize Navigation Buttons**   Hover your mouse over the thin blue bar above the Outlook navigation buttons (above the word "Mail"). When you see a double-headed arrow, drag the bar down to the bottom of the screen.

- **Favorite Folders**   Click and drag any folder up to the Favorite Folders area to create a shortcut. To remove a folder, right-click it and choose Remove from Favorite Folders. (Be careful not to hit delete!)

- **RSS Feeds**   Click Tools, then Account Settings, then select the RSS Feeds tab. Click New, then paste in the desired RSS URL. Look for RSS URL information on your favorite Web sites and blogs. Example: *http://www.example.com/feed/main.xml*

- **New Mail Desktop Alert**   To turn Desktop Alerts off or on, click Tools, then select Options. Click E-mail Options, then Advanced E-mail Options and check the box by Display A New Mail Desktop Alert. When an alert appears, click the Options down arrow in the new message notification area to Delete, Flag, Mark it as read, or Disable New Mail Desktop Alert

- **Arrange Messages by Conversation**   Click the Arranged By: bar above the message list. Make sure Show in Groups is checked, then click Conversation. To delete an entire conversation thread, right-click the conversation thread header and choose Delete.

- **Assign a Category**   Right-click the Color Category square next to an e-mail or task to choose a color. For calendar items, right-click the item and select Categorize, then choose a color. The first time you use a particular color, Outlook will ask you if you want to rename it. To customize categories or create new categories, right-click the color square and select All Categories.

- **Disable or Enable Postmarks**   Right-click any message, then click Junk E-mail, then Junk E-mail Options. Check the box next to When sending e-mail, Postmark the message... To disable postmarks, uncheck the box.

- **Turn Anti-Phishing On/Off**   Right-click any message, then click Junk E-mail, then Junk E-mail Options. Check the box next to Disable links and other functionality in phishing messages. To turn anti-phishing off, uncheck the box.

Now that you can read and sort your e-mail more quickly in Outlook 2007, let's focus on some tips and tricks for finding, and more importantly, *acting* on the information and tasks in your Mailbox.

Chapter 2
Search and Destroy— Find and Act on Important E-Mail Messages

Learn how to:

❑ Find what you're looking for in an instant

❑ Manage your daily task list

❑ Free yourself from space-hogging e-mail attachments

Finding and Acting on E-Mail

Searching for things is a natural part of life. You have to look under the bed and the couch and in the car to find your child's missing shoe. You have to take out every plastic container in the cupboard to find the lid that matches what you just put the leftovers in. And you probably have a sock drawer full of socks with no mates. Some searches, we can't spare you from, but we can teach you how to find information in your e-mail faster.

This chapter will show you how finding and acting on e-mail in Microsoft Office Outlook 2007 is easier than ever before. With new Instant Search, you can locate your target and take action (you guessed it) instantly. Flag a message as a full-blown Outlook task, or simply change the subject line to something more recognizable. You can even help your coworkers do their part by adding reminders and setting expiration dates on time-sensitive communications. Used as personal productivity tools, you can create tasks and set reminders for yourself as an alternative to holding on to numerous e-mail attachments.

As the saying goes, "seek and ye shall find." Even if your Mailbox contains more folders than Bart Simpson's permanent record.

I Still Haven't Found What I'm Looking For (In My Mailbox)

What do Bigfoot, the Loch Ness Monster, and the Abominable Snowman have in common? They're all easier to locate than that piece of e-mail your coworker sent you two weeks ago containing updated metrics for this afternoon's scorecard review.

Finding messages when you need them can be a frustrating and time-consuming process, especially when your Mailbox resembles the floor of your college dorm room. Here are a few tips to make finding information a snap.

Instant Search

Information can run but it can no longer hide thanks to Office Outlook 2007 Instant Search. Instant Search can locate the information you're looking for—across your Mailbox, Calendar, Contacts, and Tasks—and highlight the specific areas where your search term appears. Instant Search even searches inside e-mail attachments! For more refined search results, narrow the scope of your search by adding helpful criteria in the Instant Search pane (see Figure 2-1). The Instant Search pane is accessible just below the Outlook toolbar.

To search across all your Outlook items at once, click Tools, then Instant Search, then select Advanced Find. In the Look For: drop-down menu, select Any Type Of Outlook Item.

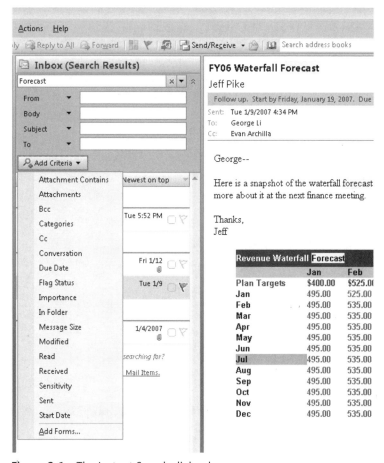

Figure 2-1 The Instant Search dialog box.

Search Folders

Search Folders, introduced in Outlook 2003, make it easy to quickly access the information you're looking for in your mailbox. However don't be misled by the name. Search Folders aren't really folders at all–they're filters. Clicking a Search Folder will filter your mailbox (Deleted Items, Sent Items, Inbox, and subfolders) based on the specific criteria of that Search Folder.

For example, there are three default Search Folders in Outlook 2007–Unread Mail, Large Mail, and Categorized Mail. Clicking the Unread Mail Search Folder will filter out all the read messages and only show you the unread ones. As you read the messages, they are filtered out of the Search Folder. Like Favorite Folders, messages in Search Folders are not moved from their original location. You are simply looking at them in a different view.

You can add as many Search Folders as you want. Right-click Search Folders and click New Search Folder. You can choose from a variety of preset folders or create your own based on custom criteria like a keyword or a person's name (see Figure 2-2). If you access the same Search Folder often, you should drag it up to the Favorite Folders list so you can access it quickly.

Figure 2-2   Create a New Search Folder.

Forget the String Around Your Finger

It's been said that elephants never forget. People, however, do. We forget birthdays and anniversaries. We forget to take out the trash. We forget to respond to an e-mail Request for Proposal by "end of day" Friday or our company will lose its biggest account forever and our manager will be really upset and we'll be searching the classifieds this weekend looking for another job.

You can avoid such embarrassment by using Outlook 2007 to mark important e-mails for future reference or follow-up. Here's how.

Change the Subject Line

Have you ever lost an important e-mail because you don't remember when it was sent or the subject line doesn't indicate what's inside the body of the message? Who knew those important numbers you needed to include in the company's 10K were hiding in a message with the subject line, "Hi!"?

You can double-click any message and change the subject of the message by highlighting it to select it and then typing over it. You can simply close the message, and Outlook will ask if you want to save the edited message. If the mail is part of a larger thread, changing the subject will not alter the way Outlook arranges the message by conversation until you reply or forward the message with the new subject.

Flagging Mail as Tasks

In Outlook 2003, there were basically three ways to flag an e-mail for follow-up—use the Colored Quick Flags, drag the e-mail onto the Tasks button, or manually create the task. Colored Quick Flags only offered a visual reminder of the activity. Dragging the e-mail onto the Tasks bar created a task for the e-mail, but had to be customized if you wanted the task to call out a specific action required by the e-mail content. Manually creating the task was the most flexible option, but also took the most time to accomplish. In the end, most people gave the colors a go for awhile and then dropped back into the habit of creating to-do lists in a blank e-mail message, Word document, or on the inside of their left hand (or right hand for you southpaws).

In Outlook 2007, flags and tasks are one and the same. When you flag an e-mail for follow-up, you are automatically creating a task. This new task appears in the To-Do Bar and can be opened and customized. To flag an e-mail as a task, right-click the Flag next to the e-mail you want to assign a task to (see Figure 2-3). Select a due date for the task or click Custom to further refine the task parameters.

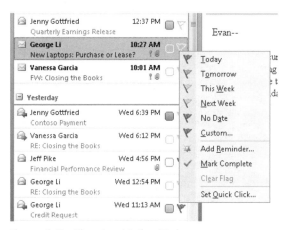

Figure 2-3 Flagging Mail as Tasks.

When viewing your Calendar in either the Day format or the Week format, tasks are instantly accessible through your Calendar by clicking the Daily Task List option on the View menu. Use the Arrange By option to specify whether tasks are to be displayed By Start Date or By Due Date. The Daily Task List displays your daily tasks directly beneath your daily appointments and meetings, so you know exactly what you have to do and when you have time to do it (see Figure 2-4). To allocate time on your calendar for working on any given task, drag the task up onto the calendar and drop it on the desired time slot. Tasks you complete remain on the day you completed them. Tasks you don't mark complete roll over to the next day's task list. (They will not, however, sit up, lie down, or play dead.)

Figure 2-4   Daily Task List.

Now That I Have Your Attention...

Turning e-mail into action can help you stay on top of your daily commitments. But what happens when finishing your work depends on someone else finishing theirs? How do you know the e-mail you sent requesting the latest revenue numbers, updated press release, or key to the executive washroom received the attention it required?

Requesting a delivery receipt and a read receipt of any message usually only accomplishes one thing—creating more e-mail in your Inbox. It doesn't actually prove your coworker read the message, although it does give you some sense of security that if they ever came back and said they didn't receive the e-mail, you could prove they did. Or could you? Did you know that if they navigate into their e-mail options they can choose to never send a response to these requests?

You could assign a task to your coworker; however, if that person does not report to you, he or she may take offense at your attempt at micromanagement. (Only our real managers are allowed to micromanage, and even then at their own peril.)

There is a better way. Send your coworker a reminder and set an expiration date for the message. Doing so may prompt your recipient to look at the message as many as four times—once when they receive it, once in the reminder window, again in their Inbox when it turns the color red and finally when Outlook crosses out the message. Here's how to set it up:

Reminders

You can send reminders to coworkers (if they have not disabled Outlook's default reminder options) by clicking the Follow Up button in the Options group of the Message tab of a new e-mail (see Figure 2-5). Click Flag For Recipients, then select a date and time to remind them. To set a reminder for yourself at the same time, check the box next to Flag for Me. Even if you have opted out of reminder pop ups, the message header turns the color red in your Sent Items folder when it's time to follow up.

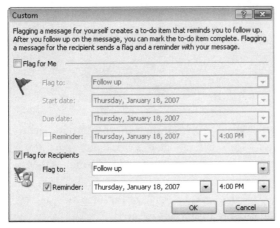

Figure 2-5   Flag for Recipients.

You can set a reminder on any message you receive by right-clicking the Flag and selecting Add Reminder. If you add the reminder when the message is in your Inbox then you will still receive the reminder at the set due date even if you move it down into a personal folder.

Expiration Date

You can send a message with an expiration date to a coworker by clicking the Message Options arrow in the Options group of the Message command tab in a new message, selecting the Expires After check box, and specifying a date and time (see Figure 2-6). This feature is perfect for those "you have until close of business" e-mails. You can also set an expiration date on a message in your Inbox. Right-click any message in your Inbox, click Message Options, then put a check box by Expires after, and choose a date and time for the message to expire.

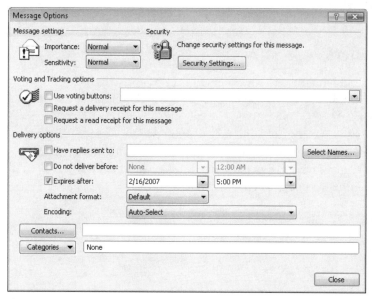

Figure 2-6 Expiration Option.

The first line of an expired message has a strikethrough through it to let the reader know the time to deal with this message has come and gone. For more sensitive communications, Information Rights Management (IRM) can prevent messages from being read again once they've expired. (For more information on IRM, see Chapter 8.) Take note that the message will not be deleted automatically just because it has expired.

Attachment Detachment

Because everything is e-mailed nowadays, Outlook is often expected to do more than just manage our e-mail; we are also asking it to manage the files associated with those messages. How many of us are saving an e-mail in our Inbox right now just because we need the attachments in it? You know, that e-mail from HR reminding you to sign up for benefits or that Excel workbook you receive every month that you might—just *might*—need to reference someday? Maybe you don't really need Outlook to save the attachment at all. Maybe you just need Outlook to remind you to go back and complete the task. Now that you know how to create a task, set a reminder and add an expiration date, let's get rid of some of those attachments.

Remove Attachments

To save incoming e-mail attachments locally or to a shared location, in the Reading Pane right-click the attachment and choose Save As. To save multiple attachments at once, select the message in the list pane, click File, then Save Attachments, then select All Attachments. If the attachment was the only reason you were holding onto this particular message, you're now free to delete the e-mail.

Now, go into your Sent Items folder, click Arranged by at the top of the Message Pane, and select Attachments. This is not a pretty picture. You already have access to these files as evidenced by the fact that you attached them to an e-mail, so why are you letting them take up space in your Mailbox?

In the preview pane, right-click the attachment and click Remove (see Figure 2-7). The attachment is permanently deleted in that it did not go into your Deleted Items folder in Outlook nor is it in your Recycle Bin on the desktop.

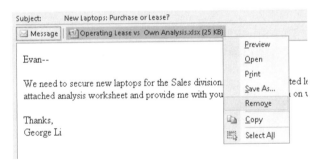

Figure 2-7 Remove Attachment.

You can do the same thing with attachments in any folder; just take care to save the ones you need somewhere safe before you remove them. The Remove option is grayed out in the Reading Pane, so you will have to open each message to remove the attachments.

Tip or Treat   Create a new folder called E-mail in your Documents folder on Windows Vista (or your My Documents folder on Windows XP) or on your personal network share drive, so you always know where to go when you're looking for a document sent to you in e-mail. Create subfolders in this folder to coincide with the subfolders in your Inbox or the types of documents you receive like "Expense Reports" and "HR Documents."

Edit Message

If—after deleting the attachment—you need to remind yourself that you did, in fact, send it in the first place, double-click the message to open it and click Other Actions in the Actions group in the Message tab. Click Edit Message for a blinking cursor in the body of the message where you can type yourself a note to remind you which attachment was sent with the original e-mail. As an alternative to editing the message after you send it, get into the habit of referencing the name of the file in the body of your original message.

Tip Jar

Here's a review of the top 10 tips covered in Chapter 2:

- **Instant Search**   Click the Search field below the toolbar. Enter your search terms or expand the search pane for additional search criteria. To search across all your Outlook items at once, click Tools, then Instant Search, then select Advanced Find. In the Look For drop-down, select Any Type Of Outlook Item.

- **Search Folders**   Click a default Search Folder to filter your mailbox on Unread, Large, or Categorized e-mail. To add a Search Folder, right-click Search Folders and click New Search Folder.

- **Change Subject Line**   Double-click any message and change the subject of the message by highlighting it to select it and then typing over it.

- **Flag E-Mail as a Task**   Right-click the Flag next to the e-mail you want to assign a task to. Select a due date for the task or click Custom to further refine the task parameters. The new task automatically appears in the To-Do Bar.

- **Create an Appointment from a Task**   Tasks are accessible through your Day format or Week format Calendar by clicking the Daily Task List option on the View menu. Drag a task from the Daily Task List and drop it onto a time slot on the calendar.

- **Send an E-Mail Reminder**   Click the red flag in the Options group in the Message tab of a new e-mail. Select a date and time. Reminder will pop up if the recipient does not have their reminder window turned off.

- **Remind Yourself**   Click the Follow Up button in the Options group of the Message tab of a new e-mail. Click Flag for Me, then select a date and time to remind yourself. It will turn the color red in your Sent Items folder letting you know it's time to follow up with them.

■ **Send an E-Mail with an Expiration Date**   In the Options section of the Message tab of a new e-mail, click the Message Options arrow to open the Message Options dialog box, then check the box next to Expires after and choose a date and time. Expired messages will be marked in the listing pane with a strikethrough through the first displayed line. To set an expiration date on a message in *your* Inbox, right-click any message in your Inbox and click Message Options. Put a check box by the Expires after and choose a date and time for the message to expire.

■ **Save Multiple Attachments**   Click File, then Save Attachments. Select All Attachments, then click OK. Navigate to the folder where you want to save the files or create a new folder by clicking the New Folder button in the Save All Attachments dialog box.

■ **Remove an Attachment**   Double click a message to open it. Right-click the attachment, then select Remove. To remove all attachments in a message, hold down the Shift key and highlight the files you want to remove from the message, then right-click the attachments and select Remove.

So now you know how to navigate Outlook's redesigned user interface and how to find and act on information in your Mailbox. And like G.I. Joe always said, "Knowing is half the battle."

It's time to put everything you've learned together and begin managing your information—instead of letting your information manage you. If only there was an equally effective way to deal with all of your meetings and appointments. Wait, there is....

Part Two

We've Got to Start Meeting Like This: An End-to-End Solution for More Effective Meetings

In this part

Have you ever played Buzzword Bingo? You know, the game where you print out a bingo card with buzzwords and phrases like "action item" and "efficiency" before going into a meeting and cross them off as you hear them said by any of your fellow meeting attendees. The game is won when you text message a coworker in the same meeting the word "Bingo" to signal you have completed a row. Invented by Tom Davis of Silicon Graphics in 1993 (and later made famous by Dilbert), Buzzword Bingo has since developed into a popular satire on the workplace, helping countless people stay awake during meetings. A group of MIT students even used Buzzword Bingo cards to liven up a 1996 commencement address by then-Vice President Al Gore. Talk about an inconvenient truth!

While office tomfoolery certainly has its place, wouldn't it be nice to get something besides your bingo card completed in a meeting? *Group Dynamics: Theory, Research, and Practice* published an article in March 2005 by Alexandra Luong and Steven G. Rogelberg titled "Meetings and More Meetings: The Relationship Between Meeting Load and the Daily Well-Being of Employees[1]." Guess what they found out? Meeting load increases feelings of fatigue and subjective workload. Apparently, meetings disrupt our primary tasks even if those meetings are a *part* of our primary roles and responsibilities. Have you ever been so frustrated during a meeting that you wanted to say, "If I spent as much time working on this project as I do talking about it, I'd be done with it by now?" If so, welcome to the club. (Meetings are Mondays at 7 P.M.—you can take notes, right?)

---

1. *http://interruptions.net/literature/Luong-PhD.pdf*

This section delivers an end-to-end solution for getting the most out of the time you and your teammates spend in meetings. We'll show you tips and tricks for connecting with colleagues, sharing meeting documents and information, and taking, distributing, and acting on meeting notes. With better access to people and information, you can contribute more in meetings and take away more *from* your meetings. Then maybe—just maybe— you won't have to attend so many meetings in the first place. Let's start by finding a time when everyone is available.

Chapter 3
Smile on Your Brother— Better Ways to Organize Meetings with Customers and Colleagues

Learn how to:

❑ Find and schedule the people and resources you need

❑ Share your Calendar with internal and external contacts

❑ Control private and archived Calendar information

I Will Meet Them, Sam and Pam

The first step toward any successful meeting is finding the right people to meet with. Your particular project or issue may require feedback or contributions from a team member, partner, customer, and occasionally all three. Sometimes you don't know *who* you need to meet with but you know you need to meet with *somebody* quick or the whole darn thing is going to fall apart. Whatever your meeting motives may be, quick and easy access to the people you need and the schedules they live by is a must; making the 2007 Microsoft Office system a must-have.

Electronic Business Cards

Business cards. Can't live with them. Can't tape them to the spokes of the wheels on your Camry. So why do so many people still use them? Why, in an era of electronic communications, does a 3.5" x 2" rectangle of heavy paper stock find its way into more pockets than a Pocket PC could ever dream of? The answer is simple. Business cards are inexpensive, easy to carry, and most of all, personal. More than just a name and number, a business card reflects the identity of a person and her company.

In Outlook 2007, you can manage your contacts as a virtual Rolodex of electronic business cards. As the default view for the Contacts folder, electronic business cards make your contacts easier to find and use. Double-click any business card to open it and view or edit the familiar Outlook contact properties. To customize your business card, click Business Card in the Options group on the Contact command tab (see Figure 3-1). Here you can customize the fields on your card and even add a photo, logo, or any other compatible image.

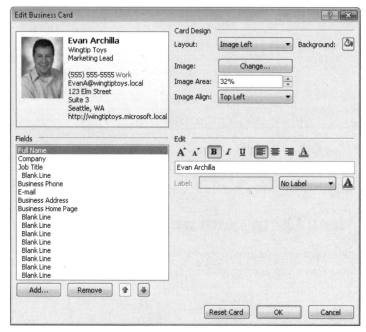

Figure 3-1 Customize an Electronic Business Card.

To e-mail your new business card to someone, click the Send button in the Actions group of the Contact command tab and select Send As Business Card. A new e-mail message will open with the contact file attached and a picture of your business card in the body of the message (see Figure 3-2). To make your business card a part of your Outlook signature, click Tools, then Options in the main Outlook window. On the Mail Format tab, click Signatures. Select an existing signature or click New to create one. Click Business Card to select a card and insert it into the signature. Click OK.

Chapter 3: Smile on Your Brother—Better Ways to Organize Meetings
with Customers and Colleagues

Part 2:
We've Got to
Start Meeting
Like This

Figure 3-2   E-mail an Electronic Business Card.

SharePoint Social Networking

Finding existing contacts is one thing, discovering new ones is something
else entirely. Microsoft Office SharePoint Server 2007 My Site personal Web
sites (more on Office SharePoint Server 2007 and Microsoft Windows
SharePoint Services in the chapters to come) help build social networks
between employees. The My Profile page includes an In Common With You
component that displays information you have in common with visiting
coworkers. Items can include the first manager, additional colleagues, or
distribution group or site memberships you both share. Discovering com-
monalities with coworkers can lead to new opportunities for collaboration
or problem-solving in the future. To create a My Site personal Web site, click
My Site on your SharePoint Server 2007 portal page and use the "Getting
Started with My Site" section to start building your social network. (see Figure 3-3).

If you're looking for someone with expertise in a particular area, you can
use the People Search Box to find them; and, unlike Cheers, you don't even
need to know their name. Every person who creates a My Site personal Web
site can provide detailed information about his skills and responsibilities,
interests, past projects, and more. This information becomes searchable by
other portal visitors, fostering new business relationships and leveraging
intellectual capital across the organization. To add the People Search Box

and People Search Core Results component to your My Site, click Site Actions, then Edit Page. Click Add A Web Part in the section of the page where you want the Web Part to appear. Expand the All Web Parts section. Check the boxes for the Web Parts you want and click Add.

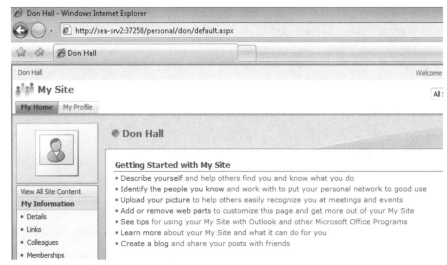

Figure 3-3   Getting Started with My Site.

Microsoft Office Communicator

Do you spend more time talking to voice mail than people? Is sending e-mail like tossing pennies down a black hole? Take a look around—the lights may be on in the cubicle next door but nobody's home. Where is everyone? Chances are they're in a meeting. Or between meetings. Or working from home to avoid meetings. Wherever they are, you need to talk to somebody. And you can't wait three weeks until the stars and the gaps in your Calendars align.

Microsoft Office Communicator, the desktop client for Microsoft Office Live Communications Server, integrates real-time presence information into your favorite Microsoft Office system applications. With Communicator, you can tell if a contact is online and available to communicate with you. Just hover over a name in the To: line of an Outlook 2003 or

Group Schedules

Have you ever created a fake appointment just to check your coworkers' availability? Save time and keystrokes by creating a Group Schedule for quick access to everyone's free/busy information. In Outlook's Calendar view, click Actions, then select View Group Schedules. Click New, name the group, and enter the names into what looks like the scheduling tab of an appointment. When you finish adding the names, click Save And Close. To open the group schedule anytime, click Actions, then View Group Schedules, and open the desired schedule from the list. This is also a great tip for keeping track of all your conference rooms and resources. Create a group schedule with all available conference rooms so you can quickly see when the room you want is available before you schedule the meeting.

Scheduling Resources

If your conference rooms are listed in your Exchange Server 2007's Global Address List, then you can schedule them as a resource in a meeting request. The advantage of doing this is the request for the conference room is automatically sent and confirmed before the meeting is sent out to the participants. This avoids having to send an update to the meeting participants if you find out later that the room was already scheduled.

To add a conference room to the list of resources for a meeting, create a new appointment, and click Invite Attendees. Click the To... button and navigate in the Global Address List to the name of the conference room you would like to schedule. Click the Resources button at the bottom of the window. Click OK. The conference room populates the Location field of the meeting. When you Send the meeting request, you will receive a notice telling you the conference room has been successfully booked or that it is not available.

2007 e-mail message and click the drop-down menu for a list of communication options. You'll also find presence information for contacts in the Office 2007 Document Information Task Pane and on Windows SharePoint Services sites and workspaces.

If your coworker is online and available to work with you, you can use Communicator to send her an instant message, place a PC-to-PC voice and video call using your computer microphone and speakers or, if Communicator is integrated with your company's phone system, you can use Communicator to place and receive phone calls using your desktop phone. You can even configure Communicator to auto-forward incoming calls to your mobile phone, home phone, or other location where you happen to be online. Throw in the ability to participate in real-time application sharing sessions, conference calls, and Microsoft Office Live Meeting online meetings (see the sidebar later in this chapter), and you have one tool that can do the work of many. If only that basket of remote controls next to the recliner was this organized.

To check the availability of the room, click Scheduling in the Show section of the Ribbon. From here you can see the free/busy bar for the resource in addition to the schedules of the invited attendees.

Tip or Treat   Microsoft Exchange Server 2007 provides additional enhancements to the Outlook 2007 Calendar. For example, Exchange 2007 analyzes the Calendars of attendees in a meeting request and proactively recommends ideal meeting times. If meeting information changes, users on Outlook 2003 or 2007 receive an informational update, instead of a request to re-accept the meeting. Outlook 2007 highlights the changes in the update so people immediately know what's different.

Sharing Is Caring

This might sting a little. In order to take your productivity to the next level, you and your teammates need to have view access to one another's Calendars. We know this may require the cooperation of others and we know you can't control what they do, but we can at least show you how to get out of the e-mail whirlpool when someone is trying to set up a meeting. The next time someone sends out a message that says, "We all need to get together. When is everyone available?," you can Reply to All, "I gave all of you access to my Calendar. Feel free to take a look, then send a meeting invite when you decide on a time." And that sense of freedom just might convince others to share their Calendars too.

Sharing Requests

A Sharing Request is an e-mail message that is generated when someone asks permission to view another person's Exchange Server 2007-connected Calendar. The Calendar owner may either Allow or Deny the request using the buttons at the top of the message. There are two ways to send a Sharing Request:

First, go into the Calendar view of Outlook 2007 and click Share My Calendar... in the navigation bar. An e-mail invitation will open. Type in the names of the people you want to grant permission to or click the To... button and select them from your Global Address List. Before you click Send, click the box next to the words Request permission to view recipient's Calendar (see Figure 3-4). Now, we'll see if your kindergarten teacher was right about that share and share alike thing.

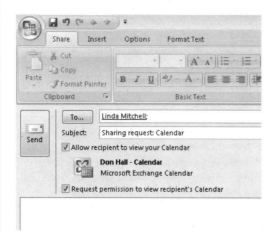

Figure 3-4   Sharing Request.

Chapter 3: Smile on Your Brother—Better Ways to Organize Meetings
with Customers and Colleagues

Part 2:
We've Got to
Start Meeting
Like This

You can also generate a Sharing Request by simply trying to open another person's Calendar side-by-side with your own. To do this, click Open A Shared Calendar in the navigation bar of the Calendar view. Type in the name of the coworker whose Calendar you would like to view. If they have already granted you permission, then their Calendar will open up side-by-side with your own. If they have not yet given you permission, a pop-up message will ask you if you would like to send a Sharing Request. A new e-mail will open giving you the opportunity to share *your* Calendar with *them* as part of the same request.

Tip or Treat   When you opened another Calendar in Outlook 2003, the new Calendar arranged itself side-by-side with your own. Outlook 2007 takes this capability one step further by allowing side-by-side Calendars to be overlaid on top of each other. Simply open another Calendar for which you have viewing permissions. Then, click the left arrow in the second Calendar name tab. The second Calendar moves on top of your Calendar. The underlying appointments appear transparent and in the same color as their Calendar tab. To put a different Calendar on top, simply click the other Calendar tab. You can overlay multiple Calendars, including Share-Point Calendars. Click the right arrow in the Calendar tab to return to side-by-side view.

Folder Permissions

In addition to sending Sharing Requests, you can assign general permissions to any of your Exchange Server-connected Outlook folders or remove permissions at any time by right clicking the folder in the navigation bar and selecting Change Sharing Permissions. For example, right-click the word Calendar under the My Calendars section of your navigation bar and select Change Sharing Permissions. You could grant everyone that can log into your corporate network Reviewer access to your Calendar by highlighting the word Default and selecting Reviewer from the permission level drop down arrow (see Figure 3-5).

Unlike Sharing Requests, this will not send a confirmation e-mail so you can grant people you may not even be working with yet permission to view your Calendar without requesting access to view their information. This is a great choice for mobile users or people who are used as a resource on multiple projects. You won't have to go through and set up permissions every time new people come into your project circle—everyone in your company has reviewer access all the time making it very easy for them to set up meetings with you.

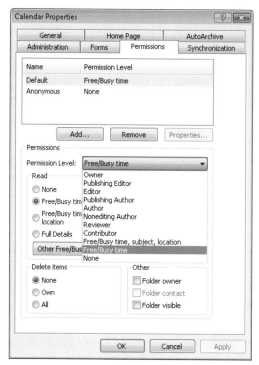

Figure 3-5   Folder Permissions.

To set up multiple folder permissions for that one special administrative assistant or for your boss, click Tools, then Options, then select Delegates. You can use the Delegate options to grant someone permission to view or edit your Inbox, Contacts, and Tasks folders, as well as your Calendar. Be sure to click the check box at the bottom to send the person an e-mail summarizing the permissions you just granted them.

I Will Meet Them Anywhere

Ah, the joys of an offsite meeting. If scheduled correctly, you don't have to go into the office before your meeting in the morning and you can slide that busy bar down through lunchtime on your Calendar. If only our external contacts knew we were available to meet. Fortunately, Outlook 2007 makes it easy to share your Calendar information outside of your organization. When it comes to your spouse and kids letting you enjoy the resulting extra thirty minutes of sleep, you're on your own.

Chapter 3: Smile on Your Brother—Better Ways to Organize Meetings
with Customers and Colleagues

Part 2:
We've Got to
Start Meeting
Like This

Internet Calendars

If you have a Windows Live ID (the artist formerly known as a Microsoft
.NET Passport) and an Exchange Server connection, you can publish your
Outlook 2007 Calendars to Microsoft Office Online at *www.microsoft.com/
office* for your clients and family to view. Click Publish My Calendar on the
navigation bar to publish your Exchange Calendar or right-click any of the
Calendars listed under My Calendars, select Publish To Internet, then Publish To Office Online. You can choose whether or not access is by invitation
only and if others can see partial details. You decide if you want to update
the Calendars periodically and how long your Calendars are viewable.

Calendar Snapshots

To send someone an HTML snapshot of your Calendar, click Send A Calendar Via E-mail on the navigation bar (see Figure 3-6). Choose a date range
and a detail view. For example, you can send someone your availability for
the next seven days. If it's your spouse, perhaps you want to send him or her
the subject lines of all your appointments for the entire month. Just make
sure any anniversaries or birthdays are properly marked before sending.

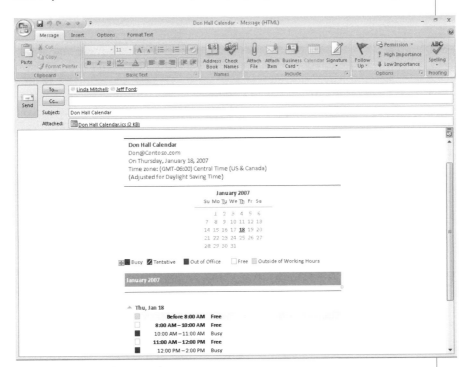

Figure 3-6   Calendar Snapshots.

Microsoft Office Live Meeting

Congratulations, the meeting was a huge success. Your boss is pleased, your client impressed, and the finance department is practically counting the money. And to think, you did it all in your underwear. Or bathrobe. Or shorts, flip-flops, and that Def Leppard t-shirt you bought during the Hysteria tour of '88. Now, *that* was a show.

Of course, nobody actually saw you dressed in your Saturday morning best. Your client is based in another state. Your boss lives in another city. And recent cuts in the travel budget made sure you won't be seeing either of them in person until the next fiscal year. Thankfully, Microsoft Office Live Meeting was there to help.

Live Meeting is an online meeting service that lets you host and participate in meetings from any computer with Internet access. With Live Meeting, you can brief Bob in Baltimore without packing a bag. You can plan with Pauline in Paris without purchasing a plane ticket. You can even find funding in Fargo in February without freezing your fanny off.

And because Live Meeting is tightly integrated with the Microsoft Office applications you use every day, you're never more than a few clicks away from a great meeting. For example, with the free downloadable Live Meeting Add-In Pack (available on Microsoft Office Online at *www.microsoft.com/office*), you can turn any Outlook 2003 or 2007 meeting request into a Live Meeting. You can also use the Live Meeting Add-In Pack to meet instantly by clicking the Meet Now button in Outlook and the other Office 2003 or 2007 applications. Even a Communicator session can be elevated into a Live Meeting.

Once in your meeting, you can upload a Microsoft Office PowerPoint presentation or other files you wish to present to meeting attendees. You can engage in real-time application sharing with another person, or create interactive slides for whiteboarding, Web browsing, and audience polling. Meeting audio can be integrated with your phone conferencing service or broadcast over the Internet to attendees' computer speakers. And the whole thing can be recorded and saved for future playback. Kind of like that mini tape recorder you used to capture *Rock of Ages*.

What Not to Share

Don't panic. There's a way to prevent even people *with* permission to view your Calendar from accessing items you want to keep private. Things like your bunion surgery and Timmy's soccer practice and Lil' Lisa's piano recital. For everything else, there's archiving.

Private Appointments

Open any appointment and click the word Private in the Options group in the Appointment tab. It has a picture of a padlock next to it (see Figure 3-7). When you mark an appointment private, other people will only see the words "Private Appointment" on your Calendar and will be unable to open the appointment and view the notes section. You, on the other hand, will

Chapter 3: Smile on Your Brother—Better Ways to Organize Meetings
with Customers and Colleagues

Part 2:
We've Got to
Start Meeting
Like This

still be able to view the details of your appointment along with the hyper-link to the map of the doctor's office. This is important to note as someone with reviewer access to your Calendar is able to view the notes section of any appointment that is not marked private.

Figure 3-7   Mark an appointment private.

Calendar Archives

When sharing your Calendar with others, it is important to consider whether or not everyone needs access to the last 14 years of your appointments. Many people do not realize their Calendar is one of the folders that counts against their mailbox size limit. If your organization allows you to create personal folders, then it is a good idea to archive your Calendar.

In Calendar view, click File, then click Archive (see Figure 3-8). Select a location where you want to store your archive file, then select a date from the drop-down box. Typically, you want to archive anything that is older than 30 days. When you click OK, a new checkbox appears under the My Calendar section on your navigation bar giving you one-click access to your previous appointments. Now your colleagues can more quickly open up your current and future appointments because their machine isn't trying to open up the events of your entire career.

Tip or Treat   By default, Outlook only shows two months of free/busy information in the scheduling window. If you do not have permission to view someone else's Calendar but you need to try to book an appointment with them further than two months out, click Tools, Options, then Calendar Options and select Free/Busy Options. Change the number 2 in the "months to publish" box. Don't forget to change it back as this will affect the free/busy bar for everyone you create an appointment with and it will take much longer for the scheduling window to populate everyone's information. Before you schedule a meeting with a large group, it's a good idea to change this setting to 1 month so the information will synchronize faster.

Exchange Server 2007 provides additional options governing who can see
your free/busy information and the level of visible detail.

Figure 3-8   Archive Your Calendar.

Tip Jar

Here's a review of the top 10 tips covered in Chapter 3:

- **Create an Electronic Business Card**   Open your Outlook contact. Click
  Business Card in the Options group on the Contact command tab.

- **Group Schedules**   To create a new group schedule, in the Calendar
  view, click Actions, then select View Group Schedules. Click New,
  name the group, and enter the names. Click Save And Close. To open
  the group schedule, click Actions, then View Group Schedules, and
  open the desired schedule from the list.

- **Schedule a Resource**   Create a new appointment and click Invite
  Attendees. Click the To button and navigate in the Global Address List
  to the name of the conference room you would like to schedule. Click
  the Resources button at the bottom of the window. Click OK.

- **Send a Sharing Request**   In the Calendar view of Outlook 2007, click
  Share My Calendar in the navigation bar. Type in the names of the
  people you want to grant permission to or click the To button and
  select them from your Global Address List. Before you click Send,

click the box next to the words Request permission to view recipient's Calendar.

- **Calendar Overlay**   Open another Calendar for which you have viewing permissions. Then, click the left arrow in the second Calendar name tab. To put a different Calendar on top, click the other Calendar tab. Click the right arrow in the Calendar tab to return to side-by-side view.

- **Change Folder Permissions**   Right-click Calendar under the My Calendars section of your navigation bar and select Change Sharing Permissions. To grant everyone on your corporate network Reviewer access to your Calendar, highlight the word Default and select Reviewer from the permission level drop down arrow.

- **Internet Calendars**   Click Publish My Calendar on the navigation bar or right-click any of the Calendars listed under My Calendars, select Publish To Internet, then Publish To Office Online.

- **Calendar Snapshot**   To send someone an HTML snapshot of your Calendar, click Send A Calendar Via E-mail on the navigation bar. Choose a date range and a detail view. Click Send.

- **Mark an Appointment Private**   Open any appointment and click the word Private in the Options group on the Actions command tab. When you mark an appointment private, other people will see the words "Private Appointment" on your Calendar and will be unable to open the appointment and view the details.

- **Archive Your Calendar**   In Calendar view, click File, then click Archive. Select a location where you want to store your archive file, then select a date from the drop down box. Click OK.

You found your coworkers, checked their availability, and decided on a time and place to get together. You're well on your way to a successful meeting. Now, you need to provide your attendees with the documents and other information they need to actively contribute to the discussion. Before you click Send on that meeting request, turn the page to Chapter 4.

Chapter 4

Prepare for Takeoff— Create and Customize an Online Gathering Place for Meeting Attendees

Chapter 4: **Prepare for Takeoff—Create and Customize**
an Online Gathering Place for Meeting Attendees

Part 2:
We've Got to
Start Meeting
Like This

Learn how to:

- ❏ Create a central online location for storing meeting documents and information
- ❏ Upload meeting content to the workspace home page
- ❏ Customize the layout and default elements of the workspace

Destination: "Same Page"

Ding! The Outlook reminder window says you've got five minutes to make it to your next meeting. You had fifteen minutes, but like an early morning alarm clock, you couldn't resist hitting Snooze. The umpteen things in your Outlook To-Do Bar will have to wait—it's meeting time.

You grab your laptop and head for the door. You can't be late for this one; after all, you scheduled it. Like a racecar driver pulling in for a pit stop, you squeal into the break room, grab another cup of coffee and a little something from the vending machine, and you're back on the track, the checkered flag of the conference room waving in the distance.

You've waited a long time for this meeting. Two weeks to be exact—that's how far out you had to search everyone's Calendars for available time. And here you are. Your coworkers greet you as you walk in the room. You're right on schedule. A minute or two of idle chit-chat, then it's down to business— or so you think.

Unfortunately, John didn't accept the fourth and final meeting update containing the revised agenda. Otherwise, he would have known his section was moved to the end and his presence wasn't required until the second half of the meeting. Meanwhile, Heather, in an effort to recover some much needed space in her Inbox, accidentally deleted the attached meeting documents from the request, without first saving them to her local machine. And just what the heck is Mike doing here? He's not even involved with this project.

Two weeks of planning and waiting for a one-hour shot at group productivity and the minutes are slipping like sand through your fingers. Why wasn't everyone prepared? You included the meeting objectives and agenda items in the meeting request. You attached all the necessary documents. When things changed, as they inevitably do, you informed your coworkers through a series of updated requests. You did everything you could to ensure Outlook contained the latest and greatest information about this meeting. Is it possible you expected too much from your e-mail and calendaring application?

SharePoint vs. SharePoint

It's one of the most frequently asked questions on any frequently asked questions list (right after "How much will this cost?" and "Will it run on my Commodore 64?"). The question that's keeping everyone up at night is this: What the heck is the difference between Microsoft Windows SharePoint Services and Microsoft Office SharePoint Server 2007? Allow us to explain...

Windows SharePoint Services is the technology in Windows Server 2003 that makes it easy to create collaborative Web sites like Meeting Workspaces, Document Workspaces, Team Sites, and more. It's so easy, in fact, that sites and workspaces tend to proliferate fairly rapidly throughout the organization. When a company reaches "critical mass," Office SharePoint Server 2007 (the successor to Office SharePoint Portal Server 2003) rides to the rescue.

As we discussed in Part I, most users have more e-mail in their Inbox than they know what to do with. Receiving one meeting request is necessary; receiving a subsequent meeting update every time someone's agenda, objectives, or mood changes can be a nightmare. And attachments? Forget about it. So, while Outlook 2007 makes it easier than ever to *schedule* meetings, it's not necessarily the best tool for helping users *prepare* for meetings.

Enter the Meeting Workspace. A Meeting Workspace is a collaborative Web site created by Windows SharePoint Services, a feature of Windows Server 2003. You can use a Meeting Workspace to store meeting objectives, agenda items, documents, and more in a central online location. Attendees receive a link to the workspace in the meeting request. When something changes, meeting information and documents can be edited on the workspace. This means fewer meeting updates and file attachments in your coworkers' inboxes. With all of this information online and easily accessible, your meeting is virtually excuse-proof.

Chapter 4: **Prepare for Takeoff—Create and Customize**
an Online Gathering Place for Meeting Attendees

Part 2:
We've Got to
Start Meeting
Like This

Create a Meeting Workspace

While Outlook itself never signed up for meeting preparation, neither will it hang you out to dry. In fact, the first step toward creating a Meeting Workspace can be found within an Outlook 2003 or 2007 meeting request. Enter your meeting attendees, subject, and location, then select your start and end times. Provide meeting details or other background information in the body of the request. Next, click the Meeting Workspace button in the Attendees section of the Meeting command tab (see Figure 4-1).

SharePoint Server 2007 is a stand-alone product that aggregates Windows SharePoint Services sites and workspaces under a single corporate Web portal. It offers enterprise search functionality, allowing users to search for people or information across the portal. It also extends Windows SharePoint Services functionality with tools for document, content, and records management.

SharePoint Server 2007 also includes an integrated version of Office Forms Server 2007 (also available as a standalone product) for streamlining forms-based business processes, as well as Excel Services for real-time browser access to Excel 2007 spreadsheets. With all of this great functionality built right in, SharePoint Server 2007 not only rides to the rescue, it brings the whole darn collaboration cavalry with it. Heigh-ho, SharePoint, away!

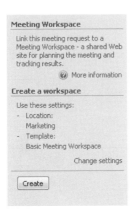

Figure 4-1   Meeting Workspace Task Pane.

Before you create your workspace, you need to provide the URL of the location where the site will live and choose the type of Meeting Workspace template you want to apply. To do this, click Change Settings in the Meeting Workspace Task Pane. Existing locations are accessible from the Select A Location drop-down menu or you can type a new URL. If you do not know which URL to use, contact your server administrator. Click the Select A Template Type for available Meeting Workspace template options (see Figure 4-2):

- **Basic Meeting Workspace**   Contains all the basic elements for a typical meeting including Attendee, Objective, and Agenda lists, as well as a Document Library.

- **Blank Meeting Workspace**   Workspace structure only; individual elements must be added manually. For more information, see the Customize Your Workspace section later in this chapter.

- **Decision Meeting Workspace**   Perfect for meetings involving document review and related decision-making. Contains the same elements as the Basic template plus Tasks and Decisions.

- **Social Meeting Workspace**   Plan the annual Holiday party and post the embarrassing after-photos on the same workspace. The Social template includes Directions, Things to Bring, and Attendees. The workspace also features a Discussion forum and Picture Library.

- **Multipage Meeting Workspace**   The best of the Basic and Blank templates in one workspace. This template includes one page with Attendee, Objective, and Agenda lists, plus two blank pages you can customize to your liking.

Figure 4-2   Meeting Workspace Options.

Select your template, click OK, then click Create. Outlook and Windows SharePoint Services will work together to build your new workspace. When the process is complete, the Task Pane changes and a link appears in the body of the meeting request. It's a good idea to click Go To Workspace in the Task Pane (see Figure 4-3) and populate the workspace with your meeting information *before* you send the request. That way, when people visit the workspace for the first time, they will experience an active site and be more likely to return in the future.

Tip or Treat   If your meeting is a recurring meeting, you can configure your Meeting Workspace with a page for each subsequent meeting date. Before creating your workspace, click the Recurrence button in the Options

Chapter 4: Prepare for Takeoff—Create and Customize
an Online Gathering Place for Meeting Attendees

Part 2:
We've Got to
Start Meeting
Like This

section of the Meeting command tab. Set your recurrence options and click
OK. Then, create your workspace. Use the list of dates in the left-hand pane
of the workspace to move between meeting pages.

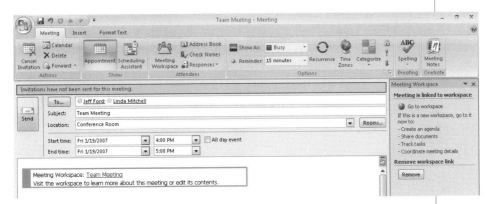

Figure 4-3   Go to Workspace.

Get to Know Your Workspace

The Basic Meeting Workspace template will fit the needs of most general meeting scenarios. This template consists of a home page with four default Web
Parts (see Figure 4-4). A Web Part is the official name of a SharePoint home
page element.

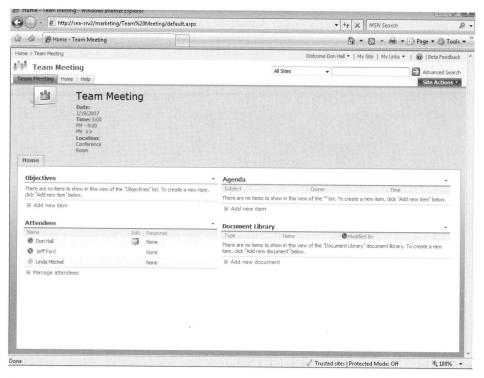

Figure 4-4   Basic Meeting Workspace.

Each Web Part has a specific purpose and content type:

- **Objectives**   Use the Objectives Web Part to inform attendees of top-level meeting objectives. To add a meeting objective, click Add New Item. Type in the objective and click OK.

- **Agenda**   The Agenda Web Part allows you to break the meeting down into specific topics for discussion. To add an agenda item, click Add New Item (see Figure 4-5). Type in a Subject, Owner, and Time. You can also enter any agenda-specific notes in the Notes field. Notice the familiar Office formatting icons in the Notes field toolbar. Even if you've never used a SharePoint site before, you should have no problem bolding text, adding a bulleted list, or changing the font color. If you can accomplish these tasks in Word or Excel, you can accomplish them in SharePoint. When you're finished, click OK.

Chapter 4: **Prepare for Takeoff—Create and Customize**
an Online Gathering Place for Meeting Attendees

Part 2:
We've Got to
Start Meeting
Like This

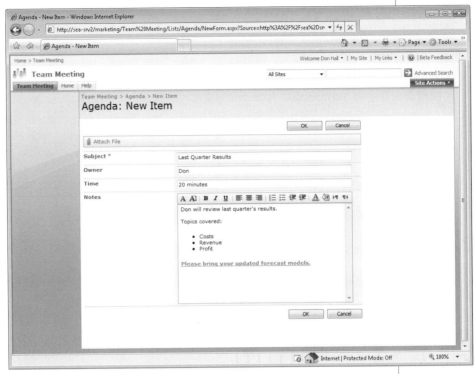

Figure 4-5   Add an Agenda Item.

- **Document Library**   The Document Library stores meeting-related documents. To add a document to the library, click Add New Document (see Figure 4-6). Click Browse to select and upload a single document. Click Upload Multiple Files to mark more than one file for upload. Click OK. For more information on working with Document Libraries, see the Shared Workspaces section in Chapter 9.

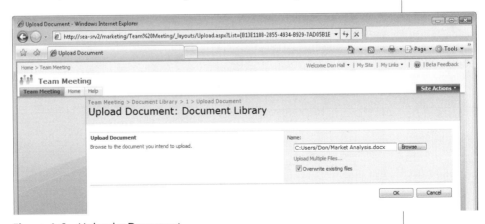

Figure 4-6   Upload a Document.

- **Attendees**   After you upload your meeting content, click Send In Your Outlook Meeting Request. The recipients will be automatically added to the Attendees Web Part and granted permission to access the workspace. You can use the Attendees Web Part to monitor Attendee responses like Accepted, Declined, or Tentative. This saves time over navigating to your Outlook Calendar and opening the original meeting request. If your organization is running Office Live Communications Server, you'll see integrated presence icons for each of your attendees, allowing you to see whether they are online then communicate with them via Communicator.

Customize Your Workspace

You don't have to be a Web designer to customize the layout and Web Parts on your workspace home page. With a few clicks, you can rearrange the home page Web Parts, add a new Web Part, or modify the properties of an existing Web Part.

- **Customize Home Page Layout**   To rearrange your home page Web Parts, you must first enter edit mode by clicking the Site Actions button, then clicking Edit Page (see Figure 4-7). Hover over an existing Web Part header until you see a crosshairs icon. Now, simply drag and drop the Web Part to another column or to a different place in the same column. When you're finished, click Exit Edit Mode to return to the normal workspace view.

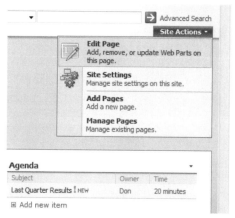

Figure 4-7   Site Actions Menu.

- **Add a Web Part**   There are two ways to add a Web Part to your home page. If you're not already in edit mode, click the Site Actions button,

Chapter 4: **Prepare for Takeoff—Create and Customize**
an Online Gathering Place for Meeting Attendees

Part 2:
We've Got to
Start Meeting
Like This

then click Edit Page. For a detailed look at available Web Parts, click
Add A Web Part at the top of the home page column where you want
the new Web Part to appear. Check the boxes next to the Web Parts
you want to add and click Add (see Figure 4-8). For faster Web Part
creation, click Advanced Web Part Gallery And Options in the Add A
Web Part dialog box. Drag the Web Part you want from the Add Web
Parts Task Pane and drop it in the desired location on the site. You can
also use the Add Web Parts Task Pane to search for available Web
Parts, browse the Web Parts galleries, or import Web Parts from
another location. When you're finished, click Exit Edit Mode to return
to the normal workspace view.

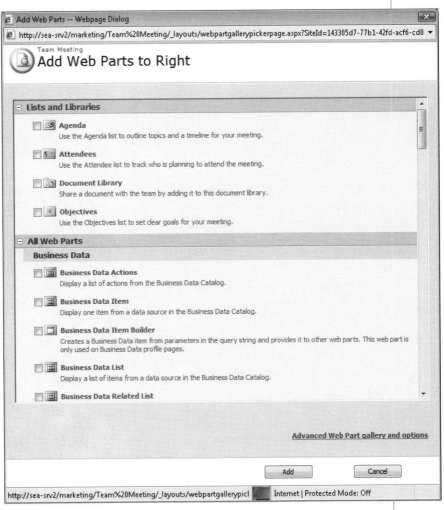

Figure 4-8   Add a Web Part.

- **Modify an Existing Web Part**   Pick the Web Part you want to modify, then click the drop-down arrow in the Web Part header. Choose Modify Shared Web Part to access a Task Pane with available customization options. You can use this Task Pane to change the Web Part view, appearance, layout, and other more advanced options. When you're finished, click Exit Edit Mode to return to the normal workspace view.

Tip Jar

Here's a review of the top 10 tips covered in Chapter 4:

- **Create a Meeting Workspace**   In an Outlook 2007 meeting request, click the Meeting Workspace button in the Attendees section of the Meeting command tab. Click Change Settings and select a workspace location. Click OK, then click Create.

- **Select a Meeting Workspace Template**   Before clicking Create, click Change Settings in the Meeting Workspace Task Pane and select the desired workspace template from the drop-down menu. Click OK.

- **Make a Workspace Recurring**   Before clicking Create, click the Recurrence button in the Options section of the Meeting command tab. Set your recurrence options and click OK.

- **Add a Meeting Objective**   To add a meeting objective, click Add New Item. Type in the objective and click OK.

- **Add an Agenda Item**   To add an agenda item, click Add New Item. Type in a Subject, Owner, Time, and any related notes. When you're finished, click OK.

- **Upload a File to a Document Library**   To add a document to the library, click Add New Document. Click Browse to select and upload a single document. Click Upload Multiple Files to mark more than one file for upload. Click OK.

- **Manage Attendees**   Meeting request recipients are automatically added to the Attendees Web Part when the request is sent. Use the Attendees Web Part to monitor attendee responses and online presence information.

- **Customize Home Page Layout**   Click the Site Actions button, then click Edit Page. Drag and drop Web Parts to the desired location.

- **Add a Web Part**   Click the Site Actions button, then click Edit Page. Click Add A Web Part at the top of a home page column. Check the boxes next to the desired Web Parts and click Add. Alternatively, click

Chapter 4: Prepare for Takeoff—Create and Customize
an Online Gathering Place for Meeting Attendees

Part 2:
We've Got to
Start Meeting
Like This

Advanced Web Part Gallery And Options in the Add Web Part dialog box. Drag and drop a Web Part from the Add Web Parts Task Pane to the desired location on the site.

- **Modify an Existing Web Part** Click the Site Actions button, then click Edit Page. Pick the Web Part you want to modify, then click the edit drop-down in the Web Part header. Choose Modify Shared Web Part to access a Task Pane with available customization options.

Well, here we are. You made all the right colleague connections. You scheduled the meeting of the century. You even created an online workspace to help your meeting attendees arrive prepared and ready to contribute. If only you could keep your fingers off the Snooze button, you might actually enjoy that long walk down the red carpet to the conference room instead of running around the hallways like a chicken with its head cut off.

While we can't help you get to your meeting on time, we can show you some ways to make better use of your time in and after your meeting with a little something called Microsoft Office OneNote 2007. Everyone's here, we have everything we need, and the clock is ticking. Let's call this meeting to order....

Chapter 5
Take Note!—Capture, Share, and Act on Meeting Information

Learn how to:

❏ Capture and organize all your notes in one place

❏ Easily share and act on your notes

❏ Quickly find what you're looking for in your notes

Where Oh Where Have My Little Notes Gone?

Time to play your favorite game, Search for the Note, with your host, Impatient Coworker. Let's set the stage: all the paper on your desk is arranged into neat little piles like "for the car," "to be filed," and "don't throw away." Ms. Coworker comes in and asks you about that new client you told everyone about in the meeting this morning. She wants to know the name and job title of everyone you met at your initial meeting with them. You remember you were using a blue pen that day and it was the second or third page in a yellow legal pad. You have ten seconds before you look like an unorganized scatterbrain—Go! As the clock ticks, how you wish all your notes lived in one magical place instead of on the backs of envelopes and receipts!

Microsoft Office OneNote 2007 is a note-taking application designed to replace the steno notebooks, the sticky notes, the legal pads, the draft e-mail messages, and the miscellaneous Word documents floating around your home and office. OneNote 2007 is available as a stand-alone application or as part of Office Home & Student 2007, Office Ultimate 2007, and Office Enterprise 2007. By having all your notes in one place, OneNote gives you the ability to instantly search across all of them by keyword or by note tag. Imagine what it would be like if you could instantly see every note you've ever put an asterisk (*) by!

Organize This

OneNote 2007 doesn't care if you're organized or not. With the instant search feature, it will always be able to find your notes no matter what Section you put them in or what Page you have them on. Still, some people love to be organized. If you want your Sections to be ordered and named, read on. If you're a mess and you're OK with that, well, then we are too.

Notebooks

OneNote 2007 is hierarchical like a three-ring binder or a filing cabinet. Each Notebook is divided into Sections and each Section is filled with Pages. These Notebooks are actually folders under *Documents\OneNote Notebooks* and the Sections are files on your hard drive.

Open OneNote from the Start Menu under Microsoft Office. By default, OneNote is set up with three Notebooks—Work, Personal, and the OneNote Guide. You can create new Notebooks by clicking File, then selecting New Notebook (see Figure 5-1). For a quick start, choose Work on the left side of the screen. You are now ready to create Sections in your electronic Work folder.

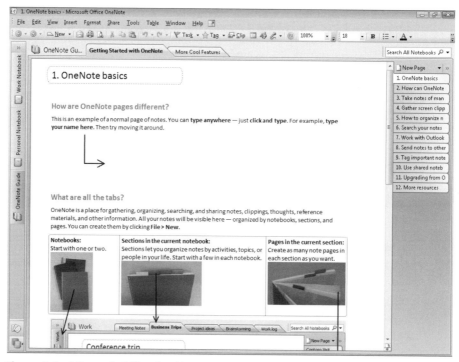

Figure 5-1 Microsoft Office OneNote 2007.

Tip or Treat   While Documents\OneNote Notebooks is the default location for storing your OneNote Notebooks, you can actually place Notebooks anywhere you want—including a network location. For network-based Notebooks, OneNote 2007 downloads a full offline copy accessible from the local machine. Changes made when the machine is offline are automatically merged with the online version.

Sections

Think of a Section as a subfolder of your Notebook folder on your hard drive. Just like you would create individual folders for each project you work on to keep all your documents organized, you could create a separate Section in your Notebook for each department, location, project, or client.

To rename one of these Sections, right-click the Section tab and click Rename. You may change the names to fit how you already organize your files on your personal drive. To add more Sections, right-click any of the tabs at the top of your Notebook and choose New Section. Type the Section title you want and hit Enter.

To rearrange these Sections, right-click the Section tab you want to move and click Move. In the Move Section To dialog box, select the appropriate Notebook, click the target tab, then choose to move the Section before or after that tab.

Section Groups

Let's go back to the filing cabinet analogy. You currently have a filing cabinet set up just for Work and you have separate drawers, or Sections, for each project you're working on. Some of these projects may span multiple drawers or relate to a larger objective. To arrange your electronic filing cabinet so related "drawers" are together and therefore easier to access, create a Section Group.

Right-click any Section tab and select New Section Group. Select the New Section Group tab, and rename the group. You can right-click and Move individual Sections into the new Group, or you can drag and drop them. Click the green up arrow in the Section Group to navigate back up to the parent Section tab.

Pages

On the right side of the screen are pages. These are your "files" and there are a number of different ways you can get information onto these pages. Each page automatically names itself whatever you type as the title in the dotted oval at the top. You can drag and drop these pages to reorder them and you can create subpages by right-clicking any page or clicking the down arrow at the top of the page list and choosing New Subpage. To move a page to another Section, simply drag it over the Section name and look for the black arrow to drop it where you want it within that Section's page order.

Type, Write, Record

So, what if you don't have a laptop? You can still capture notes a number of different ways with OneNote 2007. For those of you with Tablet PCs, you'll love the fact that you can capture and search your handwritten notes or convert the digital ink to text. Laptop users can use the built-in microphone to record staff meetings and conference calls. Desktop users will love the convenience of taking conference call notes and posting them on a Meeting Workspace within seconds. No matter what type of PC you use, there's something for you in OneNote 2007.

Type Anywhere

Taking notes with OneNote is a lot like taking notes on paper. Put your pen anywhere on the paper and write. Click in OneNote and type anywhere on any page. However, unlike paper, it's quick and easy to reorder your notes in OneNote. Mouse over a note and notice the blue border around it (see Figure 5-2). Click the top of the border and move the text box to another part of the page. To merge a note into another text box, use the crosshair icon on the left side of the note and drag it into any other note on the same page.

The more structured note-taker can add lines to a page by clicking Format, then selecting Rule Lines. There are nine choices ranging from none to a very large grid pattern. To change your default page to this setting, click File, then click Page Setup. Scroll down to the bottom of the task pane and click Save Current Page As A Template. Give your template a name and check the box next to Set As Default Template For New Pages In The Current Section. To apply this template to a page in another Section, click the down arrow next to New Page on the right side of the page and choose More Template Choices and Options. Click the plus sign next to My Templates and choose your new template.

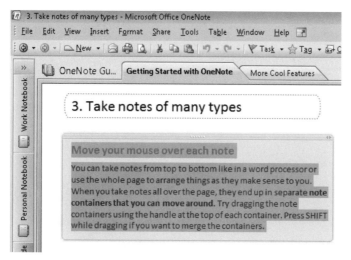

Figure 5-2   Note Container.

Tip or Treat   Need more room on a page? Click Insert, then select Extra Writing Space and drag the arrow down to create more space between two notes anywhere on your page.

Templates

OneNote also comes standard with some basic templates for meeting notes, to-do lists, and lecture notes and there are many more available on Microsoft Office Online at www.microsoft.com/office. To see the standard templates, click the down arrow next to New Page on the right side of the page and choose More Template Choices and Options. Click the plus sign next to Business and click Detailed Meeting Notes to see an example of a default template.

Tables

Here's another tip for the neat freaks. If you want to line up your text in rows and columns, you can insert a table. Click Table, then select Insert Table. Use the Table menu to add or delete rows or columns. You can even rearrange your rows by dragging and dropping. You can also create a table on the fly by typing a note and hitting Tab. OneNote will automatically format your text as a table (see Figure 5-3). Hit Enter to create a new row.

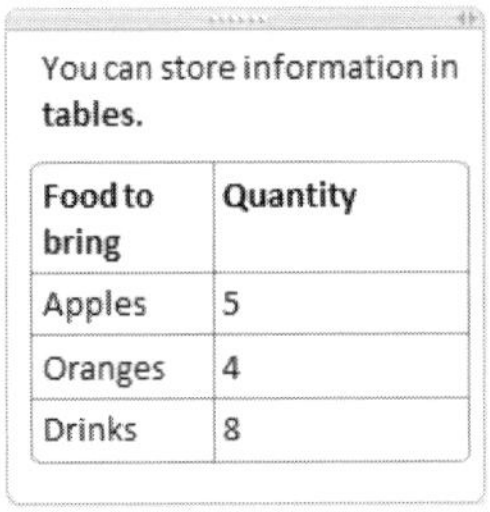
You can store information in **tables.**

Food to bring	Quantity
Apples	5
Oranges	4
Drinks	8

Figure 5-3 OneNote Table.

Keep in mind, a table in OneNote will not sort, alphabetize, do formulas or work as a data file for a mail merge. As cool as this application is, OneNote is not meant to replace what Microsft Office Word and Excel already do so effectively. If you need more advanced table functionality, you can always send your OneNote table to Word (more on this later) or paste it into Excel.

Tip or Treat OneNote is a place to take notes, not to do complex algorithms, but it can do some simple math. Type **(2*3)+(4/2)=** and then hit your space bar. Nothing as challenging as FOIL (First, Outer, Inner, Last) or the quadratic equation, but hey, it's better than using your fingers and toes to count while you're taking notes.

Digital Ink

Of course, not all notes are text-based. Anyone with a steady hand can draw diagrams or other pictures in OneNote. Click the Drawing Toolbar icon and select a pen color. Try to draw an arrow on the page by dragging your mouse. It's not as easy as it sounds but with a little practice, you may become quite the mouse artist. Click the Type/Selection Tool button at the far left of the Drawing toolbar to get your cursor back. Remember, this is *drawing*, not inking.

Only people with Tablet PCs can ink in OneNote 2007, which means the words they draw on the monitor with a special magnetic pen are searchable within OneNote as if they had been typed on the keyboard. Pretty cool, huh? To convert ink to text, highlight the ink entry and click Tools, then select Convert Handwriting To Text (see Figure 5-4). If you want to lock in your ink entry as a schematic, click Tools, then Treat Selected Ink As, then select Drawing.

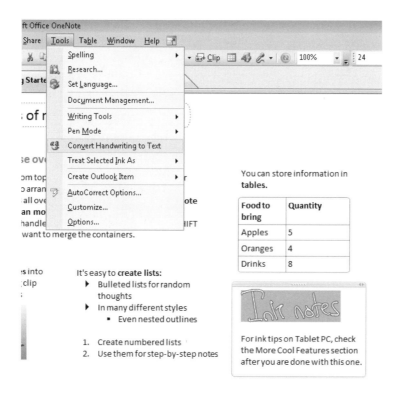

Figure 5-4 Convert Handwriting to Text.

Another neat feature for the stylus is Lasso Select which allows you to high-light areas that you circle on the page with your pen. That's under Tools, then Writing Tools.

Record

Do you ever have to wake yourself up from daydreaming in a meeting? Audio recognition can help. With the permission of everyone in the room and in accordance with your company policies and local laws, you can record audio or capture video in OneNote. The exciting part is that OneNote is able to pull key words out of the recording and index them so that things that were said in a meeting are searchable! It's like you've found a worm hole through time and we've catapulted you into the future. Imagine never having to take meeting notes again. Now, come back to reality because people are just going to freak out about that idea.

Between now and the time it takes to convince your coworkers it's possible, OneNote 2007 also synchronizes the notes you're taking with the recording, so people who missed things like training sessions and meetings can go into the OneNote page and click a topic or an agenda item. The audio will begin playing back at the point in the meeting when that note was taken so they can just listen to the parts that they are interested in instead of having to listen to the entire recording from the beginning.

If you have an external microphone at your desktop or a built-in microphone on your laptop, then test this feature out by going to a blank OneNote page. Give it the title **Testing.** Click anywhere in the notes section of the page and click Insert, then select Audio Recording. A Windows Media recording toolbar will appear and a note will appear on the page capturing the date and time the recording was started (see Figure 5-5).

Figure 5-5   Audio Recording and Video Recording Toolbar.

Now, type and say the following as you type:

Section 1–In this section, we are going to discuss the audio indexing capabilities of OneNote 2007.

Section 2–Here, we will discuss the synchronization of what we type into OneNote 2007 with the recorded audio.

Stop typing and stop recording by clicking the Stop button on the Recording toolbar. Now, click the Audio icon next to Section 2 and if you have speakers, you should hear the recording playback what you were saying when you began typing that line of text. You don't have to be Buck Rogers to think that's pretty futuristic.

Insert Files as Printouts

In addition to typing, writing, and recording your notes, you may want to import documents, images, or other items into your Notebook. If you used OneNote 2003, you may have used Insert Document as Picture and loved how it made it possible to mark up a document. The limitation of that feature was that the text inside the picture wasn't searchable. That meant you were only able to search the notes you had taken on top of the document, not the text inside of it.

As a way to capture information in OneNote 2007, a print driver was added. That means that if you can print it, you can insert it into OneNote. You're thinking, "No way, Wayne." Way, dude. Click on Insert, then select Files As

Printouts. Find the file in your directory and when you double-click it, the application it was created in will open and print the file into your Notebook (see Figure 5-6). It will also embed a copy of the file in your Notebook. Now the text inside the printout and any annotations you make are searchable. Sweet.

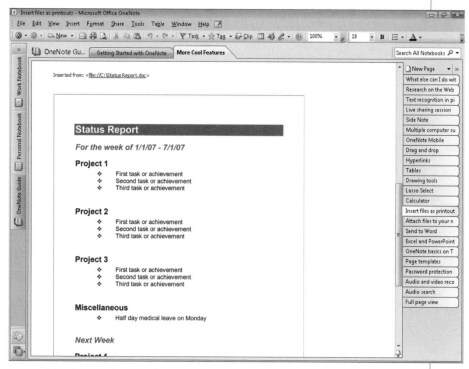

Figure 5-6   Insert Files as Printouts.

But be careful! We just got you out of the habit of keeping duplicate e-mails, let's not replace that with a habit of keeping duplicate documents in OneNote. Use this feature as a way to get all those meeting notes from Word into a searchable database of information for your team (see Shared Notebooks). After you insert your Word-based notes into OneNote, you should delete them from your file directory.

Tip or Treat   If you want to manage project-related documents within OneNote, you can insert just the embedded file by clicking Insert, then selecting Files. The embedded file is a copy of the document and it references the original location when you mouse over the icon. Again, be careful not to keep unnecessary duplicates—keep the copy you need and delete the rest. For documents stored in shared locations, consider inserting a hyperlink instead.

Insert Screen Clipping

Oh, Jeeves, is there anything you don't know? Phone books, encyclopedias, dictionaries, and even syndicated comic strips are all on the Internet. How many times have you written something down in a report that you remember seeing on a Web site? The only problem is, you didn't add that Web site to your Favorites and you've cleared out your History folder and now you have to run the search again to cite the reference? You should have used screen clippings.

Navigate to any Web site and then open OneNote 2007 on top of it. Click Insert, then select Screen Clipping. The Internet page appears washed out on the screen. Now, use your mouse to drag across a portion of that site, maybe a picture or an interesting paragraph. When you release the mouse button, you'll see your screen clipping inserted into OneNote with a hyperlink referencing the site address where you pulled the information from (see Figure 5-7). Even better, it captured the date and time you did it. You'll never have to duplicate an Internet search again.

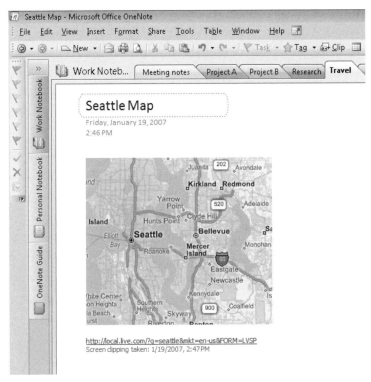

Figure 5-7   Screen Clipping.

Screen clippings also capture snippets of other types of files. If you're reading a report in Word or reviewing a spreadsheet in Excel, you can pop over to OneNote and insert a screen clipping of anything you see on your screen.

Tip or Treat If you need more than a screen clipping, you can send an entire Web page to OneNote. Navigate to any Web site in Windows Vista Internet Explorer 7, click Tools, then Send To OneNote.

Scan

Sure, OneNote is great but where was it four score and seven legal pads ago? For all the notes you've loved before, you can scan them into OneNote and the built-in character recognition will do the rest. That's right, notes that you scan in are searchable too. So, until they buy you a Tablet PC, you can insert your old paper notes as pictures from a scanner. Click Insert, then Pictures, then select From Scanner Or Camera.

Side Note

You can't always guarantee OneNote will be open and ready for input anytime inspiration strikes. If you have OneNote 2003 or 2007 installed on your machine, then you've seen the OneNote Side Note icon down by your clock on your desktop. Click it. This creates what looks a lot like a sticky note, allowing you to jot down quick thoughts or drag and drop anything you have highlighted onto the note (see Figure 5-8).

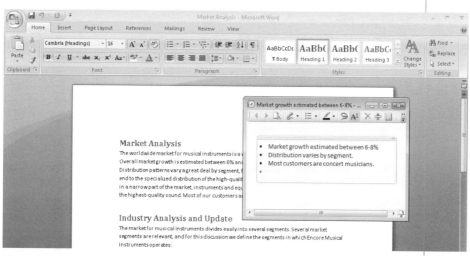

Figure 5-8 Side Note.

Side Notes reside in the "Unfiled Notes" area of your Notebook. You can find unfiled notes by running a search on the contents or by clicking the icon in the bottom left corner of your OneNote window that looks like three pages. To file these notes, simply drag and drop them into the Notebook and Section you want.

To create a screen clipping when OneNote is closed, right-click the OneNote icon in the Windows taskbar and click Create Screen Clipping. Like Side Notes, the clipping will be placed in the Unfiled Notes Section where you can move it to a more permanent location.

Automatic Save

When you finish taking notes or importing content, close OneNote. Don't bother looking for a save button because there isn't one. OneNote automatically saves as you go, so you'll never accidentally quit without saving again. Once you type a note, you know it'll be there the next time you open the page.

Action!

As any experienced note-taker knows, capturing notes is only part of the story. Chances are someone's going to ask you to *do* something with your notes, either share them, complete an action item, or both. OneNote 2007 provides a number of ways to share your notes with other people and other Office 2007 applications.

E-Mail Notes

We hate to admit it, but there may come a time when you have to e-mail your notes to someone, especially if they don't have OneNote. If that's the case, don't worry—recipients running Outlook 2003 or later will be able to view an HTML version of your notes in the body of the e-mail message. Recipients with OneNote can open the attached *.one file and automatically add the notes to the Notes E-mailed to Me Section in their Notebook. To e-mail your OneNote notes, click the E-mail icon in the OneNote toolbar (see Figure 5-9).

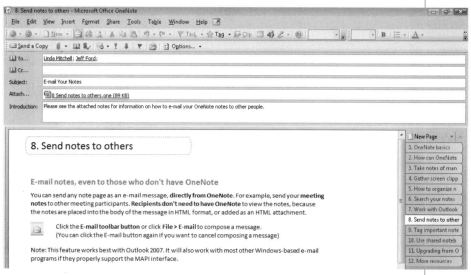

Figure 5-9 E-mail Notes.

Upload to SharePoint

You can publish any Notebook Section to any SharePoint site the same way you would upload a document. Navigate to an existing SharePoint Document Library, click Upload Document and browse for the Section you want to upload (Documents\OneNote Notebooks by default). To save an individual Page or entire Notebook to SharePoint, use the Save As command in OneNote's File menu to browse for the Document Library, then select Page, Section, or Notebook in the Page Range field. Click Save.

Live Sharing Session

That red exclamation point on an e-mail doesn't carry as much weight as it used to, does it? For teams that need to stay up-to-date with critical announcements, a Live Sharing Session in OneNote might be a better way to communicate than e-mail. Live Sharing Sessions can also be used as a kind of mini-meeting between multiple presenters before the big Live Meeting later on. We'll show you how to start the session; you decide all the ways you can use it.

Live Sharing Sessions are possible when each person invited is on your network and has a local copy of OneNote running on their PC. You can only share pages in the same Section, so you'll need to navigate to an existing page you want others to see or create a new Section and move pages to populate it. Click Share, then Live Sharing Session, then select Start Sharing

Current Section. Hold your Shift key down and click on page titles to share more pages within the same section. Click Start Shared Session, then click the Invite Participants button. An Outlook e-mail message will appear with an internal IP Address participants will automatically connect to when they double-click the OneNote file attachment in their preview pane. If you want to invite participants outside your network, you'll have to work with your IT Department to open a port.

During the Live Sharing Session, all participants are able to take notes on the Shared Pages. Each participant is automatically assigned their own ink color so it's a good idea to have everyone type their name on the top of one of the shared pages. If you want to block others from editing the pages, uncheck Allow participants to edit at the bottom of the Current Live Session task pane and check Use the pen as a pointer if you want participants to see your cursor. When anyone clicks Leave Live Sharing Session, they will have their own copy of the notes everyone took up to that point.

Shared Notebooks

If you want a more permanent sharing solution, one where everyone can take the Notebook offline for edits and automatically update all copies when they're back online, then Shared Notebooks may be the solution you've been looking for.

To create a Shared Notebook, click Share, then select Create Shared Notebook. Give it a name, a color, choose a template you want to use, and then click Next. Chose Multiple people will share this notebook and choose where you will store it. Paste in the address of your team SharePoint site if you chose to upload it onto a server or the file path where you want to store it in a shared folder if you chose that option in the previous step. Click Create. Now, everyone will access the Shared Folder via the hyperlink you e-mail to them and all offline copies will be updated when the person logs back into the network and clicks File, then Sync, then Sync This Notebook Now. This book just paid for itself.

Protect Section Content

If you have a Shared Notebook that contains sensitive or confidential information (i.e., for managers only), you may opt to password protect a Section by right-clicking the Section tab and clicking Password Protect This Section. Click Set Password. Once the password is set, this Section is no longer searchable. Keep in mind, audio and video recordings will remain unprotected, meaning even though a person cannot navigate to the page without the password, if they know where the files are located, they will still be able to listen to the audio or view video files.

Outlook Task Integration

It's so easy to commit to a task in a meeting. Sometimes, though, it happens so fast you forget you said you were going to do something until you show up at the next meeting and see your name on the agenda. Looks like we'll have to schedule another meeting to discuss what you were supposed to do before this one. Thank goodness OneNote 2007 and Outlook 2007 feature integrated tasks.

When you create a task in OneNote, it automatically shows up in your task list and To-Do Bar in Outlook. Once in Outlook, you can drag the task from the To-Do Bar onto your Calendar and schedule time to complete it before the next meeting. To flag a note with an Outlook task, click View, then select Outlook Tasks Toolbar (see Figure 5-10). Click next to the notes you want to assign a task to, ensuring the blue frame surrounds the selection, then click the appropriate task flag in the Outlook Tasks Toolbar.

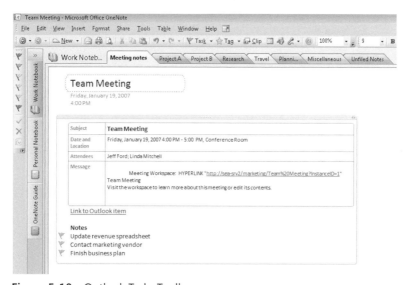

Figure 5-10 Outlook Tasks Toolbar.

Tip or Treat   OneNote and Outlook integration doesn't stop with tasks. Users of Outlook 2003 or later can turn any OneNote note into an Outlook Appointment or Contact. To do this, click Tools, then Create Outlook Item, and select the item you want.

In addition, you can link a page of OneNote meeting notes directly to an Outlook 2007 meeting request. Simply open an existing meeting request and click the Meeting Notes button in the OneNote group of the Meeting command tab. A prepopulated OneNote page will open containing the meeting Subject, Date and Location, Attendees, and Message from the meeting request. It also includes a Notes Section for capturing meeting notes.

Other integration points include the ability to link OneNote Contact Notes to an Outlook 2007 Contact and send the contents of an Outlook 2007 e-mail message directly to OneNote.

Send to Word

You've done your research and combined all your notes into one cohesive business letter that's ready to be sent out to all your clients. Now, where is the mail merge button on this thing? When you need more than just simple formatting, it's nice to know you can send your notes to Word. Click File, then Send To, then select Microsoft Office Word. If you save the new document in Word, then you can delete your working page from OneNote.

Search Me

How many times have you asked yourself, "Whose phone number is this?" while searching through your car console for change? Yesterday, you went in to check your voicemail at work. Three digits into the callback number for your first message, you scrambled to find something to write on and finally found the dry cleaning receipt on your desk. Now, that receipt is in the car to remind you to pick up the dry cleaning. It seems like every piece of paper at home or in the office has something you scribbled down on it so you wouldn't forget and now you have to go through every piece of paper because you forgot where you wrote it down.

Lucky for you, OneNote 2007 uses the same indexing system as the Windows Desktop Search Engine. This is also the engine that drives Instant Search in Outlook 2007. What this means is you will spend less time each work day searching for notes, images, audio, and video you've captured in OneNote than you would hunting through pen and paper notes or electronic files. Simply type a word or string of words into the Search text box in the upper-right corner of the OneNote window and hit Enter.

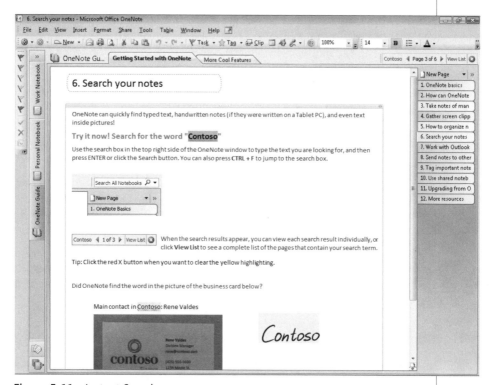

Figure 5-11   Instant Search.

Notice how OneNote highlights the search results on the page (see Figure 5-11). Scroll through your results, or click View List to see all the results in the Task Pane. From here, you can click to jump to the first result on the selected page. To expand your search to all Notebooks or narrow your search to the current Section, click the Search drop-down arrow at the bottom of the Task Pane. To start a new search, close the current search results by clicking the red X in the same line where you typed your initial keywords.

Note Tags

Do you have a review process at work? When it's time to divvy up the raises, does your boss hand you a blank sheet of paper and tell you to write down all the things you've done this year? Sure, you can remember what you did this past month and that neat relief map you made out of cotton balls and tissue paper when you were in the fifth grade, but the past year is a little hazy. Note tags to the rescue.

To Do, Important, Question, and other default note tags are accessible by clicking the down arrow next to the word Tag on your toolbar. Highlight a note, click the Tag drop-down arrow, and select the tag you want to use (see Figure 5-12). The most recently used tag will be inserted again by simply clicking the Tag button. To see all the tagged notes in your Notebook, click the Tag down arrow and select Show All Tagged Notes. Just like your Instant Search results, the Task Pane shows all of your tagged notes, giving you the opportunity to jump between them with a click.

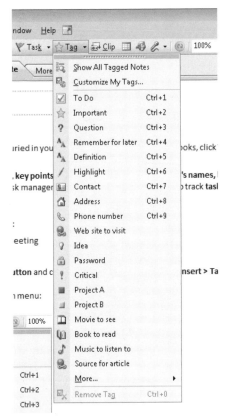

Figure 5-12   Note Tags.

To customize a note tag for your review process, click the down arrow next to Tag and click Customize My Tags. In the Task Bar, you can click Modify to change an existing tag, or click Add to create your own. Name the tag **Review**, click the down arrow next to Symbol, then choose the picture of the Award Ribbon. Now you have a Note Tag to use throughout the year when you want to highlight something to include on your review. Next year, when that blank sheet of paper comes across your desk, you'll simply Show All Tagged Notes, drag and drop them onto a single page, and send them over to Word for a little clean-up. You may even get extra credit for turning your review in early.

Hyperlinking

Another effective way to find your notes is not to search at all. With Hyperlinking, you can jump between your notes with a click. Click Edit, then Copy Hyperlink To to copy a hyperlink to a paragraph, Page, Section, Section Group, or Notebook. Navigate to the place in your Notebook where you want the link to appear and click Edit, then Paste. Click the link for instant access to the referenced notes.

Now that all your notes live in one magical place, what are your other two wishes?

Tip Jar

Here's a review of the top 10 tips covered in Chapter 5:

- ■ **Templates**   Click the down arrow next to New Page on the right side of a OneNote page and choose More Template Choices and Options.

- ■ **Record Voice Notes**   Click anywhere in the notes section of the page and click Insert, then select Audio Recording. A Windows Media recording toolbar will appear and a note will appear on the page capturing the date and time the recording was started.

- ■ **Insert Files as Printouts**   Click Insert, then select Insert Files As Printouts. Find the file in your directory and double-click it to print the file into your Notebook.

- ■ **Insert Screen Clipping**   Click Insert, then select Screen Clipping. Use your mouse to drag across a portion of an Internet site or open application. Release the mouse button to insert the clipping into OneNote. If OneNote is closed, right-click the OneNote icon in the notification area of the Windows taskbar, and click Create Screen Clipping.

- ■ **E-mail Notes**   Click the E-mail icon in the OneNote toolbar. OneNote attaches the original *.one file and pastes an HTML version of the notes in the message body.

- ■ **Live Sharing Session**   Click Share, then Live Sharing Session, then select Start Sharing Current Section. Click Start Shared Session, then click the Invite Participants button.

- **Shared Notebooks**   To create a Shared Notebook, click Share, then select Create Shared Notebook. Give it a name, a color, choose a template you want to use, and then click Next. Choose Multiple people will share this notebook and choose where you will store it. Click Create.

- **Outlook Tasks Toolbar**   To flag a note with an Outlook task, click View, then select Outlook Tasks Toolbar. Click the note you want to assign a task to, then click the appropriate task flag in the Outlook Tasks Toolbar.

- **Instant Search**   Type a word or string of words in the search box in the upper right corner of the OneNote window and hit Enter. Scroll through your results, or click View List to see all the pages that contain the search word or string in the Task Pane. Click to jump to any page.

- **Hyperlinking**   Click Edit, then Copy Hyperlink To to copy a hyperlink to a paragraph, Page, Section, Section Group, or Notebook. Navigate to the place in your Notebook where you want the link to appear and click Edit, then Paste.

Wow, what a meeting! The right people were there, everyone was prepared, and the meeting notes are already available for each attendee to see and take action on. Unfortunately, time didn't stop while you were meeting. The Word document you were editing still needs work. The Excel report your colleague sent you still needs to be analyzed. And the PowerPoint presentation for tomorrow's customer meeting still needs a little pizzazz. Looks like you could use some time-saving tips for these everyday Microsoft Office activities. Well, follow us....

Part Three

All Work and No Play... (You Know the Rest): Create More Professional-Looking Documents in Less Time

In this part

All your preparations have come down to this moment. You cleaned out your Inbox and used your Daily Task List to block off time on your Calendar. The Communicator icon in the taskbar reflects your busy intentions. Your coffee cup is full. Your bladder is empty. You are ready to get to work.

You stare at the blank spreadsheet before you, the clock starts to tick a little louder. You look at the phone, surprised no one is calling you. For once, it seems everyone is content to hold their questions until this afternoon's meeting. You look back at the blank spreadsheet. Your heart races. Then, it occurs to you that you don't know how to work without distractions. You finally have time to do all the work you put off because of fires to put out and now you don't know where to start. Remember, opportunities like this don't come along very often—let's get up into the Ribbon and enjoy it!

Raise your hand if you recall what is was like to type a document in Microsoft Word for the spell check and then copy and paste the text into a desktop publishing program to finish creating a newsletter? Microsoft Office Word 2007 has come a long way from columns and section breaks to become your headquarters for corporate communications. With new Building Blocks and Office Themes, anyone can put together a professional-looking training manual or report. However, the best thing you can do for your documents is make a resolution right now to learn how to use Styles in Office Word 2007.

And how about those spreadsheets? If we had a dollar for every time we've heard, "So, what's new in Excel?"—we'd be rich. In fact, one of our favorite new things about Microsoft Office Excel 2007 is that we now have enough cells in a spreadsheet to track the number of times we've heard that question. This section should come with a studio audience for as much applause as we get when we demonstrate how much easier it is to format spreadsheets in Office Excel 2007. Some of the same features in Word like themes and styles are also available to you in Excel 2007. And for anyone who has ever struggled with putting a header on a spreadsheet, prepare to give this section a standing ovation.

Of course, where would Excel be without PowerPoint? In previous versions, the two applications seemed like a perfect match. Why then was it so difficult to make anything that wasn't native to PowerPoint look right on the slide? With the new Shared Charting Engine, graphs look the same no matter where you put them. And if you're tired of bullet points, you're going to *love* SmartArt.

So, sit up a little straighter in your chair, get a firm grip on your mouse, and let's get to work on your next masterpiece....

Chapter 6

Frustration-Free Formatting—Get the Most from the New Document Structure and Formatting Capabilities of the 2007 Microsoft Office System

Chapter 6: Frustration–Free Formatting—Get the Most from the New Document
Structure and Formatting Capabilities of the 2007 Microsoft Office System

Part 3:
All Work &
No Play

Learn how to:

❑ Quickly format all your documents using Microsoft Office Word 2007 Styles, Themes, and Building Blocks

❑ Format Microsoft Office Excel 2007 data as a table for easier editing and analysis

❑ Easily format, customize, and repurpose Microsoft Office Power-Point 2007 slides

Our Hero

Your secret is safe with us. We know you want to be the formatting expert in the office. Everyone is always asking your officemate how to take a troubled document and line up bullet points, renumber lists, and make the text wrap around the picture just right. She seems to be the only person who can get the column widths spaced to print perfectly on the handouts page. It may take her half the day to do it, but that doesn't matter, everyone loves her because she is a problem solver.

For once, you wish you knew something that she didn't; then you could roll your chair over, lean around the cubicle and say something like, "I didn't mean to eavesdrop, but if you're having problems with that spreadsheet, I have a minute to show you how to do it if you like." You'd put on the imaginary superhero cape you keep draped over the back of your ergonomic chair and get to work doing the impossible task in the nick of time. "No, really, there's no need to thank me. I'm happy to help," you'd say, "It's no bother."

You don't have to be coy with us. We know how much fun formatting can be when you know the ins and outs of every drop-down list and dialog box. The best part of our job is seeing your eyes light up when you get a glimpse of what's new in the 2007 Microsoft Office system. This chapter is for beginners and experts alike—if you work around people that always seem to have a prettier PowerPoint than you do or if you're a self-taught information worker who's been playing around with formatting features for years. We're going to make some of you the expert others already think you are and others will get their first taste of what it's like to stand behind someone and say, "Just let me do it—it'll go faster!"

We promise not to let your secret out of the bag because with the 2007 Microsoft Office system, we can all be superheroes.

Office Word 2007—A New-Fashioned Love Song

It's the constant in our lives—the epicenter of organizational change via communications, reports, legal pleadings, contracts, correspondence, and book reports. Word is such a faithful companion that sometimes we take it for granted. We know Word can track changes and merge mail and spell check and so we go through our daily lives never really challenging the limits of what it can do for us. It's as if we don't want to tax our old friend too much. Can you hear that? It's Word 2007 crying out to be loved in new ways.

Tip or Treat   Perhaps you played around with fonts and saw Live Preview for yourself when we mentioned it in the introduction. If not, then select a paragraph of text now and from the Home tab on the Ribbon, click the down arrow next to the font you're currently using and hover over another font name. Wait for Live Preview to update the view and you can see exactly how that font will look on the page before you select it.

Style Makeover

Wait! Don't skip this section just because it's about styles. This is exactly what we're talking about—you've decided that if you can get a Word document to look the way you always have, then why bother learning styles.

Chapter 6: Frustration–Free Formatting—Get the Most from the New Document
Structure and Formatting Capabilities of the 2007 Microsoft Office System

Part 3:
All Work &
No Play

Maybe you took a class once and it all seemed a little too complicated. Stick around and see how styles have changed.

Some of you already know the thrill when you make a change to a style and the entire document updates automatically without the need to manually reformat every header. For those of you going back and forth to the toolbar 17 times to format one paragraph, you're definitely on board with this section. First, you need to understand that in Word 2007 a new blank document is simply a copy of a template named Normal.dotx or Normal.dotm if the document included one or more macros. In previous versions of Microsoft Office, if you changed Heading 1, closed the document, and didn't answer "Yes" when asked to save the changes to the template, then the changes you made to Heading 1 weren't available to you in any new documents. Many people did not use styles because they thought they had to keep recreating them.

Tip or Treat   Sometimes you need an instant formatting fix. Format Painter is used to copy the formatting of a selection instead of copying the text. Format a sentence by highlighting it yellow and making the text red. Now, select the sentence and right-click. Find the picture of the Paintbrush on the mini toolbar that pops up near the right-click menu or in the Clipboard section of the Home tab. Double-click the Paintbrush button, then select other sentences in your document to watch the Paintbrush copy the formatting of your sentence. Hit your ESC key to escape out of this feature.

To apply existing formatting using a SmartTag, copy a section of text from any Web page and paste it into a Word document. Click the picture of the clipboard that appeared at the bottom-right corner of the pasted text, then select Match Destination Formatting. You got asked one too many questions from Mr. ClipIt in previous versions of Office and you started ignoring every little thing that popped up to help you, didn't you? Don't feel too bad about it, other users did too.

Open Sesame

In the 2007 Microsoft Office system, you can open a new document and bring over the styles from any other document—it doesn't have to be a template. This is a new spin on the old File, Save As trick. Click the Microsoft Office Button, click New, and then select New From Existing (see Figure 6-1). When your file directory opens, select a document where you edited the styles or customized bullets (more on editing and customizing styles in a minute), double-click that file name, then click Create New.

Figure 6-1 Create a New Document from an Existing Document.

Notice at the top of the screen that Word did not open the file you selected, but instead created a new document based on that file. All you have to do now is delete the existing text and start from scratch, knowing your favorite styles are waiting for you up in your Quick Styles gallery on the Ribbon (see below). When you save the new file, the application will prompt you to rename it. Your other document will not be affected. No need to worry about templates just to get to your styles and no more cringing when you realize you just saved this week's report over the top of last week's report.

Tip or Treat   To get to the Style Organizer and import one or two styles from a template, click the diagonal down arrow in the Styles group of the Home tab. Click the Manage Styles icon at the bottom, click the Recommend tab at the top of the Manage Style dialog box, then select the Import/Export button at the bottom. On the right side of the screen, close the Normal.dotx file, and then click Open File. Double-click the template you want to copy a style from. In the Organizer dialog box, hold your Ctrl key down and click to select the styles from the template you just opened that you want to use in this document, and then click the Copy button. Close out of this dialog box and look for the styles in your Styles window list.

Quick Styles

On the Home tab, you'll find the Styles group. The Styles group features a gallery of the styles available for use in the document. This is your Quick Styles gallery (see Figure 6-2) and you can add the styles you want to access

Chapter 6: Frustration–Free Formatting—Get the Most from the New Document
Structure and Formatting Capabilities of the 2007 Microsoft Office System

Part 3:
All Work &
No Play

most often to this gallery and remove the ones you use less often. This is a great way to put the three styles you love most on the Ribbon for one-click access.

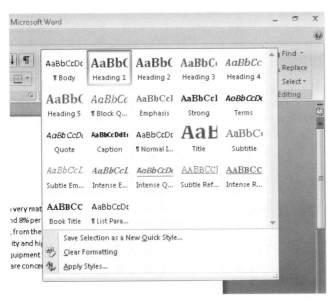

Figure 6-2 Quick Styles Gallery.

To get started, click the More button to the left of the words Change Styles in the Styles group. Note this is also where you can choose Clear Formatting (see tip below). Right-click and remove any styles you aren't using frequently in the document. You can also right-click specific styles in the Styles section of the Ribbon and remove unwanted styles from the gallery until you've narrowed down your list. If you want to access styles that are not in the Quick Style gallery, click the arrow in the bottom right of the Styles group to expand the Styles pane. Right-click the style you want, click Add To Quick Style Gallery, and then close the Styles task pane.

Depending on the number of styles in the Quick Style gallery, you may have to scroll up or down to locate a particular style. While you cannot drag and drop styles around the Quick Style gallery, the gallery will hold its position on a particular line as long as you are on the Home tab. If you leave the Home tab and come back again, the top line of the Quick Style gallery will be visible again.

Tip or Treat   Clear Formatting is a great command for those times when it's taken you 20 minutes and you still can't figure out why a bullet point isn't lining up correctly. Select the paragraphs that are giving you trouble and click the More button next to your Quick Styles gallery, and then click Clear Formatting. Now you have a clean slate to format this section of the document correctly. This is a great way to reset tabs and get rid of that line number that's in bold for no apparent reason.

To create a new style and add it to your Quick Style List, click the diagonal down arrow to open your Styles sheet and click the New Style icon at the bottom of that window. Name your style and select the formatting you want to apply to text in this and other documents. Confirm that Add to Quick Style List is checked in the bottom of this window and select New Documents Based On This Template. Automatically update is what you would check if you were re-formatting an existing style and you wanted all the other instances of that style to update. Click Format if you want to format the paragraph spacing or add a fill or border. When you are finished with your new style, click OK.

Once you have your Quick Styles gallery just the way that you want it, click Change Styles, then select Set As Default so the gallery always looks just like it does right now. If you skip this step, the Quick Styles gallery will reset the next time you open Word 2007, frustrating the heck out of you and possibly subjecting your coworkers to a string of colorful metaphors.

Ready, Set, Style

A Style Set allows you to change all the styles in your document immediately. With Live Preview, you can see how your document will look if you let Word 2007 apply styles that already look great together.

On the Home tab, click the Change Styles button, mouse over Style Set, then hover over Distinctive, now Elegant, and last but not least, Formal (see Figure 6-3). Remember to pause in between Style Sets so you can preview the styles live on your screen. Use Quick Styles and Style Sets when you don't have much time to clean something up or as a basis for all your documents. These styles are available in every Word 2007 document. Here's how you can create your own Style Set and make it available in all your documents as well.

Open the Styles pane by clicking on the diagonal down arrow in the Styles group on the Ribbon. Add or remove styles from this list by either clicking the New Style icon or right-clicking and removing styles. When you have a

Chapter 6: Frustration–Free Formatting—Get the Most from the New Document Structure and Formatting Capabilities of the 2007 Microsoft Office System

Part 3:
All Work &
No Play

list of styles that you like—and only the ones you like—click Options at the bottom of the task pane, select New Documents Based On This Template, and click OK.

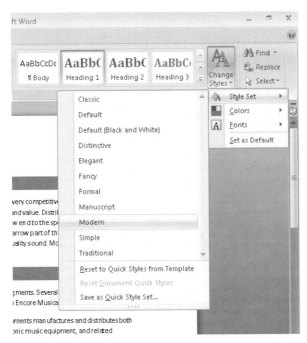

Figure 6-3   Style Sets.

Close out of your Styles pane and click Change Styles on the Ribbon. Click Style Set, then click Save As Quick Style Set. Give the Style Set a file name like your first name so you know which one is yours, then click Save. Click Change Styles, then select Style Set and look for your name. You have modified styles one time and now they are available to you every time you open a new blank document in Word 2007. While everyone else is struggling to re-format their documents, you will be one click away from all your favorites.

Tip or Treat   When you use styles, it's easy to create a Table of Contents in Word 2007. Click the References tab on the Ribbon, then click Table Of Contents in the Table Of Contents group. Click Insert Table Of Contents. Word automatically detects document headings and generates a Table of Contents from them. Use F9 inside the table to update headings and page numbers. One more reason to start using styles! Look for Table of Contents in your Building Blocks Organizer as well (we'll cover this a little later in the chapter).

Dream Themes

Like picking out clothes that match in the morning, Themes in Word 2007 ensure that even the color-blind make every hue they use in a document complement every other. In previous versions of Office, you had to pick colors from a honeycomb-looking palette and go back and forth a few times, consult a color wheel, then finally settle on something you'd never be able to match again unless you memorized the numbers for Red, Green, and Blue under the Custom colors tab. For those who loved doing that, it's still there, but for those who would rather worry about content than colors, there are Themes.

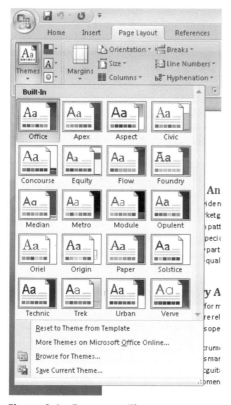

Figure 6-4 Document Themes.

Click the Page Layout tab on the Ribbon, and then click the arrow under Themes. Click Flow (see Figure 6-4). On a blank page, you won't notice a difference, but to see what it's done for you, click the down arrow next to Page Color in the Page Background group. Notice the Theme Colors? Go back to Themes and choose Verve. Click Page Color again. Notice that the

Chapter 6: Frustration–Free Formatting—Get the Most from the New Document
Structure and Formatting Capabilities of the 2007 Microsoft Office System

Part 3:
All Work &
No Play

blues of Flow changed to the purples of Verve? Themes limit your options to prevent you from making bad color choices. Too bad we can't shop for hair color or neckties by Office Theme.

It's not just page color; these Themes traverse other features in your document. Go back to the Home tab and click Change Styles, then click Colors. Notice the list of Themes. If you incorporated colors into your styles—like the shading of a text box—then selecting a document theme will automatically update the colors in your styles. It's like buying a pair of pants that you like in three different colors! Now you can have the styles you want updated automatically to match the colors used in other elements of your document.

Tip or Treat   Style Inspector takes the guesswork out of how a word or paragraph was formatted. On the Home tab, click the diagonal down arrow next to Styles on the Ribbon to open the Styles task pane. Select a paragraph in your document and click the Style Inspector icon at the bottom of the Styles task pane. It tells you the paragraph and text formatting and gives you the option to clear those elements or create a new style based on them. It's like Reveal Codes or Show Paragraph Formatting from previous versions of Word but with hot fudge, whipped cream, and a cherry on top.

With Styles, Themes, and a little help from Live Preview, you can make your documents look like a million bucks in half the time. Now that you've got some extra time on your hands, let's teach you how to quickly incorporate the new design elements introduced in Word 2007.

Putting Lipstick on a Pig

Have you ever spent so much time picking apart the way a handout looks that you don't bother to read it at all? Or made a judgment about someone you've never met by how professional their resume looks? As much as we'd like to think that everything we write is going to be carefully mulled over by our readers, the reality is that we are all influenced by the visual appeal of a document or presentation. This section is perfect for dressing up bad news and highlighting key content that might otherwise be missed by your audience.

Tip or Treat   Anytime you want to try something new without the threat of messing up one of your documents, use the random text formula in Word 2007. Type =rand(n) where *n* is the number of paragraphs of random text you want and hit Enter.

Building Blocks

Building Blocks are reusable chunks of content you can incorporate into any document. Think of them as virtual Legos you can use to build your document structure. No more fumbling around with invisible tables, indentations, and the like. With Building Blocks (also known as Quick Parts), great-looking documents are child's play.

Let's start at the top of the page with a header. Click the Insert tab, click Header in the Header & Footer group, and then select Tiles from the gallery. Notice the Design tab that appeared (see Figure 6-5). From here, you can change the location of the header on the page and insert a company logo. Double-click off the header to exit the Design tab, and double-click the header to return to it.

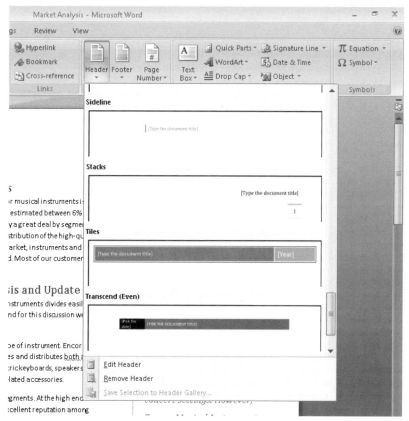

Figure 6-5   Insert Header.

For a complete list of Quick Parts, click the Insert tab on the ribbon, then click the Quick Parts button in the Text group. Go to Building Blocks Orga-

Chapter 6: Frustration–Free Formatting—Get the Most from the New Document Structure and Formatting Capabilities of the 2007 Microsoft Office System

Part 3:
All Work &
No Play

nizer. Scroll down to Page Numbers under the Gallery column and choose Circle Right (see Figure 6-6). Click Insert.

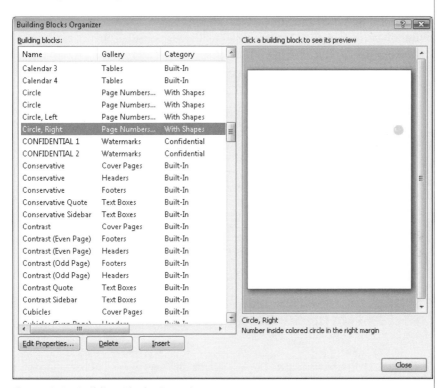

Figure 6-6 Building Blocks Organizer.

To edit the number in the circle, double-click the header, and click once on the circle. Click the pound sign (#) to change the page number, and format the font color of the number as well. Take care though, if you apply a theme now, the font of the page number will not be affected—only the shading of the circle. While you can resize the shape, you cannot move where the number appears.

Now, let's put a quote on the other side of the page. Go back up to the Text group on the Insert tab and click Text Box. Insert Tiles Quote. Click in the Quote and type, "Speak softly and carry a big stick." –Teddy Roosevelt

With Building Blocks, you can make any document look professional in just a few clicks by adding a Cover Page, a Bibliography, a Sidebar, a Watermark, and even an equation. Combine these design elements by applying goof-proof color Themes and you look like a Word Wizard. Isn't this fun?

Custom Building Blocks

Maybe you've come up with a color scheme, text box, or design that you are constantly copying from one document to another. Make that element a Building Block so that it is available in all your new documents. Select the text, then click the Insert tab. Click Quick Parts in the Text group and click Save Selection to Quick Part Gallery. Put the new Building Block in the Gallery it refers to—for example, if it is a Text Box, then choose Text Box from the Gallery drop-down menu. Under Options, you can choose to Insert content in its own paragraph. Now, your element is available any time you need it from the Building Blocks Organizer.

Office Excel 2007—Your Wish Is on My List

It's like a genie came out of the Microsoft Office Button and granted you three wishes. But you were smart: for your last wish you asked that your genie would forget he'd granted you any wishes and you got three more. Here are some of the things you can cross off your wish list for Microsoft Office Excel 2007.

Increased Spreadsheet Capacity

If you opened a new spreadsheet and populated one cell with a dollar sign each second, it would take you more than 507 years to fill in the 16 billion cells now available in one spreadsheet in Office Excel 2007. With 16,384 columns and 1,048,576 rows, that's a lot of dollar signs. Thankfully, you can also see more cells on the screen in Excel 2007 using the new Zoom slide bar in the bottom right corner of your spreadsheet. Compare that to the 256 columns and 65,536 rows available in previous versions and you'll see why Excel 2007 is like leaving spreadsheet skid row and movin' on up to a deluxe apartment in the sky.

I've Got a New, Added View

Click the View tab in an Excel 2007 workbook and notice that, in the Workbook Views group, you still have Page Break Preview. Many of us learned that this is the fastest way to fit all the columns on a printed page. If you're a wiz with scaling, Breaks is still waiting for you on the Page Layout tab, but there's no need to manage your headers and footers from this dialog box anymore.

Chapter 6: Frustration–Free Formatting—Get the Most from the New Document
Structure and Formatting Capabilities of the 2007 Microsoft Office System

Part 3:
All Work &
No Play

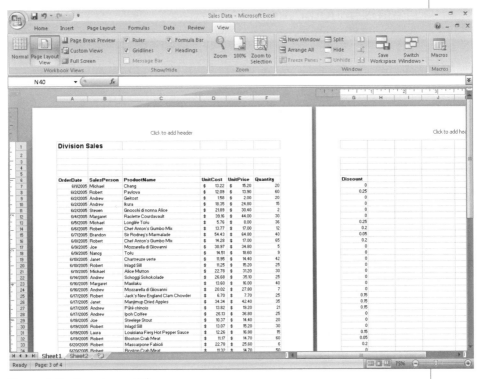

Figure 6-7   Page Layout View.

Click Insert, then Header And Footer, or click the View tab and Page Layout view to be taken into the Page Layout view of Excel (see Figure 6-7). Now you can type the header and footer directly on the page like you do in Word 2007. Your header and footer look just the way you want them to without having to go back and forth between Print Preview to check. When you are finished, click Normal on the View tab to return to the spreadsheet view. Wish granted.

Tip or Treat   In Excel 2007, when you use the close button in the upper right-hand corner to close a workbook, you aren't automatically closing out of all the workbooks you have open. Yes, it's perfectly normal that you hear baby cherubs singing off in the distance.

That's So Random

Excel 2007 is all about formatting your spreadsheets faster so you can analyze your data better. Poor Mr. ClipIt (aka, Clippy, the helpful Microsoft Office paper clip) is animating over and over in his grave right now because he can't interrupt you to ask you what you're doing.

Open a new worksheet and type the word January in cell B1. Drag the bottom, right corner (when your mouse pointer becomes a small plus sign) to autofill through September across the first row. In cell A2, type Monday, then autofill the days of the week through Friday down column A. To populate the worksheet with sample data, use the =randbetween(x,y) function where x is the bottom number in your range and y is the top number. Then autofill across your columns and rows (more on functions later—the numbers will continue to randomly generate during this exercise).

Tip or Treat   Cell Styles are a quick and easy way to format common cells in Excel—things like Grand Total rows and Headings, as well as Themed cell styles. In the following activity, if you choose a Themed cell instead of a Heading style from the gallery, then the column headings will only change when you apply a new theme to the table.

Select the cells in your header row—just the cells, not the entire row—and from the Home tab on the Ribbon, click Cell Styles in the Styles group. Click Heading 3. Click in the blank cell next to your last column heading and type in October. When you hit enter, the new column heading text will automatically format to match the others but the line does not copy over. Let's see what we can do about that. Click the Undo button twice to delete October and remove the cell styles. We'll try that again using the steps below.

Format as Table

Using the same sheet as in the above example, select cells A1 through J6. Click Format As Table in the Styles group of the Home Tab (see Figure 6-8). Click Table Style Medium 3. Click OK. Type October, November, and December to complete your header row. Notice how they formatted automatically. Autofill numbers into these new columns to complete the table. You may recognize this feature as Lists from Office 2003, but in addition to creating the autofilter for you at the top of each column, you take advantage of the autoformat and autofill functions of a table.

Chapter 6: Frustration–Free Formatting—Get the Most from the New Document
Structure and Formatting Capabilities of the 2007 Microsoft Office System

Part 3:
All Work &
No Play

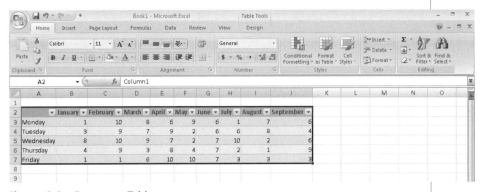

Figure 6-8   Format as Table.

Type Saturday in the first blank row under the days of the week in column A and hit the Tab key. Notice that the formula automatically populated the remaining columns of data with the randbetween formula. Try this with your own worksheets and see how converting your data to a table can help you format automatically and autofill formulas to create spreadsheets faster. With the gallery of Table Styles and Page Layout Themes, you will never have to painfully and manually draw lines around one cell at a time ever again.

Click the Design tab on the Table tools contextual command tab. Hover over the Table Styles gallery to see a Live Preview of the table styles. Click the Page Layout tab, then Themes. Hover over the Theme names for a preview of how the new colors and fonts will affect the table.

Tip or Treat   Want the table to stop generating random numbers? Copy the table and use Ctrl+V to paste it into a new spreadsheet (using the Enter key to paste does not return the Smart Tag referred to in this tip). Hover over the picture of the clipboard in the bottom, right corner of the table and click the down arrow. Click Values And Source Formatting. Made you use another Smart Tag!

Column Headings

By indicating that your table had a header row, you turned on another new feature in Excel 2007, but in order to see it in action, you'll have to copy this data all the way down the page. Select just the numbers in the table (no headings) and hover over the bottom, right corner until your mouse pointer becomes a skinny plus sign, drag down to autofill through row 50. Look at the top of your screen. Notice the names of the months docked in the column heading row (see Figure 6-9). Scroll up and down the page as much as you want using your mouse wheel so you can watch the column headings dock and undock—we'll wait. If you click out of the table and scroll down the page, the headings do not stay on the top row.

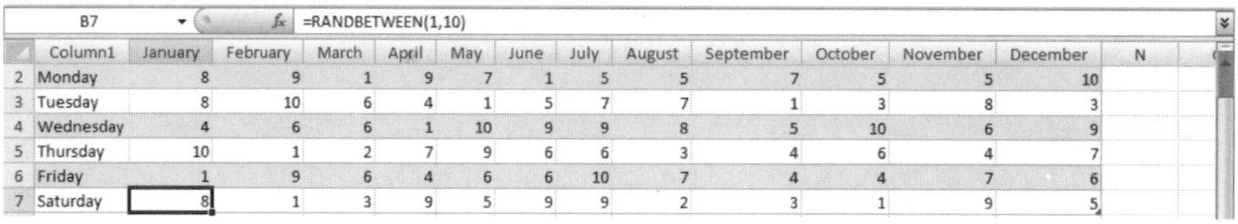

	B7		f_x	=RANDBETWEEN(1,10)										
	Column1	January	February	March	April	May	June	July	August	September	October	November	December	N
2	Monday	8	9	1	9	7	1	5	5	7	5	5	10	
3	Tuesday	8	10	6	4	1	5	7	7	1	3	8	3	
4	Wednesday	4	6	6	1	10	9	9	8	5	10	6	9	
5	Thursday	10	1	2	7	9	6	6	3	4	6	4	7	
6	Friday	1	9	6	4	6	6	10	7	4	4	7	6	
7	Saturday	8	1	3	9	5	9	9	2	3	1	9	5	

Figure 6-9 Column Headings.

A First Foray into Functions

For many, it's just easier to let Excel format text into tables. Look at the structure! The cells! It's like it was made to line up paragraphs perfectly. But it wasn't. Excel was made to do math—crazy, hard math on numbers and with strings of text. For those of you who already know an array from a hole in the ground, this discourse about formulas isn't going to teach you any new, crazy, hard math but this tip will show you how Excel 2007 makes writing formulas seem not so scary for the rest of us.

Go back to the source data we created in the example above and type =co under the January column and notice how all the functions that begin with *co* are listed on the screen (see Figure 6-10). Click once on any function in the list to see its description. Double-click the function you want to use. Then, the tip will stay with you, letting you know what values to enter to complete the function. In fact, if you click the name of the function in the tip, it will open up a Help screen with directions on how that function is used, with samples for you to look at. So, don't be afraid—foray into functions. They even manipulate text!

Chapter 6: Frustration–Free Formatting—Get the Most from the New Document
Structure and Formatting Capabilities of the 2007 Microsoft Office System

Part 3:
All Work &
No Play

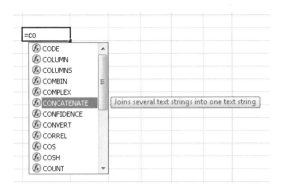

Figure 6-10   Formula Tips.

Tip or Treat   Use column headings instead of cell ranges to write formulas in an Excel Table. Select the table, click the Formulas tab in the Ribbon, and then click Create From Selection in the Defined Names group. Click OK. Now, instead of using B1:B5, you can type in the column heading (for example, January).You can also type [(that's the left bracket) in certain formulas to see a list of column headers—for example, =**sum(**[. Arrow down to the header you want, hit Tab, and type the closing parenthesis.

For example, here's a formula in Excel that takes text from two columns and combines the words into one string in a new column. In a new worksheet, Name Column A First Name and label two new column headings Last Name and Full Name respectively. Complete the First Name column with **Lisa, Jorge** and **Tonja** and the Last Name column with **Brown, Sanchez,** and **Smith**. Click in the blank cell under Full Name and click the Formulas tab on the Ribbon. Don't be scared; we're right here.

In the Function Library group, click the down arrow next to Text on the Ribbon and select CONCATENATE. Don't forget to add this word to your meeting bingo card. It's pronounced kin-kat-en-ate. Start using it in sentences like, "What we really need to do is concatenate the two teams for a more productive project" and "I don't know why we have to have so many meetings about this thing; we need to concatenate the messaging." Then, sit back and wait for everyone in the office to start saying it. See, formulas CAN be fun.

For the Text1 field, click Lisa. Then, click the Text2 field and click Brown. Click OK. Now, let's teach you how to put a space in between the two words. Click the cell with the formula in it and click your mouse next to the first cell reference to get a blinking cursor. Position the cursor after the comma, and type " ", (open quote, spacebar, close quote, comma) between the two cell references so the formula should look like this:

=CONCATENATE(A2," ",B2)

Whatever you type in between the quotes will be added to the new field. In this case, we only added a space, but in the next example, we add a comma and a space so it looks like Last Name, First Name. Click the blank cell next to Jose Sanchez and type =con. Double-click Concatenate, click the data cell with Sanchez in it, type comma, open parenthesis, comma, spacebar, close parenthesis, comma and click the data cell with Jose to populate the Text3 field. The formula should look like this:

=CONCATENATE(B3,", ",A3)

Hit Enter and...wow! It's like magic, only this is no illusion. Ever wonder how many other formulas we're not using because we don't know what the word means? We could show you more of the really cool things you can do with formulas in Excel 2007, but PowerPoint is getting impatient.

Office PowerPoint 2007—It Has a Great Sense of Humor

If you've ever played matchmaker for two of your friends, then you know what it's like to convince other people to use PowerPoint more often. When we're out on the road, we ask for a show of hands, "Of the three applications, would you say you spend most of your time in Word, Excel or Power-Point?" We rarely see an audience where more than 10 percent use PowerPoint the most, and the reality is that very few people think they have jobs that require them to use PowerPoint. You either have to be a presenter or a person who supports a presenter to get much use out of it, right?

Exactly! We find the problem is that most people don't consider themselves presenters; or worse, they don't think their meeting is important enough to create a slideshow for it. More and more people at all levels of the organization are calling meetings and fewer and fewer of those meetings are including an agenda, much less a PowerPoint presentation. No wonder we're frustrated about going to another meeting. Why am I here if the presenter didn't even take the time to come up with some key points that he or she wanted to make?

Like stumbling over how to tell one friend that the other friend is a little overweight, you're forgetting to focus on what makes PowerPoint so attrac-

Chapter 6: Frustration–Free Formatting—Get the Most from the New Document
Structure and Formatting Capabilities of the 2007 Microsoft Office System

Part 3:
All Work &
No Play

tive to the information worker: "This is the tool I can use to help alleviate some of my fear about getting up and speaking in front of other people." By having a dynamic visual aid, they won't be staring at you the whole time and when they do look over, they'll be smiling and nodding their heads. Power-Point is the kind of application you want to take to the company picnic and show off to all your friends.

Slide Style

Contrary to what you might hear in the fashion capitals of Europe, Power-Point is back in Style. There was a time when applying styles in PowerPoint meant using the Heading 1, Heading 2, and Heading 3 styles from Word to get the best results. In Microsoft Office PowerPoint 2007, you can import any Word document and PowerPoint will take a best guess at creating slides based on the actual layout of the document (see Figure 6-11). If you still have the Word file open that you created at the beginning of this chapter and you want to use it for practice in this section, be sure to name it and close it. You cannot import a Word document that you currently have open for editing.

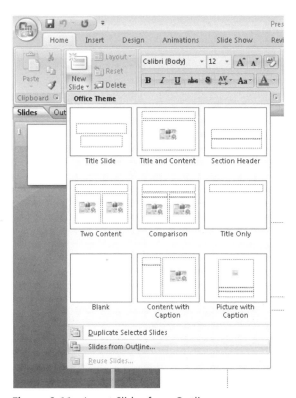

Figure 6-11   Insert Slides from Outline.

To begin, open a blank PowerPoint presentation and click the Home tab on the Ribbon. Click the arrow next to New Slide in the Slides group, and choose Slides From Outline at the bottom of the drop-down menu. Depending on how large a file you choose, this process may take a minute. If it is a complex document with embedded images, it may not work at all. Still, PowerPoint will automatically generate a presentation using the text from most Word documents.

Now that the text is in the presentation, let's get it formatted on the slides correctly. Click the Outline tab in the upper left corner of the thumbnail pane, just below the Ribbon. Click the picture of the slide next to any body text that may have slipped in and hit Delete. Use your Tab key to indent titles into subheadings, and if you need to promote an item, use Shift+Tab.

To change the order of bullet points, drag up or down onto another slide. Click the Slides tab to return to the Slides view. Delete any blank slides here. It may look a little plain, but it's a start.

Once the basic formatting is complete, you can begin to jazz up your presentation by applying a PowerPoint Theme. Themes work the same way in PowerPoint 2007 as we showed you in Word. Go to the Design tab in PowerPoint to see the gallery of Themes available in the Background group (see Figure 6-12). Click the drop-down arrow next to Background Styles to explore more options to customize your presentation.

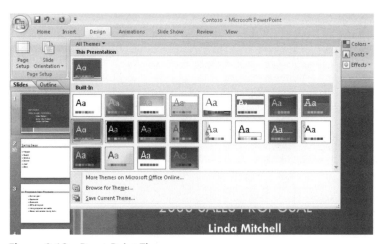

Figure 6-12 PowerPoint Themes.

Chapter 6: Frustration–Free Formatting—Get the Most from the New Document
Structure and Formatting Capabilities of the 2007 Microsoft Office System

Part 3:
All Work &
No Play

Master of Your Own Design

Sometimes you need a slide that's as unique as you are to get your point across. Creating your own custom slide layouts allows you to decide where you want slide elements, like text boxes, charts, or pictures to be positioned on a page. This takes the Slide Master concept to a whole new level.

You can place a background object, background fill, body placeholder, headers and footers, placeholder formatting, a title placeholder, and a subtitle placeholder all on one slide if you like. No more Bulleted List slides you have to modify in the Master Slide screen—you've got three columns of content to make your point now. The best part is that you can reuse these custom layouts in other presentations.

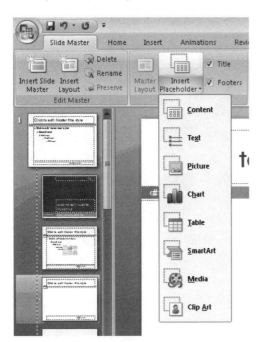

Figure 6-13 Custom Slide Layouts.

To add a custom layout, click the View tab, then click Slide Master in the Presentation Views group. Scroll down to the bottom of the list and click below the last layout. Click Insert Layout in the Edit Master group in the Slide Master tab (see Figure 6-13). Delete unwanted placeholders and click the Insert Placeholder arrow in the Master Layout group to choose content, text, picture, chart, table, diagram, media, or clip art. When you're done, click the Microsoft Office Button, click Save As, and select PowerPoint Template from the Save As Type field. Rename the file and click Save. This new layout is accessible anytime you want to use it via the layout drop-down box.

Publish Slides

Now that you've figured all that out, everyone is going to want a copy of your presentation. Don't let them down. Sharing your slides with coworkers is almost as good as being asked for your autograph. Just try and keep your mouse off the e-mail attachment button.

If your company is running Office SharePoint Server 2007, you can publish some of or all the slides in a presentation directly to an online Slide Library (see Figure 6-14). To publish your slides to a Slide Library, click the Microsoft Office Button, click Publish, then select Publish Slides. Put checks by the slides you want to publish or click Select All. Navigate your Web browser to the site where you want others to be able to pull them down and use them. Select and copy the Web address but leave off the view name from the URL (for example, /AllItems.aspx) and paste it into the Publish To: field in PowerPoint. Click Publish. By linking the presentation to the slides in the library, you will be prompted each time you open the presentation to update and synchronize any changes made online by your coworkers.

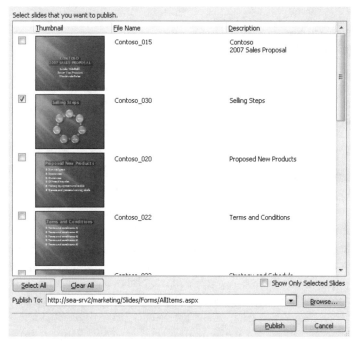

Figure 6-14 Publish Slides to a PowerPoint Slide Library.

Chapter 6: Frustration–Free Formatting—Get the Most from the New Document
Structure and Formatting Capabilities of the 2007 Microsoft Office System

Part 3:
All Work &
No Play

To reuse slides from a Slide Library in your own presentation, click the
down arrow next to New Slide and click Reuse Slides. In the Reuse Slide
task pane, select Open A Slide Library and double-click the SharePoint site
where you saved the slides (see Figure 6-15). You can even preview the
slides by hovering over the thumbnail images. Click the slide you want
and—voila!—it's in your presentation with the current design template
applied automatically. To keep the source formatting, click the Smart Tag
and select Keep Source Formatting.

Figure 6-15   Reuse Slides from a PowerPoint Slide Library.

Tip Jar

Here's a review of the top 10 tips covered in Chapter 6:

- **Reuse styles from an existing Word document**   Click the Microsoft Office Button, click New, and then select New From Existing. Select your Word document. Now, click Create New.

- **Save a Style Set in Word 2007**   Click Change Styles on the Home tab of the Ribbon, click Style Set and Save As Quick Style Set. Give it a name and click Save.

- **Use a Word 2007 Building Block**   Click the Text Box arrow in the Text group in the Insert tab. Click Exposure Sidebar (for example).

- **Apply an Office Theme to a Word document**   Click the Page Layout tab in Word. Click Themes, then select Metro (for example).

- **Adjust the Zoom of Your Spreadsheet**   In Excel 2007, slide the Zoom bar over to 20 percent and back to 100 percent.

- **Use Excel 2007 Page Layout View**   Click the View tab (not the Page Layout tab) and click Page Layout View in the Workbook Views group.

- **Format an Excel 2007 Spreadsheet as a Table**   Select your data in an Excel worksheet. Click Format As Table in the Styles group of the Home tab. Select a table style to automatically create and format the table.

- **Create PowerPoint 2007 Slides from a Word document**   In PowerPoint 2007, click the Home tab. Click the New Slide drop-down menu, then click Slides from Outline. Double-click the Word file you want to copy into PowerPoint. Click the Outline tab on the left of the screen in PowerPoint (not on the Ribbon) to quickly clean up unwanted text.

- **Create a Custom PowerPoint 2007 Slide Layout**   Click the View tab, then click Slide Master in the Presentation Views group. Scroll down to the bottom of the list and click below the last layout. Click Insert Layout in the Edit Master group in the Slide Master tab. Delete unwanted placeholders and click the Insert Placeholder arrow in the Master Layout group. Click the Microsoft Office Button, click Save As, and select PowerPoint Template from the Save As Type field. Rename the file and click Save.

Chapter 6: Frustration–Free Formatting—Get the Most from the New Document
Structure and Formatting Capabilities of the 2007 Microsoft Office System

Part 3:
All Work &
No Play

- **Re-use slides from a SharePoint Slide Library**   Click the down arrow under New Slide on the Home tab. Click Reuse Slides. Click Open A Slide Library in the Reuse Slides task pane and double click the Share-Point site where you saved the slides.

You have officially taken your rightful place as the formatting superstar in your office. Read on to attain ultimate enlightenment.

Chapter 7

Easy on the Eye Candy— Create Documents, Spreadsheets, and Presentations That Pop

Learn how to:

❏ Turn mediocre documents and presentations into mini-master-pieces with WordArt and SmartArt

❏ Create, copy, and customize charts with the Microsoft Office 2007 Shared Charting Engine

❏ Put the "show" back in slideshow with PowerPoint 2007 Presenter View

The Land of "Awes"

Welcome to the big time. This chapter should not be read by people with neck or back conditions, people with a medical sensitivity to strobe effects, fog effects, motion sickness, or those who are unable to meet the minimum height requirements. Expectant mothers or women who expect to become pregnant should consult their doctor prior to reading this chapter. To avoid serious injury, remain seated while reading, and keep your hands on the book at all times.

Yours is a journey of sight, sound, and Shared Charting Engines. The destination? A visual wonderland of 3-D text, diagrams, and conditional formatting. A place where every worker is an artist and every document is a work of art. Welcome to the land of "awes." Something tells us you're not in your cubicle anymore.

Art Appreciation

The colors. The lines. The textures. You've never seen anything like it before. As you stare in wonder, a feeling of warmth and hospitality washes over you like a warm summer breeze. It's as if the image in front of you has a direct line to your soul. It's not a Monet masterpiece; it's your officemate's Office file.

How did he do it? His degree was in anthropology, not art. You know this guy. He couldn't draw his way out of a coloring book. Heck, he even flunked the art school self-test they advertise on late night TV. So, what gives? Your coworker may not be an artist, but the 2007 Microsoft Office system is. And since software can't sign its name, you get to take all the credit.

WordArt That Wows

Open a blank Microsoft Office Word 2007 document and click the Insert tab. Look for WordArt in the Text group and click it. Don't let the familiar WordArt gallery fool you; things have changed. Choose WordArt Style 15 (as you mouse over each icon, the icon's title is displayed), type What's New, and click OK. Notice the WordArt Tools contextual command tab now on the Ribbon (see Figure 7-1).

Figure 7-1 Word 2007 WordArt Tools.

With WordArt in the 2007 Microsoft Office applications, you can apply and customize special effects like reflections and shadowing to your text. On the Format tab, in the Shadow Effects group, click the tiny Nudge Shadow Down button a couple of times. To see more options, click the down arrow of the Shadow Effects button and preview the Perspective Shadow examples. In the Additional Shadow Styles collection, click Shadow Style 15 and nudge it up and to the right several times until you get it just how you like it.

Change the Text Wrapping in the Arrange section of the Format tab to Square and drag the picture down farther on the page so you can see the Live Preview when we demonstrate the next WordArt feature. Now, click the arrow next to Change Shape in the WordArt Styles section of the Format tab. Click Slant Up.

Move your mouse over the circular rotation handle on the graphic and drag it left to rotate it just slightly. Drag the whole graphic to the upper, left corner of the page. Click Shape Fill and choose Yellow. Click Shape Outline and...you get the idea. Click the buttons in the Text group on the far left of the Format tab and notice the other changes you can make to the text. (See Figure 7-2.)

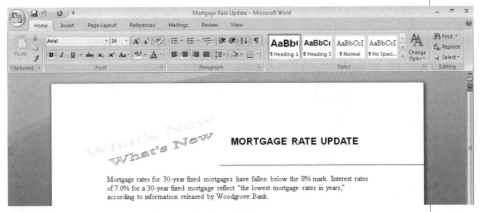

Figure 7-2 Customized WordArt in Word 2007.

To see even more of what you can do with WordArt, close Word and open Microsoft Office PowerPoint 2007. Click the title field in the default slide and type What's New. Click the Format tab on the Ribbon. Select the words and hover over the WordArt Styles gallery icons on the Ribbon. Expand the WordArt Styles gallery and select Fill - Accent 1, Metal Bevel, Reflection. Click the Text Effects button on the ribbon in the WordArt Styles group and look through the menus for Transform and 3-D rotation (this will not animate the text to rotate—that's an animation; we'll talk about those later).

Figure 7-3 Customized WordArt in PowerPoint 2007.

In the Text Effects drop-down list, click Glow and choose the orange glow on the top row. In the Shape Styles group, click Shape Fill, then click Blue, Accent 1, Lighter 60% near the middle of the gallery. Click Shape Effects, select Glow, then choose Accent Color 1, 18 pt Glow in the bottom-left corner (see Figure 7-3). Not bad for a roller coaster, but here comes the loop-de-loop.

All That and Brains Too

SmartArt might be the coolest thing to happen to the Microsoft Office system since ClipArt. Then again, we don't get out much, so our worldview may be a little skewed. You can use SmartArt to automatically convert plain old text into dynamic diagrams that more accurately represent your vision.

Start by adding a new slide to the presentation you were using above. On the Home tab, select Title And Content from the New Slide drop-down gallery. Click the text area of the slide and type the following bullets into the slide:

■ Manage e-mail

- Make meetings more effective

- Create more professional-looking documents

- Collaborate with coworkers

Select the bullet points, right-click and select Convert To SmartArt. Click
Basic Cycle (see Figure 7-4).

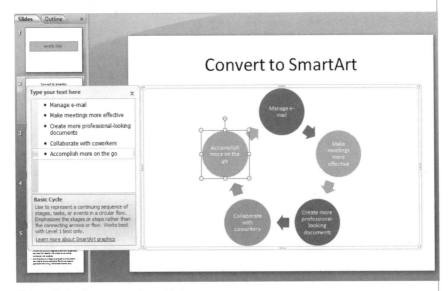

Figure 7-4   Convert to SmartArt.

Oops, we forgot a bullet. Mouse over to the Type Your Text Here box and
click to get a blinking cursor behind coworkers. Hit Enter and type Accomplish more on the go. We would like to observe a moment of silence to com-
memorate the loss of all the bulleted lists that bravely served us in past
presentations. Your memory will live on in our hearts and minds.

This looks good, you say to yourself, but it would look better in 3-D. Now,
you're talking. Notice the Design tab on the Ribbon under SmartArt Tools.
Click the More button at the right edge of the SmartArt Styles group, scroll
through the gallery and choose Polished from the 3-D collection. Click
Change Colors and choose Colorful Accent Colors. Click the Design tab,
click Effects from the Themes group, then click Technic. (See Figure 7-5.)

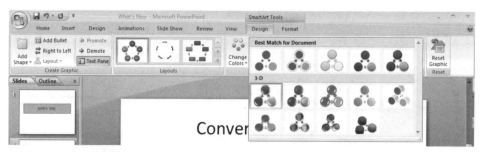

Figure 7-5 SmartArt Tools.

Tip or Treat   To make a graphic appear to rotate on the screen, select the object, then click the Animations tab. In the Animations group, click Custom Animation, then click Add Effect on the task pane. Click the arrow by Entrance, then click More Effects. Scroll down to Swivel and click OK. Click the down arrow next to the Diagram number in the task pane and click Effect Options. On the Effect tab, click Vertical from the Direction drop-down menu, then click the SmartArt Animation tab. Click the Group Graphic drop-down menu and choose One By One. Click OK.

Play your slideshow by clicking the Slide Show icon (projector screen) in the bottom-right corner of the screen and mouse click through the graphics. Go back to the SmartArt Tools Design tab and click Reset Graphic on the far right of the Ribbon. Remember when you thought this looked cool? That was, like, so five minutes ago.

Straight from the Chart

People love to look at charts. They can make all kinds of decisions once they see the biggest piece of pie or the lowest bar on a chart. Where would *Who Wants To Be a Millionaire* be without charting audience participation? If you've got numbers, then you can create charts. And if you've got the 2007 Microsoft Office system, you can create charts anywhere you want to with the new Shared Charting Engine.

Shared Charting Engine

The beauty of the Shared Charting Engine is that all your charting features are available to you no matter where the chart lives. Yes, you heard us right; charts work the same in Word and PowerPoint as they do in Microsoft Office Excel 2007! And you thought the genie had already gone back into the bottle.

When you insert a chart into a document, spreadsheet, or presentation, a contextual Chart Tools command tab appears for customizing the design, layout, and formatting of the chart. Cut and paste the chart into another application and the Chart Tools come right along with you. Click outside of the chart and the Chart Tools disappear until you need them again. (See Figure 7-6.)

Figure 7-6   Charting Tools Command Tab.

When copying charts between Excel and PowerPoint, keep in mind that charts paste into PowerPoint as their actual size. This means that if you are bringing over a chart from a dedicated chart page in Excel, you will probably want to resize it once you have it in PowerPoint. Not to worry, the placeholders are much easier to manipulate now and you'll find the experience of resizing much less stressful.

Perhaps the best part is that the chart pastes into your presentation with an automatic link to the data in Excel. If PowerPoint is closed when you update the source spreadsheet, the chart will automatically update the next time you open PowerPoint. That's right, no more "Get Updates" message. If you're thinking things can't possibly get better than this, think again.

Watch what happens when you insert a new chart in PowerPoint 2007. We'll pretend you need to manually enter your data from a piece of paper someone handed you and that there is no corresponding Excel spreadsheet to concatenate (nice word!) with this slide. Go to a title slide and click the Insert tab, then select Chart from the Illustrations group. Click Bar on the left, then click OK. Watch as your screen transforms into a half-PowerPoint and half-Excel super screen. (See Figure 7-7.)

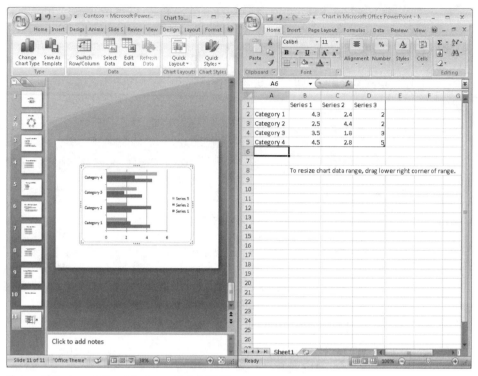

Figure 7-7 Insert Chart in PowerPoint 2007.

Type in the values you want to chart in the Excel spreadsheet. Click in the middle of the PowerPoint slide to see your chart update to reflect the new values. Close the Excel spreadsheet. If you need to edit the data in the Chart, just right-click the edge of the placeholder and click Show Data. And the crowd goes wild.

I Want to Turn the Whole Chart Upside Down

Sometimes, a spreadsheet with the best of intentions becomes cumbersome with important data. What starts as a simple product list can turn into a flat database file with everything you know about the vendors who sell it, the contact name and e-mail address of the person who invoices you, and...employee vacation time? We're not proud of the things we've seen.

Take the following spreadsheet for example—what started out tracking how many fruits and vegetables each person bought also became a tracking device for what type of bag they chose. So, how do I get the information I need to quickly report bag usage at my store?

PivotTables allow you to see and analyze your data in a whole new way, without affecting the layout of your source data. To see a PivotTable in action, type this data into a new Excel spreadsheet:

Name	Apples	Oranges	Squash	Beans	Bag
Lisa	13	13	16	18	Plastic
Jorge	8	19	12	18	Paper
Tonja	16	2	7	3	Plastic

Now, select the data, click the Insert tab, then click PivotTable. Select New Worksheet, then click OK. Drag Bag down to Row Labels and Apples, Oranges, Squash, and Beans down to Values. (See Figure 7-8.)

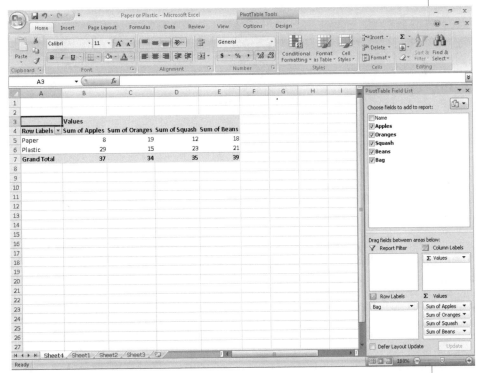

Figure 7-8   Insert PivotTable.

You can chart this data by choosing PivotChart in the Tools group in the Options tab, in the upper-left corner of the Ribbon. Click Bar from the list and click OK.

Unlike regular Excel charts, PivotCharts are not linked to your data. So, if you make a change to the source data and you want the PivotChart to reflect that, you must go back into the sheet with the PivotTable, click the Analyze tab and choose Refresh in the Data group. To see this example, change Jorge's bag choice to Plastic and Refresh your PivotTable. (See Figure 7-9.)

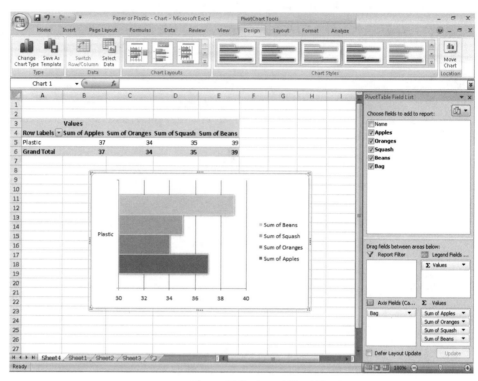

Figure 7-9   Insert PivotChart.

Data Connection Wizard

The Data Connection Wizard in Excel 2007 walks you through connecting your spreadsheet to an external database. Excel 2007 links the data between the external source and the spreadsheet. This allows Excel 2007 to update worksheets with the most recent data from your organization's other data sources and eliminates the need for you to copy and paste. Click Data, then click From Other Sources in the Get External Data group. Click From Data Connection Wizard. Work with your IT Department if you have any questions regarding connecting to external databases using this Wizard. They will have to ensure the data is in a trusted location and that connections to external data are not disabled on your computer via your Trust Center.

This is one of the reasons some people prefer pasting PivotCharts into their PowerPoint presentations instead of a linked Excel chart. You may have the best of intentions when you change the source data of a linked PowerPoint/Excel chart, but if your coworker is connected to the company network and presenting the content in another room (whether or not they pulled it down off the SharePoint site or the shared network drive), the presenter may come out of the meeting confused as to why their data kept changing throughout the meeting.

Effects and Sizzle

The following exercise is an exhaustive walking tour of the formatting options available to you in the Office 2007 Shared Charting Engine. It serves to make you comfortable with the Ribbon navigation and allows you to see an example of each effect. Be sure to write down in the margin of this book the other styles and options that caught your eye in the Live Preview so you can refer to your list of favorites later.

Use the sample data for fruits and vegetables provided above to create a new spreadsheet. Do not include the Bag column. Select all rows of data and click the Insert tab. In the Charts group, click the down arrow on Pie and click Exploded Pie in 3-D. Note that only Lisa's data is on the chart. In the table, there is a blue line around the data. Move your mouse over the top, left corner of that line and, when the mouse pointer becomes a double-headed diagonal arrow, reposition the blue line to only include Tonja's data. Notice the graph changed to accommodate the new data selection.

In the Chart Layouts group on the Design tab of the Ribbon, click Layout 2. Click the Format tab on the Ribbon. On the far-left of the Ribbon, click the arrow at the top of the Current Selections group. (See Figure 7-10.)

Figure 7-10   Chart Area Menu.

Instead of double-clicking every chart element like we used to do in previous versions, we can select exactly what it is we are trying to modify. Click Series "Tonja" from the menu. Click Shape Outline from the Shape Styles group, click Weight, then select 3 pt. Some of these choices will be overridden by future choices.

To change the individual colors of a pie piece, click one time on that piece of pie (avoid the data labels). Notice the Current Selection at the left end of the Ribbon changes to reflect what you have selected. Click Shape Fill, click Gradient, then select Linear Left in the Light Variations category. Click the

Layout tab, click 3-D Rotation, and change the Y rotation to 20°. Click
Close.

Click the Format tab and then, in the chart, click Tonja's name. Confirm
that you are editing the Chart Title by referring to the Current Selection section of the Ribbon. Click Shape Fill, then select Red Accent 2, Lighter 60%.
Click Shape Outline and select Dark Blue, Text 2, Lighter 80%. Click Shape
Effects, click Bevel, then choose Art Deco.

Click inside the chart area, then click Shape Fill, and select Red Accent 2,
Lighter 60%. Click Shape Fill again, select Gradient, then click Linear
Down. Click the Data Labels. In the WordArt Styles section of the Format
tab, click Text Effects, click Reflection, then select Half Reflection, 4 pt offset
from the gallery. Industrial Light And Magic, eat your heart out.

Working Hard or Hardly Working?

If we put that much time into customizing a chart, maybe we should save it as
a template so we don't have to do it all over again for Jorge and Lisa. Click the
Design Tab, then in the Type group click Save As Template. (See Figure 7-11.)

Figure 7-11   Save a Chart Template.

Name it Fruits and Vegetables and click Save. Click off the chart into the
datasheet, then select the data in your table. Click the Insert tab on the Ribbon, then click the diagonal down arrow at the bottom of the Charts group.
Click Templates, click the picture of Fruits and Vegetables, and click OK.
Relocate the blue line to Jorge's data. Rinse and repeat.

Show and Tell

Art and Charts aren't the only ways to express your ideas and information
visually in the 2007 Microsoft Office system. Excel cells with conditional
formatting or colored fills are virtually impossible not to notice. And what
good are PowerPoint slides without the PowerPoint slideshow? That's like
peanut butter without jelly. Peas without carrots. Sonny without Cher. OK,
maybe that last one we can do without altogether.

On One Condition

Graphs were made for people who don't like to look at numbers, but what does Excel 2007 offer the person who has to look at all those numbers to decide which ones to graph? Say hello to conditional formatting.

First, make sure you're on the Home tab of the Ribbon. Next, select the fruits and vegetables data you know and love. In the Styles group, click Conditional Formatting, click Data Bars, and click your favorite color (tough guys use purple). Click Conditional Formatting again, click Clear Rules, then select Clear Rules From Entire Sheet.

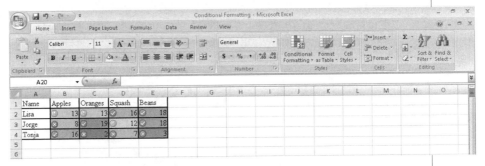

Figure 7-12 Conditional Formatting.

If looking at bars flashes you back to the time a chart killed your goldfish, try clicking Conditional Formatting, selecting Icon Sets, then clicking 3 Symbols (Circled). Click Conditional Formatting, click Color Scales, then click Red-Yellow-Green Color Scale, and you've got an easy way to spot the lowest numbers on the chart. (See Figure 7-12.)

Conditional Formatting is based on rules. You can clear these rules and make your own; you do not have to color every cell. Select your table, click Conditional Formatting, then click New Rule. Click Format only cells that contain. Use the drop-down menus to Format only cells with cell value less than and type the number 5. Click the Format button, click the Fill tab and choose Red. Click OK, twice.

Right about now, you should be wondering if you can sort your data by color. In Excel 2007, the answer is yes. As for who wrote the Book of Love, we're still wondering that ourselves.

Tip or Treat Remove Duplicates allows you to search multiple columns of data and remove duplicates. Make sure that you are searching for duplicates in text fields as some values may repeat. For example, in an address list, you could run a search on name and street address to ensure that you are not deleting people just because they have the same name. The Remove Duplicates button is located on the Data tab in your Excel 2007 Ribbon.

Filter by Color

It's the squeal of joy heard round the world. Finally, we can sort by text *or* fill color! Paste what's on your clipboard (should still be the fruits and vegetables table with the bag column) into a new worksheet in Excel 2007. Color the text of the two instances of "Plastic" red and fill the "Paper" cell with yellow. Right-click the word "Plastic" (now red) in Lisa's row, click Sort, then select Put Selected Font Color On Top. Now, right-click Paper (yellow fill) and click Sort, this time selecting Put Selected Cell Color On Top. It truly is a great time to be alive and using Office. (See Figure 7-13.)

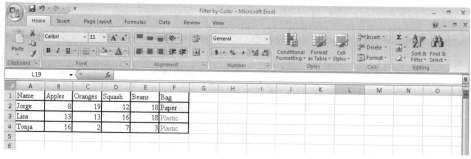

Figure 7-13 Filter by Color.

Excel Services

A component of Microsoft Office SharePoint Server 2007, Excel Services makes it possible not only to display Excel workbooks on a SharePoint site but also do calculations within the browser window. Using this technology, companies can make information available to their extranet users and clients via a secure connection with real-time data—no need to upload the document to a company Web site every time a change is made. The results are visible and data set up as parameters can be manipulated via PivotCharts,

Tip or Treat Custom sort now supports up to 64 levels. Click the Data tab, select Sort, then choose Add Level. You can sort multiple font colors, cell colors, and conditional formatting icons at the same time.

Be a Presenter—Not a Belly Itcher

There you are in the back row of the auditorium all bundled up in your sweater because it is always freezing in here. The presenter begins and you read everything on the first slide and then go back to your internal thoughts about how you're getting hungry and you should have eaten and how you had forgotten all about that pastry filled with ham and cheese that you put in the freezer in the break room last week until just now. That would taste good—all warm and cheesy in your hands. Next slide. You read everything on that slide and move on to another musing. After an hour of this, you will have survived another mandatory training event. Friends don't let friends do this to their next audience.

however the business logic (typically confidential) is hidden from the external user. You determine who has permission to view the site and to what degree they can interact with the data.

Parameters is the term for Excel Cell Ranges in Excel Services. You can define Parameters by going to the Formulas tab and clicking Define Name. You have the ability to decide which of these pre-defined Parameters are viewable by clicking the Microsoft Office Button, selecting Publish, then Excel Services, Excel Services Options, and finally Show tab. By default, the Entire Workbook is viewable, however you can select a particular sheet from the drop-down menu and check Parameters you want to be visible and uncheck Parameters you do not want to show.

To publish the spreadsheet, type in the URL of the portal you are publishing it to. Work with your IT department if you have any questions regarding whether or not Microsoft Office SharePoint Server 2007 (and therefore Excel Services) has been implemented within your organization.

Presenter View

Presenter View in PowerPoint is a way you can set up your slideshow to run on two monitors—two different views on two monitors. This means your audience will continue to see the slideshow just as they always have, but you will see thumbnails of future slides, a timer, and even your speaker notes on your laptop monitor, and that person in the back row will never be the wiser.

In order to demonstrate this feature, you will have to be connected to a secondary monitor, be that an additional monitor at your desk or a projector in a conference room. You will not be able to practice with this feature if you have only one screen in front of you right now. You can, however, practice curling your tongue, wiggling your ears, and flaring your nostrils. All you need for that is a good sense of silliness and a complete lack of something better to do.

Speaker Notes

Open an existing PowerPoint presentation and at the bottom of the screen, make the Click to add notes section larger by dragging it up. These are your speaker notes. Sometimes presenters use this area to create their audience handout. To print this section, choose Notes Pages from the Print What section of your Print dialog box. Type something helpful to the nervous speaker like, Smile. Breathe. Picture them with their teddy bear. Click the Slide Show tab, then Use Presenter View.

If your secondary monitor has not been activated, you will be prompted to click Check to go into the properties of your desktop and activate the dual monitor feature. Click the number 2 at the top of the Display Settings dialog box and put a check by Extend my desktop onto this monitor. Don't change any properties on your first monitor. Click OK and it will return you to your PowerPoint presentation. (See Figure 7-14.)

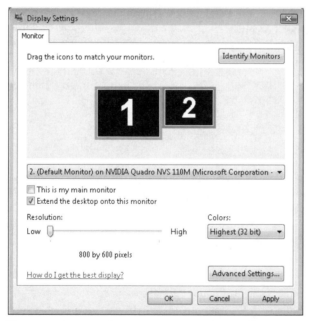

Figure 7-14 Extend My Desktop onto This Monitor.

Click the Show Presentation on arrow to choose which monitor you want to project the slideshow onto. Choose Monitor 2.

Now, when you play the slideshow, you'll see one view on your laptop while the participants see the full slideshow on the projected screen. If they are seeing your presenter's view and you are seeing the slideshow, ESC out and make sure to choose the other monitor from the Display slide-show on drop-down menu under the multiple monitors heading of the Set Up Show dialog box, accessed by clicking Set Up Slide Show in the Set Up group in the Slide Show tab. Of course, now that they've seen your speaker notes, they're all going to want teddy bears.

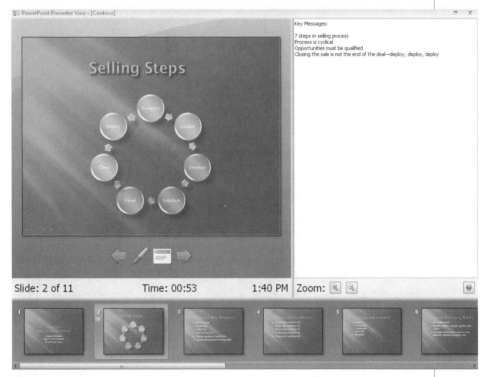

Figure 7-15   Presenter View.

Presenter View shows the slides coming up in the presentation as thumbnails on the bottom navigation panel (see Figure 7-15). This allows you to skip over a slide if it just doesn't seem appropriate to this audience. Instead of being the presenter that has to page down to get to the slide he or she wants and then page back up to find their place, you have all your slides available to you and can click once to project the one you want. This allows you to have a more dynamic presentation because you can follow the flow of the audience. If someone asks you a question that you were going to answer in a later slide, just click the slide that answers it and continue. Keep your audience engaged by giving yourself the flexibility to customize your presentation on the fly.

Don't worry about losing your place in your printed notes because your speaker notes are in this view along with a clock that lets you know how long the slide show has been running. No need to panic if there isn't a clock in the room; just start the presentation and the timer counts up to let you know how much time has elapsed. Even if you haven't completed all the slides in your presentation in the 15 minutes you've been allotted, you'll know to wrap it up and ask for a time slot in another meeting to finish the presentation. One of the secrets to delivering a successful presentation is to never go over your allotted time.

Other new features of Presenter View in PowerPoint 2007 include the ability to preview upcoming text. In a slide with animations, you'll see the upcoming bullet in the list which will prevent you from building people up for the next point, clicking the slide and then saying, "but first, we'll talk about this." With Presenter View, you don't have to memorize your animations.

Getting you to stop looking up at the projected screen is only half the battle, the other half is keeping your audience's attention.

Keep Their Eyes on the Slide

What do diversity training, safety training, and comedy defensive driving all have in common? VCR tapes that have been copied too many times with bad sound and even worse acting. Nothing ruins a perfectly executed PowerPoint presentation quite like fumbling around with a silver VCR with no one who was ever in the A/V club in the room to help you out.

See if you have any resources at your company to get those tapes converted to files and have them burned onto a DVD. When your company orders new videos, make sure they provide them to you as .avi files on the DVD. Why? Because under the Insert tab in PowerPoint is a Movie From File option.

By putting media into your PowerPoint presentations, you keep your audience's eyes on the slide and off of those sweat patches developing under your arms. But movie clips don't always have to star Troy McClure (you may remember him from such movies as...). Click Movie From Clip Organizer to see the movies that are available for you to use from Microsoft Office Online. Type meeting in the search box of the task pane. Insert one of the movies with the gavel on it into your slide by clicking the down arrow next to the picture and clicking Insert. Resize the image and play the slide show. Now, when you call the meeting to order, you've already got their attention!

Here's a trick for the last slide in your show. Click the Insert tab on the Ribbon and click Clip Art in the Illustrations group. Type applause into the search field (make sure you're connected to the Internet), click Go, and insert any of the clips named Crowd Cheer. Tell PowerPoint you want the sound to start automatically. Play the slideshow and listen to that audience—they love you! When it's time for you to end your presentation, you know you'll always get a round of applause. You can also add applause as a Transition Sound on the Animations tab.

Tip or Treat   To have the same song play throughout the entire presentation, insert the audio clip to play automatically. Under the Animations tab, select Play Across Slides from the Animate drop-down list.

Presentation Options

What about those times when you just want to tweak your presentation a little bit? Perhaps you've been asked to condense your 45-minute presentation down into 15 minutes. That should be easy enough to do, especially with custom slideshows in PowerPoint 2007.

Open an existing PowerPoint presentation and click the Slide Show tab. Select Custom Slide Show, then click Custom Shows. Click New and use the Add button to select a few of the slides. You can even re-order your slides in this dialog box. Give your custom show a descriptive name at the top like 15 minutes and click OK. Click Show to make sure you got what you wanted. (See Figure 7-16.)

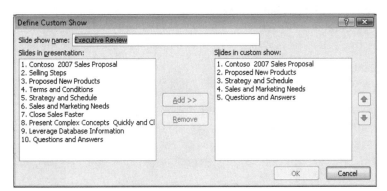

Figure 7-16   Custom Slide Show.

To edit your custom slideshow, go back up to Custom Slide Show, select Custom Shows, and click Edit. You must be a professional.

Tip Jar

Here are the top 10 tips covered in Chapter 7:

- **Create WordArt**   Type your name on a blank title slide in PowerPoint 2007. Choose a style from the Applies to All Text in the Shape section of the gallery (access it through WordArt Styles' More button in the Format tab).

- **Customize WordArt**   Choose a Transform Warp from the Text Effects drop-down menu on the Format Tab.

- **Create SmartArt**   Click the Insert tab, then click SmartArt. Click Hierarchy and select Organization Chart. Click inside the SmartArt diagram and type the names of people you know in the Type Your Text Here box. Make sure to put your name at the top of the list!

- **Modify SmartArt**   To modify the organization chart, use your Tab key to demote a block or Shift+Tab to promote it.

- **Create a PivotTable**   Select data in an Excel spreadsheet and click the Insert tab, then click PivotTable. Click OK. Drag Column Headings down to Row Labels and Values.

- **Chart Your PivotTable Data**   With the PivotTable selected, click the Options tab, then click PivotChart in the Tools group. Click Bar from the list and click OK.

- **Copy a PivotChart to PowerPoint**   Copy and Paste the chart into a PowerPoint slide. Change the data in the data spreadsheet. Reselect the PivotTable spreadsheet, then click Refresh in the Data group in Excel's Options tab to update the PivotTable and both PivotCharts.

- **Conditional Formatting**   Select a table in Excel 2007 and click Conditional Formatting on the Home tab. Click Data Bars and choose a color.

- **Sort by Color**   Select a row of data and highlight it in yellow. Select another row of data and color the text green. Right-click one of the yellow cells and click Sort, then click Put Selected Cell Color On Top. Right-click one of the cells with green text and click Sort, then click Put Selected Font Color On Top.

- **Create a Custom Slide Show**   Click the Slide Show tab, then select Custom Slide Show. Click New and use the Add button to select a few of the slides. Give it a name and click OK.

Hey, that's a great looking document! You must really know what you're doing. If only we could say the same about everyone else....

Part Four

Trust Exercises: Letting Go Through Controlled Collaboration

In this part

Ah, summer camp. An annual adventure in the great outdoors. A seven-night slumber party under the stars. Canoeing. Crafts. And, of course, Kumbaya.

As any challenge-course veteran will tell you, however, summer camp is not all fun and games. Sometimes you actually learn something. Many a camper has returned to civilization with visions of leadership, service, and teamwork dancing in his head. It seems societal escape does wonders for Junior's social skills.

Of all the tried-and-true team-building activities, there is one exercise in particular that holds a special place in the minds of campers everywhere—the trust fall. To perform a trust fall, one camper climbs up on a picnic table, tree stump, or any other sturdy object that happens to be three or four feet off the ground. The other campers form two lines on either side of the sucker...er, volunteer, and extend their arms out toward each other. Now comes the trust part. The volunteer—the guy or girl on top of the tree stump—must turn around, then fall backwards into the waiting arms of the other campers.

Trust falls build trust between team members. You have to trust your fellow campers to catch you. Because everyone takes a turn falling off the log, the generally accepted fear of "what goes around, comes around" usually prevents campers from landing in the dirt. Distributing the faller's weight evenly along the line makes catching as easy for the bookworm as it is for the captain of the wrestling squad.

What if we could bring the concept of the trust fall into the workplace? What if collaborating with coworkers was like falling back into the supportive arms of your friends instead of taking a daily nose-dive into the dirt? What if sharing a document was as easy for the new person as it is for the seasoned vets? With the 2007 Microsoft Office system, it can be.

In this section, we'll show you how the document preparation features of the 2007 Microsoft Office applications provide a sturdy foundation for any trust fall into team collaboration. You'll learn how a Windows SharePoint Services Document Workspace simplifies document sharing and fosters open communication among team members. And you'll experience the collaborative support of structured workflows and document lifecycle management available in Microsoft Office SharePoint Server 2007.

So, pack your bags and get on the bus. When it comes to working better with others, the 2007 Microsoft Office system is going to make you one happy camper. And we promise, no more Kumbaya.

Chapter 8

Prepare to Share— Share Any Document with Confidence

Learn how to:

❑ Apply formatting and content editing restrictions to your Word documents and Excel spreadsheets

❑ Ensure compatibility with previous versions of Office

❑ Preserve the integrity of your Microsoft Office documents

It's My Document, I'll Share What I Want To

Congratulations! All those hours writing and rewriting paid off—the document in front of you is 95 percent complete. After days of seeing spots, you can finally see the light at the end of the tunnel. And then in walks your manager. "The document looks great, but you should run it by so-and-so and whatshername before you publish it."

Okay, you're a team player. You're happy to send the document out for review, but you don't want your 95 percent complete document to come back to you 65 percent complete because so-and-so and whatshername made a bunch of changes you weren't expecting or, more importantly, they weren't authorized to make. What should you do?

Prior to Microsoft Office 2003, protecting documents meant requiring specific passwords to open or modify files. While this capability is still accessible in 2007 Microsoft Office applications by selecting Save As from the Microsoft Office button, then selecting General Options from the Tools menu, an all-access password does not allow for the granular level of content control desired by today's discriminating user.

While passwords remain the primary method for restricting editing rights to Microsoft Office PowerPoint 2007 presentations (you could also use Information Rights Management, also known as IRM—more on this later), Office Word 2007 and Office Excel 2007 build upon capabilities introduced in Office 2003 to help you define what in the document can be modified, how the said item will be modified, and who will do the modifying. We know, we know. You're worried your coworkers will label you a control freak. Just remind them that a little control today prevents a lot of freaking out tomorrow.

Protecting Word Documents

It's happened more than once. You created the greatest Word document the world has ever seen. Your font choices were inspired. Your magnificent use of styles reflected your inner brilliance. And your content! Your content stood alone as a shimmering reflection of your word processing wizardry. If only you hadn't shared this masterpiece with the amateur in cubicle four.

Now, your styles are in shambles. Your content...collapsed. What kind of joker considers Jokerman an appropriate font for a competitive marketing analysis anyway? Well, chin up, friend. Wipe that tear from your eye and listen closely. There is a way to prevent such document disasters from happening again.

Structured editing, a concept introduced in Office 2003, allows you to lockdown your document's structure and content *before* sharing. You can access this capability by clicking Protect Document on the Review command tab, then selecting Restrict Formatting And Editing. Checking the box under Formatting restrictions limits the available formatting options in the document to a selection of styles—styles that you define by clicking Settings and then checking or unchecking the specific styles. You can also prevent others from changing the document Theme or Quick Style Set from this dialog box. (See Figure 8-1.)

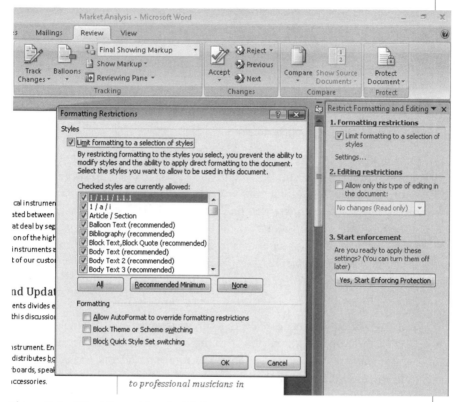

Figure 8-1   Word Formatting Restrictions.

Checking the box under Editing restrictions defines the type of editing that can take place in the document. Selecting Tracked Changes from the drop-down menu allows general editing in the document, but requires that all changes be tracked. This means the reviewer does not have to remember to turn the track changes feature on, nor can the feature be accidentally or deliberately turned off. Selecting Comments restricts general editing but allows users to make their feedback known by inserting comments. The Filling in forms option limits editing to any form fields contained within the document. And No changes (Read only) says "No way, José" to any and all document editing. (See Figure 8-2.)

Figure 8-2 Word Editing Restrictions.

Of course, there are exceptions to every rule and structured editing is...well, no exception. The Exceptions section allows you to open up specific areas of the document for editing outside of the generally enforced document protections. For example, if you had a section of the document where you wanted people to insert their name or some other type of personal information, simply select that section in the document and check the box next to Everyone. Now, everyone has permission to edit that specific section, but the rest of the document remains under the editing restrictions you previously defined.

You can take the concept of exceptions once step further. Clicking More Users allows you to add individuals to your exceptions list. Now you can assign a paragraph to Jeff and another to Jenny and each one can edit their individual section. They cannot, however, edit each other's section or any other section of the document unless allowed by the global editing restrictions. (See Figure 8-3.)

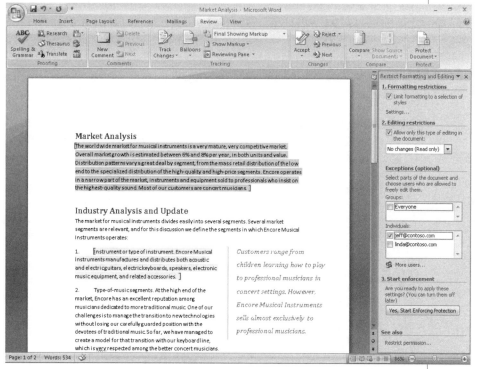

Figure 8-3 Structured Editing Exceptions.

When you are ready to share the document, click Yes, Start Enforcing Protection. To prevent others from turning document protection off, assign a password or, for a greater level of confidence, set the option to User authentication. User Authentication takes advantage of Information Rights Management technology to encrypt the document and prevent it from further unauthorized distribution. (For more on Information Rights Management, see the Restrict Permission section later in this chapter.)

Word to the Wise   When enforcing document protections, be sure to enter a password or select User Authentication. Selecting Password and leaving the password field blank will allow any user to turn off your protections with a click, leaving you right back where you started. For User Authentication to function, you must use e-mail addresses as opposed to Windows user accounts to add people to your exceptions list.

After enforcing protections, send or share the document as you normally would. You can e-mail the document, post it to a network file share, or better yet, turn it into a Document Workspace (more on this in the next chapter).

When your coworker opens the document, the Restrict Formatting and Editing task pane reflects the available options. Clicking Find Next Region I Can Edit will take the person directly to the next section available for editing. Show All Regions I Can Edit displays all of these sections at once and they can even choose to have these sections highlighted for easier identification. (See Figure 8-4.)

Figure 8-4   Restrict Formatting and Editing Task Pane.

As you can see, structured editing is a capability that benefits both sides of the collaborative equation. As a document owner, structured editing gives you the document structure and content control you've always wanted. As a document reviewer, it focuses your attention on the specific areas you have the power to impact. You get in, make your changes, and get out. The document owner saves face, the document reviewer saves time, and the document...well, it just gets saved.

Protecting Excel Spreadsheets

Microsoft Office Excel 2007 benefits from its own version of structured editing, though the way you use it is quite different from Word. Again, building upon capabilities introduced in Office 2003, Office Excel 2007 allows you to lockdown your workbook structure and data *before* sharing. To protect your Excel 2007 files from unwanted changes, use the Changes group of the Review command tab.

Let's start with the most basic functionality—protecting individual worksheets. First, click Protect Sheet in the Changes group. Next check or uncheck the protection options you want to apply to the sheet. For example, do you want to allow other people to insert or delete rows from the spreadsheet? Do you want the formatting commands available? Make your selections, then enter a password to prevent unauthorized users from turning the sheet protections off. Click OK and you're done. (See Figure 8-5.)

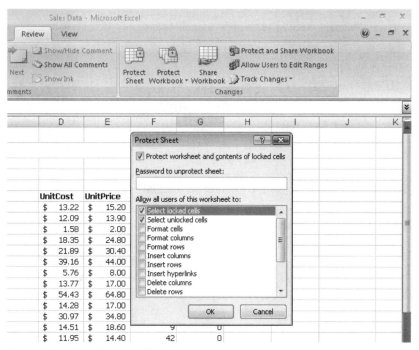

Figure 8-5 Excel Protect Sheet Options.

To preserve the structural integrity of the workbook as a whole, click Protect Workbook in the Changes group. Select Protect Structure and Windows. Check the Structure box to prevent users from adding, deleting, or moving worksheets. Check the Window box if you want the workbook win-

dows to open in the same size and position every time. Again, you should
enter a password to prevent unauthorized users from turning the workbook
protections off. Click OK and you're done. (See Figure 8-6.)

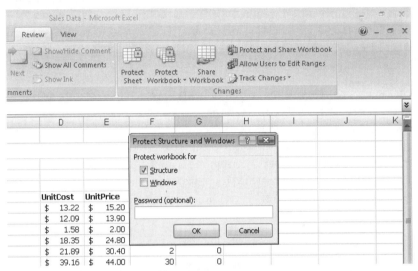

Figure 8-6 Excel Protect Workbook Options.

Now, here's where it gets really interesting. Protecting a worksheet locks
down all of the cells in that worksheet; the data is read-only. However, as we
saw with Word, limiting a file to read-only access is not always the most real-
istic way of working. Sometimes other people have legitimate and necessary
contributions to make to our work.

In these cases, you may want to open up individual cell ranges for editing by
others. To do this, click Allow Users To Edit Ranges in the Changes group.
Click New. In the Title field, give the range a name that will make it easy to
identify later on. Click the Refers To Cells field, then select the range of cells
in the workbook. You can assign a unique password to this range or you can
click Permissions and allow specific people to edit this range without a password. Click OK. When you're ready, click Protect Sheet and follow the
instructions outlined above for protecting an individual worksheet. (See
Figure 8-7.)

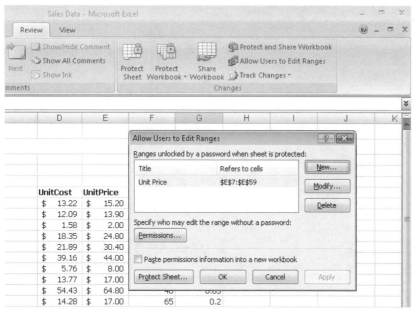

Figure 8-7   Allow Users to Edit Ranges.

Compatibility Checker

Now that you know how to protect your Word and Excel files before sharing them, it's time to focus on the other side of the collaborative coin. As the saying goes, ask not what your reviewer can do for you, but what you can do for your reviewer. And in the case of reviewers running older versions of Microsoft Office, the best thing you can do is ensure the document you're sending them doesn't utilize previously unsupported features.

Excel 2007, PowerPoint 2007, and Word 2007 feature a new compatibility checker that identifies unsupported features and gives you the opportunity to resolve simple issues. To run the Compatibility Checker, click the Microsoft Office Button, click Prepare, then select Run Compatibility Checker. Check the corresponding box to automatically run the Compatibility Checker during the save process. (See Figure 8-8.)

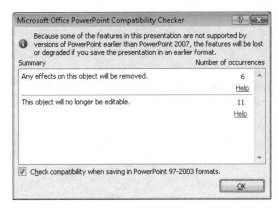

Figure 8-8   PowerPoint 2007's Compatibility Checker.

Microsoft Office Open XML Formats

Microsoft Office Open XML is the new default file format for Excel 2007, PowerPoint 2007, and Word 2007. Why would Microsoft introduce a new file format with this release? No, not to make your life miserable. In fact, Microsoft Office Open XML is designed to make working with documents easier than ever before.

Imagine two versions of the same Excel spreadsheet—one is saved using the old .xls format and the other is saved using the new .xlsm format. Two spreadsheets identical in every way, except the .xlsm file is up to 75 percent smaller than its counterpart, it comes equipped with improved damage-recovery, and the "m" in the file extension lets you know this spreadsheet contains macros *before* you open it. Throw in the inherent developer and data integration benefits of XML and you have a file format for the 21st century.

Standard Open XML file extensions end with an "x"—.docx, .xlsx, and .pptx. Open XML files containing macros, like the example above, end with an "m"—.docm, .xlsm, and .pptm. And don't worry; you can still save files in their original binary .doc, .xls, and .ppt formats for sharing with older versions of Office. However, a better option for users of Office 2000 SP3, Office XP SP3, and Office 2003 SP1 is to download the appropriate

Uncross Your Fingers

Worst-Case Scenarios: Online, the Internet companion to the best-selling *The Worst-Case Scenario Survival Handbook* offers a number of intriguing ways to escape life's most perilous situations. If you find yourself on the banks of a piranha-infested river, don't dip your big toe in the water without first consulting *Worst-Case Scenarios*. Nor should you attempt to foil a UFO abduction. Or try to extinguish a burning turkey. (Drop the baster and back away from the bird.)

Unfortunately, *Worst-Case Scenarios* is silent on the subject of sharing Microsoft Office files, a workplace activity fraught with potential peril. Consider the sales person who e-mailed a request for proposal to his customer without removing the revision marks containing the deleted lower price. Or the purchasing manager who signed a vendor contract that had been unknowingly modified. Or the executive who read her previously internal memo on the front page of the *New York Times*.

While the 2007 Microsoft Office system can't help you wrestle free from an alligator, it can help you avoid more common worst-case scenarios in the workplace. Remove hidden information from files, verify document integrity with digital signatures, and help curb the unauthorized distribution of e-mail and document content—all without breaking a sweat. With Office 2007 in your survival kit, you'll be ready for almost anything. Is that your tie caught in the paper shredder?

Open XML file converter from www.microsoft.com/office. With the file converter installed, users can open and edit the new Open XML formats in their existing version of Microsoft Office.

If you can't see your file extensions in Windows Explorer, click Organize, then Folder and Search Options. Click the View tab and uncheck Hide extensions for known file types.

Document Inspector

When was the last time you cleaned your house? Really cleaned it. Sure, the living room *looks* good, but there may be enough popcorn, M&M's, and spare change under the sofa cushions for a night at the movies. Pull out the chair in the corner and you just bought tickets to a dust bunny rodeo. And don't even *think* about looking under the rug.

Like our homes, Microsoft Office documents have lots of places for dirt, trash, and other unwanted items to hide. After a long review cycle, a document may be full of comments and revision marks. Template instructions or other internal content may be formatted as hidden text. Personal information may lurk within the document properties or other areas of the file. In most cases, these items are no longer needed. In some cases, these items are sensitive or confidential in nature and potentially damaging in the wrong hands.

Enter the Microsoft Office 2007 Document Inspector. The Document Inspector checks your document for hidden and personal information and gives you the opportunity to permanently remove such information from the file. To use the Document Inspector, click the Microsoft Office Button, click Prepare, then select Inspect Document. Check the boxes for the type of content you want the Document Inspector to search for, then click Inspect. (See Figure 8-9.)

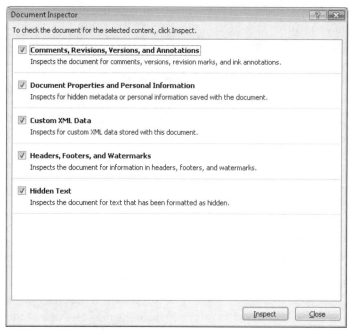

Figure 8-9 Document Inspector in Word 2007.

Add a Digital Signature

You can use the new Microsoft Office release to digitally sign your documents and, in turn, authenticate the identity of the signer and preserve the integrity of your document content.

A digital signature requires a digital ID, which can be purchased from a third-party digital signature provider (see the Microsoft Office Marketplace on Microsoft Office Online at *www.microsoft.com/office*, and search for "digital signing") or it can be created on your own in a 2007 Microsoft Office application. Keep in mind: only digital IDs obtained from a digital signature provider can be authenticated by other computers. Digital IDs you create yourself can only be authenticated on your own computer, so they are not usually appropriate for contracts or other legally binding agreements. You should also contact your legal department concerning the legality of digital signatures in your area as laws vary from place to place.

When the results are displayed, click Remove All next to each information type you want to remove. Then, click Close. The document in front of you is now clean enough to eat off of, though we recommend using a placemat.

Tip or Treat   When your document, spreadsheet, or presentation is finished, you can use the Mark As Final feature to finalize the document and make it read-only. Click the Microsoft Office Button, click Prepare, then select Mark As Final. Click OK to save the document. Most of the formatting commands for finalized documents are grayed out and therefore inaccessible as long as the document is marked as final. To unmark a document as final, repeat the above steps.

Restrict Permission

On March 28, 2004, Eric, a Department of Defense employee, visited the Starbucks at Connecticut Avenue and R Street NW in Washington, D.C. Whether Eric ordered a double tall two percent no foam latte or a grande mocha frappucino with whip remains a secret. What are no longer secrets, however, are the contents of Eric's phone log, a rude Q&A for the Sunday morning talk shows, a policy summary document, and a map to the Secretary of Defense's house—all documents found on a Starbucks table and turned over to an activist group for public drubbing. Three days later, the *Washington Post* offered its two cents on the coffeeshop controversy: "Note to Eric: U Need 2B More Careful."

There are two ways to digitally sign your 2007 Microsoft Office documents. First, you can streamline the signing process for contracts and other agreements by inserting a digital signature line into the document. To insert a signature line, click the Signature Line button in the Text group of the Insert command tab. In the Signature Setup dialog box, enter the signer's name, title, and e-mail address, then click OK. The signer can sign the document by typing their name, inserting an image of their signature, or using the handwriting functionality of a Tablet PC.

If you simply want to preserve and verify the integrity of a shared document, you can insert an invisible signature that will let readers know the document has not been modified since it was signed. To add an invisible signature, click the Microsoft Office Button, click Prepare, then select Add A Digital Signature. In the Sign dialog box, enter the purpose of the signature and click Sign.

Poor Eric. As if $4 for a cup of coffee wasn't punishment enough, stopping off for a cuppa Joe may have cost him his job. All because of four little pieces of paper. Take a step back from the details of Eric's story and there's a broader lesson we can all learn. Yes, some of us need to reevaluate our addiction to caffeine; we'll save that discussion for a future book. The point we want to make right here and now is we *all* need to be more careful with our information.

Too often, sensitive information flies through our companies with nothing more than a wink and a nod. E-mail threads are forwarded with no thought to the information contained deep within the existing conversation. Confidential documents are printed for reading on the airplane and then left sitting on the printer. Time-sensitive spreadsheets live on long after the information contained within them is out of date. And the common theme—Eric included—is not one of maliciousness, but of carelessness. Human nature at its most accidental.

The 2007 Microsoft Office system can help nip unintended exposure of sensitive or confidential information in the bud. Information Rights Management (IRM), introduced in Office 2003, is a Microsoft Office technology that takes advantage of Windows Rights Management Services (RMS) in Windows Server 2003. Because of the additional technical and licensing requirements of rights management functionality, you'll want to check with your IT department to see if your company is ready for IRM.

Word to the Wise IRM is about controlling information flow and enforcing corporate policies. It is not meant to be a security stop-gap. Malicious users will be able to work around IRM permissions. If a user can read the document, there is nothing to stop them from retyping the contents into another document or simply writing the information down on a piece of paper. Likewise, the same person could take a digital photo of their monitor and e-mail the image to an unauthorized user. However, for most cases of "casual" copying and leakage, IRM is an effective information barrier.

To use IRM in Word 2007, Excel 2007, or PowerPoint 2007, click the Microsoft Office Button, click Prepare, then select Restrict Permission. Now, click Restricted Access. Once your credentials are verified, a Permission dialog box appears. Check the box next to Restrict permission to this document. Then, enter the e-mail addresses of the people you wish to have access to the document. (See Figure 8-10.)

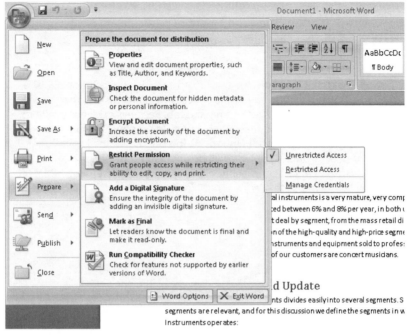

Figure 8-10 Restrict Permission.

There are three levels of access permission:

- **Read** The document can be opened and read, but it cannot be edited, copied, or printed. These commands are grayed out and therefore inaccessible to the user. People who do not have at least Read permission for the document cannot open it and therefore cannot see the document contents.

- **Change** The document can be opened, edited, and saved, but it cannot be printed. Again, the inaccessible commands are grayed out.

- **Full Control** Basically, full control equals author level permissions. If you assign full control to another person, he or she can do anything with the document you can do. You assign Full Control by clicking More Options and selecting Full Control from the drop-down menu next to the selected access-level for the individual's name.

For more detailed permission settings, click More Options. Here you can set an expiration date for the document by checking the box next to This document expires on and selecting a date. When the document expires, users without Full Control permissions will be unable to open it.

When you finish assigning permissions, click OK. Notice the "Restricted Access" message visible below the Ribbon. The document is now protected and ready for sharing. Starbucks anyone?

Tip or Treat   IRM can also be used to protect outgoing Outlook 2007 e-mail messages. In the message window, click the Permission arrow in the Options group of the Message command tab. Recipients will be unable to forward, copy, or print the message content. To set a message to expire, click the arrow to expand the Options dialog box, check the Expires after box, and select a date. Recipients will be unable to open the expired message. Microsoft Office attachments will be governed by the same IRM permissions as the message itself.

Tip Jar

Here's a review of the top 10 tips covered in Chapter 8:

- **Word Formatting Restrictions**   Click Protect Document on the Review command tab. Select Restrict Formatting And Editing. Check the box under Formatting restrictions. Click Settings and then check or uncheck the desired styles.

- **Word Editing Restrictions**   Click Protect Document on the Review command tab. Select Restrict Formatting And Editing. Check the box under Editing Restrictions and select the type of editing that can take place in a document. Use the Exceptions section to open up specific areas of the document for editing outside of the global document protections.

- **Excel Workbook /Worksheet Protections**   To preserve the structural integrity of a workbook, click Protect Workbook in the Review command tab. Select Protect Structure And Windows. Check the Structure box to prevent users from adding, deleting, or moving worksheets. To protect individual worksheets, click Protect Sheet in the command tab. Check or uncheck the protection options you want to apply to the sheet. In both cases, enter a password to prevent unauthorized users from turning the protections off.

- **Excel Range Permissions**   Click Allow Users To Edit Ranges In the Change group. Click New. In the Title field, give the range a name that will make it easy to identify later on. Click the Refers To Cells field, then select the range of cells in the workbook. Assign a unique password to this range or click Permissions and allow specific people to edit this range without a password.

- **Compatibility Checker**   Click the Microsoft Office Button, click Prepare, then select Compatibility Checker.

- **Document Inspector**   Click the Microsoft Office Button, click Prepare, then select Inspect Document. Check the boxes for the type of content you want the Document Inspector to search for, then click Inspect. When the results are displayed, click Remove All next to each information type you want to remove. Then, click Close.

- **Mark as Final**   Click the Microsoft Office Button, click Prepare, then select Mark As Final. Click OK to save the document.

Chapter 9

Life in the Sandbox— Better Ways to Distribute, Review, and Manage Shared Work

Learn how to:

❑ Create a centralized workspace for storing and working on documents

❑ Take the pain out of document review cycles

❑ Manage document properties, content, and lifecycle

\\attachments\fileshares\gone

You protected your Excel worksheet, inspected your Word document, and
checked your PowerPoint presentation for Office 2003 compatibility. You're
prepared to share. The only question is, how?

If you answered "e-mail," you're in good company. Attaching files to e-mail
messages is the most popular way to send work to others. But is it the best
way to *share* work with others? Before you click Send, consider the effects of
collaborating via regular e-mail attachments.

You create a rough draft of a document and e-mail it to five people on the
team—number of copies = 7 (one for each of the five people on the team, the
one in your Sent Items folder and the one on your hard drive).

Three of your teammates send the document back to you saved as a new
filename, but don't dare delete the rough draft still in their Inbox—number
of copies = 16.

You pick and choose from those three documents and put it all back into a new filename to denote the second draft and send it back out to the team again—number of copies = 23–26 (depending on whether or not you saved those alternate versions to your hard drive).

Repeat until no one knows what the most recent version of the document is, you have to resend it to everyone again—number of copies now totals more than 30, and we risk sending the wrong one to the client because you're not even the one putting the PowerPoint presentation together; that's someone else's job. And if you're out of the office when it comes time to cut and paste this information, then that person is going to ask one of your five coworkers for it and they haven't read this book, so their Inbox is a mess and they will send the wrong one. But you're going to get blamed for it because it was your document, and that's why you have to keep every single e-mail with every single version attached to prove it wasn't your fault that they sent the wrong one to the person who sent the presentation to the client.

Whew! Sound familiar? And just think—you could have saved yourself a lot of time and trouble by ditching the attachments and uploading your files to a network fileshare. Or could you?

As anyone who's ever received an "access denied" message knows, working with documents on a network fileshare is no picnic. First, all contributors must have access to the specific fileshare. Those without access must request access through the server administrator. Once access is granted, collaborating on the shared documents is a little like riding the bumper cars at Six Flags; contributors constantly "bump" into each other as they attempt to open, edit, and save the document. It is impossible to tell at a glance who has the document open or what changes they may have made to it.

A Windows SharePoint Services Document Workspace combines the central location of a network file share with the collaborative capabilities people need to store, edit, and manage shared documents and information. Because Document Workspaces are tightly integrated with your favorite Office 2007 applications, you can create and manage your workspace right from within the application you are using. This means you can stay focused on the task at hand and lend a hand to someone else at the same time. You can check your documents in and out—even track and restore multiple versions—all with a couple of clicks.

Think about it—if sharing was this easy in preschool, there would have been a lot less biting and hair pulling. Wait, that was last week's budget meeting.

Creating Document Workspaces

Like the Meeting Workspaces discussed in Chapter 4, Document Workspaces are collaborative Web sites built with Windows SharePoint Services—
a feature of Windows Server 2003. Creating a Document Workspace
requires no knowledge of HTML, XML, or any other geeky sounding acro-
nym ending with the letter "l." With the server infrastructure in place, all
you need to create and use a Document Workspace is Internet Explorer and
your favorite 2007 Microsoft Office application.

Shared Attachments

There are two ways to create a Document Workspace with the 2007
Microsoft Office system. If you're not quite ready to end your love affair with
attachments, send your document, spreadsheet, or presentation as a shared
attachment. When you send a shared attachment, the recipients receive a
linked copy of the document along with the location of the Document
Workspace where the original document resides. They can edit the attachment and then update the online copy, or better yet, save the workspace
URL as a Favorite in their browser, delete the e-mail, and edit the document
from the workspace.

To send an e-mail message with a shared attachment, click the New Message
button in the Outlook toolbar. Click the Attach File icon in the Include
group of the Message command tab. Browse for the file and click Insert.

At the bottom right of the Include group, click the Attachment Options
arrow and select Attachment Options. The Attachment Options task pane
will open. Click Shared Attachments. A Document Workspace text box and
link will appear in your message. Next, you'll need to provide a location for
your Workspace. Existing locations are accessible from the Create Document Workspace at drop-down menu or you can type a new URL. If you do
not know which URL to use, contact your server administrator. (See Figure
9-1.)

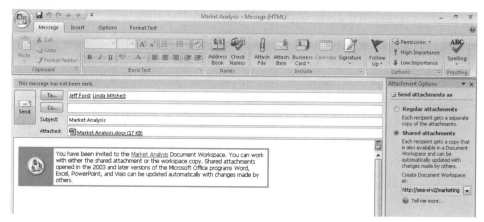

Figure 9-1 Outlook 2007 Shared Attachment.

When you are ready to create the workspace, enter your recipients' information and click Send. In a minute or two, you'll receive an e-mail indicating the successful creation of the workspace. Click the link in the e-mail to visit your new workspace. Notice your **To** and **Cc** recipients are visible in the Members area of the workspace home page. When creating a workspace with a shared attachment, the e-mail recipients in the **To** and **Cc** fields are automatically added to the workspace with contributor permissions. People in the **Bcc** field are not granted any permissions. We'll talk more about workspace permissions in a few pages.

Document Management Task Pane—Part I

In addition to shared attachments, you can create a Document Workspace in a couple of clicks from any open Word, PowerPoint, or Excel file. First, click the Microsoft Office Button, click Publish, then select Create Document Workspace. The Document Management task pane will open on the right side of the screen. (See Figure 9-2.)

This time, you'll need to provide a name *and* location for your workspace. Again, existing locations are accessible from the Location for new workspace drop-down menu or you can type a new URL.

When you are ready, click Create. Choose Yes when prompted to save the file. Now, sit back and relax as Office and Windows SharePoint Services work together to build a site for your document. When the process is complete, the task pane will change to reflect the document's new Document Workspace capabilities. Click Open site in browser to view your new workspace in all its glory.

Figure 9-2   Document Management Task Pane—Create.

Team Sites and My Sites and More, Oh My!

Meeting Workspaces and Document Workspaces are just two examples of the different sites and workspaces you can create with Windows SharePoint Services and Office SharePoint Server. To see the full list of Windows SharePoint Services default site templates, click the Site Actions button on your site, workspace, or portal home page, then select Create Site. You may need to click the Sites and Workspaces link under Web Pages. Scroll to the bottom of the New SharePoint Site page to the Template Selection box.

On the Collaboration tab, you'll find easy-to-use site templates for creating your own Team Sites, Blogs, Wikis, News and Publishing Sites, and Records Repositories. Click the Meetings tab for five different Meeting Workspace templates (you can also access these templates from the Meeting Workspace Task Pane in an Outlook meeting request). The Enterprise tab includes enterprise-ready templates for Document Centers, Report Centers, and Search Centers. Select the template you want to use and click Create.

With an Office SharePoint Server 2007 portal deployed in your organization, each individual employee can create and manage their own personal My Site. Your My Site is the place to store and edit personal documents, manage shared documents and tasks, and keep track of colleagues. Each My Site contains personal and public views of your information allowing you to share information about yourself and your role while keeping private information private. To automatically create and configure your own My Site, simply click the My Site link from your Office SharePoint Server portal home page. Then repeat after us, "There's no place like my home page. There's no place like my home page." Ruby slippers are optional.

Home Page Navigation

Your Document Workspace home page consists of a Quick Launch navigation pane on the left side of the screen, a Site Actions button on the top right, and a collection of five default Web Parts in the middle. (See Figure 9-3.)

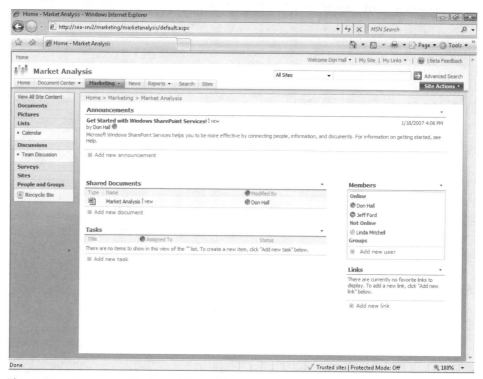

Figure 9-3   Document Workspace Home Page.

- **Announcements**   You can use the Announcements Web Part to post general communications for workspace members and visitors. Click Add New Announcement, then enter a Title and Body for your announcement. If you want your announcement to have a limited lifespan, set an expiration date. Otherwise, click OK.

- **Members**   The Members Web Part provides an at-a-glance view of your workspace members. To add a new Member, click Add New User. Enter an alias in the Users box or search for the desired person in the Address Book. Next, you'll need to assign permissions to the new member. Should they have read access to the workspace? Will they need editing (contributor) rights? Or do they require something more? Finally, you have the option of sending an e-mail notification to your new members along with a link to the workspace. Add a Personal

Message and click OK. If your organization is running Microsoft Office Live Communications Server and Microsoft Office Communicator, a presence icon will appear next to each of your workspace members. This icon will let you know whether or not a particular member is online and available to communicate with you. Click the Presence icon for a list of available communications options.

Tip or Treat   To change existing member permissions, click People And Groups, then Site Permissions in the Quick Launch pane. Click the name of the member whose access rights you want to modify, check the appropriate permissions box, and click OK.

- **Links**   If your team needs quick access to related internal or external links, add those links to the Links Web Part. Click Add New Link. Enter a URL and click Click Here To Test to make sure the link works properly. Enter a Description or additional Notes and click OK.

- **Tasks**   You can track team- or project-related tasks with the Tasks Web Part. Click Add New Task. Enter a Title for the task and set a Priority level and Status. If the task is in progress, enter a completion percentage. Add the task owner to the Assigned To field and enter any additional information in the Description field. Select a Start and Due date and click OK. You can manage your shared tasks alongside your personal tasks by clicking the Tasks link at the top of the Web Part then, on the next page, click the Actions button and select Connect To Outlook. Click Yes when prompted. Your workspace task list will appear under Other Tasks in the Task window of Outlook. Your workspace tasks will also be visible on the To-Do Bar.

- **Shared Documents**   The Shared Documents Web Part provides a home page view of the documents stored in the Shared Documents document library (more on document libraries in the next section). To add a document to the library, click Add New Document. Click Browse to select and upload a single document. Click Upload Multiple Files to mark more than one file for upload. Click OK.

Tip or Treat   To customize the layout and Web Parts of a Document Workspace, follow the same steps for customizing Meeting Workspaces outlined in Chapter 4.

Using Lists and Libraries

Now that you're familiar with how to create a Document Workspace and add content to the home page, it's time to dig a little deeper into the workspace structure. At its core, a Document Workspace is a collection of lists and libraries. These lists and libraries can contain everything from shared documents and pictures to team contacts and Calendars to imported Excel spreadsheets. Each of the Web Parts on the home page is essentially a view into one of your workspace lists or libraries. Let's take a look at some common lists and libraries you can use to manage team documents and resources.

Document Library

The Shared Documents Web Part on the workspace home page is an example of a document library. To access the full library, click the Shared Documents link at the top of the Web Part. Notice the toolbar across the top of the library. From here, you can create a new document or folder, upload additional documents, perform various actions like view the contents of the library in a Windows Explorer interface (for copying and pasting between libraries) or sign up for e-mail notifications, and adjust the document library settings. Every list and library will have a similar set of options in the toolbar.

You can create additional document libraries by clicking Documents in the Quick Launch pane, then clicking Create. Under Libraries, select Document Library. Enter a Name and Description for the library. If you want a shortcut to this library displayed on the Quick Launch pane, set the Navigation option to Yes. If you want to turn on document versioning for this library, set the Document Version History option to Yes (more on document versioning in the next section). Set the default document template for new documents created from the library and click Create. (See Figure 9-4.)

Figure 9-4   Document Version History Option.

Tip or Treat   In addition to uploading an Excel file to a document library, you can publish just the data contained in an Excel table to a custom SharePoint list. The custom list can be analyzed in a data sheet view in the browser and synchronized with the original file. In Excel 2007, click Format As Table in the Styles group in the Home command tab and select a table layout. In the External Table Data group in the Design tab of the Table Tools contextual menu, click Export, then Export Table To SharePoint List. Enter the URL where you want to publish the list. Enter a Name and Description and click Finish. Click the link when prompted to visit your new online list.

Picture Library

A Picture Library allows you to store and edit team or project-related images. To create a picture library, click Pictures in the Quick Launch pane, then click Create. Under Libraries, click Picture Library. Picture library setup options are basically the same as those for a document library. Enter the necessary information and click Create.

Calendar List

The Calendar list provides a shared location for team meetings, appointments, and other important events. You can access the workspace Calendar by clicking Calendar in the Quick Launch Pane. To add new items to your shared Calendar, click the New button. Enter a Title, Location, Start and End times, and a Description of the event, meeting, or appointment. If the item will occur more than once, check the Recurrence box. If you'd like to create a Meeting Workspace specific to this particular item, check the Workspace box. Click OK.

To view and edit the shared Calendar beside your personal Outlook Calendar, click the Actions button, then select Connect To Outlook. Click Yes when prompted. You can now view the two Calendars side-by-side in Outlook. To copy items from the shared Calendar to your personal Calendar, simply drag and drop.

Contacts List

Similar to a shared Calendar, a Contacts list provides a central location for storing team contacts. A Contacts list is not created by default in a Document Workspace, so you'll need to create one. To do this, click Lists in the Quick Launch pane, then click Create. Under Communications, click Contacts. Enter a list Name and Description and click Create.

To add contacts to your list, click the New button. Complete the contact fields and click OK. Click the Actions button, then Import Contacts to import contacts from your Address Book.

To view and edit shared contacts in Outlook, click the Actions button, then Connect To Outlook. Click Yes when prompted. Your shared contacts are now accessible below the Other Contacts header in the Contacts window in Outlook. To copy a shared contact into your personal contacts, simply drag and drop.

Discussions & Surveys

Discussion Boards and Surveys are lists designed to improve team communications. Discussions provide an opportunity for people to brainstorm and resolve issues outside of e-mail, conference calls, meetings, and other traditional communication venues. Surveys allow you to gather feedback or poll your team on project-related ideas and suggestions.

To access the default discussion board, click Team Discussions in the Quick Launch pane. To start a new discussion thread, click the New button. Enter the Subject and Body information and click OK.

To respond to an ongoing discussion, click the thread, then click Reply. Enter your response and click OK. Click the View button to view the postings as flat or threaded discussions.

To create a Survey, click Surveys in the Quick Launch pane. Click Create, then click Survey under Tracking. Enter a Name and Description for the survey, then click Next. For each survey question, enter the question, select the question type, and select additional question options as appropriate. Click Next Question to add a new question. When you are ready, click Finish.

To respond to a survey, click the survey you want to complete, then click Respond To This Survey. Complete the survey questions, then click Finish Survey. To view survey responses, click Show A Graphical Summary Of Responses or Show All Responses. Click the Actions button for options to import the results into an Excel spreadsheet or Access database.

As the Document Turns

You created your workspace. You customized your home page. You graduated at the top of your class from Lists and Libraries 101. Now it's time to get to work. There are documents to edit and you're just the person to edit them. And so is Jenny. And Jeff. And George. So buckle up, keep your hands and arms inside the vehicle at all times, and enjoy the ride.

Check In/Check Out

One advantage of a Document Workspace over a network fileshare is the ability to reserve a particular document for editing. Any document uploaded to a document library can be checked out, thereby securing the editing rights to one person. You can configure the check out process so other users who try to open the document while it is checked out will be given read-only access. The document library shows who has the document checked out, so you'll know who's working on the file at any given moment.

Tip or Treat   If you don't see a Checked Out To column in your document library, click the View drop-down and select Modify This View. Check the box for Checked Out To and click OK. You can use this same process to add other columns to the document library view.

To check out a document, hover over the document and click the drop-down menu. Select Check Out. You are now the sole editor of this document. Click the drop-down again and open the document for editing. When you finish editing an Office 2007 document, click the Microsoft Office Button, click Server, then select Check In. Or simply save and close the document and select Yes when prompted to check the file in. (See Figure 9-5.)

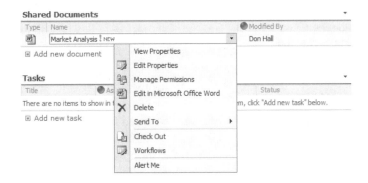

Figure 9-5   Shared Document Options.

If you want SharePoint to track the different versions of your shared documents, you need to enable versioning for your document library. To do this, click the Settings button in the document library, then select Document Library Settings. Under General Settings, click Versioning Settings. Under Document Version History, select Create Major Versions or Create Major And Minor (Draft) Versions. From this page, you can also set up an approval process for submitted content, as well as require documents to be checked out prior to editing. Now, every time a document is checked out, modified, and checked back in, SharePoint will save it as a new version.

Microsoft Office Groove 2007

How do you work with people in other organizations? These could be partners, vendors, or even customers. Sharing documents and information across multiple network boundaries is often a cumbersome process, with participants almost solely dependent on sending and receiving e-mail attachments.

As we've seen, the problem with e-mail attachments, apart from server space issues, is the existence of multiple versions of the same document floating around the organization. Sending e-mail attachments between organizations further complicates matters because now these multiple versions have the potential to take on lives of their own within multiple locales.

Microsoft Office Groove 2007 makes it easy to work across network boundaries by bringing people together in decentralized workspaces. Decentralized workspaces securely operate outside the network firewall, allowing people from multiple companies to share documents and information with each other in a controlled environment.

Office Groove 2007 is installed locally on each participant's computer. Only people running Groove can access Groove workspaces, and they can only access the workspaces to which they've been invited. Each workspace member receives a local copy of the workspace documents and discussions. You can even add and synchronize documents stored in a Windows SharePoint Services document library.

When changes are made, the changes—and only the changes—are synchronized between each member's computer. This means you can work seamlessly with documents online or offline, updating your virtual team when you happen to have an Internet connection. Groovy.

To see the version history, hover over the document, click the drop-down, and select Version History. You can also view the version history inside your Office 2007 application by clicking the Microsoft Office Button, then Server Tasks, and selecting View Version History. You can then choose to Open, Restore, or Delete other versions.

Compare Word 2007 Documents

With multiple people checking in multiple versions of the same Word 2007 document, you may eventually need to compare one version against another in order to see what changed. Click the Compare button in the Compare group of the Review command tab to see options for document comparison. If version history is enabled on your document library, you can compare the current version with the Last version saved to the server, the last Major version checked into the server, or a Specific version on the server. Word will open both document versions and then display the changes in a third document, allowing you to see everything in one place. The compared documents themselves remain unaffected. (See Figure 9-6.)

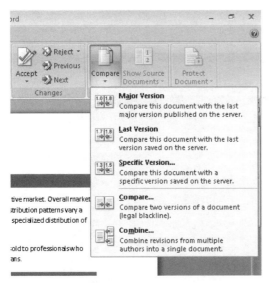

Figure 9-6   Word Compare Options.

If you're sharing Word documents the old-fashioned way (aka sending regular e-mail attachments or saving to a network file share), you can still take advantage of Word's document comparison feature. Click the Compare button in the Compare group of the Review command tab, then select (you guessed it) Compare. Then, browse for the original and revised documents. It's a good idea to label your documents with unique identifiers so you know exactly which document you're looking at. Select the option button next to New document to view the combined changes in a third document window. Click OK. Documents are displayed by default in the new Tri-Pane view, allowing you to see the original, revised, and combined documents at the same time. To change this view, click the Show Source Documents button and select Hide Source Documents. (See Figure 9-7.)

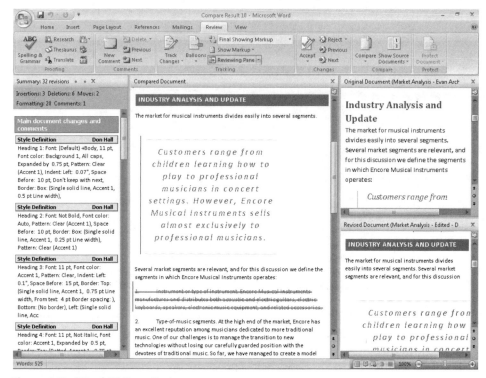

Figure 9-7 Word Tri-Pane Review.

Keep in mind that document comparison features only identify the changes between two documents. Comparing documents will not reveal who made the changes and therefore should not be used when you are compiling versions sent to you by multiple contributors. In these situations, click the Compare button in the Compare group of the Review command tab, then select Combine. Browse for the two documents, then decide whether to merge the changes into the original document, the revised document, or a third combined document. Reviewer information will be visible in the document by hovering over the change or clicking the Reviewing Pane button in the Tracking group of the Review command tab.

Document Management Task Pane—Part II

Two windows—one Internet Explorer, one Microsoft Office application. And this screen's not big enough for the two of them. The clock strikes high noon. Your left hand moves slowly into position. The cursor blinks. You draw your weapon. Alt-Tab! Alt-Tab! They don't call you the fastest thumb and forefinger in the West for nothing. When the dust settles, your original window remains—like you never even left it.

But you did leave it. And in the time it took to go back to your Document Workspace to view a task, click a link, or communicate with a workspace member you lost your place and your train of thought. When editing a document stored on a Document Workspace or other SharePoint site, you can use the Document Management Task Pane to view your workspace information within the context of your Office application. This means you can holster your Alt-Tab and stay focused on the work at hand.

To open the Document Management Task Pane, click the Microsoft Office Button, then Server Tasks, and select Document Management Information. The task pane consists of five tabs, each containing information from your workspace. (See Figure 9-8.)

1. The **Status tab** shows who has the document checked out, allows you to get updates from the workspace, and check the document back into the site when you're finished working on it.

2. The **Members tab** allows you to add new members to the site and see the presence information (online, offline, away, busy, etc.) and communication options for existing members.

3. The **Tasks tab** displays the workspace tasks list along with opportunities to create new tasks, sign up for task alerts, and view tasks associated with existing document workflows (more on workflows in the next section).

4. The **Documents tab** displays the workspace document library along with the ability to upload new documents and sign up for document alerts.

5. The **Links tab** provides access to the workspace links list and the opportunity to add new links to the workspace.

Figure 9-8   Document Management Task Pane—Status Tab.

Click the Options button at the bottom of any tab for options related to the automatic startup of the Document Management Task Pane and the frequency of document updates.

This Is Your Lifecycle

"...a recent study conducted by Accenture indicates more content will be created in the next two years than in the entire previous history of mankind, and over 93 percent of it will be electronic."[1]

Wow. That's a lot of content. Most people we know have a hard enough time managing the contents of a couple of file cabinets. The Library of Congress in Washington, D.C. maintains a collection of over 130 million items. It's the largest library in the world, yet this bibliographic behemoth pales in comparison to the annals of recorded history.

Who's going to manage this new content? Who's going to archive these records? Who's going to make us a turkey sandwich? While we can't solve the world's content problem, we can teach you a few ways to manage your own. As for the turkey sandwich, we just wanted to see if you'd do it.

Document Information Panel

When was the last time you edited the properties of a document? Not sure? Try this. Go into Documents and hover over any given file. If the floating tooltip for Business Plan.doc shows the document author as "Memaw" and the document title as "Holiday Cookie Recipe," chances are good these document properties haven't been edited in quite awhile.

Why are document properties important? Quite simply, document properties make basic document information like authorship, title, subject, and keywords visible to other users and, more importantly, to search engines looking for your document. The more content haystacks we create, the more difficult it becomes to find the needle. Updating your document properties is like placing a homing beacon on the needle.

In the past, updating document properties was an afterthought at best. The process itself wasn't difficult, just inconvenient. You had to right-click the file and choose Properties, or access the Properties command from the File menu in your Office application. The subsequent dialog box contained mul-

---

1. Microsoft Enterprise Content Management White Paper. Published November, 23 2005 at *http://www.microsoft.com/office/preview/ecmwhitepaper.mspx.*

tiple tabs to navigate and, in the case of Office, had to be closed before you could do anything else.

The Document Properties panel in Office 2007 is different. To access it, click the Microsoft Office Button, then Prepare, and then select Properties. The Document Properties panel appears below the Ribbon, allowing you to edit your document properties while you work. You can define custom properties by clicking the Document Properties arrow and selecting Advanced Properties. This needle is as good as found. (See Figure 9-9.)

Figure 9-9   Document Properties Panel.

Document Workflows

Oftentimes, our documents require some kind of feedback or approval before we can finalize them. With more documents created every day, the need for a good content management process grows with every click of the Save button. With the built-in workflow functionality of Office SharePoint Server, you can initiate and manage document workflows on any document stored in a Windows SharePoint Services document library. Now, when your coworker tells you to "go with the flow," you can be sure they mean it.

Approval Workflow

To start an approval workflow, hover over a document in a document library and click the drop-down menu. Click Workflows, then select Approval. Enter the approver names and the message you want to appear with the workflow request. Enter the number of days or weeks the approver has to approve the document, then click Start. (See Figure 9-10.)

Figure 9-10   Start a Workflow.

To approve a workflow document, open Outlook 2007. Select the workflow message and click Edit This Task at the top of the Reading Pane. The workflow dialog box opens. Click the document link to view the document. Enter your comments in the workflow dialog box, then click Approve or Reject. You can also use the links at the bottom of the dialog box to assign the task to someone else or request that the document owner make a change to the document prior to approval.

Collect Feedback Workflow

To start a feedback workflow, hover over a document in a document library and click the down arrow to access the document menu. Click Workflows, then select Collect Feedback. Enter the reviewer names and the message you want to appear with the workflow request. Enter a due date to remind the reviewer via e-mail to review the document, then click Start. (See Figure 9-10.)

To review a workflow document, open Outlook 2007. Select the workflow message and click Edit This Task at the top of the Reading Pane. The workflow dialog box opens. Click the document link to view the document. Enter your feedback in the workflow dialog box. Click Save to respond at a later time or Send Feedback to respond immediately. Again, you can use the

links at the bottom of the dialog box to assign the task to someone else or
request that the document owner make a change to the document.

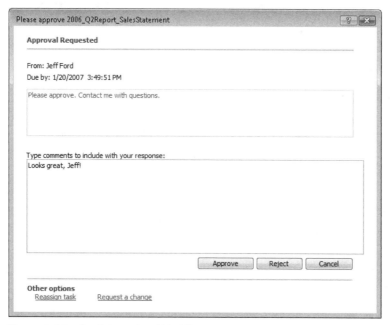

Figure 9-11   Participate in a Workflow.

Manage Workflows

You can view existing workflow tasks in the tasks list on your Document
Workspace or in the To-Do Bar and Tasks window in Outlook. To view
workflow status, hover over a workflow document in a document library,
click the down arrow to access the document menu, then select Workflows.
You will see Running and Completed Workflows. Click any existing workflow to view its progress, add approvers or reviewers, or delete the workflow.

Managed Document Repository Site Template

A Document Workspace is a great way to store and manage a few project-
related documents. But what happens when the project is over and the documents are ready for primetime? A Managed Document Repository is an
enterprise-ready site designed to hold large amounts of document content.
Think of it as the Library of Congress of SharePoint sites.

To create a Managed Document Repository, click the Site Actions button on your site, workspace, or portal home page, then select Create Site. You may need to click the Sites And Workspaces link under Web Pages. Complete the necessary site information, then click the Enterprise tab in the Template Selection box. Select Document Center, then click Create.

Managing E-Mail and Records

Do you work in an industry where every piece of e-mail you send (or sometimes even *think* about sending) has to be archived for legal purposes? In today's regulation-heavy environment, if you're not careful, cleaning out your Mailbox can lead to cleaning out your desk. To make the process of archiving e-mail easier, you can use Managed E-Mail Folders in Microsoft Exchange Server 2007.

Once setup by the administrator, Managed E-Mail Folders are accessible in Outlook 2007 and Outlook Web Access 2007. You can drag messages required for archival to these folders where they will be governed by administrator-defined retention and expiration policies.

Likewise, an Office SharePoint Server Records Repository can help you archive and manage important documents of record. IT personnel, lawyers, and records managers can use the Records Repository site template to quickly create an online records vault and apply information management policies to govern record labeling, auditing, and expiration. Documents can be uploaded to the repository directly from your favorite 2007 Microsoft Office applications.

Managed E-Mail Folders and SharePoint Records Repositories are an easy way to stay compliant with external regulations and internal policies.

Tip Jar

Here's a review of the top 10 tips covered in Chapter 9:

- **Create a Document Workspace**   In a new e-mail message, click the Attach File icon in the Include group of the Message command tab. Browse for the file and click Insert. Click the Attachment Options arrow in the Include group. Click Shared Attachment in the Attachment Options task pane. To turn an Office 2007 document directly into a Document Workspace, click the Microsoft Office Button in your Office 2007 application, click Publish, then select Create Document Workspace.

- **Integrated Task List**   To view your workspace tasks in your Outlook 2007 To-Do Bar, click the Tasks link on your workspace home page, then click Actions and select Connect To Outlook. Click Yes when prompted.

- **Shared Calendar**   To view your workspace Calendar side-by-side with your Outlook 2007 Calendar, click the Calendar link on your workspace Quick Launch pane, then click Actions and select Connect To Outlook. Click Yes when prompted.

- **Shared Contacts**   To create a shared contacts list, click Lists in the Quick Launch pane, then click Create. Under Communications, click Contacts. Enter a list Name and Description and click Create. To import contacts from your Address Book, click the Actions button, then select Import Contacts. To view and edit shared contacts in Outlook 2007, click the Actions button, then Connect to Outlook. Click Yes when prompted.

- **Document Check In/Check Out**   To check out a document, hover over the document and click the down arrow to access the document menu. Select Check Out. Hover over the document again, click the down arrow, and open the document for editing. When you finish, click the Microsoft Office Button, then click Server Tasks, then select Check In. Or simply save and close the document and select Yes when prompted to check the file in.

- **Version History**   Click the Settings button in the document library, then select Document Library Settings. Under General Settings, click Versioning Settings.

- **Compare Word Documents**   Click the Compare button in the Compare group of the Review command tab. For SharePoint document libraries, compare the current version with the Last version saved to the server, the last Major version checked into the server, or a Specific version on the server. For other documents, click Compare (look for "legal blackline" in the feature description). For documents with multiple reviewers, select Combine. For Tri-Pane Review, click Show Source Documents and select Show Both.

- **Document Properties Panel**   To access the Document properties panel, click the Microsoft Office Button, then Prepare, and then select Properties. Define custom properties by clicking the Document Properties arrow and selecting Advanced Properties.

- **Document Workflows**   To start a workflow, hover over a document in a document library and click the drop-down menu. Click Workflows, then select the desired workflow. Enter the workflow information and click Start. To approve a workflow document, open Outlook 2007. Select the workflow message and click Edit this task at the top of the

Reading Pane. Enter your comments in the workflow dialog box, then click Approve or Reject.

- **Managed Document Repository**   Click the Site Actions button on your site, workspace, or portal home page, then select Create Site. If necessary, click the Sites And Workspaces link under Web Pages. Click the Enterprise tab in the Template Selection box and choose Document Center.

Great work! Your documents are readily available, easy to work with, and on their way toward a long and fruitful lifecycle. You deserve a breath of fresh air. Let's take Microsoft Office out of the office for the afternoon....

Part Five

You *Can* Take It With You: Working Remotely With or Without Your PC

In this part

BZZZZZ. Is it us or do those fluorescent lights sound a little louder today? Does your cubicle feel a little smaller? Has Richard from accounting stopped by one too many times asking for your latest budget report? Snap out of it. You don't need Calgon to take you away, you have a laptop computer.

No laptop? No problem! You can use Exchange Server 2007's Outlook Web Access to read and send e-mail messages from any computer with a Web browser and Internet connection. Remote e-mail not enough? How about browser-based access to your Calendar, contacts, tasks, and linked network documents? With Outlook Web Access, you get all of this and more.

As any road warrior will tell you, working away from the office wasn't always this easy. Traditionally, the barrier to mobile productivity was the inability to connect to the people and information you needed. Today, with the proliferation of wireless broadband technology, the barrier to remote connectivity is coming down faster than you can say "56K." Throw in a Windows Mobile device like a Pocket PC or Smartphone that takes advantage of existing over-the-air mobile phone networks and you have virtually seamless connectivity to the information you need the most, when and where you need it.

The 2007 Microsoft Office system—and specifically Microsoft Office Outlook 2007 and Exchange Server 2007—is built with this connected world in mind. In this section, you'll learn tips and tricks for working remotely with and without a laptop computer. We'll show you tips for configuring Office Outlook 2007 for mobile use, as well as working offline with documents stored in Windows SharePoint Services document libraries. We'll take you on a guided tour of the latest release of Outlook Web Access, and share some important information on the integration between the 2007 Microsoft Office system and Windows Mobile devices.

Like your parents always said, there's a great big world waiting for you out there. Thank goodness a lot of it has broadband.

Chapter 10

Your PC or Mine—Access Your Information from Any Internet-Connected Computer

Learn how to:

❑ Be productive with Microsoft Office Outlook 2007 on and off the network

❑ Edit Windows SharePoint Services documents offline and synchronize the changes

❑ Access your Office Outlook 2007 information and Windows SharePoint Services documents from any computer with a Web browser and Internet access

Have Laptop, Will Travel with Office Outlook 2007

Thanks to an increase in mobile processing power and longer battery life, more and more people are looking at laptop computers as replacements for traditional desktop machines. However, desktop replacement shouldn't imply that your new laptop never leaves the top of your desk. Yes, it serves the same function as your old computer, but this one is designed to give you the flexibility of working *anywhere* you want to—your office, your home, the local coffee shop, and all points in between.

Whether you are a full-time road warrior or occasional office escapee, the 2007 Microsoft Office system helps put the lap back in laptop. But first, you need a few tips and tricks to help you maximize your newfound freedom.

Improved Out of Office Assistant

It's the day before vacation and you are ready to go. So ready in fact that you turned off your computer before you remembered to turn on your Out of Office Assistant. You've got a plane to catch to Orange County and five days off. In the "use it or lose it" world of vacation, you're at a crossroads here. Do you wait for your computer to reboot or do you go to Disneyland?

Exchange Server 2007's improved Out of Office Assistant makes it easy to avoid such Disneyfied dilemmas by allowing you to schedule your out of office reply to turn on and off automatically based on specific dates and times you define. So, on the day you're vacation is approved, you can set your out of office reply to turn on the day you leave and turn off again the day you return to the office. No more forgetting to turn your Out of Office Assistant on before you run out the door, and better yet, no more annoying "You forgot to turn off your out of office reply" e-mails clogging up your Inbox a full week after you're back.

The improved Out of Office Assistant also features tools for formatting rich HTML content, allowing you to compose out of office messages using your choice of fonts, font colors, bulleted or numbered lists, and other formatting characteristics. You can also include hyperlinks to Web sites that may benefit recipients in your absence.

To configure the Out of Office Assistant, Outlook 2007 must be connected to Exchange Server 2007. Click the Outlook Tools menu, then select Out Of Office Assistant. To turn the Out of Office Assistant on, click the radio button next to Send Out Of Office Auto-Replies. Check the box next to Only Send During This Time Range to schedule start and end dates and times for your Out of Office reply. Type and format your reply and click OK. You can also configure how Outlook processes your incoming messages while you are away by clicking the Rules button at the bottom left of the Out of Office Assistant window. (See Figure 10-1.)

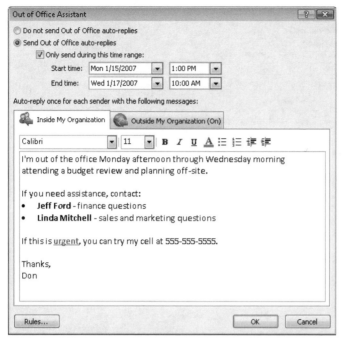

Figure 10-1   Exchange Server 2007 Out of Office Assistant.

Tip or Treat   You can also access the Out of Office Assistant from Outlook Web Access and from Outlook Mobile on a Windows Mobile device.

You may want to customize your out of office reply based on an internal or external recipient. For example, you may want your reply to coworkers to read something like "At Disneyland all week. See you, wouldn't want to be you," while your customer reply is more along the lines of "Thank you for your message. I am out of the office this week on vacation. I appreciate your business and will respond to you at my earliest opportunity." With the improved Out of Office Assistant, you can send separate out of office replies inside and outside your organization.

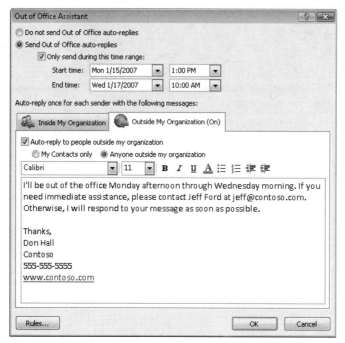

Figure 10-2   External Out of Office Reply.

To create a separate Out of Office message for external recipients, click the Outside My Organization tab. Check the box next to Auto-reply to people outside my organization. Click the radio button to send the reply to My Contacts Only or Anyone Outside My Organization. Type and format your reply and click OK. (See Figure 10-2.)

Connect to Outlook

Your ex-girlfriend or boyfriend was right. The world doesn't revolve around you. Whether you're in a meeting, in an airport, or in line for your fifth ride down Splash Mountain, work doesn't stop working. There are deadlines to meet, projects to manage, and documents to finish.

In Part IV, we introduced you to Windows SharePoint Services document libraries. Document libraries are a great tool for storing and collaborating on Microsoft Office documents and other files. In the olden days of Office 2003, opening and working with SharePoint documents required you to be connected to the network. To take a SharePoint document offline, mobile users would have to check the document out and save a copy to their laptop. When the person reconnected, they would replace the server copy or try to compare and merge the changes between the server and local versions. Offline productivity was possible, but not necessarily practical.

With Windows SharePoint Services 3.0 and Microsoft Office Outlook 2007, you can connect a SharePoint document library to Outlook and open these shared documents within the same application you use to manage your e-mail, Calendar, and other everyday information. To connect a document library to Outlook, click Connect To Outlook on the Actions menu of the document library you want to work with. Click Yes if prompted. Connected documents appear in the SharePoint Lists folder in the Outlook 2007 navigation pane. (See Figure 10-3.)

Figure 10-3 Connect to Outlook.

To edit connected Microsoft Office Word, Excel, and PowerPoint documents offline, expand the SharePoint Lists folder, click the document library where the document resides, then open the document you want to work with by double-clicking it (just like you would open an e-mail message). While still connected to the network, click Edit Offline in the Offline Server Document bar below the Ribbon. Click OK if prompted. Outlook will check the document out from the SharePoint document library. (See Figure 10-4.)

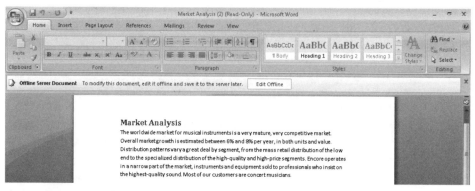

Figure 10-4 Edit Offline Button.

When you are offline and ready to work, follow the same steps to reopen the document. Make your changes and click Save. You will be prompted to Update or Do not update server when you close the document. Select the appropriate choice based on your connection status.

Cached Exchange Mode

It's 10:00 PM You swipe your hotel key and slowly push open the door to your room. After a long day of delayed flights, missed connections, and too much airport food, you've got an appointment with the Sandman. And you don't want to be late.

Before you can go to bed, however, you have to check your e-mail for a confirmation of tomorrow's meeting location. Unfortunately, this hotel doesn't offer high-speed Internet access. You turn on your laptop, dial into your network, launch Outlook, and wait...and wait...and wait. You can actually feel yourself aging in your seat as Outlook downloads all of the e-mail—and e-mail attachments—you received over the past twenty-four hours.

Well, cheer up, Sleepy Jean, there's a better way. Exchange Server 2007's Cached Mode detects the speed of your Internet connection, then optimizes the information it downloads to Outlook 2007. For example, on slower connections, you can configure Cached Mode to download only the headers of your e-mail messages. The header displays who the message is from, the subject, the size of any attachments, and the first few lines of the message body. You decide which e-mail messages are worth waiting for and click Download The Rest Of This Message Now at the bottom of the header to download them. After all, there's no reason to wait for the 3MB PowerPoint presentation of next month's revenue forecast when all you need is the 25K e-mail with tomorrow's meeting location. (See Figure 10-5.)

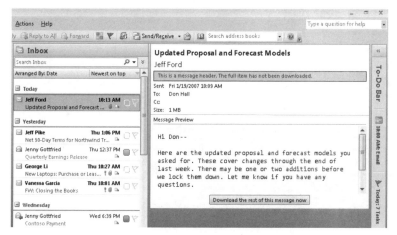

Figure 10-5 Cached Mode Message Header.

Cached Mode does more than improve your remote download experience; it stores a complete copy of your Outlook mailbox on your local machine. On broadband connections, any changes to your mailbox—and only the changes—are synchronized immediately.

If you lose connectivity or go offline, you can continue to read and send e-mail normally. Sent items are held in your Outbox until the server connection is restored, at which time these items are processed and delivered to your recipients. No more hourglass or annoying server communication pop-ups during synchronization.

You can enable Cached Mode through Outlook 2007. However, because it is a server-based feature, you should check with your IT department before doing so. To enable Cached Mode, click Account Settings on the Outlook 2007 Tools menu. On the E-mail tab, select your Exchange Server account, then click Change. Check the box next to Use Cached Exchange Mode and click Next. Click Finish and close the Account Settings window. (See Figure 10-6)

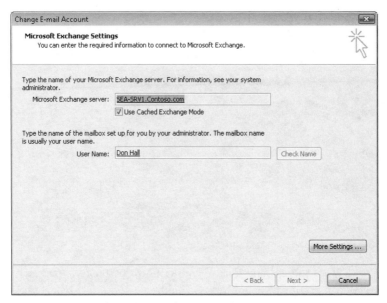

Figure 10-6 Enable Cached Exchange Mode.

To control how Cached Mode operates over slower network connections, click Cached Exchange Mode on the Outlook 2007 File menu. Click On Slow Connections Download Only Headers. A checkmark will appear to the left of this command when set. (See Figure 10-7.)

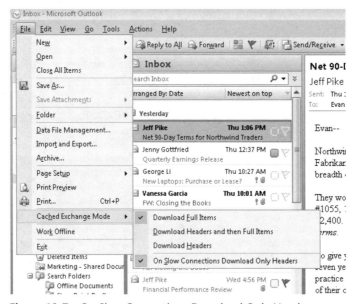

Figure 10-7 On Slow Connections Download Only Headers.

Outlook Anywhere

As of August, 2006, Starbucks Coffee Company owned or licensed over 12,000 locations in 37 countries around the world. The company's Fiscal 2007 plan calls for the opening of an additional 2,400 stores. At this rate, people from Terlingua, Texas to Timbuktu will be ordering double tall blended caramel macchiatos with extra foam in no time flat.

What does Starbucks have to do with mobile computing? Many of these locations, especially in the United States and Canada, are wireless hotspots, offering partner-provided wireless broadband access. Millions of people are never more than a few blocks away from Internet connectivity.

Starbucks isn't your cup of tea...er, coffee? No worries. Independent coffee shops, restaurants, public libraries, hotels, and airports are also investing in the wireless revolution. Even some mobile phone providers are getting in on the act, offering wireless Internet access through mobile phone networks using proprietary wireless cards and subscriptions.

While connecting to the Internet is easier than ever before, using that Internet connection to access corporate data can still be difficult. Many users "tunnel" through their existing connection using something called a Virtual Private Network (VPN). VPNs require the creation of a new Windows network connection. Many companies—Microsoft included—also require employees to insert and validate a Smart Card in order to successfully establish a VPN connection. All of this can be frustrating and time-consuming for the mobile worker.

With Exchange Server 2007's Outlook Anywhere (formerly known as RPC over HTTP, just FYI), you can synchronize Outlook 2007 to the server over any standard Internet connection—without a VPN. Just connect your laptop to your home network, airport kiosk, or wireless hotspot, launch Outlook, and log in with your regular user name and password when prompted.

Like Cached Mode, Outlook Anywhere is a server-based feature. You should check with IT before using Outlook Anywhere on your laptop. To enable Outlook Anywhere, click Account Settings on the Outlook 2007 Tools menu. On the E-mail tab, select your Exchange Server account, then click Change. Click More Settings. On the Connection tab, check the box next to Connect to my Exchange mailbox using HTTP. Contact your IT department for the appropriate Exchange Proxy Settings. Click OK. Click Next, then Finish. Close the Account Settings window.

Office in Your Pocket

No discussion of mobile productivity would be complete without a look at Microsoft Windows Mobile. Windows Mobile is the power behind handheld devices like the PocketPC and Smartphone. With a Windows Mobile device in your hand and Exchange Server 2007 in your office, the information you need most is always at your fingertips.

Every Windows Mobile device comes complete with Outlook Mobile, ensuring you have access to your e-mail, Calendar, contacts, and tasks wherever you are. Outlook Mobile also supports Exchange Server 2007's Unified Messaging, a capability that, when configured by IT, delivers voice mail and faxes directly to your Outlook and Outlook Mobile inboxes.

Exchange Server 2007's ActiveSync technology ensures your device is connected to the server and ready to receive new Outlook items as they arrive. This "push" technology makes manual synchronization a thing of the past, ensuring your device always has the latest and greatest information. Over-the-Air Search functionality allows you to search your entire mailbox from your device, whether or not the items you're looking for have been downloaded to the local store.

But wait, there's more! Windows Mobile Pocket PC devices may also include Office Mobile, powerful pocket-sized versions of the applications you know and love. With Office Mobile, you can create, edit, and open Word, Excel, and PowerPoint documents on your device. Combine Office Mobile with Exchange Server 2007's LinkAccess, and you can even open linked documents stored on internal shares or Windows SharePoint Services sites right from your device. If OneNote Mobile is installed on your device, you can take notes on your device and synchronize them to Office OneNote 2007.

Ultimately, the files you can open depend on the version of Windows Mobile installed on your device. Windows Mobile 5.0 can open files created in Office 2003 or earlier. Windows Mobile 2007, available sometime around the second quarter of 2007, will be compatible out-of-the-box with the Office 2007 file formats. Stay tuned to *www.microsoft.com/windowsmobile* for more information on Windows Mobile 2007 or potential updates to Windows Mobile 5.0.

We hear what you're saying. "All this information in my pocket is great, but what if my pocket gets picked?" Not to worry. You can use the newest version of Outlook Web Access (more on OWA in the next section) to remotely wipe your device. The Artful Dodger will have your device, but not your data. You can even use Outlook Web Access to reset your device password. So, go ahead. Put a Windows Mobile device in your pocket. Just make sure you pay for it first.

No Laptop? No Problem with Outlook Web Access

We know what you're thinking. All this mobility stuff sounds great, but you don't have a laptop. That company-issued dinosaur under your desk is as good as it's going to get. Au contraire, mon frère. With Outlook Web Access, you too can be a mobile user.

Office Outlook Web Access (OWA) is a feature of Exchange Server 2007. If OWA is enabled by your IT department, all you need to remotely access your Outlook information is a computer with a Web browser and Internet access. Your home PC, an Internet kiosk, even your Apple-loving friend's Macintosh can connect you to the information you need right now. All you have to do is log on.

Tip or Treat The full version of Outlook Web Access is designed to run in Internet Explorer 6 or higher. If you need to access OWA from a computer running an older version of IE or another browser like Firefox or Safari, you can use Outlook Web Access Light. OWA Light is also a good option for restricted browsers like those on Internet kiosks or other public Internet terminals. While some advanced features are disabled in OWA Light, you'll still be able to read and send e-mail, as well as view and manage your Calendar items, contacts, and tasks.

Logging On

To use OWA, you need to know the URL for your company's OWA Web site. The OWA URL is customizable by IT, so you should check with your IT department for the correct URL before attempting to use OWA. Typically, an OWA URL will read something like *https://mail.yourdomain.com/exchange* or *https://mail.yourdomain.com/owa*. Notice the "s" in "https:". This indicates OWA is a secure site and you need to include this "s" in your URL in order to access the logon page. Correct URL in hand, all you need to log on to OWA is the same user name and password you use to log on to your local network.

Figure 10-8 Outlook Web Access Logon Page.

You'll log on to OWA based on one of two security options:

- **Public or shared computer** This is the default option and the one you'll use most often. You should always select this option when accessing OWA from a computer that is not your own. You may also wish to select this option when logging on to OWA from a family-accessible home computer. OWA sessions in this mode will automatically log off after 15 minutes of inactivity.

- **Private** You should only use the Private option when you're sure you are the only person with access to the computer. OWA sessions in the Private mode will automatically log off after 24 hours of inactivity.

Select the appropriate security option, enter your user name and password, and click Log On. (See Figure 10-8.)

Word to the Wise When you finish using OWA, always click Log Off in the upper right of the OWA user interface. While OWA sessions do expire based on the security setting you select when logging on, you should never leave your information vulnerable to attack or compromise.

Familiar Interface

No, it's not déjà vu all over again. Microsoft redesigned Outlook Web Access
to look and function even more like the Outlook you know and love. In
some cases, it's the little things—like e-mail address auto-complete and
improved spell checking capabilities—that make a big difference when working between Outlook 2007 and OWA. You'll also appreciate the fact that
you don't have to leave the color categories and improved task management
of Outlook 2007 at your office door. (See Figure 10-9.)

Figure 10-9   Outlook Web Access.

Find People and Information

OWA makes it easier to find the people and information you need when
working away from your regular computer. Utilizing the same search technology as Instant Search in Outlook 2007, your Exchange Server 2007 mailbox is indexed for faster searching from OWA. You can search for
information contained within your e-mail and e-mail attachments. The
Search field in OWA is located in the same place as Outlook 2007, just
above your messages in the message pane.

You can also use OWA to search for people in the Global Address Book and view detailed information related to someone's organization and future availability. You can even view detailed member information for various Distribution Lists. To search the Global Address Book, type a name in the address search box at the top right of the OWA screen and hit Enter.

Tip or Treat Need to know how big your mailbox has grown during your absence? Hover over the top header in the OWA navigation pane. OWA will display a popup containing your current mailbox size compared to your server size limitations.

Scheduling Assistant

Like Outlook 2007, the process of scheduling a meeting in OWA is more efficient with the Exchange Server 2007 Scheduling Assistant. The Scheduling Assistant analyzes the availability of invitees and recommends an ideal time to meet. Recipients can accept, decline, or tentatively accept meeting requests by clicking the appropriate button in the OWA Reading Pane, without having to open the actual request.

To use the Scheduling Assistant, click the Scheduling Assistant tab in a new meeting request. Click the desired time slot from the list of recommendations on the right-hand side. Click back to the Appointment tab, complete the request, then click Send. (See Figure 10-10.)

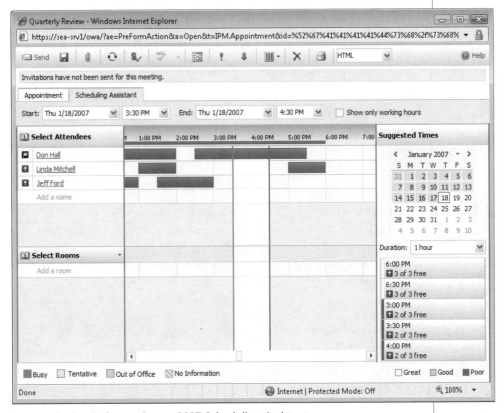

Figure 10-10 Exchange Server 2007 Scheduling Assistant.

LinkAccess

Similar to Outlook Anywhere in Outlook 2007, LinkAccess provides access to your information without a complicated VPN connection. Specifically, LinkAccess allows you to open a link to a document or document library on a Windows SharePoint Services site from an e-mail in OWA. For example, a colleague e-mails you a link to a document on a Document Workspace. You check your e-mail from home or another remote location using OWA and click the link. Without LinkAccess, you would be unable to open the document unless you first connected to your corporate network by dialing directly into the server or tunneling through your existing Internet connection using VPN. With LinkAccess, the link works and the application opens. No VPN required.

WebReady Document Viewing

What if the computer you're using to access OWA isn't running Microsoft Office 2007? WebReady Document Viewing allows you to open Word, Excel, PowerPoint, and PDF files as HTML Web Pages. OWA automatically converts the files to HTML and displays them in a browser window for easy reading. To use WebReady Document Viewing, click the Open As Web Page link to the right of the attached file. To print the document, click the Print button in the top right corner of the WebReady Document window.

Outlook Voice Access—No Computer Required

What would you say if we told you that you could check your Outlook e-mail without a computer or mobile device? Now, try saying it *without* profanity.

Outlook Voice Access allows you to dial-in to your Exchange Server 2007 mailbox from any telephone and *listen* to your e-mail using text-to-speech technology. And Outlook Voice Access doesn't just read you your e-mail. It can also play back calendar items, contacts, and tasks.

Hear something that deserves a reply? Don't go running to your laptop. Use Outlook Voice Access to reply to or forward messages, as well as send a pre-configured "I'll be late" notice.

Need to call someone at the office but don't remember their extension? Use Outlook Voice Access to search the company directory for a person to call or initiate a phone call from one of your Outlook contacts.

You can navigate Outlook Voice Access with your telephone keypad or, better yet, by using the built-in speech recognition. Let your fingers do the walking some other time.

OWA Options

With OWA, using a Web browser to check your e-mail does not mean giving up the control and customization you expect from your full Outlook client. Click the Options button at the top right of the OWA user interface to access a list of familiar tools for customizing messaging and calendaring options, managing junk e-mail settings, and even scheduling internal and external out of office auto-replies.

Tip or Treat   You can also use OWA to view your Outlook information on your Office SharePoint Server 2007 personal My Site. If you have not yet created your My Site, click the My Site link at the top right of the Office SharePoint Server 2007 portal home page.

The My Calendar Web Part is a default component of your My Site home page. To configure this Web Part to display your OWA Calendar, click the Open The Tool Pane link in the Web Part. Enter the OWA URL and your mailbox name (e-mail address). Then, click OK.

To add other OWA Web Parts to your My Site, click the Site Actions button, then Edit Page. Click Add A Web Part in the zone where you want the Web Part to live. Scroll down to the Outlook Web Access Web Parts section. Check the boxes next to the Web Parts you want to add and click Add. Follow the

same steps you used to configure My Calendar to configure the new OWA
Web Parts.

Tip Jar

Here's a review of the top 10 tips covered in Chapter 10:

- **Schedule the Out of Office Assistant** Click the Outlook Tools menu, then select Out Of Office Assistant. Click the radio button next to Send Out Of Office Auto-Replies. Check the box next to Only Send During This Time Range: and select start and end dates and times.

- **Send external Out of Office replies** Click the Outlook Tools menu, then select Out Of Office Assistant. Click the radio button next to Send Out Of Office Auto-Replies. Click the Outside My Organization tab. Check the box next to Auto-Reply To People Outside My Organization.

- **Connect a Windows SharePoint Services document library to Outlook** Click Connect To Outlook on the Actions menu of a document library. Click Yes if prompted.

- **Edit a connected Windows SharePoint Services document offline** Expand the SharePoint Lists folder in Outlook 2007, click the document library where the document resides, then open the document. While connected to the network, click Edit Offline in the Offline Server Document bar below the Ribbon. Click OK if prompted. Make your changes offline and click Save. Close the document; click Update or Do Not Update Server when prompted.

- **Enable Cached Exchange Mode** Click Account Settings on the Outlook 2007 Tools menu. On the E-mail tab, select your Exchange Server account, then click Change. Check the box next to Use Cached Exchange Mode and click Next. Click Finish.

- **Download only headers on slower connections** Click Cached Exchange Mode on the Outlook 2007 File menu. Click On Slow Connections Download Only Headers.

- **Enable Outlook Anywhere** Click Account Settings on the Outlook 2007 Tools menu. On the E-mail tab, select your Exchange Server account, then click Change. Click More Settings. On the Connection tab, check the box next to Connect to my Exchange mailbox using HTTP. Contact your IT department for the appropriate Exchange Proxy Settings. Click OK. Click Next, then Finish.

■ **Log on to Outlook Web Access**   Check with your IT department for the correct OWA URL (usually https://mail.yourdomain.com/exchange or https://mail.yourdomain.com/owa). Be sure to include the "s" in "https:". Enter your user name and password and click Log On.

■ **Outlook Web Access Security Options**   Select This Is A Public Or Shared Computer when accessing OWA from a computer that is not your own. OWA sessions in Public mode will automatically log off after 15 minutes of inactivity. Select This Is A Private Computer when you're sure you are the only person with access to the computer. OWA sessions in the Private mode will automatically log off after 24 hours of inactivity.

■ **WebReady Document Viewing**   Click the Open As Web Page link to the right of the attached file. To print the document, click the Print button in the top right corner of the WebReady Document window.

Conclusion

Whether it's your favorite dessert or a much-deserved day off, all good things must come to an end. So it is with this book. Like Mr. Rogers before us, it's time to change sweaters and slip into our comfy shoes.

We've been through a lot together these past few hundred pages. We stared down your monster of an Inbox. We carved some valuable "me" time out of your meetings. We gave life to the document you always knew was inside you. We played well with others. And we cut the network ties that made you feel like a desk-bound puppet on a string. (For information on becoming a real boy or girl, see Appendix A.)

We hope you enjoyed reading this book as much as—at times, maybe even more than—we enjoyed writing it. We know from experience that reading time comes at a premium and we thank you for spending your time with us. If you'd like more information on the tips, tricks, products, and solutions discussed in this book, here are a few links to check out:

- Microsoft Office Online (user assistance, training, templates, clip art, and more)—*www.microsoft.com/office*

- 2007 Microsoft Office System Product Information (marketing focused)— *www.microsoft.com/office/prodinfo.mspx*

- Microsoft Office System Tips & Tricks (tips and webcasts)—*www.microsoft.com/office/greattips*

- Microsoft Office Work Essentials (Microsoft Office tips for your job or role)—*www.microsoft.com/workessentials*

- Windows Vista (general information)—*www.microsoft.com/windowsvista*

About the Authors

A seven year veteran of Microsoft Corporation, Evan Archilla is now the owner and president of Archilla Marketing, a technology marketing and training company dedicated to helping end users get the most out of Microsoft products and technologies. Evan lives with his wife and daughter in the beautiful Texas Hill Country. For more information, visit *www.archillamarketing.com.*

Tiffany Songvilay is a professional speaker and a consultant engaged in enterprise accounts as a liaison between IT and the end-user. She lives in Houston, Texas, with her husband, dogs, and Southern flying squirrels.

For more information about book events and to read the official blog, visit *www.sothatshow.com.*

Index

Additional Resources for Home and Business

Breakthrough Windows Vista™: Find Your Favorite Features and Discover the Possibilities

Joli Ballew and Sally Slack
ISBN 9780735623620

Jump in for the topics or features that interest you most! This colorful guide brings Windows Vista to life—from setting up your new system; accessing the Windows Vista Sidebar; customizing it for your favorite gadgets; recording live television with Media Center; organizing photos, music, and videos; making movies; and more.

So That's How! 2007 Microsoft® Office System: Timesavers, Breakthroughs, & Everyday Genius

Evan Archilla and Tiffany Songvilay
ISBN 9780735622746

From vanquishing an overstuffed inbox to breezing through complex spreadsheets, discover smarter ways to do everyday things with Microsoft Office. Based on a popular course delivered to more than 70,000 students, this guide delivers the tips and revelations that help you work more effectively with Microsoft Office Outlook®, Excel®, Word, and other programs. Also includes 'webinars' on CD.

Look Both Ways: Help Protect Your Family on the Internet

Linda Criddle
ISBN 9780735623477

You look both ways before crossing the street. Now, learn the new rules of the road—and help protect yourself online with Internet child-safety authority Linda Criddle. Using real-life examples, Linda teaches the simple steps you and your family can take to help avoid Internet dangers—and still enjoy your time online.

The Microsoft Crabby Office Lady Tells It Like It Is: Secrets to Surviving Office Life

Annik Stahl
ISBN 9780735622722

From cubicle to corner office, learn the secrets for getting more done on the job—so you can really enjoy your time off the job! The Crabby Office Lady shares her no-nonsense advice for succeeding at work, as well as tricks for using Microsoft Office programs to help simplify your life. She'll give you the straight scoop—so pay attention!

Microsoft Office Excel 2007: Data Analysis and Business Modeling

Wayne L. Winston
ISBN 9780735623965

Beyond Bullet Points: Using Microsoft Office PowerPoint® 2007 to Create Presentations That Inform, Motivate, and Inspire

Cliff Atkinson
ISBN 9780735623873

Take Back Your Life! Using Microsoft Office Outlook 2007 to Get Organized and Stay Organized

Sally McGhee
ISBN 9780735623439

See more resources at **microsoft.com/mspress** *and* **microsoft.com/learning**

Microsoft Press® products are available worldwide wherever quality computer books are sold. For more information, contact your bookseller, computer retailer, software reseller, or local Microsoft Sales Office, or visit our Web site at **microsoft.com/mspress**. To locate a source near you, or to order directly, call 1-800-MSPRESS in the United States. (In Canada, call **1-800-268-2222**.)

What do you think of this book?

We want to hear from you!

Do you have a few minutes to participate in a brief online survey?

Microsoft is interested in hearing your feedback so we can continually improve our books and learning resources for you.

To participate in our survey, please visit:

www.microsoft.com/learning/booksurvey/

...and enter this book's ISBN-10 number (appears above barcode on back cover*). As a thank-you to survey participants in the United States and Canada, each month we'll randomly select five respondents to win one of five $100 gift certificates from a leading online merchant. At the conclusion of the survey, you can enter the drawing by providing your e-mail address, which will be used for prize notification only.

Thanks in advance for your input. Your opinion counts!

* Where to find the ISBN-10 on back cover

ISBN-13: 000-0-0000-00000
ISBN-10: 0-0000-00000

00000

Example only. Each book has unique ISBN.